African Americans and ROTC

# African Americans and ROTC

*Military, Naval and Aeroscience*
*Programs at Historically*
*Black Colleges, 1916–1973*

*by* CHARLES JOHNSON, JR.

*[handwritten inscription: 2LT Curtis R. Phillip, Best Wishes, Charles Johnson, Jr.]*

McFarland & Company, Inc., Publishers
*Jefferson, North Carolina, and London*

Library of Congress Cataloguing-in-Publication Data

Johnson, Charles, Jr., 1937–
    African Americans and ROTC : military, naval and aeroscience
programs at historically Black colleges, 1916–1973 / by Charles
Johnson, Jr.
        p.      cm.
    Includes bibliographical references and index.
    ISBN 0-7864-1324-7 (softcover : 50# alkaline paper) ∞
    1. United States. Army Reserve Officers' Training Corps—
History — 20th century.    2. United States. Naval Reserve Officers
Training Corps— History — 20th century.    3. United States. Air Force
ROTC — History — 20th century.    4. African American college stu-
dents— History — 20th century.    5. African American universities and
colleges— History — 20th century.    I. Title.
    U428.5 .J64    2002
    355.2'232'071173 — dc21                                    2002002798

British Library cataloguing data are available

Cover photograph: Watson's Rangers, Morgan State University. (Courtesy
of the Morganiana Collection, Prints and Photographs Collection, Beulah M.
Davis Special Collections Department, Morgan State University)

Manufactured in the United States of America

*McFarland & Company, Inc., Publishers
  Box 611, Jefferson, North Carolina 28640
  www.mcfarlandpub.com*

This book is dedicated to Morgan State University Professor Emeritus Roland McConnell, who inspired my interest in military history; to Administrative Sergeant Major Richard Robinson, retired, who taught military science at Morgan State University; to Major General Frederic E. Davison, retired, who graduated from Howard University and became the first African American commissioned ROTC officer from a historically African American institution to attain flag grade rank in the United States Armed Forces; to Major Robert E. Greene, retired, a commissioned officer from Lincoln University in Missouri, who encouraged me to complete this manuscript; to Cathy Taylor-Core, who shared my interests in military history and influenced my career at Howard University; to coed students who formed marching units or supported their respective collegiate detachments; to female graduates who received commissions prior to the enrollment of women into aeroscience, military science, and naval science programs; to all cadets, midshipmen and midshipwomen who enrolled into ROTC detachments at historically African American colleges and universities; to students inducted into the Arnold Air Society, the Scabbard and Blades Society, and the National Society of the Pershing Rifles, especially members of the Morgan State University Drill Team; and to General Larry R. Ellis, who was commissioned in 1969 at Morgan State University and nominated by President George W. Bush in 2001 to become the first African American from a historically African American institution to attain the rank of a four-star general, the highest peacetime rank for an Army officer. Students who enrolled in basic or advanced aeroscience, military science or naval science courses and achieved success in their civilian or armed forces careers have established a legacy which has become a significant aspect of African American history.

# Acknowledgments

The author is grateful to National Archives II personnel, especially Richard Boylan, Becky Collier, Thomas C. Lipscomb, Morret Ozlar, Frederick W. Pernell, and Louis Smith, for documents which provided the basis for this study; to Regina T. Ackers in the U.S. Naval Historical Center; to personnel in the U.S. Army Military Institute who located records that improved the scope of this study; and to university archivists, librarians and their assistants who identified references which enabled the collection of significant materials for this study.

Among those who rendered assistance are Howard University archivist Clifford L. Muse, Jr., research associate Esme Bhan, manuscript curator Joellen El Bashir, and Moorland-Spingarn curator Janet Simms-Wood; Alabama A and M University archivists Mildred Stiger and Ethel L. Alexander; Deborah Green and Cynthia Poston in the Hampton University Archives; Tuskegee University archivist Daniel T. Williams and his assistant Cynthia B. Wilson; Jacqueline Brown of Wilberforce University; Yvette A. Ford in the Ethnic Studies Department at Lincoln University in Missouri; and Karen A. Robertson, director of the Morgan State University Library, and the staff in the Beulah Davis Room.

Aeroscience, military science, and naval science detachment cadres who provided valuable service include Captain Willie E. Almond at Central State University, Captain Rodney Connors at Fort Valley State College, and Captain Ira O. Credle at Virginia State University in addition to archival and military staffs at Hampton University, Morgan State University, Prairie View A and M University and Southern University and A and M College.

The author is extremely appreciative of the tremendous support and recommendations provided by his sisters, Iolas J. Drake and Pauline J. Harris, and wife and daughter, Willigean H. Johnson and Hausalynn H. Johnson, who read earlier drafts of this manuscript.

# Contents

# *Preface*

The procurement of African American commissioned officers was not a major objective of military officials prior to the enactment of the National Defense Act of 1916. The majority of the African American officers were assigned to National Guard organizations in states where companies were organized. With the exception of personnel assigned as chaplains, three officers commissioned by the United States Military Academy and a relatively small quantity of commissioned officers from the enlisted ranks, opportunities for African American cadres were negligible, limited to filling vacancies in the 9th and 10th Cavalry and 24th and 25th Infantry Regiments. Land grant provisions under the Morrill Acts of 1862 and 1890 authorized military training, but programs implemented at African American institutions did not include the commissioning of officers.

The enactment of the National Defense Act of 1916 with the provisions to establish a Reserve Officer Training Corps (ROTC) changed the perception of military training at African American institutions. The War Department was concerned with military preparations for American involvement in World War I and the necessity of training personnel in the effective use of the weapons and technology of modern warfare. The immediate plan for college students was training in the Student Army Training Corps. With a military camp initially established at Howard University for African American students and collegiate officials, the participants were designated to organize detachments at their institutions. This designation initiated the first federal military affiliation with most of the historically African American colleges participating in the Student Army Training Corps. Chapter One of this study is an assessment of the interests and aspirations of college students and their efforts to obtain training programs for the institutions as well as their participation in the Student Army Training Corps.

After the armistice was implemented on November 11, 1918, institutions with Student Army Training Corps organizations were authorized to request the conversion of their units into Reserve Officer Training Corps detachments. Revision of the National Defense Act in 1920 influenced reductions in personnel and the amount of ROTC detachments, and the realignment and reorganization affected the status of some detachments because of the lack of qualified noncommissioned officers and commissioned officers to serve in the ROTC programs. The impact of World War II with emphasis placed on massive recruitment and the effective deployment of personnel prompted an expansion in the procurement of commissioned officers. Military officials relied heavily on Officer Candidate Schools to rapidly produce commissioned officers in ninety days instead of the four years required through the ROTC programs. Therefore, ROTC was discontinued as a source of providing commissioned officers. The effort to retain ROTC detachments that included the basic two year and advance two year programs which resulted in the commissioning of officers is the focus of Chapter Two.

Near the conclusion of World War II, attention was given to the reestablishment of a program for procuring officers through ROTC detachments, and African Americans recognized the opportunity to gain detachments for their institutions, especially the land grant colleges and universities. Chapter Three evaluates the wartime collegiate experiences and the tremendous efforts of the presidents of Negro land grant colleges and influential citizens to obtain Army ROTC detachments. Chapter Four is an analysis of African American efforts to receive Air Force and Navy ROTC detachments and the obstacles which were surpassed to establish these organizations.

Howard and Tuskegee universities were the only African American institutions with Army Air Force detachments when the War Department reestablished the units because the institutions had had Air Force training prior to the revisions in the program during World War II. The establishment of the Department of the Air Force within the Department of Defense encouraged institutions to seek the organization of campus units. Simultaneously, African Americans, recognizing that the Navy ROTC program was organized in 1926, were interested in taking part in the development of Navy ROTC. The Air Force established several detachments by 1951, but the Navy was reluctant to expand the established program of 52 detachments under its Hollaway Plan which required students to interview, compete and qualify for nominations into Navy ROTC programs. The major obstacle for the large proportion of African American students was the limited quantity of programs in areas where admission into Navy ROTC was not available.

This problem was intensified by the Navy Department, which prevented the formation of Navy ROTC units at historical African American colleges or universities prior to 1967. Finally, beginning with Prairie View Agricultural and Mechanical University, Navy ROTC, which included commissioning officers into the Marine Corps, would expand to other African American institutions, and Army ROTC and Air Force ROTC programs were similarly expanded to provide the procurement of commissioned officers to additional historically African American institutions.

The successful establishment of aeroscience, military science or naval science detachments at all of the seventeen land grant institutions and other private and state African American colleges and universities by 1973, through the perseverance of James C. Evans, assistant civilian aide to the secretary of defense; Carl Murphy, editor of the Baltimore *Afro-American*; and other collegiate officials was a major accomplishment. African American institutions which had received support from female marching units enthusiastically endorsed the Department of Defense initiatives which extended ROTC, Air Force ROTC and Navy ROTC to female students by 1973. The aeroscience and military science policies pertaining to the officers' requirements and training are evaluated in Chapter Five. In Chapter Six, revisions and extensions of military science, aeroscience and naval science detachments are emphasized.

The objective of organizing military training programs in African American colleges and universities with the implementation of the National Defense Act of 1916 was achieved by 1973. This success was influenced by the mandatory participation of students in basic programs to ensure the enrollment of cadets into advanced programs, which in turn would enable their institutions to attain their assigned procurement of commissioned officers. However, opposition to the war in Vietnam inspired student protests against the draft, and the majority of African American students refused to enroll into ROTC, Air Force ROTC and Navy ROTC programs. Many were involved with the civil rights and Black Power movements, and many had strong feelings about the injustice imposed against Muhammad Ali, who refused military induction based on his Muslim beliefs.

Professors of Military Science, Aeroscience and Naval Science realized that the retention of their detachments was in jeopardy, and they were confronted with problems of influencing students to voluntarily enroll in their programs when the majority of their peers and the general public were protesting and demonstrating their anger about issues pertaining to mandatory service in the armed forces. Incentives were required not only to attract students but to ensure that qualified students with the potential to become effective commissioned officers would become involved with military, naval or aeroscience programs. However, a major recruitment advantage for detachment commanders in African American colleges and universities after 1973 was the successful careers of officers commissioned prior to the implementation of the All-Volunteer Armed Forces program, who had served in significant assignments with many attaining the rank of flag and general officers in the armed forces.

The story of African American involvement in ROTC has generally been omitted from references pertaining to ROTC programs. This study is unique because of its evaluation of African American efforts to establish ROTC at historically African American colleges and universities. It offers full coverage of the problems encountered in maintaining viable Army, Air Force and Navy detachments that produced commissioned officers to accept leadership roles in the armed forces.

# 1

# Student Army Training Corps

The procurement of officers was emphasized with the establishment of the United States Military Academy at West Point, New York, in 1802 and other private and state institutions which provided military training for their male students. Segregationist policies within the nation ensured that African Americans were excluded from the institution until the admission of Michael Howard from Mississippi and James Webster Smith from South Carolina. Twenty-three others were influenced to seek admission into the USMA and the applicants who were granted admissions were socially ostracized and hazed by the other cadets. The cadets who endured under the system and were commissioned prior to 1936 were Henry O. Flipper in 1877, John Hanks Alexander in 1887 and Charles Denton Young in 1889.[1]

Congressional interests in providing opportunities to encourage the knowledge and higher production of agricultural crops and to increase the mechanical and industrial quantity of qualified personnel influenced the enactment of the Morrill Land Grant Act on July 2, 1862, which authorized the establishment of state land colleges with military instruction offered to students. Alcorn Agricultural and Normal College under this legislation was organized as the first African American land grant college in 1871 and received three-fifths of the endowment for Mississippi.[2] However, the incentive of military training and commissioning of Alcorn A and N students was not an objective of the program. A revision of the legislation, entitled the Second Morrill Act, on August 30, 1890, encouraged additional states to provide African American land grant colleges with similar military requirements for male students. Cognizant of the value of military training and discipline, the Howard University Board of Trustees on August 2, 1869 appointed General Oliver O. Howard, Henry A. Brewster and D. W. Anderson, the first African American to serve on the executive committee, to serve as the Military Committee that organized the Military Department which formed the Howard University Cadets. Captain Melville C. Wilkinson, who served as the commandant, formed several infantry companies and cadets were required to purchase their uniforms. Retrenchment influenced by the loss of appropriations from the Freedmen's Bureau in 1872 and the affects of the Panic of 1873 motivated the board of trustees to discontinue the Cadet Corps after 1874.[3]

Hampton Institute and Wilberforce University were private institutions, but their students especially benefited from programs which provided military discipline and training, since Virginia and Ohio respectively had not organized colleges for African American students. Hampton from its establishment by Brigadier General Samuel C. Armstrong in 1868 had instituted a strict form of military discipline and training, and male students were organized into a regiment. The Virginia General Assembly on March 19, 1872 designated Hampton as a land grant college. This military training was not designed to prepare cadets for commissioned service as officers.

Training was also offered to Native American students after their arrival on November 5, 1878 with Captain Richard H. Pratt who previously had served with the 10th Cavalry Regiment and remained at Hampton until the following year. Captain Pratt was reassigned to Carlisle Barracks in Pennsylvania where he organized a school for Native Americans with the assistance of Native American students who had previously attended Hampton. Captain Henry Romeyn had been assigned to Hampton on March 13, 1878 under the provisions of the Morrill Act which detailed officers to state agricultural schools and he succeeded Captain Pratt as the commandant of cadets.

Hampton lost its land grants funding when Virginia established Virginia Polytechnic Institute at Blacksburg in 1884 but was entitled to receive a third of the appropriations under the Morrill- Nelson Acts of 1890 and 1907. Commandant George LeRoy Brown, who had succeeded Captain Romeyn, was reassigned and replaced by a civilian, George L. Curtis. In November 1884 Arthur T. Boykin became the first African American drillmaster, the highest African American position on campus until Robert Russa Moton was appointed as acting commandant in May 1889 while Commandant Charles W. Freeland was recruiting Native American students. Moton was assigned to the Wigwam after the return of Freeland and was placed in charge of Native American male students who formed Company C in the Hampton battalion. The battalion was integrated during the first twelve years of the Indian program but became segregated in 1890 when Native American students demanded that their daily formations be conducted at their quarters instead of assembling at other quarters. The battalion was reintegrated in 1909 primarily because of the lower enrollment of Native American students which continued to decline to sixteen in 1919. Moton was appointed the commandant in June 1891 upon the resignation of Freeland and was assisted by Allen Wadsworth Washington, a Tuskegee graduate, who served as the commandant when Moton succeeded Booker T. Washington in 1915.[4]

Wilberforce University on March 19, 1887, in an unprecedented arrangement between a private sectarian institution and the Ohio legislature, accepted the establishment of the state funded Combined Normal and Industrial Department at Wilberforce University. With the enactment of the Morrill Act on August 30, 1890 that guaranteed equity to African Americans from grants providing educational aid to states and artfully defined a doctrine of separate but equal through the establishment of African American land grant institutions, some officials opposed legislation by W. T. Wallace to share land grant funding to Ohio State University with Wilberforce. Several legislators debated extensively and denounced the sharing of federal funds with Wilberforce, and some African Americans considered that the department jeopardized opportunities to matriculate at other private and public colleges in Ohio and threatened the repeal of public school integration. African Americans were also concerned that with the approval of funding in 1892 and the gubernatorial appointment of the majority of board of trustees the control of the campus would shift to the state. With funding of the Combined Normal and Industrial Department through direct taxation in 1896, the power of the department resided more with the board of trustees than with Wilberforce officials. State appropriations increased from $2,000 in 1889 when the last state grant was awarded to $16,000 for 1893 with higher appropriations projected for 1894 and 1896. Some African Americans were not surprised when the office of the superintendent was separated from the office of the president of Wilberforce in 1896.[5] However, the extension of state involvement on the campus enabled the inclusion of military training under the Morrill Act.

Wilberforce established a military program when Senators John Sherman, Calvin S. Brice and George W. Hulick influenced President Grover Cleveland to authorize the establishment of a federally sponsored military training program at Wilberforce. The War Department appropriated $4000 for the issuance of equipment, supplies and weapons and on May 23, 1892 a favorable inspection was conducted by CPT Heisland. Lieutenant John Hanks Alexander, an African American officer who had graduated from the United States Military Academy in 1887, was detailed on January 9, 1894 to organize the Military Department in his capacity as Professor of Military

Science and Tactics. He began the assignment of the professor of military science and tactics on February 12, 1894 and performed excellent service until his death which occurred in Springfield on March 26, 1894. The commitment of the War Department to Wilberforce was not interrupted since Lieutenant Charles Young, who also graduated from the United States Military Academy on August 31, 1889, was appointed to command the Military Department. He assumed command of the department immediately after his arrival on May 21, 1894. The resignation of MAJ Charles W. Fillmore as commander of the Ohio 9th Infantry Battalion on March 25, 1898 and a declaration of war against Spain the following month caused the transfer of Lieutenant Young to the battalion. Although several officers who were Wilberforce graduates commanded the cadets until August 27, 1905, the next experienced regular military officer assigned to Wilberforce was LT Benjamin O. Davis. In 1909, he was succeeded by LT John E. Green who previously was assigned to the 25th Infantry Regiment. The departure of LT Green in 1913 prompted the reassignment of CPT Davis in 1914 to the Military Department at Wilberforce which had graduated nine cadets. CPT Davis considered the caliber of military training at Wilberforce distinguished the university from other African American institutions that provided military training to theirs students. University officials were extremely proud of the federal support its military department received and its unique African American relationship with the national government.[6]

The West Virginia Institute was established as a land grant institution by legislation enacted on March 17, 1891. The Institute commenced military training according to Reed's Military Science and Tactics manual and students performed company and battalion exercises. Training was officially conducted in 1895 by the Master of Military Drill until the title was changed in 1899 to the Commandant of Cadets. Interest in the advantages of military instruction influenced J. McHenry Jones to petition state legislators to introduce a Cadet Bill that was approved in February 1899. The Institute was authorized to provide free admission, uniforms, tuition, books and stationery to sixty students. John H. Hill, who had served as principal of the Institute before enlisting into the 10th Cavalry Regiment where he became Regimental Quartermaster Sergeant, and who had also served in the 8th (Immune) Volunteer Regiment during the Spanish-American-Cuban-Filipino War where he was commissioned a lieutenant and appointed the Regimental Commissary Officer, was discharged from the military on March 6, 1899, and returned to the Institute as a professor of mathematics and the Commandant of Cadets. The Military Department conducted theoretical courses involving the study of drill regulations and tactics, military organization, administration and discipline and small arms instruction. Practical courses provided included skills pertaining to drill and gymnastics, target practice, signal instruction and minor exercise in military tactics. Adverse reactions toward the training by the Military Department occurred when the State Militia was directed to withdraw sixty Winchester rifles which had been lent to the department. Efforts to replace the loss of arms and equipment were unsuccessful since the cadets were not under the supervision of a regular Army officer. However, the purchase of sixty Remington rifles by the board of regents and Senator S. B. Elkins restored student morale which had been affected by public criticism. Enthusiasm for the military program was evident in the cadet discipline and in their response to the bugler's call which announced significant weekly events. However, the state legislature in 1907 failed to provide provisions for the appointment of cadets and during the 1911-1912 academic year the president and board of trustees requested the reinstatement of military training. Whether military training was reinstituted is difficult to ascertain but on December 6, 1916 the Commandant of Cadets at West Virginia University inspected the Cadet Corps at West Virginia Collegiate Institute which had officially been redesignated on February 17, 1915.[7]

The Delaware General Assembly enacted legislation which established Delaware State College for Agriculture and Mechanical Arts on May 15, 1891. William C. Jason, president of the college, in 1905 authorized Commandant Joseph E. Cogbill to provide military training for two companies of cadets. Delaware State College later provided military instruction under War Department General Order 70 that was enacted in 1913 with forty of forty-four students receiving military training.[8]

Claflin University had served as the land grant college for African American students until March 3, 1896 when the South Carolina State legislature separated the campus and organized the Normal, Industrial, Agricultural and Mechanical College of South Carolina as the land grant college. At the first meeting of the new college board of trustees on April 10, 1896, a recommendation was approved which supported the submission of an application to the secretary of war for the assignment of an officer to teach military science and tactics. Notified of the nonavailability of an African American officer, professor Robert S. Wilkinson provided military training until the program was terminated in 1910.[9]

The introduction of Council Bill 87 by J. W. Johnson on February 4, 1897, that was supported by Henry S. Johnson, who was destined to become a governor of Oklahoma, and enacted on March 12, 1897, established the Colored Agricultural and Normal University of Oklahoma which became Langston University in 1941. Inequities of higher education were extremely obvious since African Americans were obligated to provide forty acres of private property for public utilization, and the university was assigned multiple functions which included the major aspects of a liberal arts college, an agricultural and mechanical college. Langston University officially became operational on September 4, 1898 without any buildings on its campus and conducted classes in the Cumberland Presbyterian Church with President Inman E. Page, who had served as president of Lincoln University in Missouri for eighteen years, and a faculty of four who taught forty-one students and nine elementary students. Therefore, the effort to sustain the institution did not immediately involve military training although uniforms were provided to the band.[10] Maryland did not establish a state land grant institution for African Americans but on December 31, 1890 an agreement between the Morgan College Board of Trustees and Maryland Agricultural College of Prince George's County designated the Delaware Academy at Princess Anne in Somerset County as the Industrial Branch of Morgan College and the land grant institution for African American students. The site became the Eastern Branch of the Maryland Agricultural College for persons of African descent. The campus was redesignated as Princess Anne Academy but military training was not an essential part of student activities.[11]

Warfare in Europe offered an opportunity to obtain commissions after the enactment of the National Defense Act in 1916 which influenced the formation of a National Army, the Student Army (and Navy) Training Corps and the Reserve Officer Training Corps.[12] The Operations Division of the War Department General Staff planned the mobilization and deployment of 80 divisions in France and 18 divisions for the continental United States by June 30, 1919. Military officials realized early in their attempts to recruit soldiers for combat in Europe that they were required to formulate special instructions to accommodate personnel who were unable to read and understand military orders or comprehend the meaning or significance of communication, tactical operations and technical training. In view of the serious problem of officer procurement, a plan was developed to utilize the facilities of educational institutions and organize the SATC commanded by BG General Robert I. Rees. The acquisition of 518 academic colleges and universities and 80 for vocational training academic facilities initially excluded the participation of African Americans but Special Assistant to the Secretary of War Emmett J. Scott urged C. A. Prosser, Director of the Federal Board for Vocational Training, and his assistant, W. L. Hamilton, who were responsible for developing a vocational program, to expand the training to all soldiers since the Army had already inducted African Americans and more would soon join the military. Congress created the Committee on Education and Special Training on February 10, 1918 to administer this extensive program. Provisions granted under the Selective Service Act of May 18, 1917 and War Department General Orders 79 issued on August 24, 1918 granted the committee authority to establish the SATC on September 15, 1918. Chief of Staff General Peyton C March considered the implementation of the SATC was essential since the age limitations under the draft were increased and procurement of officers from established agencies was limited. African American institutions initially selected for participation in the program were Howard, Atlanta University, Florida Agricultural and Mechanical College, Georgia State Industrial College, Hampton, Agricultural and Technical College of North Carolina, Branch Normal School at Pine Bluff in Arkansas, Tuskegee, Western University at Quindaro, Kansas, and State Agricultural and Mechanical College at Orangeburg, South Carolina in addition to Wendell Phillips High School in Chicago, Illinois and Sumner High School in St. Louis, Missouri.[13]

SATC formally became operational on October 1, 1918 with the muster of approximately 140,000 men enrolled at 525 educational institutions where executive and teaching personnel were available. The physical equipment at these institutions also provided immediate training facilities with the capacity to train 200,000 men. SATC provided training for officer candidates and enlisted personnel for service as trade technicians or specialists for the armed forces in a protracted war, provided additional training camps to accommodate new draftees, and in the process supported higher education which was experiencing a reduction in male student enrollment because of military manpower requirements. Officials further concluded in March 1918 that in addition to a shortage of technicians there was a serious shortage of personnel in higher technical professions and a reserve of potential officer candidates. To facilitate the accomplishment of its objectives, the committee divided SATC detachments into collegiate sections and vocational sections which were formerly identified as National Army Training Detachments. A plan was devised to permit students between the ages of eighteen to twenty-one to voluntarily enlist in SATC detachments as privates. Although they were placed on furlough status, received thirty dollars per month, were subject to military orders, and received military training, they were still liable to be called to active duty at anytime. The students were expected to maintain high academic standards, and graduates were eligible for active duty. In the implementation of this plan colleges with more than 100 male students were invited to send faculty and student representatives to summer camps where training was scheduled for assistant SATC instructors.[14]

Students enlisted in both sections of training and depending on their academic qualifications were permitted to select their branch of service. Collegiate and vocational sections were initially divided into four groups and given two months of industrial or academic training before becoming eligible for an additional two months of higher academic training with military value. Collegiate students with acceptable achievement were given the opportunity to transfer to a Central Officers' Training School, a noncommissioned officers' school or be assigned to collegiate institutions for intensive study in curricula which involved instruction in chemistry, engineering or medicine. Students not enrolled in the advanced training program were transferred to a Vocational Training Section or to a cantonment for duty with troops as privates. However, personnel in vocational units were given equal opportunities with men in collegiate units to demonstrate their qualifications for officers' and noncommissioned officers' schools or for continuance at institutions for more advanced study. SATC regulations also provided for the transfer of student-soldiers into the active Army at intervals with their places taken by new men inducted for similar training. Institutions with Vocational Sections were Tuskegee, Hampton, Howard, Atlanta, Georgia State Agricultural and Mechanical College, Agricultural and Technical College of North Carolina, State Agricultural and Mechanical of South Carolina, Prairie View N and I College, Lincoln University in Chester County, Pennsylvania, West Virginia Collegiate Institute, Wilberforce, Alabama State A and M College, Tennessee A and I College and Louisiana A and M College. Collegiate sections were established at Howard, Lincoln University in Chester County, Pennsylvania, Fisk University, Meharry Medical College, Talledega College, Virginia Union University and Wilberforce in addition to combined sections at Atlanta and Morehouse College, and Wiley University and Bishop College.[15]

Students who attended African American colleges and universities did not experience any significant difficulty with volunteering for SATC service but African Americans attending other institutions did not share the same experience. Students complained that officials at several colleges in Nebraska, Ohio, Pennsylvania and other states denied their admission into SATC detachments. John P. Shillady as secretary of the National Association for the Advancement of Colored People shared their views and urged Emmett J. Scott to use his influence to gain admission of students in organizations where admission had been denied. Scott informed Shillady that a statement issued by COL Robert I. Rees denounced the exclusion of eligible African Americans and that students seeking induction in detachments at their institutions would not be required to transfer to other institutions. Commanding officers of SATC detachments were advised to use tact and discretion in providing mess and quarters, and in arranging such segregation as necessary under local conditions in cooperation with their educational officials. The statement by COL Rees for the War Department clearly emphasized that the military did not attempt to eliminate the color line at colleges and universities where it was enforced and issues concerning racism were merely relegated to college authorities where they were resolved to the satisfaction of the institutions. Oberlin College officials were instructed that integrated barracks and detachments were not permissible and African American students were advised to transfer to nearby Wilberforce University or to other African American colleges and universities where SATC programs were available. The War Department's denial to extend the policy to include African Americans students at Oberlin College caused the students to refer to the SATC as a *Sad Attempt to Cooperate.*[16]

On June 3, 1918, the War Department established Reserve Officers' Training Corps camps at Plattsburgh Barracks in New York, Fort Sheridan in Illinois, and Presidio of San Francisco, California, where 6,500 students were trained personnel but not commissioned. The camps were continued for SATC training from July 16, 1918 to September 15, 1918 when students would be commissioned as Infantry officers. Exclusion of African Americans influenced Howard officials to request the extension of the program to African American colleges and vocational schools. As a result, War Department authorization was granted on July 16, 1918 and the instruction camp for African American schools and college was conducted at Howard with training anticipated from August 1 to September 16, 1918. Participating colleges were requested to send a student representative with each group of twenty-five students and a faculty member for each 100-student attendees. To maximize the inordinately short period of time to establish a successful summer camp, Howard organized a committee on military instruction and information which coordinated with CEST. The committee also received assistance from the Central Committee of Negro College Men, an organization which was formed at the urging of Joel Spingarn and consisted of African American students and graduates from Lincoln of Pennsylvania, Fisk, Atlanta, Morehouse, Morgan, Virginia Union, Columbia, Harvard, Yale and Brown, to pursue the issue of officer training for African American students at separate camps. Within two weeks Howard had recruited its established quota of 200 by August 5, 1918, which included forty-seven faculty representatives, from as far as Florida, Michigan and Oklahoma and representing seventy colleges and schools assembled at the university. However, the SATC Instruction Camp trained 457 collegiate students from seventy colleges by September 1918. This unexpected but enthusiastic large training class taxed the university's physical plant since Howard was training and providing quarters and commissary provisions for 300 soldiers in its detachment of the National Army Training Corps. Although many thought COL Charles Young would be assigned to command the SATC summer camp, a cadre of officers from the 349th and 350th Field Artillery was selected by the War Department and it was commanded by Lieutenant Russell Smith. All were graduates of Fort Des Moines and were detailed from Camp Dix, New Jersey to conduct the summer camp. Spingarn was given the major credit for the establishment of the camp at Fort Des Moines, Iowa where the 17th Provisional Training Regiment commissioned African American officers on October 15, 1917.[17]

The experimental test summer camp at Howard was significant in several respects. The exceptional successes of military instruction in conjunction with excellent cooperation by the academic officials were recognized by military officials during their inspections and reviews of troops. The camp afforded the association of many students from several institutions where friendships were formed that outlasted the beneficial aspects of military training. The formation of the Negro Student Army Association revealed to Howard officials a new mission in educational leadership, and a vibrant determination to inculcate practical aspects of the military and physical training of SATC into the university's program. The decision to combine the SATC graduation with that of the second contingent of the National Army Training Corps on September 14, 1918 was also a notable historical event since it symbolized the sensitivity of the university and SATC officials to the common interests of African American soldiers. The joint graduation gained added distinction since Special Assistant to the Secretary of War Emmett J. Scott presided, and presentations were given by CEST representative MAJ Robert B. Perry and the Honorable William H. Lewis. This occasion also marked the first university appearance of President-Elect J. Stanley Durkee who accepted a commemorative bronze tablet from the Negro Student Army Association. National Army officials awarded 320 certificates to summer camp participants who qualified as sergeant instructors, and recommended 101 for training at officer training camps.[18]

The selection of Howard as the training camp was an excellent decision. Students had earlier formed a Howard battalion, and personnel with previous military training in the Washington High School Cadet Corps became the officers who commanded the battalion. When war was declared on April 6, 1917, military training was intensified and students organized themselves and urged the establishment of a Plattsburgh camp for African Americans which was later established at Camp Des Moines where Howard University had more graduates than any other African American institution. The formation of SATC was ideal for its students who desired to continue their education while receiving the military benefits of the program. With the School of Manual Arts and Applied Sciences already involved in a program sponsored by the Federal Board for Vocational Education that trained personnel for service in the Signal Corps, a training course was organized on November 7, 1917 with sixty-five men that was expanded to 135 personnel. Many of the enlisted men who were recommended for service with the 325th Field Signal Battalion at Chillicothe, Ohio later served as instructors because of the excellent training they received at Howard University. The presence of enlisted personnel who were quartered in Clark Hall and portions of the old Main Building after the formation of the SATC detachment on September 1, 1918 assisted in establishing *esprit de corps* among the students.[19]

Walter S. Buchanan as president of Alabama State Agricultural and Mechanical experienced difficulty in receiving an SATC detachment. The Educational Director of Vocational Instruction, C. R. Dooley, questioned the feasibility of establishing a detachment there and felt that it was wiser to place detachments at institutions where maximum achievement could be obtained at the earliest possible date with the minimum outlay of equipment. However, by October 18, 1918, a detachment was granted and two officers had arrived to organize a Section B detachment.[20] South Carolina State A and M formed a military organization consisting of a headquarters corps, six companies and a band with MAJ Grover Harden serving as commandant.[21] Several West Virginia Collegiate Institute personnel had been qualified for service during the Howard SATC camp and on September 19, 1918 the college was authorized to establish a SATC detachment that was commanded by 1LT Robert M. Hendricks. The institute was approved to provide Section A training but the CEST modified the organizational plan for Section B training.[22] Military training at Wiley and Bishop provided an opportunity for the commissioning of LT Elijah H. Goodwin from the United States 24th Infantry Regiment who commanded the detachment while Private Archie Price served as acting Corporal at Wiley and Privates Wilfred Lamb, Arthur N. Simmons and Claude Simpkims served at Bishop. LT John R. Finley with prior service as a corporal in the Ohio 9th Battalion from 1910 to 1913 was assigned to the Medical Corps and joined the detachment on September 21, 1918.[23] LT Leonard L. McLeod had served with LT John A. Love in the 350th Field Artillery and upon their arrival in September 1918 at Hampton were respectively assigned as commanders of Companies A and B with CPT Charles W. Fairfax becoming the battalion commander. LT Love was subsequently transferred to Howard and LT Lee J. Purnell assumed command of Company B on October 5, 1918.[24] Although CPT Edward Clayton Foster commanded the Atlanta and Morehouse SATC detachments, the other African Americans commissioned at Fort Des Moines were CPT Joseph Hurlong Scott, LT Richard Carlisle Thompson and LT Eugene Waldo Hardimen. LT Thompson had served three years in the 10th U.S. Cavalry Regiment and LT Hardimen was assigned to the Dental Corps. The university section included instructor Lewis A. Dominis with fifty-three students from Atlanta University and a Morehouse detachment with thirty-eight students.[25] Meharry Medical College was unique in that its SATC detachment was assigned the responsibility for training personnel in the Medical and Dental Enlisted Reserve Corps.[26]

The presence of military personnel was a concern for some collegians, including Samuel H. Archer, Dean of Morehouse College and acting president, who felt that smoking by soldiers would influence and affect the behavior of Morehouse students. He met with the president of Atlanta, Edmund A. Ware, to discuss this problem with students to explain the traditions of Morehouse. The commanding officer of the SATC detachment concurred with a nonsmoking policy at the college and restricted smoking from the lower portion of all campus buildings. Archer shared this policy with president George Rice Hovey of Virginia Union and urged that the implementation of policies denouncing smoking, swearing and gambling be sent to the Committee on Education and Special Training. The president of Morehouse, John Hope, was visiting African American soldiers in Europe under the auspices of the YMCA to assist their response against discriminatory practiced by United States military and to seek the elimination of the racial policies.[27]

Military organizations on the campus of Howard had the opposite affect and influenced the brief formation of a Girl's Battalion. During the fall of 1918 when the university closed because of an influenza epidemic, it was deemed best to place the female students in a dormitory under military discipline. At the initiative of Durkee, a Girl's Battalion was organized and after a short period two companies of uniformed women students participated credibly in battalion reviews and drills. The lack of any cases of influenza in the dormitory was attributed to lectures given to the students and the spirit of cooperation and *esprit de corps* fostered by the battalion which was discontinued with the reopening of the university in 1918.[28]

Demobilization immediately after the armistice of November 11, 1918 affected the status and the continuance of SATC organizations.[29] War Department officials determined that the profitability of the detachments to the federal government and students could only be maintained until the end of the fiscal year. Major Ralph Barton Perry as executive director of CEST advocated the views of the War Plans Division of the General Staff of the Army. He stressed that SATC was not an educational methodology assumed by many institutions but only a plan for creating a reservoir of officer candidates for Officer Training Camps and personnel with technical skills. Major Perry explained that approximately 25 percent of the educational institutions were opposed to maintaining their detachments and individual soldiers desired discharge to pursue their civilian education, and the War Department was not authorized to retain them for military service. In some instances, he realized that demobilization had caused some individual hardships for some students and inconvenience to institutions relying on the continuation of the corps. These concerns influenced Secretary of War Newton D. Baker to announce on December 21, 1918 that with the termination of SATC detachments, eligible colleges and universities would participate in the establishment of a Reserve Officers Training Corps which had been authorized on June 3, 1916.[30]

# 2

# *Establishing ROTC Detachments*

Demobilization of SATC relieved CEST of most of its responsibilities but the reestablishment and development of ROTC became its main function. On August 25, 1919, the administration of ROTC was transferred from CEST in the Office of the Chief of Staff to the Office of the Adjutant General. The War Department Plans Division on August 29, 1919 created an ROTC Branch to supervise, direct, and control affairs pertaining to ROTC, and CEST was demobilized on September 1, 1919. The War Department also had announced within days after the armistice the reestablishment of approximately 100 of the detachments in existence, and institutions were granted permission to submit their applications. Some institutions were given until January 1919 to dissolve their SATC detachments in order to establish ROTC detachments without discontinuing military training or financial benefits received from the federal government. The ROTC programs which included land grant colleges consisted of two years each of basic and advanced training. Compulsory enrollment was required at land-grant colleges and some private institutions, but advanced training which led to a reserve commission was based on a selective and voluntary basis. Legislation also allowed institutions to organize detachments which were given specialized instruction in infantry training as well as field artillery, engineer, coastal artillery, ordnance, medical, and aeronautical training. This training was significantly different from SATC programs which were essentially formulated for meeting the emergency requirements of providing technical support to combat organizations. The focus of SATC was not to train officers for the immediate war or to retain a reserve officer cadre capable of commanding soldiers in future wars. In June 1919, ROTC detachments had been established in 191 colleges and universities, and 128 secondary institutions with an enrollment of more than 90,000. However, interest in the program made it apparent that personnel available for duty was significantly reduced especially with the discharge of temporary officers.[1]

The reduction of temporary officers allotted to educational institutions to maintain ROTC detachments caused the withdrawal of many organizations. Institutions that desired to continue military training programs under War Department General Order 48 issued in 1916 were not required to maintain ROTC detachments and students were required to provide their uniforms. Each institution was obligated to offer at least three hours of instruction to 100 or more students who were at least age fourteen and bonds were also required for security of military property. In instances where the War Department was unable to detail officers, the institutions were responsible for designating an individual responsible for administering military science departments through the utilization of volunteer retired officers, reserve or discharged officers and faculty or students with active duty commissioned service. Institutions that desired to continue military training under the established conditions were required to submit applications to their local ROTC district inspector. On April 4, 1920, a War Department circular announced a policy that curtailed ROTC detachments at institutions where it appeared that maximum benefits were not obtained, and to facilitate the maximum advantage of limited manpower all personnel were transferred to more productive detachments. African American institutions discontinued under this procedure included Straight College in New Orleans, Louisiana, Prairie State Normal and Industrial College in Prairie View, Texas, Branch Normal College at Pine Bluff, Arkansas, South Carolina State A and M in Orangeburg, South Carolina, Alabama State A and M College in Huntsville, Tennessee Agricultural and Industrial State Normal School in Nashville, Tennessee and West Virginia Collegiate Institute located in Institute, West Virginia.[2]

The transition from SATC to ROTC detachments coincided with the ending of Red Summer in 1919, when twenty-five major racial disturbances troubled the nation, with the most serious occurring in Chicago, Illinois; Knoxville, Tennessee; Omaha, Nebraska; Longview, Texas; and Elaine, Arkansas. Several African American veterans returning from Europe were confronted with racial violence and fought to protect themselves and other civilians. William E.B. Du Bois recognizing the sentiments of many African Americans who had supported the efforts to make the world safe for democracy, emphasized, "We Return. We return from Fighting. We return fighting" — to improve conditions at home. Claude McKay recognized the increased violence toward African Americans incited by organizations that included the Ku Klux Klan in his poem, "If We Must Die," which stressed aggressive resistance toward violent mobs and aggressive reactions in defense of themselves and their communities. State officials in Arkansas feared the military attitude among cadets. Branch Normal College at Pine Bluff in Arkansas had the bolts of its rifles removed by the commanding general at Camp Pike, who anticipated trouble with the return of the bodies of four African American soldiers who had been killed during a riot. Although the bolts were to be returned after the termination of the unrest, the failure of the military to return the bolts prompted a protest from Superintendent J. G. Ish, Jr. to the military district inspector.[3]

South Carolina State A and M established its ROTC detachment on January 21, 1919 with 1LT Samuel A. Hull assigned as PMST. The detachment was withdrawn by the War Department on December 17, 1919 but on January 20, 1920 the college was authorized to continue military training under Section 56 of the National Defense Act. First Sergeant Denver F. Frasier was appointed commandant and PMST and Sergeant George A. Holland remained unassigned there until the Adjutant General G. M. Holley of the Southeastern Department requested his reassignment to another organization or institution with an established military department. The adjutant general alleged that since the withdrawal of the previous ROTC detachment military instruction had become unpopular and the insistence by Sergeant Holland that the college officials adhere to military regulations regarding military instructions had caused negative relations between Sergeant Holland and collegiate president Robert Shaw Wilkinson. He recommended that the War Department send no military personnel to the college since South Carolina State A and M had a faculty member qualified to perform the duties of a professor of military science and tactics.[4]

Wilkinson explained to MAJ James E. Ardrey during the annual inspection of 1922 that the uncertain attitude of the War Department officials toward the college and the withdrawal of the PMST did not influence the most effective military organization and efficient instruction. Wilkinson petitioned for the continuation of ROTC since the college recognized the benefits derived from military training and the students were willing to accept instruction offered by the military department. He also requested the issuance of uniforms and other equipment that was available to the former ROTC detachment to ensure the highest maintenance of military efficiency. Wilkinson claimed that the required standards were not met because of the inability of a small proportion of students to meet the financial requirements of the organization. He withdrew the request for the assignment of a PMST to succeed Sergeant Denver Frasier who had been transferred to Camp Benning, Georgia where he was in the process of obtaining his discharge to return to South Carolina State A and M. The favorable attitude of the faculty and students influenced MAJ Ardrey but he recommended the elimination of target practice from the program because the college was located in a southern community where white citizens were fearful of any conditions that might result from issuing ammunition to African American cadets. This issue undoubtedly contributed toward the withdrawal of government aid to the college on November 3, 1923.[5]

The intention of the War Department to withdraw ROTC from Agricultural and Technical College of North Carolina, established on December 26, 1918, was devastating to president James B. Dudley. He informed TAG that the college had maintained the required strength through a special arrangement that permitted the institution to extend the enrollment to students in its trade department. He emphasized that the institution was a land grant college charged with the mission of having military instruction and it was the only African American land grant college which gave attention exclusively to training men with an average age of twenty-two. The college had advertised ROTC and many of the incoming students were encouraged to enroll during the next semester because of the availability of military training. Sixty-eight enrolled students received instruction from a military officer and the elimination of ROTC would entirely destroy the splendid student morale and the confidence of the students and general public in the reliability of the college to offer ROTC as advertised. The War Department agreed to reconsider the status of the detachment and provide assistance in military training if a minimum of 100 were enrolled. Dudley according to War Department direction requested the continuation of the military department under War Department General Order 48 enacted in 1916 and the retention of a noncommissioned officer to assist in the reorganization of the detachment. He also reported that the ROTC enrollment had reached 121 and was expected to increase to 300 by October 1, 1919.[6]

CPT Robert L. Campbell served as PMST until discharged in November 1919 and Dudley obtained temporary approval to retain Sergeant William C. Greene to ensure the success of ROTC until the detail of a commissioned officer. The discharge of temporary officers prevented the War Department from detailing officers to detachments which previously had failed to maintain the required student strength. Dudley was also notified that SGT Greene would be relieved of his temporary duties at North Carolina A and T and he attempted to reassure the War Department that a faculty member who had served in France as a commissioned officer would be used to train students. However, MAJ Person Mencher of the Office of the Chief of Staff in the War Department reported on October 4, 1919 that North Carolina A and T had enrolled only twenty-two from its collegiate department and 100 from its trade section or preparatory department. He stressed that ROTC regulations prohibited the enrollment of students in the preparatory department into the ROTC division.[7]

Senator F. M. Simmons on October 1, 1919 questioned the legality of the discontinuance of the ROTC detachment and informed TAG that information received from the University of North Carolina did not give the impression that Agricultural and Technical College of North Carolina failed to meet the required enrollment and that there was not a scarcity of officers there since two faculty members had served in France. Confident of the issuance of appropriate orders to maintain ROTC, Senator Simmons supported the splendid efforts of the college and praised the accomplishments of Dudley to strengthen racial relations. On October 10, 1919, TAG advised the senator of the extension of government aid to the college and that the noncommissioned officer formerly assigned to duty there would be reassigned to the institution. However, TAG had given only the continuance of military training for JROTC under the National Defense Act.[8] With the exception of five salvageable rifles and gun slings, the balance of the government property was destroyed by fire on January 27, 1930 and no other military property had been issued since 1931. MG Edward L. King of the Fourth Corps Area requested the withdrawal of military property since the college was also unwilling to furnish the required surety bond for the security of government property which was necessary for military training. Therefore, the War Department disbanded the JROTC program at Agricultural and Technical College of North Carolina.[9]

Although not officially redesignated as Agricultural and Technical College of North Carolina, the college, on April 30, submitted an application to reestablish military training but it was rejected. The Chief of Infantry, who was requested by TAG to survey the educational institutions qualified to receive new detachments, reported that his branch had an excess of officers under the 1933 revision of the War Department Mobilization Plan and the existing ROTC detachments were producing a strength larger than necessary. Since the combined output was approximately 750 in excess of the requirement during the last five years, he requested that the advance course for ROTC detachments be reduced to a maximum of 500. It was obvious the Infantry was unable to justify the establishment of new ROTC detachments but a priority list was presented to TAG. The Chief of Infantry considered the geographical area where detachments should have been organized, the probable enrollment of institutions, the early application of qualified institutions and the present status of Section 55c institutions.

MG George Van Horn Moseley, Commanding General of the Fourth Corps Area, informed TAG that there was no requirement for African

American reserve officers in his corps area. The Chief of Infantry felt that insufficient grounds was given by the corps area commanding general for the disapproval of the application. The Army Mobilization Plans specially specified that thirty-six battalions and fifteen regiments of African American personnel would be included in the Organized Reserves. The establishment of ROTC at Howard and Wilberforce clearly indicated an apparent intention to commission and utilize African American Reserve Officers. For as long as this policy remained in effect, it would have been an injustice to discriminate against African American students and deny them an opportunity to qualify for reserve commissions. The Chief of Infantry on July 18, 1935 placed Agricultural and Technical College of North Carolina on the list of qualified institutions scheduled to have new JROTC detachments, but it was placed below several colleges and high schools in the twenty-sixth priority position. TAG on August 16, 1935 rejected the recommendation of the Chief of Infantry because of the shortage of available commissioned and enlisted personnel. This rejection did not deter the board of trustees from authorizing Ferdinand D. Bluford to reapply for a detachment on July 27, 1936. Granted a JROTC detachment under Section 55c, CPT Robert L. Campbell relieved Clyde DeHuguley who had served in the department since 1929. Warmoth T. Gibbs provided military instruction after the departure of SGT Green in 1926.[10]

Cognizant that War Department officials would not provide high priorities to the placement of military personnel at African American institutions, some college presidents provided the initiative to establish detachments and received government aid under section 56 of the National Defense Act of June 3, 1916. MG J. T. Dickman of the 8th Corps Area recognized the interest of W. B. Bizzell, who was president of Texas A and M College as well as Prairie View Normal and Industrial College. He recommended military training for college under Special Regulations 45 without the preliminary inspection from his headquarters since Prairie View N and I had formed an ROTC detachment on December 15, 1918 that was disbanded together with other detachments. However, MG Dickman requested that SGT Horace G. Wilder of Company C, 24th Infantry Regiment, stationed in Columbus, New Mexico, be detailed to train the students if the detachment was reestablished. Secretary of War Newton D. Baker approved the reestablishment of the detachment under the amended Section 55c of the National Defense Act and the reassignment of SGT Wilder on January 6, 1921. Prairie View with a JROTC detachment was assigned to the Civilian College category as a nonessential military institution.[11]

William Hale, president of Tennessee A and I State Normal School, State Superintendent of Public Instruction Albert Williams and Governor

A. H. Roberts were extremely displeased with the discontinuance of the JROTC at Tennessee A and I. An officer had not been detailed to the detachment but SGT Vance H. Marchbanks with twenty-four years of Regular Army service and service as a captain during the recent war, and SGT Allen Turner had rendered excellent service to the institution. The district military inspector was satisfied with the performance of the noncommissioned officers but speculated that the efficiency of 146 students would have been higher under the leadership of an officer. Soliciting the assistance of Senator K. D. McKellar, State Superintendent of Public Instruction Williams considered retention of the detachment because of its great value and tendency to promote racial harmony. Governor Roberts was anxious to retain the detachment because its discontinuance was viewed as discriminatory by African Americans. With the encouragement of the governor and Senator McKellar, Hale requested an investigation by the secretary of war concerning the withdrawal of the ROTC detachment.[12]

After careful reconsideration of the issue at the request of the governor of Tennessee, Secretary of War Baker emphasized the necessity of adhering to legislation implemented on December 22, 1919 which he did not consider deliberately discriminatory toward African American institutions. Eliminations at African American and other civilian colleges were necessary because of the shortage of military officers available for ROTC duty. He stressed that institutions could avoid radical changes in their programs with the acceptance of military aid under Section 56 of the National Defense Act and whenever possible with the assignment of a regular Army officer.[13]

Tennessee A and I complied with the military instructions contained in General Order 48 and CPT Glenn P. Anderson from the ROTC detachment at Vanderbilt University in Nashville inspected the proposed detachment. CPT Anderson reported that SGT Marchbanks, discharged as a captain from the Army on April 14, 1919, was a soldier of excellent bearing and was qualified to conduct military training. In the event that SGT Marchbanks was not eligible to command a detachment because of his status in the regular Army, professor G. O. Carrington with eleven years with the United Boys Brigade of America in Boston, Massachusetts was available. He recommended Carrington primarily because of his enlisted service in the Field Artillery Central Officers Training School where he would have been commissioned if the armistice had not been signed. CPT Anderson recognized the excellent reputation of Tennessee A and I and encouraged the reestablishment of a detachment. COL E. H. De Armond, Chief of Staff for Headquarters of the Southeastern Department, recommended approval of government aid, and the retention of SGT Marchbanks or the assignment of Carrington as military science instructor. The request for government aid was approved by the secretary of war on March 8, 1920.[14] Although an inspection by MAJ J. E. Ardrey of the Fourth Corps Area indicated that faculty and students were interested in military training but no action had been initiated to begin the program, MAJ Ardrey did not recommend the establishment of an ROTC detachment and recommended the withdrawal of the JROTC detachment if the institution delayed the beginning of military instruction. The War Department withdrew its authorization of this detachment on September 25, 1923.[15]

Withdrawal of the ROTC detachment may have been influenced by politicians who opposed the administration of Hale and raised allegations concerning the mismanagement of military funds. Accusers alleged that Hale misappropriated checks by failing to issue checks to soldiers in accordance with scheduled payments. They further alleged that Hale had habitually extended loans to military personnel at exorbitant rates of interest with their bimonthly salaries serving as security. Although most loans were granted a few days prior to the issuance of military checks, a United States attorney general concluded that Hale had the checks in his possession when loans were granted but retained them for several days to benefit from the accrued interest. The Coordinator of the Veterans Bureau at Tennessee A and I, H. N. Robinson, was implicated in the allegations and was arrested with Hale on Federal warrants charging them with extortion on February 4, 1922.

Hale explained that the local and district offices of the Veterans Bureau had urged his support in providing financial assistance to SATC personnel and defended his loan policy as acts of goodwill that were not designed to secure interest. Supported by influential interest groups within the state which included local newspapers, a motion submitted by the only woman on the State Board of Education to suspend Hale until the charges against him were settled was defeated. The chairman of the Board of Education declared that the board had fulfilled its obligations to the Federal government in reference to the administration of SATC at Tennessee A and I. The board had not received an official complaint and was first informed of charges through a news dispatch that originated from Washington. The chairman was dismayed that two Federal agents arrived in Nashville and arrested Hale and Robinson without informing members of the State Board of Education. The board expressed complete faith in the honesty, integrity and ability of Hale and advised the Veterans Bureau that "unless it recognized the supremacy of Tennessee authorities in the operation of the state's schools where rehabilitation training was carried on, the Board of Education would request that such training be discontinued."[16] Clearly the board resented the actions of the federal agents and Hale was unable to prevent the negative recommendation of the inspector which caused the removal of the ROTC detachment.

With the reestablishment of military training after the World War, Delaware State College had thirty-five eligible students who were exempted from military training because of the distance they walked daily to get to the college, and military instruction consisted mostly of close order drill. Professor William H. Lee, a graduate of Hampton, had the additional duty of maintaining the detachment in the absence of commissioned or noncommissioned personnel. From a national defense standpoint there were no material benefits gained from the existence of the detachment and it required practically no maintenance to retain. The War Department did not implement measures to withdraw the detachment. In 1926 S. J. Lewis, who graduated from Hampton, gave military training to thirty-six students. Although the detachment was initially given Springfield rifles and other obsolete and worthless equipment, ammunition and uniforms were not issued. Therefore, a request to withdraw government aid from Delaware State was submitted on April 27, 1927.[17]

Lincoln University in Jefferson City, Missouri was originally established as Lincoln Institute by African American enlisted men and officers of the 62nd and 65th Regiments on September 11, 1866 and became a land grant college in 1891. Although an Army officer was not assigned, preparations were made by the Industrial Arts department to secure uniforms for students in September 1919. A decision of the Board of Curators at Lincoln University on May 15, 1923 to establish a military department was approved by the university board on August 10, 1923. N. B. Young as university president requested military aid from the War Department and the assignment of a retired African American noncommissioned officer who would be provided board and lodging. LTC Fred V. S. Chamberlain inspected the institution and recommended the establishment of a detachment whenever a suitable instructor was available and that a retired African American noncommissioned officer be detailed to Lincoln. Sergeant Arthur P. Hayes was assigned in June 1924 together with funding for the purchase of arms and equipment and the secretary of war granted the establishment of a JROTC detachment on July 3, 1924.[18] However, limited appropriations for the faculty influenced the president of Lincoln to request the Seventh Corps Area commanding general to withdraw government aid and remove all government property. TAG complied with the request on September 27, 1927.[19]

Kansas Vocational Institute in Topeka which was previously known as the Industrial and Educational Institute was granted government assistance on April 20, 1922 but enrollment of eligible cadets never reached 100. When the Seventh Corps Area commanding general recommended the withdrawal of government aid in 1925, Congressman Daniel R. Anthony, Jr. aggressively opposed the termination of military aid. Declining enrollment during the two years, from forty-eight to thirty-three, compelled the Seventh Corps Area to initiate measures to withdraw the detachment but the principal of the Kansas Vocational Institute requested an extension of the detachment since efforts were being made to increase the number of cadets. Anthony was appraised of the situation on December 29, 1927 to ascertain his views on the matter but he did not respond to the Corps Area commander. COL Edward Croft in the Operations and Training Division determined that the government received little or no return for military aid given to the institute and on April 8, 1929 he recommended the withdrawal of government aid from Kansas Vocational Institute. The War Department again sought the opinion of Anthony to determine the desirability of maintaining the detachment since an inspecting officer and the Corps Area commander had indicated that the prospect of the institute to meet the legal requirements was negligible. Anthony admitted that the institute was struggling to provide an education for African American male students and it was entirely supported by the State of Kansas, but he still thought it necessary to continue the government aid. With the assurance of Congressman Anthony who was supported by John S. Dean, a former officer during the World War, Acting Secretary of War Patrick J. Hurley approved the continuation of the aid. Enrollment improved from thirty during the next academic year to 70 but by March 23, 1931 the students receiving military training had declined to sixty-six. Although Senator Arthur Capper supported the retention of the program, Secretary of War Hurley notified the Kansas Vocational Institute of the elimination of government aid at the end of the 1931 academic year.[20]

The War Department authorized West Virginia Collegiate Institute to establish a Junior ROTC detachment on December 23, 1918, five days prior to the disbanding of SATC. CPT John H. Purnell organized the detachment which was disbanded in 1920. West Virginia State College reapplied for a detachment and was granted approval to establish a detachment from the State Board of Education in 1929. Attempting to meet the requirements of a land grant institution, the faculty adopted a special recommendation of the Committee on Collegiate Aims which required the reestablishment of military training. On January 27, 1936, John W. Davis, president of West Virginia State College, envisioned a new responsibility of training African American officers for the organization which was approved by the State Legislature during its last session. LTC R. B. Patterson, Acting Adjutant General of the Fifth Corps Area, considered the allocation of an infantry

detachment for the college because of the corps area justification that eliminated an infantry detachment at Ohio State University. He also felt the
establishment of an additional detachment at West Virginia State should
have been considered only with the question of continuing the detachment
at Wilberforce. Although this attempt failed to gain TAG approval, Davis
was informed by Congressman Joe L. Smith of the Sixth West Virginia Congressional District that the appropriation bill approved by Congress on
March 15, 1936 provided for the establishment of additional ROTC detachments.[21]

When another affirmative faculty vote was endorsed by the West Virginia State Board of Education, Davis on March 21, 1936 requested assistance from President Franklin D. Roosevelt in obtaining approval for an
ROTC detachment. Davis had attained support of Senators Rush D. Holt
and Matthew M. Neely, Congressmen Andrew Edmiston, George W. Johnson, John Kee, Robert L. Ramsey, Jennings Randolph and Joe L. Smith in
addition to the Command General Guy Ash of the West Virginia National
Guard. Supporting resolutions were also passed by the West Virginia Congress of Parents and Teachers, the West Virginia High School Principals'
Conference, and the American Legion Department of West Virginia. Davis
stressed that African Americans were excluded from receiving the benefits
of ROTC partly because of the attitudes of officials in states where African
American institutions were located and partly because of policies imple-
mented at integrated universities that did not encourage the enrollment of
African American students. State Supervisor of Negro Schools and chairman of the National Negro Democratic Committee of West Virginia, I. J. K.
Wells, explained the difficulties confronting African Americans when they
attempted to enlist into the military or gain admission into the USMA or
Naval Academy. Denying the reestablishment of ROTC at West Virginia
State would be an injustice since there was not a single state National Guard
organization for African Americans. TAG confirmed congressional funding
for establishing additional ROTC detachments but provisions to assign personnel to these detachments would not be finalized until after a study was
conducted to determine which institutions would receive the ROTC
detachments.[22]

West Virginians launched a massive campaign to regain an ROTC
detachment for West Virginia State after the West Virginia State House on
February 5, 1937 and the Senate on February 8, 1937 passed a resolution
requiring ROTC for West Virginia State. Senator Neely and Congressman
Edmiston queried respectively Secretary of War Harry H. Woodring and
MG Edgar T. Conley to ascertain what action was needed to expedite the
ROTC application of West Virginia State. They were informed that with the

exception of medical detachments the lack of funds prohibited the organization of new ROTC detachments. The responsibility of training 1,000 Reserve officers under the Thomason Act in addition to other demands placed upon the Army forced the War Department to the reluctant conclusion that new detachments would be delayed until there was an increase in commissioned personnel. Acting Assistant Chief of Staff L. D. Gasser investigated the issue and stated that the Bureau of the Budget must provide a commissioned strength of 14,459 before the Personnel Division would issue a statement regarding legislative action necessary to provide additional officers. He maintained that it was more efficient and economic to eliminate the existing deficiencies in the established ROTC detachments and recommended to Chief of Staff Malin Craig that Senator Neely be assured that the War Department appreciated his interest in matters affecting the national defense. Although assured that all ROTC applications were retained for future consideration, Daniel W. Ambrose, Jr. of the State Auditor's Office, who was also a member of the Business and Professional Men's Club, together with Senator Neely and Congressman Joe L. Smith remained vigilant in their efforts to attain military training at the college.[23]

African Americans refused to relent in the struggle to achieve the reinstatement of ROTC. David A. Lane, Jr., Dean of West Virginia State and a comrade of Charles Young American Legion Post 57, and Daniel L. Ferguson, chairman of the American Legion ROTC Committee, and Tau Chapter of Kappa Alpha Psi Fraternity joined the effort to persuade the War Department to extend military training to West Virginia State.[24] Physician D. T. Murray of the Young Democratic Club of McDowell County and member of the Negro State Board of Education questioned Assistant Secretary of War Louis Johnson concerning establishment of an ROTC detachment in addition to the organization of a National Guard detachment for African Americans and the abandonment of the Civilian Conservation Corps Camp at Berwind. Assistant Secretary of War Johnson emphasized that funds were not available for the organizations and the Forest Service was the technical branch of the Department of Agriculture which made recommendations to the director of the Civilian Conservation Corps concerning the disposition of its camps.[25] Charles E. Hodges of the Charleston Chamber of Commerce also informed TAG that the establishment of ROTC would significantly broaden career opportunities, improve the morale and spirit of the students, and enable the program to make a distinct contribution in the training of African Americans. He also informed Secretary of War Harry H. Woodring and TAG of the West Virginia State Legislature of his affirmation of the ROTC detachment on February 8, 1938. The Logan County Civic League endorsed the movement on March 22, 1938 while H.

D. Hazelwood on April 4, 1938 led a special committee of the Frederick Douglass Luncheon Club in Huntington in presenting their appeals to the War Department.[26]

John W. Davis gained support of others in urging the formation of 400 students into an ROTC detachment. D. L. Ferguson serving as a chairman of the Student Military Training Committee of the El Cubo Club, in explaining the patriotism of faculty and students, stated that John H. Hill resigned from the presidency of the college to serve as a commissioned officer during the Spanish-American-Cuban-Filipino War together with several students. Solomon Brown returned to serve on the faculty and the Student Military Training Committee. Ferguson further explained that during the recent world war the college lost its detachment because of low enrollment since approximately a third of the male students volunteered for the military. He emphasized that the West Virginia Department of the American Legion, the West Virginia Congress of Parents and Teachers in Negro Schools, the West Virginia State Teachers Association, the Charles Young American Legion Post in Charleston, and the Charleston Business and Professional Men's Club endorsed reinstatement of the detachment. On March 4, 1939 after recognizing that the Reserve Officers Association had unanimously approved a resolution requiring the extension of ROTC to all institutions which had submitted applications to the War Department, Davis requested that Congressman George W. Johnson, John Kee and A. C. Schiffler assist in the continuation of an eight-year effort to regain its detachment. Congressmen Andrew Edmiston reiterated his request for an ROTC detachment since the Civil Aeronautics Authority had designated the college as a possible site for training pilots, and Civilian Conservation Corps reports emphasized that West Virginia African Americans had adapted splendidly to the opportunities offered to them.

Assistant Secretary of War Louis Johnson emphatically stressed the training appropriations were only sufficient for maintaining existing detachments at their current levels and that the House Army Appropriation Bill for fiscal year 1940 did not contain provisions for establishing additional detachments. Howard P. Jeter explained that radio broadcasts implied that Germany was winning the European war and that it was imperative for West Virginia State students to receive military training. Assistant Secretary Johnson stated the diversion of funds to organize a detachment at one school would place the War Department in an untenable position with all of the other institutions whose applications had been denied. He stressed that demands of regular Army personnel precluded assigning officers to complete the requirements of existing detachments or providing instructors for schools desiring new detachments. The implication of these factors nullified an immediate expansion of ROTC since the War Department believed it was unwise to augment until the existing detachments were properly funded and all of the necessary personnel were assigned.[27]

Failing to induce the War Department to allocate an infantry detachment to West Virginia State, Davis referred Secretary of War Henry Stimson to House Resolution 10572, Public Law 800, 3rd Session, 76th Congress, Chapter 756, which appropriated funds for establishing additional ROTC motor-transport and tank detachments. The acquisition of 700 additional acres of land which provided the capability of offering mechanized training influenced Davis to seek the allocation of an ROTC motor transport and tank detachment for the college. Aware of the considerable misunderstanding in the nation concerning the training of African Americans, he stressed that this would be an excellent opportunity to dispel the misperception while serving the best interest of the entire country. Governor Homer A. Holt considered the college as an ideal location for motor transport and tank detachments and urged Secretary of War Stimson to investigate the possibility of establishing such detachments at West Virginia State College. Congressmen George W. Johnson, John Kee, M. M. Neely, A. C. Schiffler, and Walter R. Thurmond, president of the West Virginia Board of Control together with L. A. Toney, a past vice commander of the Department of the West Virginia American Legion and S. S. Gordon who had served as a commissioned officer in the 370th Infantry Regiment during World War I, were confident that a mechanized detachment would become a valuable asset and an integral component of the national defense. David Kirby, Secretary of the State Board of Education, in support of the allocation stressed that the college had made rapid strides in strengthening its faculty and had increased its student enrollment to nearly 1,300 from thirty-two states. The college was an excellent institution with accreditation from the North Central Association of Colleges and recognized by the Association of American Colleges and other national education organizations. However, I. J. K. Wells stressed that African American citizens felt the national administration was attempting to placate them by denying less than their full share of citizen participation.[28]

The War Department admitted that considerable attention had been given to establishing new ROTC detachments after receiving seventy-two applications which did not include many institutions which had applied to various Corps Area headquarters. Expansion of ROTC required increased manpower that would divert personnel and materials to the extent that the immediate and vital tasks of expediting the organization and training of combat forces would be jeopardized and an exception in favor of any one institution would be imprudent. General George C. Marshall stated that with the exception of a medical detachment at the University of Alaska, new ROTC detachments had not been established for several years and the intent of House Resolution 10572 was to remove restrictions formerly placed on the establishment of additional motor transport and tank detachments in order to organize those detachments whenever feasible. The War Department did not contemplate the establishment of ROTC motor transport or tank detachments but General Marshall reassured Congressman Johnson that the application of West Virginia State would be considered whenever it was feasible to expand college military training.[29] MG E. S. Adams, TAG, further explained to Daniel W. Ambrose that the War Department was charged with the responsibility of organizing, training and equipping an Army of 1,400,000 personnel and any proposal which interfered with that task would not be given favorable consideration. The procedure of producing Reserve Corps officers through ROTC, flying cadet schools and the establishment of an Officer Candidate Course were adequate to meet the contemplated requirements.[30]

Hampton was not immediately affected by War Department efforts to withdraw ROTC detachments from deficient institutions. Under the National Defense Act, Hampton had organized an SATC detachment that was demobilized after the armistice and formed an ROTC detachment on February 1, 1919. The legality of maintaining ROTC was raised on September 24, 1919 when the War Department questioned whether Hampton fulfilled the requirements of Section 40 of the National Defense Act because of the enrollment of preparatory students. The legislation also required the enrollment of 100 students who matriculated in curricula at colleges which granted academic degrees. William H. Scoville, Secretary of Hampton, stated that the institute was a land grant institution and was entitled to an ROTC organization. He candidly admitted that Hampton was not a college nor a college preparatory school although its graduates were capable of meeting collegiate entrance requirements and 256 students were enrolled in the military training program. The Judge Advocate General E. H. Crowder evaluated the status of Hampton based on the requirements of the National Defense Act which authorized ROTC detachments at four-year colleges and universities that offered collegiate degrees. He determined that legislation enacted on July 2, 1862 specially provided for the organization of ROTC detachments at essentially military schools that did not confer academic degrees but were inspected annually by War Department officials. The opinion of JAG was that Hampton was a State institution which met the requirements of the Morrill Act.[31]

Secretary of War Baker was confident that Hampton, with approximately 50 percent of the students at twenty years of age upon graduation, met the academic requirements of an essentially military school. The Hampton Board of Trustees on April 29, 1920 agreed to request essentially military status for Hampton to enable the retention of ROTC. Secretary of War Baker concurred with James E. Gregg in his desire to maintain as many ROTC detachments as possible in African American colleges and after Hampton was inspected he would make a decision. CPT A. G. Hixson, a district inspector of the ROTC visited Hampton on May 5, 1920 and according to Gregg was favorably impressed with the condition and performance of the ROTC battalion. An inspection by COL A. Thayer from the Eastern Department revealed the battalion consisted of three ROTC companies and two preparatory companies. COL Thayer recognized that relatively few African American colleges offered military training and recommended that full encouragement be given to Hampton to retain its military tradition. He recommended the retention of ROTC but concluded that Hampton's incorporation act of 1870 clearly indicated that the purpose of the institute was not essentially military. On May 27, 1920, COL F. E. Lacey, Jr. as assistant director of the Personnel Division recommended to TAG that Hampton retain ROTC until November 20, 1920. Gregg was informed of the decision on June 23, 1920 but was advised that Hampton was authorized to provide JROTC upon the withdrawal of ROTC.[32]

LT Leonard L. McLeod was performing duty at Camp Custer in Michigan where nineteen Howard University cadets and twenty-two Tuskegee cadets together with approximately thirty-nine high schools cadets from schools in Cleveland, Ohio, St. Joseph, Missouri, and Chicago, Illinois were assigned for summer training when he became aware of the planned elimination of ROTC at Hampton. Scheduled to appear before an Army Examination Board at Camp Sherman in Ohio before returning to Hampton and cognizant that CPT John Greene, the Wilberforce PMST had completed his examination, and MAJ Arthur Dean, the Howard PMST had left Camp Custer to appear before a similar examination board at Camp Meade, Maryland, LT McLeod was confident of passing the examination if given a fair chance. Failing the physical examination, he was notified that his discharge would become effective on October 31, 1920.[33]

A Virginia General Assembly decision on March 19, 1872 that designated Hampton as a land grant institution was rescinded on March 19, 1920 and the land grant was transferred to Virginia Normal and Industrial Institute in Petersburg became effective on December 1, 1920. Gregg realized the transferal and essentially military classification aggregated even further the disparity that existed in providing military training in African American colleges. He informed MG Adelbert Cronkhite, Commanding General of Third Corps Area, and Secretary of War Newton Baker on September 24,

1920 of his acceptance of the withdrawal of the ROTC detachment without a formal complaint. Expressing the military tradition of Hampton, Gregg requested the retention of LT Leonard L. McLeod as the PMST and urged the War Department to grant him a commission in the regular Army. Until a decision was reached concerning the PMST, J. L. B. Buck, who was commissioned a major during the war and succeeded William H. Scoville as director of Extension Work, would provide leadership for the detachment. TAG regretted the impracticality of maintaining the ROTC but expressed a desire that the previous high standard of excellence would be exhibited when JROTC was established on November 20, 1920. He regretted that LT McLeod had not qualified for a regular Army commission but stated he would be retained until November 30, 1920 after which a suitable replacement would be appointed.[34]

Hampton did not have adequate military officer quarters but civilian accommodations were available in the campus Holly Tree Inn. Although Gregg endeavored to have an African American assigned to the institute, since the majority of the faculty was not African American he felt there would not be any theoretical inconsistency with an appointment of a white officer. It was more important that the officer was competent, experienced and possessed the right attitude and spirit than his ethnicity. Informed that MAJ John E. Green desired to remain at Wilberforce to establish a successful ROTC detachment and that COL Charles Young was not available for reassignment to Hampton Institute, Gregg accepted MAJ Clifton R. Norton who was relieved of duty at Camp Pike in Arkansas and detailed as PMST on November 12, 1920. LTC Nathaniel N. Cartmell, a retired officer, succeeded COL Norton in 1921 and Gregg urged the continuation of service by Warrant Officer Charles C. Cooper because of his familiarity with faculty, administrators and students. Gregg was also influenced by the competency of WO Cooper and had previously requested that he command the JROTC detachment if another officer was not assigned to Hampton Institute.[35]

Establishing the organization with limited government aid in accordance with a War Department circular issued on September 15, 1921 was embarrassing for Gregg who was unable to alert new students to the impending cost of uniforms. He received the circular two days after the arrival of the students, and the policy affected approximately 300 students, approximately two third of the detachment. Gregg requested the suspension of the circular to permit students who enrolled before January 1, 1922 to have an opportunity to learn of their requirements in relation to compulsory ROTC. Gregg felt that an early notification was necessary since nearly all of the students were obligated to work and the substandard financial condition of southern African American families prevented them from paying tuition. Admitting students and announcing the change upon their arrival Gregg argued would have been detrimental to students, Hampton and the JROTC program. With the assistance of LTC Cartmell, Gregg persuaded TAG to accept the merits of his argument. The War Department concluded that Hampton was a preparatory school with some collegiate courses, that only qualified students in the highest four years were accepted into the ROTC program and that Hampton qualified as an essential military school under Special Regulations 44 which pertained to ROTC detachments. This designation automatically increased the ROTC enrollment from 134 to 519 students.[36]

On January 30, 1926, the board of trustees directed by LTC Cartmell requested the withdrawal of the JROTC detachment but military regulations required the submission of the notification three months prior to the effective removal of the detachment. However, the Third Corps Area headquarters, commanded by MG Douglas MacArthur, suggested that it was more logical to terminate the detachment at the closing of the academic year. After reviewing an inspection report which indicated an unsatisfactory management of the detachment, MG MacArthur concluded the withdrawal would not cause a material loss to the ROTC project and the funds and effort spent on Hampton would be better applied elsewhere. TAG concurred with his decision and the reassignment of COL Cartmell after the withdrawal was completed.[37]

The decline of military training coincided with the rise of the New Negro movement and the attitude of students toward the Hampton administration. Students were cognizant of the philosophies of Alain Locke and Marcus Garvey, and were influenced by the Harlem Renaissance and the attempts of students at Fisk, Howard and Lincoln to have African Americans appointed as their university presidents as well as the appointment of more African Americans to the faculty. Hampton students were also aware of protests by Howard students against mandatory ROTC attendance. Although a student strike did not occur at Hampton until October 1927, the students specifically were displeased with a rigid segregation policy initiated by Gregg after whites who attended a dance performance were unable to find seats in a reserved section for whites only. They were also concerned that some of the trade departments were under the control of white faculty members who were allegedly from Ku Klux Klan areas of Virginia. The strike was ended quickly and disturbances were subsiding by the end of the academic year but some students were suspended or dismissed and some transferred to other African American colleges.[38]

Military training of the Industrial Detachment at Tuskegee was conducted by CPT Edgar Bonsall until SATC was placed under the command of LT Charles M. Thompson and four other African American officers from October 1918 until the detachment was disbanded after the armistice. On January 11, 1919, Warren Logan was serving as acting principal of Tuskegee when he announced plans to commence ROTC instruction on February 1, 1919. Robert R. Moton, principal of Tuskegee, was primarily concerned with maintaining African American officers for the ROTC detachment to coordinate military instruction with his commandant. Emergency officers recruited during the war were scheduled for discharge by September 30, 1919 unless they had been examined and recommended for regular Army commissions. Discharge pertained to nearly all African American officers who applied under this procedure and were classified as class three personnel. CPT Russell Smith who commanded SATC at Howard was assigned as PMST in February 1919, but LT James C. Pinkston who arrived for duty in April 1919 and LT Harry J. Mack were not scheduled for military retention. CPT Smith while attending an ROTC Camp at Camp Custer in Michigan urged Moton to retain the assigned officers since the Regular Army did not have sufficient personnel available for duty with ROTC detachments. Influenced by officers who were urging their collegiate administrators to implement measures to ensure their retention, CPT Smith stressed to Moton the significance of retaining African American officers since there were few African American regular Army officers who could be detailed to ROTC detachments and all officers assigned to ROTC detachments were emergency personnel. Their discharge would ensure the placement of white officers who probably were not sympathetic toward the ROTC movement among African American colleges and would not ensure maximum cadet achievement in colleges where detachments were established.[39]

Moton conferred with Emmett J. Scott, who had served as the Special Assistant to Secretary of War Newton D. Baker, and MAJ Walter H. Loving, who served as director of the Philippine Constabulary Band and was serving in the Care Intelligence Bureau, concerning the status of African American commissioned and noncommissioned officers. With an excess of officers assigned to ROTC and other elements of the military, Scott considered the retention or reassignment of other excellent young officers was nearly impossible. Secretary of War Newton D. Baker informed Moton that the discharge of 1LT Pinkston would not be delayed due to the absolute necessity of reducing the Army to 18,000 commissioned officers by October 31, 1919. TAG realized the urgency of selecting a regular Army officer to ensure that the ROTC detachment would not be withdrawn. On July 31, 1920, MAJ Benjamin O. Davis was detailed as the Tuskegee PMST but General Peyton C. Harris stated that if Moton considered the performance of MAJ Davis unsatisfactory, he would implement measures to relieve him. Moton was confident that the assignment would fulfill his expectations and improve the education program at the institute. An increased enrollment into the detachment which had been converted into a JROTC detachment and the assignment of LTC Davis influenced Moton on November 4, 1920 to request the establishment of ROTC.[40]

LTC Davis disagreed with policies instituted by Moton and felt that the PMST position did not require a field grade officer to manage the JROTC program. He determined that any viable military science program required small arms weapon target practice and sought to obtain the necessary ammunition. The denial of an ammunition requisition by Moton influenced LTC Davis to request a change of assignment. He viewed the denial as a lack of administrative support of the military program and considered the adverse social conditions in the Tuskegee community as restrictive and disadvantageous to his family. LTC Davis recommended that TAG consider transferring him to either the 8th Illinois National Guard Infantry Regiment which was composed entirely of African Americans or the 369th New York National Guard Regiment which consisted of an integrated officer cadre. Reassignment to Howard University where it was also possible to render service to the District of Columbia 24th Regiment of High School Cadets was another recommended option. In fact anyplace in the continental United States, except the south, or foreign service assignment with the Philippine Constabulary or Haitian Constabulary were acceptable locations for military service. He was encouraged when Garnet C. Wilkinson, an assistant superintendent of Public Schools in the District of Columbia, informed him that COL Harrison Hall in TAG would immediately detail him to Howard and the Colored High School Cadet Corps which were under the control of the War Department, contingent upon his filing a request for transfer. On July 2, 1922, LTC Davis informed COL Hall of his desire for transfer by September 1, 1922 to enable him to assist in the planning and preparation of the academic year and to locate suitable quarters in Washington. Immediate concerns of Wilkinson and CPT Arthur C. Newman, who had accompanied him to the War Department, was the detail of an African American to command the Cadet Corps together with several noncommissioned officers to assist the JROTC band, provide maintenance to equipment and to administer routine matters.[41]

Moton felt that Tuskegee was more significant to the African American community than providing training for some African Americans. He acknowledged racial prejudice and segregation existed in the Tuskegee vicinity and explained to the Fourth Corps Area adjutant general at Fort McPherson, Georgia that he did not want to retain LTC Davis at the institute against his will. Regarding the denial of an ammunition requisition, he was unwilling to authorize the receipt of any ammunition regardless of the caliber since local racial tension at that time was untenable and any marksmanship training was deemed unwise. Opposition by white residents in Tuskegee to ROTC at the institute was quite evident and Moton did not want the occurrence of incidents that intensified racial tension that later caused riots in Elaine. Moton was aware of the efforts to select an African American PMST for the Howard ROTC detachment and the War Department's dilemma of allocating appropriate regular Army assignments for MAJ John E. Green at Wilberforce and LTC Benjamin O. Davis. He considered the Tuskegee assignment more critical than the position at Howard since its president and many of its faculty were white and felt it was less difficult to assign a white officer there as PMST than in the case of Tuskegee Institute where the president and the entire faculty were African American. He was disappointed and surprised that LTC Davis wanted a transfer after he had convinced the trustees to provide additional funding to construct a larger house than normal which was occupied by the Davis family. Moton did not envision maintaining the JROTC detachment unless an officer of similar caliber as LTC Davis was assigned in accordance with laws and regulations governing ROTC. Notified by the Fourth Corps Area chief of staff that a noncommissioned officer was not eligible to command JROTC, Moton requested that MAJ Green replace LTC Davis. MG David C. Shanks, Fourth Corps Area Commanding General denied the transfer of LTC Davis on July 25, 1922 although Wilkinson and Emmett J. Scott enthusiastically urged his reassignment.[42]

Emmett J. Scott, the Secretary-Treasurer at Howard, was accused of attempting to take LTC Davis away from Tuskegee. He acknowledged correspondence from LTC Davis concerning an assignment to the university prior to his departure for the Philippines but the vacancy was later occupied by MAJ Milton T. Dean. Scott denied any attempts by Howard, either directly or indirectly, to disturb the status of LTC Davis at Tuskegee although Howard with an ROTC detachment was more suitable for his rank as the senior African American officer in the regular Army. He explained that Howard would not seek his transfer until university officials were sure of his availability but he was sure that LTC Davis would find an assignment at Howard agreeable. LTC Davis assured Scott that his attitude toward service in the south had not changed.[43]

MG David C. Shanks inspected the detachment at Tuskegee on May 11, 1923 and was impressed with the policies of Moton concerning utilization of weapons by students. He recommended to TAG that it was in the best interest of the military to relieve LTC Davis whom he considered unfit for the important duty of PMST but supported the retention of the detach-

Tuskegee Institute Detachment, ca. 1920s. (Courtesy of Tuskegee University Archives, Tuskegee, AL)

ment. MG Shanks recommended that MAJ Green succeed LTC Davis but if that was impossible he urged the appointment of an African American WO. Commanding General of the Fifth Corps Area, MG J. H. McRae, in response to a request from TAG to relieve MAJ Green for assignment to Tuskegee disapproved the request since the embarrassing situation in the Fourth Corps Area would only be transferred to his corps area. MG McRae stated that the detail of MAJ Greene would expire at the end of the next academic year and he alleged that with the exception of race, MAJ Green had not developed any outstanding qualifications as a PMST. He foresaw the same situation confronting the Fourth Corps Area occurring in the Fifth Corps Area after the completion of MAJ Green's four-year assignment.[44]

The reassignments of MAJ Green and LTC Davis were scheduled respectively for July 1, 1924 and July 10, 1924 but neither officer was scheduled for foreign service. TAG considered their assignment to organizations within the United States was imperative but regarded duty with regular Army regiments as highly undesirable. TAG determined the only feasible alternative was to transfer the officers to assignments in the Organized Reserves or National Guard. However, the Chief of the Militia Bureau informally denied the transfer of LTC Davis to a National Guard organization and stressed the only suitable duty was as an instructor for African American guardsmen. An opinion of the JAG concluded that Section 40 of the National Defense Act made it mandatory for each ROTC detachment to have a commissioned officer. Therefore, TAG informed the Third Corps Area that a WO could not succeed LTC Davis and if a white officer was not acceptable to Moton the only viable alternative was to reorganize the detachment under the amended provisions of Section 55c of the National Defense Act. Moton explained to MG Shanks the conditions in the Tuskegee community that had compelled him to adhere to his decision of having an African American replacement and recommended Cleve L. Abbott as a possible candidate for commissioning. Moton also recommended the assignment of a WO from nearby Fort Benning or having a white officer from Auburn University visit the campus to conduct training several days each week to retain the JROTC. However, TAG on April 10, 1924 recommended the withdrawal of the detachment and the extension of government aid under Section 55 of the National Defense Act. On June 16, 1924, Moton had surmised the elimination of JROTC which was directed by the Secretary of War on July 1, 1924 and implemented by the Fourth Corps Area commander. The Tuskegee JROTC detachment was officially withdrawn on July 3, 1924.[45]

The successful completion of the first Reserve Officers Camp for African Americans, conducted at Tuskegee by the Fourth Corps Area with the assistance of LTC Davis influenced Moton on June 6, 1929 to request the reestablishment of JROTC and the reassignment of LTC Davis as the PMST. Secretary of War James W. Good denied his request because of the previous opposition of the corps area commander to Moton and the pending detail of LTC Davis to Wilberforce University on May 29, 1929. The lack of funds also prevented the establishment of JROTC detachments at institutions other than essentially military schools. The promotion of military training by Moton was gratifying to Secretary of War Good who regretted that unfavorable conditions made compliance with his request impractical.[46] A similar Moton request in 1930 caused the War Department to reconsider the next assignment for LTC Davis who was scheduled to become the Military Attaché to Liberia. Moton believed the military training of a large group of African American students would more than compensate the government for changing the contemplated assignment. He appealed to Walter H. Newton, Secretary to the President, that an assignment to Liberia as requested by the State Department was not advisable since LTC Davis had suffered a near fatal illness during his last duty in Liberia. Cognizant of the status of LTC Davis in the regular Army and the alleged difficulty of the War Department in allocating an acceptable position for him, Moton felt that it was inadvisable to jeopardize his health and possibly cause his death in order to alleviate what was considered an embarrassing assignment for the government. Moton urged the assignment of a WO as Military Attaché in Liberia to resolve the issue and without sacrificing the service of an officer who was more useful elsewhere.[47]

Secretary of War Patrick J. Hurley initially considered not changing the State Department request but after conferring with Walter H. Newton, who explained the circumstances of the case to the secretary of state, he recommended that if the State Department relinquished its prior claim for the service of LTC Davis the War Department would take immediate measures to relieve him of the pending service as Military Attaché to Liberia. Secretary of War Hurley also informed Newton that it was customary to notify each officer prior to making assignments in areas like Liberia and only after officer consent were orders issued. He assured Newton that had LTC Davis objected to the duty the reassignment orders would not have been issued. With the assignment of an African American minister to Liberia instead of a white minister, the State Department considered the urgency for the assignment of LTC Davis had become less relevant and requested the revocation of his orders. The War Department on December 8, 1930 relieved LTC Davis from his temporary duty in the District of Columbia where he had been since leaving Wilberforce and two days later notified MG Frank R. McCoy, Commanding General of the Fourth Corps Area of his reassignment to Tuskegee.[48]

Moton had renewed his efforts to obtain an ROTC detachment for Tuskegee in 1927 after the Institute had established some curricula offering Bachelor of Science degrees in agriculture, education, home economics, technical arts and business. LTC Davis submitted a program of instruction which provided for the organization of a Cavalry ROTC detachment which would have given a distinctive feature to Tuskegee since Howard and Wilberforce Universities had infantry detachments. Informed that congressional legislation enacted on May 28, 1930 forbade the formation of additional mounted, motor transport or tank detachments of ROTC, he recommended the establishment of an ROTC detachment by employing reserve officers as instructors with no expense to the War Department. LTC Davis urged Moton to authorize Cleve L. Abbot, directors of Physical Education and Athletics, and Charles Ecton, both of whom were commissioned officers in the Reserve Officer Corps and consented to serve as Assistant PMST, to form the basic cadre of an Infantry ROTC detachment. They would receive military credit for the service and maintain their good standing within the military. A detail of regular Army noncommissioned officers with the capability of providing machine gun instruction would complete the cadre. The elevation of the military science detachment to ROTC status would have been commensurate with the rank held by LTC Davis who was systematically denied the same military opportunities and assignments offered to white officers, many of whom were junior officers. LTC Davis remained firm in advocating an ROTC detachment and the reorganization of the Boys Department with the implementation of a strong disciplinary policy to enable the development of the students by military tradition.[49]

With support from prominent white officials and citizens in the

Tuskegee community and others within the Fourth Corps Area and a favorable interview of Moton by the Corps Area ROTC officer, the Corps Area Adjutant General W. T. Bates recommended that TAG grant an ROTC detachment to Tuskegee. The financial obligation which would have been incurred to establish the detachment did not impress TAG which emphasized that during the previous year there was an excess of 1,450 Reserve Infantry officers and undoubtedly this number would increase in 1931. The establishment of an infantry detachment at Tuskegee would further increase the over production of Reserve Infantry officers in an area where they were not needed and would not serve the requirements of the General Mobilization Plan. The allocation of five commissioned officers and the necessary enlisted personnel was not possible because of the demand to send needed personnel to existing detachments. COL Laurence Halstead in the Office of Infantry recommended the disapproval of the Tuskegee application. The War Department Operations and Training Division with concurrence from TAG maintained that it was imperative to retain good faith with institutions whose applications had been refused. The division also stressed that the reestablishment of another detachment would raise the issue of detailing a white officer to Tuskegee, and probably would cause a second withdrawal with the acute shortage of regular Army African American officers. Chief of Staff Douglas MacArthur on December 29, 1931 informed Moton that the increasing necessity of maintaining economy during the depression prevented favorable consideration to his request but Tuskegee had established its eligibility for a detachment. COL Davis who had been detailed for duty with the pilgrimage of mothers and widows to cemeteries of Europe was also returned to Tuskegee in 1933.[50]

Frederick D. Patterson who succeeded Moton in 1936 expressed disappointment that the expansion of ROTC detachments within the Fourth Corps Area did not include Tuskegee. He renewed the ROTC application process and solicited the assistance of Senator Hugo Black who inquired about availability of ROTC for Tuskegee. TAG stated that time was required to formulate plans and perfect the establishment and maintenance of new ROTC detachments. Tuskegee required additional officer and enlisted personnel and more significantly the Fourth Corps Area commanding general disapproved a reorganization at the institute since he considered there was no demand for African American Reserve Officers in the area. In a reversal of a previous decision, the Office of the Chief of Infantry disagreed with the Fourth Corps Area commanding general and stressed that the Army Force Plan specified the organization of thirty-six battalions and fifteen regiments for African American Infantry in the Organized Reserve. Although TAG correspondence concerning the procurement objectives did not include or exclude the organizations, TAG authorization to Howard and Wilberforce clearly indicated an apparent intention to commission and utilize African American reserve officers. COL J. B. Woolnough felt any unfair or unjust policy was discriminatory against African American students and denied them the opportunity to receive military training that was necessary to quality for reserve commissions.[51]

Patterson refused to accept the rejection of the War Department and on June 28, 1937 he submitted another application to Chief of Staff Malin Craig. The War Department had twenty-two applications for ROTC and fifty-four for JROTC detachments but the appropriations bill for fiscal year 1938 included funding for approximately fifty new detachments. In addition to Tuskegee, the University of Florida in Gainesville, Georgia School of Technology in Atlanta and Louisiana State Normal College in Natchitoochee were the only institutions applying for ROTC detachments in the Fourth Corps Area. Detachments for the University of Florida and the Georgia School of Technology were approved but TAG disapproved a detachment for Louisiana State Normal College because its mathematics curriculum did not meet the Coastal Artillery requirements. Tuskegee was also disapproved because there was not a need for an African American ROTC detachment nor an established quota for African American reserve officers in the corps area. LTC Fred G. Wallace inspected Tuskegee in July 1937 and alleged that the institutional curriculum was not acceptable to maintain ROTC although he recommended the continuation of government aid under Section 55c of the National Defense Act. CPT Charles Ecton, a retired officer, served as PMST and despite the lack of ROTC recognition, the Cadet Officers Corps maintained its military tradition and selected students preferably from the senior class, who possessed the highest qualities of leadership and knowledge of military science and tactics, to lead the corps of cadets. Noncommissioned assignments were given to students in the lower classes to encourage their participation in the military organization.[52]

Patterson on September 19, 1939 was confident that with LT Benjamin O. Davis, Jr., Sergeant Patton, faculty, and an enrollment of 600 male students, Tuskegee would make the transition to ROTC when the military appropriations bill for fiscal year 1940 providing for 54 additional ROTC detachments was submitted. However, the bill approved by Congress and President Franklin D. Roosevelt on April 28, 1940 omitted ROTC detachments. Patterson was informed by Secretary of War Harry H. Woodring that Tuskegee would receive every consideration for a detachment and that Tuskegee might obtain special equipment, materials and personnel to train pilots and mechanics. Although the War Department did not have any

direct connection with the training of civilian pilots and mechanics, he was advised to contact the Civil Aeronautics Authority.[53]

LT Campbell C. Johnson served as the SATC senior instructor at Howard until the organization was demobilized on December 21, 1918, and was promoted and detailed on January 14, 1919 to establish the Howard ROTC detachment. The formation of the detachment was advantageous for the university since university officials had agreed on a program of prescribed physical education after the conclusion of a conference of associated colleges on physical training and education. Students enrolled in the ROTC program received credit for physical education after the detachment was officially organized on February 3, 1919 by the PMST, CPT Johnson, and his assistant, LT James H. Love.[54]

MAJ Milton T. Dean was assigned to Howard and with the assistance of Cavalry First Sergeants Edward Yorke and W. R. Sanders the ROTC program was expanded. An inspection on April 19, 1920 revealed that the PMST was also the chairman of the department of physical training which included the military science department. MAJ Dean was praised by president J. Stanley Durkee who was eager to make ROTC a prominent feature to provide officers for the Officer Reserve Corps. The inspector recommended that the War Department aggressively support the university in its effort to obtain congressional appropriations for an armory, gymnasium and drill hall. He also stressed that the size of the military staff was insufficient to train the detachment of 361 students which was expected to increase to approximately 600 during the next academic year. The ROTC detachment was expected to reach its maximum strength within the next three years when compulsory military training would have been implemented for all classes except the senior class.[55] The expected enrollment increase and the expansion of university programs influenced Durkee to include an athletic field, gymnasium and armory to his list of requirements which was sent to the Secretary of Interior Franklin K. Lane. Emmett J. Scott, the secretary-treasurer of Howard University and former special assistant of Secretary of War Baker, requested that Secretary Baker support the university by endorsing the efforts of the university which were included in the appropriation recommendations of the Department of Interior. Emphasizing the absence of African Americans at the Military or Naval Academies, Scott stressed the special relation Howard had with the Federal government and how that offered an excellent opportunity to recognize the

*Opposite:* Tuskegee Institute ROTC Review. (Courtesy of Tuskegee University Archives, Tuskegee, AL)

military contributions and character of the Howard faculty and students during the war and to establish a nucleus of commissioned African Americans for service in the Officer Reserve Corps. With the assistance to Secretary Baker and sustained efforts of the Department of the Interior and Howard, congressional approval was granted on June 7, 1924 for the construction of an athletic field and gymnasium.[56]

Another inspection conducted by MAJ Harry L. Jordan on May 27, 1921 was severely critical of the ROTC program. Although the administrative records were in excellent condition and the rifles were in good condition, MAJ Jordan observed the detachment transferring rifles to the African American JROTC detachments for use during their annual high school competitive drill. This transferal of weapons delayed his inspection of the detachment and contributed to an unsatisfactory rating since the weapons were returned in a filthy condition. MAJ Jordan further complained that the majority of the cadets including the band were not in formation during his inspection. Durkee explained to MAJ Jordan that Emmett J. Scott had approved a request from MAJ Dean to lend weapons to the high school cadets since the superintendent of the African American schools had previously lent rifles to Howard when weapons were not available to the ROTC detachment. He also stated that the majority of the 425 students were not in formation because their chemistry and other professors refused to excuse them from their classes. However, the issue that caused the most significant aggravation for MAJ Jordan was a replacement for MAJ Dean, the Commandant of Cadets and the Physical Education Director, who was denied an extension of commission service. After queries concerning his departure from the military with twenty-three years of service, MAJ Dean replied that he did not voluntarily leave the military but the War Department disregarded his military service and refused extension of active duty commissioned service because he was an African American. When MAJ Jordan attempted to explain the difficulty of detailing an African American to Howard, Durkee stated that Howard would consider it an insult to African Americans if a white officer were assigned to the university since many African American officers had served in the Army during the national emergency and not one of them had been commissioned in the regular Army. Durkee explained that since the discharge of MAJ Dean on November 20, 1920 the university had urged the War Department to assign another commissioned African American officer.[57]

Third Corps Area Chief of Staff P. K. Ferguson apparently concluded that Howard did not value the importance of student military training because of the failure to make reasonable arrangements for the inspecting officer. He recommended to TAG the immediate withdrawal of the ROTC detachment, and the elimination of government aid under Special Regulations 44 and the transferal of all regular Army personnel. However, he recommended the extension of government aid under Special Regulations 45 and the retention of a noncommissioned officer in the event that Howard accepted the assistance. All government property not authorized would also be withdrawn if Howard refused aid. On June 29, 1921, TAG informed Durkee of the withdrawal and the revocation of the authority which granted ROTC to Howard because Section 40 of the amended National Defense Act required a commissioned regular Army officer as PMST because of the nonavailability of an African American officer and the opposition of Durkee to accept the assignment of a white officer. Howard could accept a JROTC organization under the provisions of Section 55c of the National Defense Act which did not require the acceptance of a regular Army officer and permitted the retention of the most essential military equipment. Required to respond to the War Department by August 15, 1921, Durkee was dismayed that the major factor for denying the retention of ROTC at Howard was his opposition to the assignment of a white officer as PMST. He emphasized that it was in the best interest of Howard to have an African American PMST and urged the secretary of war to rescind the order revoking the detachment.[58]

Emmett J. Scott informed Howard Trustee Theodore Roosevelt of the planned reassignment of MAJ John E. Green from Wilberforce to Howard and the revocation of ROTC. An investigation by Assistant Secretary of War Jonathan M. Wainwright at the request of Roosevelt determined that MAJ Green would not be transferred to Howard and without an available African American officer for duty at Howard during the past eight months the decision by Durkee left the War Department no other alternative except to withdraw the detachment. With acceptance of the War Department directive Durkee would be authorized to petition for the reestablishment of the detachment. Durkee applied for the restoration of the ROTC Detachment on August 24, 1921 and welcomed the opportunity to confer with the officer designated to serve at Howard by September 15, 1921.[59]

The Third Corps Area designated LTC E. E. Fuller to confer with Durkee on September 28, 1921 concerning the reinstatement of ROTC. LTC Fuller reported that Durkee insisted that MAJ Jordan had given a false impression of his position concerning the assignment of a white officer although they had debated extensively the assignment of an African American officer. He informed Durkee that the War Department could only conclude that his denial to accept white officers who were interviewed was a decision to accept only African Americans. LTC Fuller emphasized that the lack of funding required MAJ Samuel D. Crawford, who had served with

Filipino troops and was serving in Cleveland, Ohio, to finance his transfer to Howard. LTC Fuller also met with WO Edward Yorke, Sergeant Smith and several students and concluded the most regrettable features of the discontinuance of the detachment was the prevention of approximately fifteen students from completing the last year of training to receive their commissions and the fact that some were prevented from completing their curriculums because of their dependence on commutation paid to them during the academic year.

LTC Fuller anticipated protests and criticisms influenced by the African American press and other newspapers when the War Department announced the withdrawal of the ROTC and he had no doubts that some individuals and groups would politicize the issue. He claimed that the Third Corps Area and the War Department were not responsible for the withdrawal of the detachment but alleged that it was the insistence of Durkee to have only African American officers assigned to Howard as the failure of the university to meet the requirements of SR 44. His recommendation that an ROTC detachment should not be reestablished at Howard was approved by BG H. F. Hodges, Commanding General of the Third Corps Area, who believed there was no reassurance that Howard would more effectively support another detachment. BG Hodges also stated that before another detachment was assigned Howard would have an opportunity to select a white officer to serve as PMST.[60] Obviously, War Department officials refused to recognize that racism and discrimination were the main reasons for denying service in the regular Army to African Americans and Durkee knew that some African American organizations would not accept the assignment of a white officer at Howard.

Acting Chief of Staff of the Operation and Training Division, BG William Lassiter, recommended that the War Department disapprove the retention of ROTC and approved a recommendation by Third Corps Area Assistant Adjutant E. H. Metzer concerning Durkee's application submitted on October 1, 1921 for the extension of government aid to Howard under Section 55c of the National Defense Act. BG Lassiter complained that Assistant Secretary of the Navy Theodore Roosevelt had repeatedly appealed for the reestablishment of the ROTC detachment. Roosevelt argued the reestablishment would be a concession to wise governmental policy and remove any basis for African American accusations that claimed the War Department was guilty of racial discrimination. He stated that Howard was the most advanced African American collegiate institution and to deny it an ROTC detachment would prejudicially affect African American relations. BG Lassiter consented to reestablishing the detachment and urged the assignment of an experienced officer as PMST. Third Corps Area Assistant Adjutant

Metzer recommended the dismissal of SGT Dorsey Rhodes and retention of WO Edward York, who held a commission of an infantry captain in the Officer Reserve Corps, and Sergeant Darwin E. Smith. TAG Horace F. Sykes authorized the reestablishment of ROTC on November 5, 1921.[61]

Third Corps Area officials did not consider CPT Julian De Court qualified to serve as PMST for Howard but he was acceptable to Durkee and reluctantly the Corps Area detailed CPT DeCourt as the acting PMST on December 27, 1921. CPT DeCourt was relieved of duty on June 28, 1922 by the Third Corps Area commanding general after LTC Nathaniel M. Cartmell alleged that Howard students did not receive an antityphoid treatment prior to their arrival at summer camp. CPT DeCourt explained that the treatment was initiated on April 22, 1922 with a second treatment administered to some cadets on April 28, 1922. Physicians at Freedmen's Hospital had refused to administer the last treatment which necessitated a repeat of the entire process at the beginning of the final examinations which prevented the reinoculation of the cadets. The cadets arrived at camp on June 15, 1922 and were immediately sent to the infirmary for medical examinations and typhoid inoculations before receiving their equipment and clothing. Cognizant of the incomplete treatment, CPT DeCourt arranged typhoid treatment for the cadets during the encampment which caused little interference with the training cycle but LTC Cartmell alleged that CPT DeCourt had failed to comply with orders. CPT DeCourt denied the allegation but the Third Corps Area headquarters concurred with LTC Cartmell about his failure to comply in the inoculation process. His conduct during the past academic year was also a factor for his removal from the position of PMST. LTC J. Van Schaick advised CPT DeCourt that any inference by him would jeopardize his case and he recommended his retention to the commanding general. He surmised that LTC Cartmell was an efficient officer and any action taken would not adversely affect his record. Emmett J. Scott and Durkee supported the PMST but Assistant Secretary of War J. M. Wainwright informed Durkee that the decision to relieve CPT De Court was approved by the War Department. The rationale for the removal was that he was not qualified for the assignment and therefore was officially assigned as an assistant PMST, and his removal was in the best interest of the military. LTC Charles E. N. Howard was transferred from Fort Williams in Maine to become the Howard PMST in November 1922. With the commissioning of seventeen officers in February 22, 1922 which represented the first time in United States history of such recognition for African Americans, the ROTC program continued to expand with the dedication of a new gymnasium and armory on February 26, 1926 and a military staff of six under COL Howard who remained as PMST until 1929.[62]

Improvement of the ROTC program continued under the leadership of officers assigned to Howard. CPT Edward A. Kimball made significant advances during his tenure by winning two excellent ratings at annual inspections, winning the highest marksmanship rating in the Third Corps Area in 1934, enlarging and improving the band and having advanced classes attend War Department lectures designated for African American reservists in the corps area, and reconstructing the rifle range which revived interest in the rifle team. MAJ C. H. St. Germain as PMST maintained the excellence established by his predecessors and continued the Student Aid Fund which was previously supported by CPT Kimball. MAJ Lloyd Zuppann was assigned as PMST in 1936.[63]

A military inspector in December 1924 criticized excessive student absentees from ROTC instruction, inadequate discipline measures instituted by the military science department, the lack of practical emphasis on certain military subjects, and the attention the PMST gave to administrative details instead of delegating these issues to subordinate cadre. Durkee acknowledged the responsibilities of the PMST to conform to Third Corps Area instruction regarding the discharge of students who failed to attend the required ROTC classes and that the issue of penalties for absentees had been considered by the Faculty Business Committee. Durkee was assured of an affirmative vote on suggested penalties during its next meeting but stressed Third Corps Area instruction was not in compliance with university rules and regulations. He never concurred with prescribed military penalties which he believed were not enforced at other institutions. Although supportive of Third Corps Area and attempting to advance ROTC through the implementation of military instructions, Durkee felt Howard was not a military school compelled to rigidly conform with military bearing and discipline and cadet performance was satisfactory and compatible with other civilian institutions.[64]

The Howard Academic Council had initially agreed to establishing ROTC and making physical education optional courses in the spring of 1921 but the courses became requirements for graduation in the fall of that same year. The Student Council opposed compulsory ROTC and urged the selection of physical education as an elective. The adoption of penalties by the faculty concerning ROTC training and physical education became the central issues of a student strike in 1925. Among the student grievances was the special rule which permitted expulsion after the accumulation of twenty combined absences from ROTC and physical education courses within a quarter semester. The PMST was authorized to grant excuses for absences from ROTC, and after 10 absences accrued the student received a warning from the appropriate dean. The rule was announced in ROTC classes at the beginning of the quarter but signs were not posted until March 14, 1925. Students who were expelled for violating the rule by May 8, 1925 included

Norris W. Cuney, George H. Dabney, John S. George, Owen S. Edwards and Gilbert L. Edwards. Students held a mass meeting at the nearby Lincoln Theater on May 10, 1925 to reaffirm their opposition to the twenty-cut rule and to demand its abrogation. They also wanted the compulsory educational core requirements reduced to two years, student representation on the Academic Council and Student Council control over all social activities of students.

A faculty vote on May 12, 1925 required that all students who failed to terminate the disorder on May 13, 1925 and return to their classes on the following day be notified of their suspension from the university. Seven days after student compliance to terminate the strike and return to their classes on May 14, 1925, the faculty granted the substance of their requests which were presented on May 19, 1925 by the student council president Arthur M. Brady. With the exception of reported cases of misconduct, any penalties assessed against the strikers and absences from classes between May 7-14 were not counted. The faculty referred the 20-cut rule to a special committee that submitted a report after the summer action which reduced physical education requirements from four to two years. This revision made ROTC more attractive, influenced an increase in the size of the ROTC detachment and improved esprit de corps. Complaints from students and the General Alumni Association against Durkee influenced the Board of Trustees to review the dismissal of four faculty members and accept the resignation of Durkee, which became effective on June 30, 1926. The board appointed Mordecai W. Johnson, the first African American president of Howard, who was opposed to ROTC. The faculty knew the necessity of commissioning officers to command African American enlisted personnel and on February 28, 1928 they overwhelmingly defeated his proposal to abolish ROTC.[65]

Wilberforce after the elimination of the SATC retained an ROTC organization and although there was a rotation of PMSTs, the detachment provided assignments for LTC John Green and LTC Benjamin O. Davis. The major problem was which officer should be assigned to Wilberforce and how to achieve and maintain the minimum required cadets in the program. LTC Davis was transferred to Wilberforce in 1929 after the university was inspected and received an unsatisfactory inspection rating because of its low enrollment.[66] He attempted to improve military training but the lack of supplies and uniforms, the financial and demographic conditions and the academic curricula forced some students to withdraw from the program. Despite the handicaps, the military recognized his achievements and based on his seniority Davis was promoted to the rank of colonel in March 1929 prior to his departure to escort African American Gold Star Mothers to Europe.[67]

MAJ Joseph W. Whitney became PMST and he was assisted by WO

Orestus J. Kincaid who retired on June 30, 1936. WO Aaron R. Fisher with more than eight years of foreign service in France, Hawaii and the Philippine Islands was selected on July 29, 1936 to replace WO Kincaid. During the following year at the request of Ormonde Walker, president of Wilberforce, COL Davis began his fourth tour as PMST. This assignment was due partly to the refusal of the Chief of Cavalry to reassign him to the 10th Cavalry and the insistence of Walker to have the white officer replaced by COL Davis.[68] One of the students, David A. Blake, cognizant of the strength of the advanced course, requested on February 13, 1939 that the Secretary of War increase the detachment from fifteen to thirty. With only seven in the first year of the advanced program and eight in the second year, this size did not provide the required battalion organization strength. He requested a strength of thirty and urged the Ohio congressional delegation to support his efforts. Blake also emphasized that two African American ROTC detachments did not satisfy the aspirations of fifteen million African Americans and requested that the War Department authorize the redesignation of the Wilberforce detachment from infantry to a chemical warfare organization. The establishment of a chemical warfare detachment and the enlargement of the advanced course were rejected by MG E. S. Adams, TAG, on February 17, 1939 who maintained that the funds appropriated were sufficient only to maintain the existing detachments.[69]

Summer training was not always provided for African American cadre and cadets but in 1919 LT McLeod and a military assistant were detailed to Camp Devens in Massachusetts where he commanded a company of fifty cadets which included eight African American cadets. This was a rare opportunity for LT McLeod who taught cadets from Yale, Harvard, Kemper Military Academy and the University of Alabama. The southern cadets were adamantly opposed to instruction by African American cadre and openly displayed disdain, but after two weeks the company rapport and sentiment within the company was generally good and there was no trouble. At the termination of the camp only one Alabama student visited the African American quarters to convey his farewell and offer an invitation to visit the University of Alabama. The student who received the highest rating and was proclaimed the best cadet within the company was a Howard cadet.[70]

During the summer of 1928 an incident occurred at the Fort Leonard Wood Infantry summer camp which involved Howard cadets. Equipped with weapons and ammunition to practice on the target range, two cadets attempted to transport a target through a column of white cadets. A white student ordered the Howard students to keep away from their column and began using profanity when the African American students disregarded his statements. A Howard student aggressively responded to the offensive remarks and other Howard cadets left their formation to rush to his assistance. The white company similarly broke their ranks but Captain F. A. Byrne who commanded the Howard detachment quickly restored order over his men and a white officer rushed from the rear of his column to assume order and reform his company. During the incident it was alleged that an African American student was ready to use his rifle butt against a white cadet, and had he succeeded the possibility of serious injuries to some cadets would have been unavoidable. This incident caused Captain Byrne to station an officer daily in the company street until nightfall to prevent any further racial troubles. LTC A. F. Dannemiller commended Captain Byrne and CPT W. C. Rathbone, who were with the Howard detachment, for prompt action which quelled what might have been a serious riot and for their energy and good judgment in handling an extremely difficult situation which continued in their company areas until the termination of the camp. LTC Dannemiller recognized the seriousness of the confrontation and commended the action of each detachment commander in preventing a racial riot, but he obviously did not appreciate the complaints from Howard students. He alleged that African American cadets were constantly looking for acts of mistreatment and discrimination and complained when the band failed to march past their entire formation during a battalion formation. When Howard students complained of the absence of swimming pool facilities, LTC Dannemiller insisted that the camp commander had not issued orders denying the use of the camp swimming pool and their own fear of possible consequences was the sole prohibition against their using it. The camp commander complained that the presence of African Americans in camp effectively prevented the ROTC battalion from conducting marches off the reservation since property owners would not permit African American students on their property.

The Third Corps Area commander was informed that racial incidents had occurred during each summer camp held from 1924 to 1927. In 1924 near the termination of the camp, Howard students were chased out of their barracks by white cadets with sabers and other weapons because, allegedly, an African American cadet had cursed and assaulted a white cadet. It was necessary to use armed regular Army troops to protect African Americans and to release the Howard company a day early to avoid possible trouble during the last night of camp. In 1925 the Howard Infantry company and the ROTC cavalry and field (dismounted) detachment met while marching and each refused to yield the right of way but a clash was averted by the camp commander. During the next two subsequent camps students in white detachments refused to obey orders from a regular Army African American sergeant and they wanted the sergeant to salute them. The arrival of a camp officer prevented trouble in each case. All of these occurrences were consid-

ered embarrassing to African American and white students but any indis-
cretion or thoughtless word by students may have been the potential cause
of a serious disturbance. The presence of African Americans was allegedly
considered a constant menace to the preservation of an effective ROTC program and the camp commander did not perceive any appropriate reason for
the continuation of their training at Fort Wood. LTC Dannemiller recommended to the Third Corps Area commanding general the disassociation of
Howard University from the Fort Wood ROTC Infantry Camp and that a
separate camp be established in the corps area or another corps area. His
justification was the violent antipathy of the southern white students and the
equal jealousy of African American students in claiming equal privileges.
The practice of training both races in close contact with each other in future
camps LTC Dannemiller concluded would inevitably lead to violence.[71]

The Third Corps Area commanding general concurred with the recommendation and evaluated the possibility of establishing a separate camp
for African Americans. The location of Fort Wood was considered too far
north and simultaneously too far south for integration and the District of
Columbia was considered a political center that offered Howard students
support from their friends. The longstanding feud that existed between
Howard cadets and other cadets influenced a corps area recommendation
requiring that in the succeeding years Howard cadets would train with
Wilberforce cadets who had participated in Third Corps Area summer
training. This arrangement would equalize the responsibilities and incon-
veniences between the Third Corps Area and the Fifth Corps Area. It would
also remove the Howard contingency away from antagonistic conditions
that had developed between particular detachments and take Howard students away from the District of Columbia which served as a major source
of student morale and activities against discrimination. The reassignment
would further offer the same privileges and opportunities accorded to
Wilberforce students who had broadened their experiences by visiting new
localities. The corps area commander concluded the permanent reassignment of Howard to a northern camp where it could train separately or with
other African American detachments was the only feasible solution.[72]

The War Department considered the transfer of Howard students to
the Fifth Corps Area during its planning for the 1929 summer training. The
Fifth Corps Area commander concurrently requested that the Third Corps
Area commanding general accept students for training from five universities in his corps area. Wilberforce with its infantry training requirements
was included in the request although the summer program at Camp Knox
in Kentucky was established to train Infantry, Field Artillery and Coastal
Artillery ROTC students. However, the War Department Operations and

Training Division on December 1, 1929 directed the Fifth Corps Area commanding general to submit recommendations pertaining to the practicability of establishing a separate ROTC camp to train between forty and fifty students from Howard and Wilberforce. A report submitted to TAG on December 13, 1928 stressed that ROTC summer training within the corps area was conducted at Camp Knox. Facilities were not available at Fort Benjamin Harrison in Indiana or Fort Thomas in Kentucky and personnel had not been sent from these military sites to Camp Knox because of their commitment to the training of Citizens' Military Training Camp trainees at their respective locations. Accommodating Howard and Wilberforce students at Camp Knox would have necessitated the construction of separate facilities since it was not advisable to integrate African American and white students from Kentucky and West Virginia. The corps commander also alleged that if African Americans were not permitted the use of post facilities they would have grounds for claims of discrimination.

It was possible to establish a separate camp at Wilberforce with the consent from university authorities and the National Guard to utilize the firing range in Harrison, Ohio. The nearest regular Army target range was located adjacent to Fort Thomas but it would be used by Citizens' Military Training Camp trainees and was judged too distant for travel by the students. A separate camp would further require additional expenditures to ship equipment and to provide essential maintenance similar to other military camps. The corps commanding general concluded that whether training was held at Camp Knox or Wilberforce University it would require two officers from the Third Corps Army and would cost more to train the students at Camp Knox than at Wilberforce. Since training Howard and Wilberforce cadets at Camp Knox would essentially transfer problems from the Third Corps Area to Fifth Corps Area, the latter concurred that a separate camp was desirable if not necessary but it was more practical and economically more feasible to have the camp in the Third Corps Area. The Fifth Corps Area requested that the transfer be reconsidered by the Operations and Training Division. The Secretary of War in December 1928 directed TAG to notify the Third Area Corps commanding general that after an exhaustive study the best solution was the training of students from Howard and Wilberforce in his corps area.[73] The combined Howard-Wilberforce camp was obviously successful by the summer of 1934 when African American cadets in the Third Corps Area had the highest rifle and pistol scores with four qualified as experts, five as sharpshooters and twenty-eight as marksmen with the rifle, and five as experts, four as sharpshooters and twenty-three as marksmen with the pistol.[74]

Planning summer training and locating acceptable camps for African

American cadre were also problems for military officials. In addition to training performed at Fort Howard in Maryland by COL West A. Hamilton, MAJ Davis informed Moton that the War Department had authorized the establishment of CMTC in several locations and encouraged the establishment of a camp at Tuskegee Institute. The Fourth Corps Area Assistant Adjutant General Robert Whitfield concurred with establishing a separate camp for African Americans but the decision about where to locate the camp was not resolved. The practice of conducting ROTC camps at institutions within the corps area had been unsatisfactory and resulted in the discontinuance of the policy. Conducting camps at locations other than military stations had not been considered but the ROTC inspector was instructed to examine the facilities at Tuskegee. The desirability to avoid a mixed camp alleviated the requirement of releasing information to the public which may have been injurious to the CMTC movement in the corps area. After the decision to organize a camp at Tuskegee, LTC Davis was detailed from his duty as advisor to the 2nd Battalion, 372nd Infantry in Cleveland to serve as instructor at the Colored Reserve Officers' Camp in May 1929.[75]

The expectation of establishing ROTC at African American colleges and universities was dispelled with the relegation of all programs and their detachments to JROTC status with the exception of Howard and Wilberforce which maintained infantry detachments. The Office of the Executive for Reserve and ROTC Affairs reported that two detachments from 1921 to 1942 graduated 574 commissioned reserve officers while white detachments graduated 126,000 reserve officers. The policy which denied the service the opportunity for African American officers to command organizations of active African Americans personnel prevented reserve officers from gaining the experience or stimulus of active duty training which was available to white reserve officers. The 428th Infantry Regiment under the leadership of COL West A. Hamilton, headquartered in the District of Columbia, provided the only opportunity for the majority of African American reservists to received military training. Approximately 350 officers joined a variety of reserve detachments but most lost interest and left the Reserve Corps in part because of the lack of glamour or tradition of the detachments. COL Hamilton provided the major effort to sustain reserve training and unfortunately during the era of the depression most civil rights organizations and the African American press devoted little attention to African American reservists and their limited opportunities for training and promotion.[76]

*Opposite:* **Howard University cadets training at Camp Meade, MD. (Courtesy of the Moorland-Spingarn Research Center, Howard University Archives)**

# 3

# *Reactivation, Reorganization and Expansion of ROTC*

There were approximately 56,000 reserve officers who for the first time in the American military experience were activated for extended duty in 1941. Since many were ROTC graduates, this was the first opportunity for War Department officials to make an adequate appraisal of their efficiency in the program. The success attained by their mobilization indicated the significant role of ROTC, and without their availability the immediate requirements of Army rapid expansion would have been impossible. African American graduates from Howard and Wilberforce universities were primarily assigned to National Guard organizations which formed the 372nd Infantry Regiment, and the 366th Infantry Regiment that consisted of nearly all ROTC commissioned officers in addition to LT James Fowler who was a Howard cadet prior to graduating from the USMA in 1941. With the expansion of military operations, ROTC commissioned officers were assigned to many organizations which included the 92nd and 93rd Infantry Divisions. The dynamics of battlefield activities in Europe, Asia and Africa influenced the mobilization of armed forces within the United States, and African Americans were concerned with their potential involvement. During the early activation, the Secretary of the Cleveland Medical Association, W. B. Hatcher, contacted President Franklin D. Roosevelt on October 25, 1940 concerning service of African American physicians and explained that during the last world war physicians and dentists were inducted in the military in many cases as privates and assigned to branches which did not utilize their skills. He emphasized that it was regrettable and morally discouraging for African Americans, who composed one of the largest minorities, with a long and unblemished record of loyalty, to be denied representation in the mobilization of professional medical personnel. The Cleveland Medical Association had a roster of fifty physicians who appealed to Roosevelt to appoint African Americans to local draft and appeal boards. This issue was referred to TAG which stated that selection of physicians was under the jurisdiction of MG Lewis B. Hershey, the director of Selective Service.[1]

MAJ Campbell C. Johnson, who was serving as the Special Aide to Clarence Dykstra, Executive Director of the Selective Service System, on March 4, 1941 recognized that the problem confronting commanding officers of newly activated African American detachments was the availability of adequate cadres and personnel with previous military experience and other special qualifications necessary for the development of noncommissioned personnel. He specifically cited the Third Corps Area where training opportunities were probably higher than anywhere in the country. Approximately 90 percent of African American reserve officers came from the District of Columbia where ROTC training was received in high schools and Howard University, and some had participated in a CMTC conducted at Fort Howard in Maryland. MAJ Johnson emphasized that personnel with training would be indispensable in the development and mobilization of new organizations and urged that classification officers make an effort to distribute them where they would render the greatest service. He wanted a plan that extended beyond the Third Corps Area to give the new detachments the best chance for satisfactory development. Envisioning a large concentration of personnel joining the military, he urged the expedition of a plausible plan of action.[2]

The assignment of medical officers was extremely acute and MAJ Johnson together with Judge Hastie was instrumental in resolving this issue. African Americans serving as examining physicians by January 15, 1942 reached 204 while eight were on medical advisory boards. The first civilian examining panel composed of all African American physicians and employed by the War Department was located at the Army Recruiting and Induction Center at Fort Myers, Virginia in November 1942. Many physicians, including Robert B. Hill, a member of the Pennsylvania State Medical, Dental and Pharmaceutical Association, who graduated from the Philadelphia College of Pharmacy and Science and was serving as chief pharmacist at Douglass Hospital in Philadelphia, requested assistance in joining the proposed hospital which was scheduled to have an African American staff.[3]

Among the organizations involved in the realignment and reorganization were regular Army regiments of the 9th Cavalry, 10th Cavalry, 24th Infantry, 25th Infantry and the newly organized 47th and 48th Quartermaster Regiments as well as a few small detachments. Civilian Aide William H. Hastie stated a month later that this contingency was expanded with the organization of the 76th and 77th Coastal Antiaircraft Artillery Regiments and the scheduled formation of three additional coastal artillery regiments, two engineer regiments, eight separate engineer battalions, and two additional quartermaster regiments which were scattered among several camps, posts, fields and depots. The announcement to train African Americans as pilots and technicians led to the establishment of the 99th Pursuit Squadron, the 1st to the 9th Separate Aviation Squadrons, the 31st, 34th, 35th Quartermaster Truck Regiments, and the 810th Engineer Battalion. African American National Guard regiments which included the 372nd Infantry, 184th Field Artillery, and 369th Coastal Antiaircraft Artillery, were activated and brought to wartime strength. The War Department had planned African American cadres for the National Guard organizations which consisted of approximately 322 line officers and thirty medical and dental officers which would constitute the cadre of these regiments. Final plans for the admission of officer and enlisted personnel included more extensive use of professional personnel and a committee of the National Medical Association which made recommendations for the admission of fifty physicians and dentists and an equal number of nurses.[4]

Civilian Aide to the Secretary of the War Department Hastie criticized the 1941 Troop list for African Americans because of the disproportionate dispersal of personnel in small detachments which were widely scattered and insufficient to accommodate the selectees scheduled to fill the authorized organizations. Stressing the desirability of integrated forces initially on a modest basis, he complained that they had not been permitted to examine the 1942 Troop list containing combat divisions, army troops, corps troops, general headquarters reserve troops, harbor defense detachments, military police detachments, and tank destroyer battalions. Expecting the recruitment of additional selectees to reach an estimated strength of 155,000, he was uncertain of the strength that would be provided to the Army Air Corps and its services which represented one of the more substantial examples of disproportionately small African American representation in the Army as a whole. His analysis of the Troop Unit Basis for 1942 revealed approximately 3 percent of the troops organized in divisions would be African American but most of the African American infantry and field artillery detachments in early 1942 remained in General Headquarters Reserve status. Hastie was particularly concerned with reserve status involving a small percentage of African Americans in higher detachments since he regarded the divisional organization as the best method of modifying the scattered assignments.

Hastie further criticized the types of branch assignments allocated for

African Americans. The most glaring was the Medical Corps where African Americans, excluding the attached medical detachments, constituted 11 percent of the total strength but were assigned to sanitation companies where the Army plan did not contemplate the inclusion of European American sanitation companies. In the Corps of Engineers, their employment was almost exclusively as general service battalions and regiments and not as combat engineer organizations. The Ordnance Department envisioned forming scattered Ammunition companies while in the Quartermaster Corps practically all of the service battalions were composed of African Americans. Hastie concluded that despite the disavowal of interest other than military considerations, plans for the utilization of African American soldiers reflected the prevailing view that the smallest possible number of African Americans would receive combat training.[5]

The Secretary of War had not increased ROTC detachments since August 1937 but interest in military science and requests for applications for submission of new detachments had increased by 1940. Students were interested in flight training under Public Law 18 and inquiries from collegiate officials influenced the Civilian Aeronautical Authority in 1939 to grant civil pilot training programs at Howard, North Carolina A and T, Tuskegee and West Virginia State. Howard cadets began flight training on January 19, 1940 from Hybla Valley in Virginia and instruction was later provided by the Cloud Club at Riverdale Flying Field on the Patuxent River near Upper Marlboro, Maryland. On August 12, 1941, BG Benjamin O. Davis at Tuskegee informed C. Alfred Anderson, director of the Department of Mechanical Industries at Tuskegee that sixty-eight had completed the private course, thirty-nine had completed the secondary course and sixteen had completed the student instructor course. The program became coeducational in 1941 when Frances Pinkett enrolled in the course. However, Army Air Corps aviation training for African Americans was consolidated at Tuskegee where African American pilots were trained for combat service in the 99th Pursuit Squadron and the 332 Fighter Group.[6]

Military science at Tuskegee gained momentum in 1939 when all male students were required to attend ROTC classes. With the implementation of the Selective Service Act and the departures of CPT Benjamin O. Davis, Jr. and SGT Beuregard King to Fort Benning, CPT Charles Ecton as commandant together with CPT Walter J. Love to Fort Riley, LT John W. Godboldte, LT John D. Patton, and SGT Henry G. Beasley were responsible for military training before COL John F. Waterman commanded the ROTC detachment at Tuskegee in addition to serving as PMST at Alabama Polytechnic Institute. A War Department authorization which expanded the advanced ROTC program enabled the enrollment of 1,000 students during the 1940-1941 academic year. New detachments established to meet the special requirements of mobilization were allocated to Tuskegee, the University of Alaska and the Harvard School of Business Administration. MAJ John A. Welch replaced COL Waterman and succeeded in maintaining an excellent military record at Tuskegee.[7]

On February 24, 1941 Truman K. Gibson, an assistant to the Civilian Aide to the Secretary of War expressed interest in the ROTC quotas allocated to institutions within the Third and Fifth Corps Areas where Howard and Wilberforce were located. A review of cadets participating in the ROTC camp held at Fort George G. Meade revealed that fifty-four of fifty-five authorized for training attended the camp. Thirty-four of the African American cadets were from Howard, eighteen were from Wilberforce and one was from an institution in the Second Corps Area.[8] Ironically on December 6, 1941, GEN George C. Marshall serving as the War Department Chief of Staff directed the Assistant Chief of Staff for Operations to recommend two or three African American institutions where ROTC detachments could be installed during the fall of 1942. Although the War Department had applications from four institutions and letters of inquiry from eight others, the Assistant Chief of Staff, BG Harry L. Twaddle, requested that TAG, MG Carl Robinson, issue applications to all institutions which had formally or informally requested the establishment of Senior ROTC detachments since their applications contained insufficient information. War Department officials were selected to inspect the institutions with officers from the respective area corps commanders since it was necessary to conduct comparative inspections to determine the institutions. All recommendations by the inspecting officers and the corps area commander were submitted to the Chief of Staff. The submission of applications for ROTC detachments did not commit the War Department to the selection in Lincoln in Pennsylvania.[9]

Applications were sent to Hampton, Lincoln in Pennsylvania, Virginia State College in the Third Corps Area, Alcorn A and M College, Georgia State College, North Carolina A and T, Fisk and Xavier in New Orleans in the Fourth Corps Area, Kentucky State College, West Virginia State in the Fifth Corps Area, and Langston University, Paul Quinn College, Prairie View A and M College, Wiley College and Texas College in the Eighth Corps Area by December 18, 1941.[10] Fisk on April 4, 1942 requested an ROTC detachment with the voluntary enrollment but since the unit would have only fifty students the application was not seriously considered by the Deputy Director of Training for the Service of Supply. Georgia State which was supported by Senator Walter F. George, Chairman of the Committee on

Finance, failed to receive favorable consideration because of its small enrollment and Class B rating by the Association of Southern Colleges. Representative Lindley Beckworth's inquiry concerning the application submitted by D. R. Glass of Texas College revealed that the institution was not selected for an ROTC detachment because there were other African American colleges with the appropriate facilities and the capability to fulfill the specified military requirements to a greater degree.[11]

The acting adjutant general of the Third Corps Area accepted the recommendation from Malcolm S. MacLean, president of Hampton, to establish a Quartermaster detachment. The corps area commanding general was also influenced by W. L. Wright who stated that Lincoln in Pennsylvania was the only African American institution in the northeast where more than a million African Americans resided and was located near metropolitan areas in Pennsylvania, New Jersey and New York, where an African American ROTC detachment had not been established and where there was little opportunity for African Americans to enroll in ROTC detachments. COL F. G. Kellond inspected the campus and was definitely impressed with the university and recommended the formation of a detachment for Lincoln. The Fourth Corps Area commanding general supported the establishment of ROTC at North Carolina A and T. In the Fifth Corps Area the inspection officer recommended Infantry ROTC for West Virginia State but MAJ E. W. Dennis, Assistant Adjutant General of the Third Corps Area, recommended the formation of Field Artillery ROTC. Major Jesse H. Ruder, Assistant Adjutant General of the Eighth Corps Area, considered Prairie View A and M which had an ROTC detachment under Section 55c and Langston University as the best institutions where detachments could be operable in a relatively short period of time. Wiley College was favorably considered but along with Paul Quinn College and Texas College which were not favorably evaluated they were unlikely to receive a detachment. Jarvis College was located in oil fields near Hawkins, Texas and with excellent facilities was expected to submit an application and the Eighth Corps Area was prepared to grant its approval if more African American detachments were needed. College Dean H. Lister of Knoxville College recognized that his institution would not have a detachment but with the issuance of a War Department announcement on January 29, 1942 which referred to the establishment of Army Officer Candidate Schools he was hopeful that this program applied to students at his college.[12]

Aware of a War Department decision to establish at least three additional African American ROTC detachments, college officials sought assistance from Civilian Aide William Hastie and assurance in expediting their applications.[13] Hastie assured each college president seeking ROTC that before a decision was reached an Army representative would survey each institution but an announcement was not anticipated until Spring of 1942. MAJ Campbell C. Johnson informed MAJ Walter R. Brown at Hampton that while he did not have encouraging information it seemed that an exception was made in granting Tuskegee a detachment because of the presence of JROTC with an officer detailed as PMST and the local support which influenced Chief of Staff George C. Marshall to revise the ROTC status. MAJ Brown was informed that an exception would not be made for Hampton and only GEN Marshall had the authority to implement the change. Malcolm S. MacLean felt that Hampton was an exceptional institution with valid potential with an established military battalion supervised by a Fortress Monroe officer who voluntarily accepted the task. Authorization to reorganize another detachment would not have caused difficulty for MacLean who emphasized the ability of the Division of Trades and Industries faculty to provide instruction in thirteen trades at the collegiate level, many of which were applicable to national defense training. Hampton also offered evening courses to personnel from the Norfolk Navy Base, Newport News Shipyard, Fortress Monroe and Langley Field. With this capability, he stressed that an experimental tank or transportation service ROTC detachment was possible in addition to a signal corps organization stressing radio and telegraphic communication and maintenance. He did not exclude the possibility of infantry training and asserted that while neither state nor federal funds were allocated for training African American students within Virginia, Hampton had 600 uniformed men with four months to more than three years of infantry drill without arms.[14]

With an application filed since 1937 and support from the American Teachers Association, the Supervisor of Negro Schools of the Department of Education, West Virginia Governor Matthew M. Neely, Congressman George W. Johnson, the West Virginia Congress of Colored Parents and Teachers at Charleston, and Howard P. Jeter, Chairman of the West Virginia State College National Defense Committee of the Student Council, John W. Davis appealed to Hastie to intervene on behalf of the college because many of the leading state officials and citizens endorsed an effort to secure a motor transport ROTC detachment. Acutely aware of the limited expansion of African American detachments and confident of the economic feasibility of establishing military training at the college, he reported a campus inspection by COL Bolton E. Brewer from the Fifth Corps Area at Fort Hayes to Hastie.[15]

The War Department approved the organization of detachments at North Carolina A and T, Hampton, Prairie View A and M, and West Virginia State. Each institution was assigned a maximum strength of 350 cadets in the basic course and fifty in the advanced course. Each institution was authorized a cadre of three officers and two enlisted men but the assignment of cadres was a major issue for corps area commanders who were instructed by TAG to form cadres with a regular active or retired Army officer, two reserve officers preferably African American as well as two enlisted men in grades four or above. However, West Virginia State requested six enlisted men because of the requirement to have a sergeant major, motor sergeant and a clerk. The normal strength of other field artillery detachments was eight enlisted men, including two noncommissioned officers and six technical specialists, but Fifth Corps Area complained that personnel could not be authorized for West Virginia State without reducing the standard of maintenance of artillery and motor vehicle equipment at other institutions within the corps area. However, LTC E. W. Dennis in TAG requested that the Army Ground Forces located at the Army War College in the District of Columbia provide six enlisted men to West Virginia State. The Army Ground Forces selected COL Fred M. Green, a white coastal artillery officer for Hampton since the ROTC allocation was changed to Coastal Artillery.[16]

The cadre of African American officers selected for Prairie View State N and I was rejected by Willette R. Banks the college president, although Hastie explained that the cadre was carefully selected and that it was extremely difficult to locate more suitable officers particularly in the absence of any information concerning the rationale for his disapproval. Banks advised Hastie on June 12, 1942 that several officers were recommended from a list which was submitted to the college but he only recommended officers where information was available. He requested information concerning MAJ Raymond Contee in the 366th Infantry Regiment who had trained cadets in the District of Columbia, LTC Alexander W. Thomas at Wilberforce and LT Roy F. Greenwood. Hastie concurred with Banks that MAJ Contee was a competent officer but he doubted whether he wanted to leave his battalion for ROTC duty and the Department of War did not contemplate the utilization of individuals directly from civilian life to serve in Senior ROTC detachments. Banks approved the assignment of COL West A. Hamilton who effectively organized the ROTC detachment but he complained of the mediocre performance of the other officers who were not contributing to the effort of making the organization an outstanding detachment. COL Hamilton had served in the 366th Infantry and recommended the transfer of LT James W. Jones from the regiment to the ROTC cadre. Hastie empathized with Banks but stated the War Department was reluctant to transfer additional officers from troop duty to ROTC.[17]

The War Department announcement authorizing an Artillery ROTC for West Virginia State electrified the campus with excitement and John W.

Davis expressed his indebtedness to Hastie. On June 25, 1942, a campus news release stated that LTC Peyton Winlock, a white veteran of the last world war and former faculty member of the military science department at the University of Iowa, had arrived to organize the ROTC detachment which was the only artillery organization established at an African American college. In connection with this establishment, Davis compiled a list of personnel who had completed Civilian Pilot Training at West Virginia State and urged Hastie to have them request transfers for aerial reconnaissance or similar air service to make them eligible for participation in the Field Artillery ROTC detachment at the college. Hastie concurred with the possibility of aerial reconnaissance training but was unaware of War Department planning in that connection. However, he believed pilots serving in the Army in other aviation capacities would have first preference for specialized training and he was not certain of the necessity to call the Civilian Aeronautics Administration for additional pilots. Davis was further discouraged when LTC Winlock indicated that the ROTC quota of fifty made it extremely difficult to request assistance from the Civilian Aeronautics Administration. Advised to coordinate directly with the Civilian Pilot Training organization, Hastie confidentially informed Davis that the War Department had submitted a request to the Civilian Aeronautics Administration for additional civilian pilot training for African Americans but the department had not indicated any particular institution. He suggested that Davis continue to pressure the Civilian Aeronautics Administration to obtained the desired training but a request on October 2, 1942 from Davis to Charles I. Stanton who administered the Civilian Aeronautics Administration program produced no tangible results.[18]

Hastie realized the selection of four colleges caused disappointment for colleges that desired ROTC detachments. He informed Felton G. Clark of Southern A and M that despite a general policy against the formation of new detachments, ROTC at North Carolina A and T, Hampton, Prairie View A and M and West Virginia would provide a more equitable share in the ROTC program.[19] The Presidents of Negro Land Grant Colleges were aware that Howard and Wilberforce had commissioned a significant portion of the military officers but stressed the urgency of expanding ROTC to other colleges. Hastie shared the issue of annual officer production with Mordecai W. Johnson at Howard and was concerned that Howard would not meet its quota in 1941 since other schools were requesting additional allotments. The transfer of seventeen advanced allocations reduced its 1941-1942 allocation to thirty-three. A transfer of allocations by Wilberforce, during the 1940-1941 academic year, reduced its officer production to sixteen. A review of each university from 1935 until 1941 by the Operations and

Training Division of the War Department revealed that each had exceeded the basic quota but Howard had graduated forty commissioned officers and Wilberforce had graduated fifteen. Dean Charles H. Thompson of Howard and LTC Zuppman assured Johnson that special efforts would be implemented to increase the advanced course enrollment for the 1941-1942 academic year. An analysis of the advanced class enrollment revealed that of thirty-eight students, one student did not desire to continue the course because of his graduation within the year, two did not return to the program, six failed to maintain acceptable academic status, twelve were rejected and seventeen were admitted into the ROTC advanced course. Thompson maintained that a deterrent to ROTC enrollment for some students was insufficient time to pursue the course for the amount of credit offered. Military science met five times a week for four semesters and yielded only four credits toward graduation which compelled many students to devote the same time to other subjects which resulted in twelve to twenty credits. However, Mordecai W. Johnson requested Thompson and LTC Lloyd Zuppann to submit a recommendation to increase the advanced ROTC quota for the university.[20]

Cognizant of the formation of the four ROTC detachments, an educational meeting was held at St. Mark's Congregational Church on May 3, 1942 by the Sigma Chapter of Alpha Phi Alpha in Roxbury, Massachusetts where a resolution explaining the dilemma of African Americans attending colleges in northern states was submitted by Samuel Darrell to Secretary of War Henry L. Stimson on May 14, 1942. The resolution stressed that northern colleges and universities did not encourage the admission of African Americans into ROTC courses and urged Secretary of War Stimson to use his influence to change the admission policies of the institutions that did not extend military science enrollment to their African American students. MG J. A. Ulio informed Darrell that enrollment in ROTC was open to all qualified students and the basic courses did not have enrollment limitations. Whether participation is compulsory or elective was determined by each educational institution and not dictated by the Army. He emphasized that the Army made no distinction between racial groups or enemy aliens within ROTC detachments but Alpha Phi Alpha received no encouragement to pursue ROTC training.[21]

An expansion of ROTC was considered after the attack at Pearl Harbor and the increase of contracts included African Americans institutions. However, the assistant chief of staff for personnel withheld concurrence on an expansion but supported the purpose of ROTC to provide officers in peacetime to meet the requirements of mobilization. This responsibility continued until OCS and Flying Schools established during wartime were

Howard University PMS&T with staff, cadet commander, and coed commander. (Courtesy of the Moorland-Spingarn Research Center, Howard University Archives)

capable of meeting the additional wartime needs for officers. He further stated that there were very serious objections to the overproduction of reserve officers during either phase. The opinion of the Assistant Chief of Staff for Operations was that the serious shortages of officers, reserve or otherwise, was of great concern and placed the War Department in an untenable situation by establishing in the colleges an Enlisted Reserve Corps while refusing to expand ROTC. He explained that military officials had been severely criticized for refusing to rely more heavily upon this excellent resource, and the Army Air Force desired advanced course contracts available to college juniors and seniors who were in the Enlisted Reserve Corps. He concluded that any significant objections inherent in an increase in the production of reserve officers was a matter which would be considered after winning the war. Assistant Chief of Staff BG I. H. Edwards recommended to GEN Marshall that the commanding general of Services of Supply be authorized to expand ROTC to the extent practical in order to secure the maximum production of officers. This expansion was restricted to the existing framework without any additional personnel, equipment or materiel, and additional contracts were based on the past record, merit and capability of each institution. Consideration of contracts was given to members of the Army Air Forces Enlisted Reserve and depended on the ability and flexibility of each Corps Area to adjust to the additional quotas.[22]

The Director of Training for the Service of Supply, BG C. R. Huebner, estimated that 2,000 additional advance contracts would be absorbed without affecting the quality of instruction or the allocation of the quantity of equipment and material. He also envisioned an increase in the quality of material with the addition of a minimum allotment of modern weapons. Since substantial increases had been authorized in the Signal Corps, Engineers, and Quartermaster Corps, the major increases would be in the arms under the jurisdiction of the Army Ground Forces. BG Huebner concluded that the ROTC graduate was more desirable than the average OCS candidate although he admitted that the OCS candidate immediately upon graduation was more polished, more experienced and more valuable. However, a comparison of a refresher course and OSC revealed that the ROTC graduate made sounder decisions in leadership although the difference between the officers was slight. He further concluded that the average ROTC graduate developed more rapidly and at the end of six months, with or without special school, the ROTC graduate was superior to the average OCS graduate and therefore ROTC was the supply base from which to draw superior officers. He recommended that all enlisted reserves be required to take ROTC training and that Army Air Corps Enlisted Reserves be eligible for selection for advanced course contracts.[23]

TAG announced on April 21, 1942 that with the exception of Medical Corps detachments and for the duration of the emergency, ROTC students were required to enlist in the Army Enlisted Reserve Corps as a prerequisite for enrollment into the ROTC advanced course. Students under age eighteen were not to enlisted in the Enlisted Reserve Corps but could enroll in the ROTC advanced course upon signing an agreement to enlist upon

reaching age eighteen. Enrollment obligated students to complete their requirements for graduation with their class and separation from college for any reason prior to graduation was sufficient reason for immediate call for enlisted active duty.[24] On January 27, 1943 TAG clarified the responsibility of commanding generals of service commands who were charged with the responsibility of calling Enlisted Reserve Corps students to active duty. Senior ROTC students enrolled in the Enlisted Reserve Corps were to be called to active duty upon the initiation of the Army Specialized Training Program at their institutions where they would remain until graduation, provided that graduation occurred prior to June 30, 1943. Students were detailed to their respective branch schools for the completion of a three-month basic training course before being commissioned into the Officers' Reserve Corps. Students in the senior ROTC program who were not scheduled to graduate by June 1943 were also assigned to the Army Specialized Training Program where they remained until the termination of the first full semester or academic corresponding period that began in 1943, after which they received military training in replacement centers, and selected candidates designated for further technical training were detailed for instruction under the provisions of the Army Specialized Training Program. Other successful candidates were sent to the appropriate officer candidate schools where they were commissioned into the Officers' Reserve Corps after graduation. Arrangements were also made for the induction of students into the advanced ROTC program who were not in the Enlisted Reserve Corps. Medical students, including dental and veterinary, were also called to active duty upon the initiation of the Army Specialized Training Program. However, pre-medical and medical students enrolled in the advanced course which was not a medical detachment were permitted to accept a discharge from their ROTC contracts and continue their education under the Army Specialized Training Program. Students who failed to complete their medical courses were assigned to OCS for qualification for reserve commissions.[25]

In the unassigned Enlisted Reserve Corps, medical students, including dental and veterinary students, were scheduled for active duty at the end of their first full semester or the corresponding academic period beginning in 1943, and then detailed to continue their medical instruction under contracts negotiated by the War Department with the appropriate medical

*Opposite:* Company A, 2515th, Student Unit, Army Specialized Training Program, Howard University, March 1, 1944. (Courtesy of the Moorland-Spingarn Research Center, Howard University Archives)

schools. Students commissioned into the Medical Administrative Corps could resign their commissions, enlist as privates and in the same manner be detailed as medical students in the Enlisted Reserve. Pre-medical students in the Enlisted Reserve Corps who were selected for induction or chosen at the end of basic training for further medical or pre-medical training were detailed for instruction under the ASTP. Medical and pre-medical students not in the Enlisted Reserve Corps and inducted under the Selective Service Act were placed on inactive duty to continue training under the ASTP. Seniors in the technical engineering program and not enrolled in ROTC or the Enlisted Reserve Corps were given the same time limitation and placed in an inactive duty status until their graduation, but underclassmen inducted were eligible for ASTP after the completion of their basic training. Normally, unassigned Enlisted Reserve Corps students were ordered to active duty fourteen days after the completion of the semester terminating after December 31, 1942 or as soon as practical to avoid congestion in the reception centers. Assigned to replacement training centers of the Services of Supply or Army Ground Forces, students with advanced ROTC training were assigned to a replacement training center of the branch in which they had received prior training.[26]

The induction of personnel assigned to the Enlisted Reserve Corps caused several problems for collegiate officials. The loss of students obviously lowered the enrollment of male students and caused the replacement of many students who served in key student organizations and organized athletics. In some instances graduation requirements were altered and social events were held earlier to permit the participation of the departing students. Revisions in the Enlistment Reserve Corps program negated efforts by Dwight O. W. Holmes to establish an Air Corps detachment at Morgan State.[27]

The massive operational planning which required the establishment of field armies and their component army corps and divisions for the Normandy invasion on June 6, 1944 caused the curtailment of ASTP. War Department officials were aware that the decision to curtail ASTP was unpopular but military necessity required the formation of innumerable special detachments for transportation, supply and service to the field armies. Students were disappointed with the elimination of the program and some complained that the Army was wasting intelligent personnel with assignments that did not require intelligence, and thereby jeopardizing the

*Opposite:* Team 3, Basic Engineers, Company A, 2515th, Student Unit, Army Specialized Training Program, Howard University, March 1, 1944. (Courtesy of the Moorland-Spingarn Research Center, Howard University Archives)

DENTAL UNIT...ARMY SPECIALIZED
TRAINING PROGRAM...HOWARD
UNIVERSITY...SEPT. 8, 1944

future of the nation by needlessly risking the lives of their most intelligent young men in especially hazardous assignments. Paradoxically, the Army response was that it was because intelligent trained personnel were needed to raise the efficiency of the organized divisions that the chief of staff recommended the curtailment of ASTP in order to provide personnel to the Army Service Forces for allocations to the Signal Corps, the Corps of Engineers, Chemical Warfare Service and Surgeon General as well as to the Provost Marshal General who trained and supplied men for the administration of civil affairs by Allied Military Government detachments in addition to their military police duties.[28]

Students completing training at ROTC summer camp and in the advanced course were usually assigned to infantry after their graduation. Although some Wilberforce graduates were assigned to Chemical Warfare School, three Infantry students at Howard were discharged from ROTC after the completion of their advanced course on June 4, 1943 in order to attend the Howard University School of Medicine.[29] The Hampton ASTP detachment was scheduled to disband on March 31, 1944 but Ralph P. Bridgman announced that the assignment of three to Yale University for predental training, and two others entered premedical training. Eighty-nine honor men in the Hampton program completed the equivalent of thirty semester hours within six months. Meharry Medical College in Nashville, Tennessee in 1944 had established ASTP which included 211 medical students and sixty-four dental students. Equally impressive was ASPT at Howard where the majority of its medical and engineering students completed their training after military service.[30]

Inspections of ROTC detachments were usually in the excellent and superior range, but were below the requirement of 100 students in October 1943. The enrollment at West Virginia State was ninety-eight and at Wilberforce the enrollment had declined to thirty-five. COL Robert S. Walsh as chief of the Civilian Components Section questioned TAG concerning the withdrawal of the ROTC detachments at West Virginia State and Wilberforce but the detachments were retained. However, the enrollment at Wilberforce had fallen to fourteen by June 1944 and the PMST at the University of Dayton had the additional responsibility of serving as PMST at Wilberforce which only had a CWO.[31] MAJ Wilfred I. Freel, the Wilberforce PMST, recognized that the ROTC enrollment had failed to reach the required minimum during the past two years but explained the

*Opposite:* Dental Unit, Army Specialized Training Program, Howard University, September 8, 1944. (Courtesy of the Moorland-Spingarn Research Center, Howard University Archives)

failure was not due to the institutional attitude of the administration, faculty or students. Military training was compulsory but the Selective Service was responsible for drafting most of the eligible students. He urged the retention of the detachment since the wartime emergency had interrupted the normal enrollment at the institution. Charles H. Wesley, president of Wilberforce, stressed that the university had a long tradition of offering military science and was the first African American institution to have a regular Army officer PMST when President Grover Cleveland appointed LT John Alexander, the second African American USMA graduate, the PMST of its ROTC detachment. The adjutant general of the Army Service Forces at Fort Hayes, LTC Gene A. Robens, concurred with MAJ Freel and recommended to TAG that no withdrawal action be taken for the duration of the war or until six months after the termination of hostilities. Therefore, this decision retained not only the ROTC at Wilberforce but benefited other ROTC detachments at the University of Cincinnati, East Kentucky State Teachers College, Rose Poly Institute, West Kentucky State Teachers College, and Xavier University.[32]

Interest in reestablishing ROTC influenced an inquiry on September 24, 1944 from the War Department to the Major Service Commands, the Military District of Columbia and the Antilles Department concerning military credit for discharged personnel matriculating in institutions with reorganized ROTC detachments. The JAG determined that under Section 47 of the National Defense Act there was no authority for granting credit for military or naval service in lieu of any part of the required basic course. War Depart-

Graduation Ceremony for the Army Specialized Training Unit, Howard University, 1944. (Courtesy of the Moorland-Spingarn Research Center, Howard University Archives)

ment officials questioned whether veterans desired active duty for expanded periods and believed that many veterans admitted to colleges would not continue their military service unless they were accepted into advanced ROTC programs with credit for their military service. The Senate Committee on Military Affairs accepted the views of War Department officials and on April 24, 1946 approved ROTC credit for military training while on active duty.[33]

A War Department press release on October 7, 1945 announced the restoration of ROTC advanced courses and the implementation of a new interim ROTC program which affected 129 colleges and universities. The age limitation for eligible students was placed at nineteen to accommodate the Selective Service draft system. African American institutions included in the postwar program were Howard in the Military District of Washington, Hampton in the Third Service Command, North Carolina A and T and Tuskegee in the Fourth Service Command, Wilberforce and West Virginia State in the Fifth Service Command, and Prairie View A and M in the Eighth Service Command.[34]

Reactivation notification of ROTC at Prairie View A and M was received from Texas A and M College by Willette R. Banks who had anticipated a large veteran enrollment to comply with the advanced course requirement

Hampton Institute ROTC Commissioning Ceremony (Courtesy of Hampton University Archives, Hampton, VA)

of 125 students. BG Benjamin O. Davis, assigned to the Office of the Inspector General, inspected the ROTC detachment in April 1946 and Banks expressed his primary concern for acquiring capable instructors for the detachment. BG Davis had experienced similar difficulties with personnel changes at Tuskegee as PMST when the Army appeared to allocate the first available African American soldiers regardless of their education. However, revisions with higher standards had the potential of improving ROTC cadres because officers were required to have college degrees or comparable education and noncommissioned officers were required to have high school degrees or comparable education. BG Davis emphasized the necessity of securing competent military instructors especially with the reservoir of young infantry officers assigned to the Infantry School at Fort Benning, Georgia and was equally confident that Banks would have little difficulty in locating noncommissioned officers. Prairie View A and M had excellent facilities with an opportunity to develop a superior ROTC detachment.[35]

On August 20, 1946 prior to the reactivation of the advanced course program, Banks reiterated his difficulty in acquiring a PMST to replace CPT John R. Reaves who had been reassigned. He concurred with regulations requiring PMST to have bachelor degrees from reputable colleges and considered it important in maintaining an outstanding ROTC organization but complained that during the prior four years he had experienced considerable trouble with some officers who lacked character and were unsuitable for the environment of a coeducational campus. Some of the assigned enlisted men with an educational achievement below the eighth grade had adversely affected training and discipline. With the endorsement of the Eighth Service Command to obtain a cadre capable of providing leadership and ROTC instruction, Banks requested Civilian Aide to the Secretary of War, James C. Evans, to assist in the selection of personnel who were academically prepared, morally sound and capable of effectively exercising good judgment and initiative. Conferring with COL West A. Hamilton, who previously had served as Prairie View A and M PMST, about the detachment, Evans expressed his assurance of securing an appropriate staff for Prairie View A and M. Relying on COL Hamilton's high regard of LTC Robert L. Pollard, Banks recommended the officer for duty as PMST but TAG indicated that he was still overseas and information concerning his return was not available. Two other officers were also assigned to ROTC and neither had returned from overseas duty. On June 22, 1946, the Fourth Army commanding general recommended that Prairie View A and M continue to be considered as a separate detachment although the parent institution was Texas A and M University.[36]

The Bureau of Naval Personnel had contemplated an expansion of

NROTC with detachments geographically dispersed throughout the nation. On March 19, 1945, institutions were informed of the selection criteria which included an appropriate recognition by regional and national accrediting associations, personnel and facilities for instruction in basic engineering, the ability to meet space and financial considerations specified by the Navy, financial resources to ensure adequate maintenance of facilities and academic instruction, a minimum enrollment of 850 to provide approximately 300 qualified trainees, and a geographical spread between enrolled male students and where institutions had V-12 detachments or other Naval training schools. Success in preparing trainees for subsequent reserve midshipmen school and other duties was essential. Hampton Institute did not receive the expansion notification until many other colleges had submitted their applications. Bridgman informed Lester B. Young of the National Urban League of his intention to request NROTC for Hampton Institute. He also stated that on April 26, 1945 there were thirty-eight commissioned African Americans in the Navy, consisting of two Waves, twenty-two line officers and fourteen staff officers. On April 10, 1945 there were only seventy-five trainees in the general service school at Great Lakes but by April 28, 1945 only three remained at the school. The Hampton V-12 program had 33 enrolled on April 25, 1945 but the Hampton Service School was scheduled for decommissioning on August 13, 1945. Young urged Secretary of the Navy James Forrestal to establish a detachment at Hampton but was informed that Hampton did not have the required enrollment and the Navy was attempting to widely distribute the new organizations that provided three detachments to the existing eight ROTC detachments. The Navy stressed that from 1937 to 1938 the enrollment of male students at Hampton did not reach the minimum requirement and based upon that data a committee composed of prominent civilians did not recommend NROTC for Hampton. However, Secretary of the Navy Forrestal emphasized that denial was not based on the academic quality of the Institute.[37]

Hampton anticipated the extension of ROTC and had organized a Committee on Navy and Army Air Corps ROTC which reported its findings and recommendations to the Administrative Council on August 28, 1945. The committee considered the geographical location of the campus in comparison to other African American colleges, the familiarity of the curricula, physical plant and services by the Naval Bureau of Personnel, and naval training provided during the war which produced two of the first commissioned African American officers. The committee further concluded that Hampton had established excellent relations with the military through its Department of Military Science and Tactics, Automotive Transport, ASTP, and its civilian pilot training program offered prior to 1942 would impress

Army Air Corps officials. The institute had also distributed a questionnaire requiring student interest in Air Corps ROTC and envisioned a conversion of instruction in trades and industries to automotive trade and aviation mechanics. Precise information indicating the approximate percentage of students interested in or able to qualify for NROTC was not available. Opportunities to utilize the armed forces training would be largely limited to military activity. Proud of the Navy Bureau of Personnel's familiarity with the Institute's curricula, physical plant and services during the V-12 program, its unique pioneering contributions to the Navy, the probability that the two first African Americans to be appointed received their initial training at the Hampton Naval Training School, the committee concluded that their findings indicated there was a potential for professional careers in the Navy but Hampton did not meet the enrollment requirement of 850 qualified students. The committee concluded that the establishment of Air Corps ROTC would be affected by competition primarily from Tuskegee, West Virginia State, Wilberforce and Tennessee A and I. Since Hampton did not own an airport or employ a certified CAA instructor, the committee's recommendation to the Administrative Council was the formation of an Army Air Corps ROTC detachment. However, plans were implemented to organize a Coastal Artillery Antiaircraft ROTC and COL Richard H. Grinder, who was relieved of duty at the Replacement Pool at nearby Fort Monroe, was detailed to Hampton as Assistant PMST where the cadre consisted of LTC Harry Reubel, MAJ Clarence M. Davenport, Jr., LT J. H. Jemison and four sergeants.[38]

Charles H. Wesley after conferring with MAJ Freel of the University of Dayton, who was responsible for the supervision of the Wilberforce ROTC, and MAJ Edmonds of the Fifth Service Command had difficulty in recommending a regular Army officer capable of reactivating the detachment by January 1946. The nomination of LTC Allen H. Foreman, assigned to Fort McClellan, Alabama, on February 8, 1946 as Assistant PMST coincided with a difficult situation at the university. Wilberforce was experiencing the affects of a division which separated the university into two colleges, one a church and the other a state college. The Combined Normal and Industrial Department had official became the College of Education and Industrial Arts at Wilberforce on May 14, 1941 and relations with Wilberforce University became more tenuous. On September 9, 1947, Judge Frank L. Johnson of the common pleas court sanctioned the separation of Wilberforce University and decreed the utilization or exchange of property was illegal until the two institutions agreed to the mutual interchange of church and state property. The separation necessitated a review of military science by the Department of the Army and the formulation of a plan by MG John T.

Lewis which was provided for consideration by Wesley. The major aspects of the plan required the president of the College of Education and Industrial Arts to submit an application for an Infantry ROTC detachment which would be activated at the beginning of the 1948 academic year and the Wilberforce Assistant PMST would be transferred to the College of Education and Industrial Arts upon the establishment of the ROTC. However, students in the College of Liberal Arts would not be permitted to enroll in the organization, and Wilberforce ROTC would continue after the formation of the new detachment, if desired by the administration. With support from his PMST, COL James A. Nichols, and COL John E. McMahon the Executive of the Ohio Military District, Wesley applied for Infantry ROTC. The College of Education and Industrial Arts at Wilberforce, Greene County, Ohio became Central State University in 1951.[39]

Bishop Frank Madison Reid expressed reservations concerning the survival of Wilberforce since many of the privately owned African American institutions were not able to withstand the pressure of Ohio politics. He maintained that African Americans were parasites in regard to supporting education and especially religious educational institutions. He emphasized the experiences at Lincoln, Morgan State, Simmons University which became Louisville Municipal College Kentucky, and Cheyney State Teachers College of Philadelphia were indications that Wilberforce would not succeed as a state college. Citing the increased African American enrollment at Ohio State University, Reid concluded that migration of Ohio students and others from southern states would be weakened by changing educational systems.[40]

The Howard ROTC detachment was authorized five officers but with only two assistant CPTs, a request for two field grade officers was submitted in August 1946. COL James J. Barnes became PMST and was assisted by CPT Lewis C. Smith who had served with the 99th Pursuit Squadron in Sicily and Italy, and Warrant Officer Douglass A. Gaskins with fourteen years of service with the 10th Cavalry Regiment and three campaign stars from service in both the European and Pacific theater.[41]

On March 20, 1946 Bluford of North Carolina A and T complained to COL LeRoy W. Nichols, the Director of the Army Special Training Division, Fourth Service Command, that ROTC requirements were extremely excessive for LTC Raymond F. Edwards and CPT Arthur W. Ferguson and urged the expansion of the cadre with the reassignment of CPT Roger B. Kyles from Camp Knight, California. CPT Kyles was commissioned at Howard University and was highly recommended by LTC Edwards and CPT Ferguson. This situation was aggravated by the overseas transfer of LTC Raymond F. Edwards which was deferred until the arrival of his replacement and the

Tuskegee Institute ROTC Cadet Staff. (Courtesy of Tuskegee University Archives, Tuskegee, AL)

transfer of CPT Ferguson on approximately July 10, 1946. CPT Raymond A. Montgomery, Jr. was tentatively selected for duty at the college but failed to meet the overseas requirement of War Department Circular 58. Therefore, CPT Roger B. Kyles was relieved of duty with the 5th Training Regiment, Replacement Training Center at Fort Bragg and assigned to the A and T College ROTC. MAJ Edward C. Johnson also requested the transfer of LT Otis O. Zachary, who previously served with the 366th Infantry Regiment, from the 3th Training Battalion, Infantry Replacement Training Center at Fort McClellan, Alabama. Although his regimental commander denied the transfer because of the nonavailablity of a suitable replacement and a regimental shortage of officers, an appeal from LT Zachary to COL Marcus Ray, Civilian Aide to the Secretary of War, resulted in his nomination for ROTC duty at North Carolina A and T College on August 29, 1946.[42]

Patterson's request for the establishment of a Transportation ROTC detachment at Tuskegee was approved by the Fourth Service Command on November 24, 1945 but ironically a request for the establishment of an Air Force ROTC detachment was returned for additional information concerning the availability of facilities. However, the Army Service Forces Headquarters recommended to the Executive for Reserve and ROTC Affairs that the request for a transportation detachment be delayed until the revision of military policy was completed and the receipt of a sufficient number of applications that warranted the selection of additional ROTC detachments. Although Patterson inferred that a senior officer was not assigned to the institute, the Civilian Component Branch of the AGF confirmed that COL Herbert A. Barrow was assigned to Tuskegee on September 10, 1946 where he joined MAJ John A. Welch and LT Cecil W. White who had been assigned to ROTC by July 19, 1946.[43]

James C. Evans, Assistant Civilian Aide to the Secretary of War, informed R. B. Atwood during the Annual Conference of PNLGC—which represented the land grant institutions that consisted of Alabama A and M, Arkansas AM and N, Delaware State, Florida A and M, Georgia State Industrial College, Kentucky State, Southern A and M, Maryland State, Alcorn A and M, Lincoln, North Carolina A and T College, Langston A and M University, South Carolina State A and M, Tennessee A and I, Prairie View A and M and West Virginia State, and the associate members that included Atlanta University, Fisk, Fort Valley State, Hampton, Howard, Morgan State, Tuskegee, Wilberforce, Wilberforce College of Education and Industrial Arts, and Bordentown Manual Training School in New Jersey—convened in October 1945 in Chicago, that more attention would be given to the issue of ROTC with or without compulsory military training. Evans emphasized that the two issues were not the same and he clearly concurred with the PNLGC on the possibility of confusing the issues. Without arguing against compulsory peacetime training programs, Evans agreed to assist the PNLGC in separating the issues and providing maximum concentration on ROTC for African American colleges. He advised Atwood of the reactivation of ROTC detachments in the Fifth Service Command which included an Infantry at Western Kentucky State Teachers College and a Field Artillery at Eastern Kentucky State Teachers College. Evans further advised him of the success of Florida A and M in securing state authorization to file an application for a detachment. It was Evans' intention to collaborate with interested presidents to ensure an opportunity for every African American to be prepared for leadership roles pertaining to national security. The PNLGC indorsed efforts of Alabama A and M, Delaware State, Florida A and M, Kentucky State, Southern A and M, Tennessee A and I and Virginia State, all of which sought Army ROTC detachments except Southern A and M College which was seeking an AFROTC detachment since Hardin Field, a former Army Air Base, was located within a mile of its campus. Southern University and A and M College by January 27, 1948 were seeking ROTC and were encouraged by Evans to reiterate their interest especially since Kentucky State and Morgan State had submitted their applications for ROTC detachments.[44]

Expansion of ROTC to African American colleges was affected by recommendations contained in the McCloy Committee Report and Gillem Report concerning the utilization of African American manpower in the

Army during the postwar period. Released in 1946, a conclusion of the Gillem Committee was that regardless of the procurement or source and the racial composition of officers of Army components each officer should be accorded equal rights and opportunities for advancement and professional improvement. Equally significant was the ruling that all officers were required to meet the same standards of appointment, promotion and retention, and the potential source of officers was extended and fostered through the medium of a more comprehensive ROTC and an Army leadership school program. The committee recommended the procurement of African American officers through the expansion of the regular Army and with personnel obtained for the Organized Reserve Corps which included ROTC graduates and the USMA.[45]

The headquarters of the Army Ground Forces coordinated with each technical service concerning establishing additional ROTC detachments. Coordination with the Army Air Force was attempted but was only advanced slightly since planning by Air Force officials was behind the schedule planned by the AGF. A report by CPT John L. Pfeiffer revealed that contracts were offered to 145 institutions representing all arms and services and of them 107 were completed and 12 others required further consideration by their boards of regents. Thirty-three detachments were not desired by their institutions because of unsettled conditions in their institutions and the desire to view the results of pending legislation that would affect ROTC directly or indirectly prior to initiating an application. CPT Pfeiffer recommended to the War Department Director of Organization and Training the institutions where ROTC detachments should be activated on April 25, 1947. The activation list included a Quartermaster Corps for Virginia State and an Infantry detachment for South Carolina State A and M College at Orangeburg which became effective July 1, 1947.[46]

The selection of only two African American colleges prompted Senator William B. Umstead, who intervened on behalf of North Carolina College at Durham, to emphasize to TAG on June 19, 1947 that the institution was ranked among the leading African American colleges and James E. Shepard, president of the college, was an eminent scholar and highly respected by African Americans and European Americans throughout the United States. Senator Umstead urged that every consideration be given to establishing ROTC at the college. MG Edward F. Witsell, TAG, recognized that a 1942 request was not granted but he assured Senator Umstead that when another application was submitted TAG would consider it together with applications from other institutions.[47]

ROTC allocations to South Carolina State A and M and Virginia State prompted an inquiry from Felton G. Clark to the Chief of Staff of the Executive Reserve and ROTC Affairs concerning the length of time required for Southern A and M to acquire a detachment. Clark questioned the issue of establishing ROTC detachments at institutions which offered specialized curricula that included business administration. Since the college not only was offering business administration and would have conducted a business administration training detachment during World War II as requested by the War Department if most of its male students were enrolled in ASTP, Clark maintained that if this was the only approach to obtaining an ROTC detachment the college would accept it. Cognizant of the tremendous correspondence the War Department was receiving for the establishment of detachments, he considered that Southern University, one of the largest land grant colleges, should have an ROTC for the same reasons as South Carolina State and Virginia State.[48]

Ambrose Caliver, Specialist for Higher Education of Negroes and Adviser, as well as John W. Davis, chairman of the Executive Committee of the PNLGC, inquired concerning the establishment of ROTC detachments. The presidents of Florida A and M, Lincoln, and Southern A and M were among those who kept James C. Evans informed of their attempts to gain ROTC detachments. Morgan State expressed interest in ROTC but by March 1, 1948 an application was not filed with the Department of the Army. However, Dwight O. Holmes assured Evans that an application for an ROTC detachment would be submitted to the Department of the Army. A regional conference held at Georgia School of Technology in Atlanta gave the college presidents with ROTC detachments an opportunity to express their concerns about the program.[49]

African American interest encouraged the Department of the Army to reconsider the activation of additional ROTC detachments at African American educational institutions. James C. Evans, Civilian Aide to the Secretary of Defense, in response to an inquiry on February 12, 1948 by Carl Murphy, president of the *Afro-American*, was informed by MG Howard F. Witsell that TAG was revising the postwar ROTC program and had on file 248 applications from 198 colleges and universities. Impressed with the coverage of opportunities for African Americans in the *Afro-American* on February 17, 1948, Evans endeavored to ensure that Murphy received accurate information concerning the ROTC program and he requested information from TAG to assist in interpreting and disseminating information to the news media about the status of African American institutions in regard to the ROTC. Evans also urged the editor of the newspaper, William I. Gibson, to thoroughly disseminate their treatment of the ROTC program and he provided Murphy with correspondence he planned to distribute to African American colleges and university presidents to alert them to efforts of the

*Afro-American.* He informed Murphy on February 24, 1948 that Morgan State had not filed an application but a letter of inquiry concerning the activation of an ROTC was filed.[50]

Murphy supported the PNLGC and urged the Department of Defense to grant ROTC detachments to the remaining African American land grant colleges and the other colleges which met the qualifications. Emphasizing that only five of twelve land grant colleges had ROTC, he denounced the military explanations that African American colleges were too small to have detachments and that military appropriations were insufficient to establish additional detachments. He further alluded to statements alleging that trustee board members opposed military training and some college Presidents feared the presence of military cadre issuing orders to students. These statements were incompatible and inconsistent with the efforts of some college Presidents who had sought ROTC detachments for more than ten years and contended that ROTC provided leadership training, ensured competent officers for military service during an emergency, subsidized student clothing expenses through the issuance of military uniforms, and permitted students to accrue cash benefits that they would not have otherwise received. While there was little expansion of African American ROTC detachments, there was significant expansion of ROTC detachments among white institutions, especially in Minnesota where eight ROTC detachments were organized. Texas A and M had 9,000 ROTC commissioned officers who served during the last war as compared with 8,000 from the USMA which equaled the 8,000 officers from all the African American colleges and Army schools. The primary objective of the *Afro-American* campaign was the establishment of ROTC detachments in twelve colleges which were denied detachments.[51]

Ferdinand D. Bluford was inspired by the *Afro-American* and hoped a methodology was available for all land grant colleges to have ROTC detachments. He also informed James C. Evans of an executive committee meeting of the PNLGC that was held in Atlantic City where a telegram was sent to the Department of Defense recommending their establishment. He also congratulated Evans on his appointment as Civil Aide to the Secretary of Defense. Evans' primary responsibility was to advise the Department of the Army about special problems affecting African American personnel in all branches of the military with special attention given to future programs and polices regarding their service in the armed forces.[52]

The efforts of Evans and Murphy accelerated the movement to gain additional ROTC detachments. Alabama A and M which requested a detachment on December 19, 1946 had a male enrollment of 520 which included 366 veterans in March 1948. The increased enrollment encouraged

Joseph F. Drake as president to resubmit an application on March 8, 1948 for an Infantry, Quartermaster or Artillery ROTC detachment.[53] Fort Valley State had been recently designated the land grant college for African Americans in Georgia and C. V. Troup was actively engaged in clearing through the Georgia Board of Regents the issue of securing an ROTC detachment for the college.[54]

Evans was extremely interested in the assessment of Assistant Secretary of War John J. McCloy issued on September 1, 1944 when he concluded that the increased minority participation in the military would continue. Any exclusion of African Americans from reserve components Evans informed Fred Dearborn, Executive Secretary of the Civilian Reserve Components Committee, on March 3, 1948, would make a mockery of arguments advanced for universal military training and any restriction to a small number of branches was bound to adversely effect the military since African Americans would be deployed as they were in the past. Obviously, it was more advantageous to induct personnel who possessed some training, and racial restrictions only deprived the Army of trained specialists. There were seventeen African American land grant colleges and only five had ROTC detachments. Six other applications were filed, two of which already had detachments. Among the non-land grant colleges there were 158 applications from white colleges, thirty-nine of which already had detachments. This compared to seven African American non-land grant colleges which had established programs.[55]

Special Consultant L. Eugene Hedberg considered the Army was confronted with a definite public relations problem which he anticipated would spread to the Air force. Pressured by the *Afro-American* and the PNLGC which met in Atlantic City, he realized that only Howard and Tuskegee had AFROTC detachments of the ninety-six organized detachments. The Navy had fifty-eight NROTC detachments but none were established at African American colleges. If all Air force ROTC cadets were required to enroll in technical courses, this was a factor since few African American institutions offered approved engineering curricula.[56]

William A. Fountain of Morris Brown College reminded Evans on March 23, 1948 that the administration, faculty and students were anxiously awaiting the establishment of a detachment. He was informed that the PNLGC was making preparations to appear before a board appointed by Secretary of Defense James V. Forrestal.[57]

John T. Williams of Maryland State informed the Executive for Reserve and ROTC Affairs of the intense interest of the college faculty, administration and students in having an ROTC detachment established at the college. Conscious of the planned presentation of the PNLGC scheduled before the Gray Board, he was informed by COL Arthur L. Shreve that colleges were permitted to request only three branches of ROTC. Williams was not aware of the stipulation when he applied for a detachment on April 30, 1948 and on May 4, 1948 he revised his application by requesting a detachment of Quartermaster Corps ROTC.[58]

MG Witsell stated that every consideration would be given to Morgan State but activations for 1948-1949 had been completed and there was no guarantee that new applications would be considered until the next academic year. Dwight O. W. Holmes, president of Morgan State, explained the enrollment of the college was 1300 and that 900 qualified students were not admitted because of the lack of accommodations. With a potential enrollment of 2,000 that was approximately half male and with an increase in accommodations to permit the enrollment of 3,000 by 1956, the board of trustees approved his efforts to acquire ROTC, although the Executive for Reserve and ROTC Affairs, BG Wendell Westover, regretted that no assurances could be given to his request. In accordance with Holmes' desire to have a Military Police Corps, Quartermaster Corps or Artillery ROTC, the Department of the Army requested that the services consider allocating a detachment to Morgan State College in 1948. The Provost Marshal General, B. M. Bryan, did not consider it feasible to allocate a military police corps detachment since the active Troop Basis and the mobilization did not contain regular Army or Organized Reserve Corps detachments for African Americans. Therefore, available assignments for African American graduates would have been relatively few and temporary, providing an insufficient return for the government expense and involvement of military personnel. The Quartermaster General also refused to activate a quartermaster detachment and an artillery detachment was not feasible although Holmes had gained support from Senator Herbert R. O'Conor.[59]

William H. Gray, Jr., president of Florida A and M, notified Senators Claude Pepper and Spessard L. Holland of his difficulty in understanding why an ROTC detachment had not been formed since land grant colleges in South Carolina, North Carolina and Virginia had ROTC. In his last application he clearly stated preference for a Quartermaster Corps detachment or any other available detachment. He was not particularly interested in Infantry or Field Artillery which were allocated to other African American colleges. COL S. P. Walker, Chief of the Liaison Group Legislative and Liaison Division, affirmed that after Florida A and M's earlier application, on January 14, 1946, and a subsequent request for an engineer or transportation Corps, an inspection would be conducted by MAJ Mark J. Leonardi that revealed the college met had Army regulations pertaining to the establishment of ROTC. The Quartermaster General, MG T. B. Larkin, denied the activation of a detachment since the Quartermaster ROTC detachment at Virginia State would provide the requirements for the Quartermaster Corps.[60]

Florida A and M applied for a detachment in 1945, and was advised as was Morgan State regarding the activation of ROTC at the selected institutions in 1948, that its application would be maintained by the Department of the Army. Gray was disappointed with the manner in which the college was treated and expressed difficulty in understanding the criteria used by the Department of the Army in judging the merits of his request. He disagreed with the assumption that Virginia State was capable of meeting the future Quartermaster Corps requirements and stressed that MG Larkin's view seemed at variance with the spirit of policies designed to unify the armed forces. Gray alleged the policy of the Quartermaster General established arbitrary quotas which would lead to wasting human resources, a position he questioned whether the nation could afford during such critical times. The practice of refusing Florida A and M from any consideration of having Quartermaster ROTC because of the accomplishments within another southern state was unfair and denied their youth the same opportunity of advancement in the event of another war.[61]

Coordinating his efforts with the PNLGC regarding training opportunities for African Americans, Evans requested that John W. Davis, L. H. Foster and R. B. Atwood present the views of the conference to the Gray Board which was appointed by Secretary of Defense Forrestal and chaired by Assistant Secretary of Defense Gordon Gray. He especially wanted to highlight the drill corps organized at Florida A and M and compare it with an earlier unofficial drill corps at Hampton and Tuskegee. Evans also felt the pre-war civilian pilot training detachment at Lincoln was pertinent because it exemplified the commitment of the institution to uniformed students before they were permitted to qualify for commissions in the Army Air force. Evans supported Wilberforce and urged Charles H. Wesley to submit evidence of recent campus improvements. Evans felt the ROTC situation was more promising than most individuals believed and he was confident that the PNLGC would actively pursue the acquisition of ROTC detachments.[62]

Evans conferred with several Army officers to ascertain their views regarding African American possible participation in the military, their presence before the Gray Board and their thoughts concerning the extension of the ROTC program. LTC Herbert A. Barrow, Tuskegee PMST, critical of the assessment of the Gillem Board recommendations, revealed the necessity of assigning qualified African American officers to fill composite organizational vacancies. He recommended the transfer of COL Robert L.

Pollard to the 2nd Battalion, 25th Infantry Regiment at Fort Benning upon his release from Tilton General Hospital in March 1948. African American officers for all African American detachments was the best possible implementation of the Gillem report and integration of African American detachments under white commanders was equated to marching 30 years to the rear. COL Barrow informed Evans that the 82nd Airborne Division chief of staff stated that the 2nd Battalion, 25th Infantry would be assigned to the 325th Infantry Airborne Infantry Regiment prior to the Camp Campbell maneuvers in May 1948 for possible integration into the regiment. The chief of staff also stated that the 758th Tank Battalion with a white officer cadre at Fort Knox would be assigned to the division after the completion of the maneuvers. COL Barrow felt that this was almost criminal since this battalion had established an enviable combat record during the war and since most of its former African American personnel were still in the military and were making strenuous efforts for reassignment to the reactivated detachment. Some were actually stationed at Fort Knox but assigned to a training company which participated in training along with the 758th Tank Battalion. COL Barrow also concluded that the integration and redesignation of the 555th Parachute Infantry Battalion as 3rd Battalion, 505th Airborne Infantry Regiment was an excellent example of the misinterpretation of the Gillem recommendations. Although he felt the intentions of MG James M. Gavin were honorable, when the transfer was accomplished, CPT Joseph Gates was relieved as battalion commander and CPT Richard W. Williams as battalion executive officer, indicating noncompliance of military officials with the Gillem report.[63]

COL West A. Hamilton, a reserve officer who had attained the age of retirement and was scheduled to be relieved from active duty by June 30, 1948, appeared before the Gray Board. With the support of the president of Prairie View A and M where he was serving as PMST and the Executive of the Texas Military District, the Fourth Army commanding general approved the extension of his military career. COL Hamilton had seen references in the press concerning the Gray Board and desired to participate in the conference. However, it was imperative that he return to Prairie View A and M by April 6, 1948 for the Army Day celebration. Arriving at the college a day before the celebration, COL Hamilton was not notified of his extension of service to July 1, 1949.[64]

A delegation that consisted of Atwood, Davis and Foster appeared before the Committee on Civilian Components on April 2, 1948 to express the concerns of the PNLGC.[65] The delegates urged an increase of college and high school ROTC detachments in states where segregation prevented the inclusion of African Americans, improved benefits and financial aid for

ROTC students, improved selection standards of ROTC students, improved selection standards of personnel appointed for ROTC Detachments, and increased emphasis on the value of military training and its relationship to civilian occupations. They were disturbed by misleading comments regarding the alleged substandard achievement of African Americans during the war and urged the military officials to review and correct their records. Seven land grant and associated African American institutions with ROTC detachments collectively provided training in the branches of field artillery, antiaircraft artillery, coastal artillery, infantry, quartermaster and air force reserve training. Equally disturbing was the nonexistence of ROTC programs in land grant colleges in Alabama, Arkansas, Delaware, Florida, Georgia, Kentucky, Louisiana, Maryland, Mississippi, Missouri, Oklahoma and Tennessee where approximately fifty percent of African Americans resided. The delegates stated nearly all of their institutions had completed applications for ROTC organizations except Arkansas AM and N where the board had deferred a decision until June 1948, and Tennessee A and I State and Alcorn A and M where their boards similarly had not approved the submission of ROTC applications. Particularly distressing was the lack of recognition for Florida A and M which had maintained a marching corps at its own expense while seeking approval for an ROTC detachment. With AFROTC located only at Howard and Tuskegee, the delegation recommended the expansion of the program especially to West Virginia State which had sought an AFROTC detachment for several years.[66]

Evans provided each military branch with statements presented before the Gray Board by Davis, Foster and Atwood and urged their consideration of a more equitable assignment of commissioned officers from African American institutions. He recommended that their report together with the report of the Gray Board on Civilian Components be studied by appropriate staffs to indicate methods of enhancing through ROTC the quantity and caliber of future African American officers.[67] COL Henry F. Hannis in the Executive Office of the Office of the Corps of Engineers concurred and agreed that the inclusion of a higher quantity of qualified students in Engineer ROTC would raise the caliber of future African American officers in the Corps of Engineers. However, the ultimate Engineer ROTC program provided for fifty-five detachments of which forty-five were established or scheduled for operation in 1948. The Office of the Chief of Engineers favorably considered the desirability of including at least one African American college with the appropriate accredited curricula. COL Hannis alleged that none of the African American colleges had curricula approved by such accrediting agencies but upon notification of the accreditation by one or more of the accredited engineering or architectural programs his office would be in a position to favorably grant the establishment of a Corps of Engineers ROTC detachment. He also affirmed that his office was awaiting the report of the Gray Board on Civilian Components with considerable interest and a thorough study would be made concerning the utilization of African American personnel in the various components of the Corps of Engineers.[68] The Chief of Finance, MG W. H. Kasten, viewed the proposals and recommendations by the college presidents. However, the limited number of commissioned officers utilized by his office and the highly technical training required for the Finance Department officers did not warrant the establishment of ROTC detachments.[69]

COL G. C. Bunting in the Office of the Chief of Transportation stated on June 1, 1948 that activation of ROTC detachments in colleges and universities with strong undergraduate curricula in one or more subjects involving economics, business administration, transportation, civil engineering, mechanical engineering or transportation engineering was advisable since graduates in these disciplines would learn more easily the varied technical duties of a Transportation Corps officer. Engineer graduates were expected to become specialists in rail, marine or highway operations and those with degrees in economics, business and business administration would become specialists in traffic management, procurement, labor relations, and general administration. COL Bunting also emphasized those graduates in these fields would usually find civilian employment in civilian transportation or allied fields and occupy positions with duties closely related to many of the Transportation Corps specialists. Therefore, a reservoir of qualified transportation specialists would be available in the event of another war. The Transportation Corps had established only 16 ROTC detachments between 1946 and 1947, and during the summer of 1948 only six more were scheduled for activation. The Office of the Chief of Transportation had received only two applications from African American colleges but the alleged lack of capable undergraduates in related academic disciplines caused the rejection of the applications. Concluding the curricula of African American land grant colleges were based on agricultural and mechanical arts, COL Bunting alleged difficulty in locating an institution which met the Transportation Corps requirements. Although the Transportation Corps had a considerable number of African American detachments in its basic troop requirements and desired an African American officer pool, he further alleged difficulty in obtaining accurate information on curricula and facilities at African American colleges. COL Bunting suggested that if Evans recommended three or four outstanding institutions which came closest to the established criteria, the Chief of Transportation would include in his activation plans the establishment of one ROTC detachment for the next year.[70]

The Office of the Quartermaster General did not envision an immediate need for African American Quartermaster ROTC detachments because the Virginia State ROTC detachment commissioned approximately 10 percent of the Quartermaster ROTC requirement since its initial year of operation. With the expansion to its branch in Norfolk in 1948, the Quartermaster General, MG T. B. Larkin, expected an expansion more rapid than any other Quartermaster ROTC organization. The combined increase was expected to be more than adequate to fulfill the Quartermaster Corps' requirement of maintaining the percentage of African American officers in consonance with the total training of Quartermaster ROTC cadets. Representatives from the Office of the Quartermaster General and the Quartermaster Center at Fort Lee, Virginia maintained close liaison with Virginia State College, and extensive efforts were exerted to ensure that ROTC met the Quartermaster Corps' requirements. The excellent rating attained on its annual inspection conducted by the Second Army attested to the progress and achievement of the ROTC detachment. MG Larkin believed the success at Virginia State negated the establishment of additional Transportation Corps ROTC detachments at African American institutions.[71]

Congressional pressure influenced Secretary of War Kenneth Royall to have Evans initiate another follow-up evaluation of ROTC activations. Evans conferred with Chief of Staff, General Omar Bradley, and other officials concerning the expansion of African American ROTC from one to four or five detachments. Secretary of War Royall directed that until a firm decision was made on this issue that all communications with outside agencies such as Congress and the White House be channeled through his office. Evans encouraged Clark and Gray to persevere in their attempts to secure ROTC detachments.[72]

The Gray Board report, entitled Reserve Forces for National Security, was submitted to the Secretary of Defense by the Committee on Civilian Components by June 30, 1948 and released to the public on August 11, 1948. Evans was confident that with presidential approval of a $6,098,000,000 global foreign aid program with initially $1,105,000,000 advanced by the Reconstruction Finance Corporation, the comparison with respect to funding ROTC programs and federal aid to education and a similar program for internal development of national strength was obvious.[73]

Senator Barkley on June 8, 1948 was concerned over the absence of a detachment at Kentucky State and was informed that the matter was being carefully and diligently reviewed by the Army and that Secretary Kenneth C. Royall would ensure that an equitable distribution of ROTC detachments was made to qualified African American colleges.[74]

The Department of the Army submitted a list of Distinguished Military Students scheduled for commission to the president and congress for approval. Effective July 1, 1948 or upon each commissioned officer reaching age twenty-one, the list included thirteen African American ROTC graduates and two AFROTC graduates. All of the officers had attended African American institutions where nine ROTC programs were established with an enrollment of 3,035 or 4.3 percent of the entire ROTC enrollment. The extremely low enrollment influenced the Organization and Training Division to contemplate increasing the number of African American ROTC detachments by allocating one service and two combat detachments to increase the number of participating students in advanced ROTC training and by potentially increasing the number of DMS. The increase of ROTC detachments obviously contributed entirely to the effort of Evans, the PNLGC, and other college officials who had advocated the extension of ROTC detachments in their institutions since the beginning of the revision of the program after WWI. LTG Willard S. Paul, Assistant Chief of Staff of Personnel, was also influenced by African American editors who toured European installations and were critical of the assignments and location of African American soldiers and the absence of African American officers at several installations. Deputy Chief of Staff, GEN J. Lawton Collins, acknowledged the Secretary of the Army Kenneth C. Royall's desire for a careful study of the issue and implementation of corrective action. Secretary Royall recognized the Army had taken the lead among the Armed Services in appointing African American commissioned officers but there was a need for a larger quantity of African American officers. Stressing that the Army must not lower its standards to commission any officer, steps would be taken to encourage competent personnel to qualify for commission into the Reserve Officer Corps. The establishment of three detachments certainly did not satisfy the African American requirement even with the admission of nine cadets into the United States Military Academy and three midshipmen into the Navy Academy. MG John E. Dahlquist, acting Director of Personnel and Administration, recognized Evans' effort to expand African American ROTC detachments but he felt that Army staff personnel had not adequately answered Evans' basic concerns by predicating the expansion of African American ROTC detachments that were necessary to increase the officers requirement under the War Department Circular 124. He stressed that information regarding the quantity of African American officers and detachments was needed to ascertain the extension of ROTC detachments.[75]

An analysis of the numerical officers' strength for the implementation of the planned Army expansion to twenty-five divisions necessitated an

Dr. Martin Jenkins, president of Morgan State College, and ROTC cadre officers (Harris and Haines), July 13, 1950. (Courtesy of the Morganiana Collection, Prints and Photographs Collection, Beulah M. Davis Special Collections Department, Morgan State University)

increase in the procurement of personnel. The Army Organization and Training Division concluded that ten African American ROTC detachments would eventually commission 400 graduates annually and although detailed branch requirements were not completed the strength necessary to satisfy the overall requirement, including future projections and replacements to offset annual attrition, would be attained with the activation of three additional ROTC detachments. Since all of the established detachments were combat arms with the exception of a quartermaster corps at Virginia State, and the Troop Basis of the twenty-five divisions indicated a need for African American ROTC detachments in technical and administrative services, an investigation determined that the facilities at Florida A and M were acceptable for antiaircraft artillery, Southern A and M for transportation and Morgan State for infantry. The major concern was that Morgan State did not guarantee the required minimum of 100 students according to Section 40 of the National Defense Act. The concern was quickly eliminated when Martin D. Jenkins, president-elect of Morgan State, amended the college's application on June 22, 1948 to require compulsory instead of elective military training for freshmen and sophomore students. Felton G. Clark, William H. Gray, Jr. and Martin D. Jenkins were invited to meet with Secretary of the Army Kenneth C. Royall on June 28, 1948. They were officially informed that effective July 1, 1948, an Antiaircraft Artillery ROTC was granted to Florida A and M, Infantry ROTC to Morgan State, and Transportation Corps ROTC to Southern A and M. Their institutions were selected because of their curricula, male enrollment, facilities, and geographical locations to meet the requirements of Reserve Component detachments. The commanding generals of the Second, Third and Fourth Armies were notified of the activations and Evans expressed his appreciation for the attendance of each of the college presidents and the publicity they generated in local press within their respective areas.[76]

The approval of the establishment of an ROTC detachment at Morgan State coincided with attempts by Harry C. Byrd, president of the University of Maryland, to eliminate Morgan State Board of Regents and relegate the college to a status similar to that of the Eastern Branch of the University of Maryland at Princess Anne. Byrd also attempted to remove control of the African American out-of-state scholarships away from Morgan State which was administered by Thomas G. Pullen, State Superintendent of Schools, John T. Williams, president of Princess Anne, and Martin Jenkins, president of Morgan State. However, Jenkins recognized the intentions of Byrd and sought to have Morgan State regain the land grant status which was allocated to its predecessor, Morgan College, on December 31, 1890. An agreement between the Morgan College board of Trustees and Maryland Agricultural College of Prince George's County designated the Delaware Academy at Princess Anne in Somerset County as the Industrial Branch of Morgan College which became the Eastern Branch of the Maryland Agricultural College for persons of African descent. The campus was redesignated as the Princess Anne Academy and sold to the University of Maryland in 1935. After the Supreme Court decision in *Murray v. University of Maryland* concerning desegregation of the university's law school, a recommendation was made to relegate the academy to high school status with special emphasis on vocational training. Concurrently, the Morgan board of trustees negotiated with the state commission on higher education which on September 28, 1939 approved the transfer of Morgan College to state control and the official designation of the college became Morgan State College. Together with transferals of land and institutions the land grant status was retained by the Princess Anne Academy and controlled by the University of Maryland. Cognizant of the lack of past appropriations under land

Morgan State College ROTC, 1950. (Courtesy of the Morganiana Collection, Prints and Photographs Collection, Beulah M. Davis Special Collections Department, Morgan State University)

grant legislation to the Eastern Branch of the University of Maryland at Princess Anne which were retained by the University of Maryland which gained the campus through purchase from Morgan College but had exercised control of the institution since 1928, Jenkins encouraged state officials to implement a recommendation of the 1947 Marbury Commission which provided for the transferal of the land grant for African Americans from Princess Anne to Morgan State. Jenkins was extremely knowledgeable of the study completed by the Marbury Commission since he was appointed by the commission as an educational expert to complete preliminary research which was internalized and included in the final recommendations. Judge Morris A. Soper of the Morgan State Board of Trustees further criticized the incredulous manner in which the University of Marland governed Princess Anne College where a president had not been installed from 1937 to 1947. Although the recommendation by Jenkins was not approved by the Commission to Study the Question of Negro Higher Education in Maryland on October 17, 1949, the commission did not eliminate the Morgan State College Board of Regents or place the college under the administrative control of the University of Maryland.[77]

There were other pertinent factors which led to the allocation of these ROTC detachments since an analysis of African American officers in the Army had revealed several major deficiencies in the involvement of African Americans in the military. The strength of African American officers in the Regular Army prior to WWII was five and all of them were chaplains except COL Benjamin O. Davis. Mobilization efforts increased the total strength to 520 by December 1941 which continued to rise until an apex of 7,211 was reached in December 1945. Demobilization created a rapid decline to 3,803 in January 1946 that further declined to 1,773 by October 1946 but that was an increase of 68 over the previous month. The officers' strength began to stabilize but it continued a gradual decline to 947 by April 1947. A survey of seventy-eight of the ninety-eight African American Tables of Organization and Equipment for detachments in the Zone of the Interior was completed to determine the implementation of War Department Circular 124 regarding the replacement of white officers with qualified African American officers and the assignment of additional officers to detachments having a greater than normal percentage of personnel within the Army General Classification Test score of IV and V. The survey indicated similar shortages in 315 TOE detachments located in overseas areas or the Tables of Distribution detachments in the Zone of the Interior. It was apparent from the results of the survey that the procurement of additional personnel was needed with the contemplated expansion of the Army. The Organization and Training Division initiated action to secure the immediate recall of approximately seventy-two company grade officers to fill the Tables of Organization TOE vacancies in the Zone of the Interior by requesting Army commanders to requisition officer replacements. However, African Americans recall eligibility or initial entry on active duty was limited by the relatively small number of personnel who were granted commissions in the active reserves or National Guard. A Department of the Army Troop List revealed there were only 2,515 officers in the active reserves on December 31, 1947, and the National Guard Bureau reported on May 31, 1948, that there were only 297 federally recognized officers in National Guard organizations. Although the combined African American strength was 2,794, there were only thirty-nine officers and a nurse with permanent rank on active duty. A retired officer on active duty increased the total to forty-one. An additional 927 African American applicants were evaluated by the Army Selection Board but only ninety-six qualified for military service. One of the applicants declined acceptance and of the remaining applicants, sixty-four were commissioned in the Air Corps and thirty-one accepted regular Army commissions. The survey also revealed that thirty-two African American officers were integrated into seven branches. The aggregate African American officer strength in the Army by April 30, 1948, was 947.[78]

COL West A. Hamilton had expected LTC Harry S. Reubel to initially join his staff at Prairie View A and M as Assistant PMST and succeed him. Although he was informed while attending the hearing of the Gray Board that LTC Reubel was not enthusiastic about a college assignment and desired an assignment in the First Army area, he expected his arrival at Prairie View A and M in August 1948.[79] However, E. B. Evans, president of the college, was informed by James C. Evans that it was deemed advisable and necessary to relieve COL Hamilton of his duty at Prairie View State and reassign him to Morgan State on July 1, 1948. The Advisor to the Secretary of Defense was cognizant of the objections raised by COL Hamilton, E. D. Evans and the Fourth Army commanding General especially since Prairie View A and M ROTC had attained a high state of proficiency. It was exactly for this reason why COL Hamilton was selected to inaugurate the new Infantry ROTC detachment at Morgan State. With LTC Reubel already designated to succeed him, the transfer of command at Prairie View A and M did not impose an undue burden upon the college. CPT John C. Harlan was appointed as COL Hamilton's Assistant PMST at Morgan State.[80]

After the ROTC activations, University of Maryland president H. C. Byrd, on July 16, 1948, requested that LTG L. T. Gerow, Commanding General of the Second Army, form an ROTC detachment at Maryland State College at Princess Anne since the college was a land grant institution under the jurisdiction of the University of Maryland, and the university under Federal law was obligated to provide similar military training for students attending Maryland State College. Governor Earle C. Clements of Kentucky also wanted ROTC for Kentucky State and was confident that an investigation would disclose that Kentucky had not received its proportionate share in the allocation of ROTC Detachments. LTG Gerow informed Byrd and Clements that each institution failed to meet established requirements that were attained by other institutions.[81] MG H. R. Bull, acting Director of Organization and Training, also did not take action on a Lincoln in Pennsylvania application because of its December 30, 1941 submission date.[82]

Evans stated to Luther H. Foster, president of the PNLGC, that this was the first tangible result of the movement to secure additional ROTC for African American colleges. The allocation of the types of detachments was based on the respective resources at each institution and the needs of the service. Secretary of the Army Kenneth C. Royall emphasized that while the needs of the service were the governing factor it was particularly important to provide an opportunity to expand the ROTC program that conformed with project objectives. Evans was extremely appreciative of the service rendered by the PNLGC and announcements were circulated to the press which emphasized the formation of ROTC at Wilberforce in addition to detachments at Florida A and M, Morgan State, and North Carolina A and T.[83]

Determined to manage the ROTC initiative with the utmost efficiency, Evans selected LTC James H. Robinson, the South Carolina State PMST, for temporary duty in the Office of the Civilian Aide to the Secretary of the Army to give special attention to the ROTC program in African American colleges. LTC Robinson was an excellent choice for this task because of his familiarity with ROTC programs and his military experience during the war. Initially commissioned in 1925 at Howard, he entered active service with the 366th Infantry Regiment in 1941 at Fort Devens, Massachusetts and served with the regiment and the 226th Engineer Regiment during the Rome-Arne, North Apennines and Po Valley Campaigns where he was awarded a Bronze Star, Purple Heart and Combat Infantryman Badge. Appointed to the War Department Discharge Review Board upon his return to the United States where he served from February 8, 1946 to June 21, 1947, BG Pearson Menoher recommended that he receive the Army Commendation Ribbon because of his outstanding knowledge of human relations, penetrating judgment of human character, important interpretations of problems encountered in combat and elsewhere by African American soldiers, and for his significant contributions toward the development of general policy and the effective resolution of cases which were referred to him. LTC Robinson was assigned to South Carolina State A and M in July 1947 and with the retirement of BG Benjamin O. Davis he became the senior African American officer in the Regular Army. He assumed his duty as Executive to the Civilian Aide to the Secretary of the Army on June 21, 1948.[84]

Evans regretted that the ROTC activations did not include the extension of detachments to Atlanta, Kentucky State, Langston and Lincoln. He realized that all of the college presidents were concerned with the effects that Selective Service legislation would have on their students.[85] When the PNLGC met on August 17, 1948 at Virginia State, a major priority was petitioning President Harry S. Truman to establish detachments at Kentucky State, Langston, Lincoln and Alabama A and M.[86] Carl Murphy supported the initiative and emphasized to Truman that approval of an application from Rufus B. Atwood, president of Kentucky State, had the support not only of his board of trustees but also of the governor, the state adjutant general, both state senators, congressmen, the state teachers' association, and the mayor of Frankfort. MG Witsell explained the existing ROTC detachments were adequate to meet combat requirements for African Americans, and he alleged difficulty in determining suitable institutions for technical service ROTC detachments because of the limited academic fields of a technical nature offered in the curriculums of African American institutions. The need for officers was governed by branch and service and the three additional colleges had the capability and potential for producing the needed officers. Authorization of additional detachments in subsequent years would also be based on planned military needs and contingent on the availability of qualified instructors, personnel and funding. He was unable to predict whether Kentucky State would be selected to receive an ROTC detachment during the next year.[87]

An issue which affected West Virginia State ROTC was the reassignment of LTC Leon F. Lavoie to the Armored School at Fort Knox in September 1948. John W. Davis was extremely pleased with his performance and endeavored to protect the splendid *esprit de corps* and enthusiasm which was manifested at the college. Davis requested that LTG L. T. Gerow, Second Army Commanding General, provide an immediate replacement with rank not less than that of LTC Lavoie. Giving assurance that race was not a factor and that the college preferred an integrated cadre, Davis felt it was detrimental to the ROTC program to be without a PMST since a previous experience with an acting PMST did not obtain creditable results for the college or the War Department.[88]

The Executive for Reserve and ROTC Affairs was informed by the Office of Education for the Federal Security Agency that African American land grant colleges were notified of a legal opinion of the General Counsel of the Federal Security Agency that required them to offer military science and tactics. COL John R. Monnett, the Assistant Executive Officer for RROTC Affairs, recommended to the Director of Organization and Training and the Director of Personnel and Administration that the necessary action be implemented to preclude the possibility of a college having any legitimate cause for claiming discrimination against the Department of the Army, cognizant that only seven of the seventeen had ROTC detachments. A survey revealed that Arkansas AM and N and Maryland's Princess Anne Academy were not accredited, Alcorn A and M and Georgia State College were classified as B institutions, and of the remaining six colleges and universities that included Alabama A and M, Delaware State, Kentucky State, Lincoln, Langston and Tennessee A and I, all but one met the minimum enrollment requirement. The survey did not specify which institution was eliminated but Delaware State had the lowest enrollment with only 184 male students. However, MG Clift Andrus, Director of Organization and Training urged support of JAG opinions rendered on March 8, 1948 which stated that there appeared to be no Federal law requiring the establishment of ROTC detachments and the authority given the president to establish and maintain ROTC detachments was permissive and not mandatory. The Morrill Act requiring military courses at land grant institutions was an obligation that was separate and distinct from the maintenance of ROTC in such institutions by the Federal government and ROTC merely provided a medium through which the institutions met their obligations. The Office of Education in the Federal Security Agency was responsible for implementing the Morrill Act. MG Andrus contemplated the establishment of thirty-one additional detachments primarily in the technical services during the next year and urged the maintenance of ROTC standards without favoring any category.[89]

LT John T. Martin emphasized the status of African Americans in the postwar Army by stressing that of a total of 1,158 officers in the Army there were only 53 Regular officers in the Army, 63 in the Air Force, five in the Navy and 1 Marine. The prospects of having the service academies provide needed African American officers was dismal since only nine were attending the USMA, three were enrolled in the USNA, only 11 had graduated from the USMA and none from the USNA. Although an accurate total of African Americans enrolled in 218 ROTC detachments at predominately white institutions was not available, there were 3,633 cadets enrolled in thirteen African American ROTC detachments by March 1, 1949 and 715 of the cadets were members of the advanced corps of cadets. Nine students were distinguished military graduates and were among 88 cadets commissioned into the Regular Army in 1948. African Americans were integrated into composite detachments in the 2nd Infantry Division at Fort Lewis, 3rd Infantry Division at Fort Benning, 9th Infantry Division at Fort Dix, 10th Division at Fort Riley, 25th Division in Gifu, Japan, 2nd Armored Division at Camp Hood, 3rd Armored Division at Fort Knox, and the 82nd Airborne Division at Fort Bragg. LT Martin further stressed that LTC Hyman Y. Chase, a Howard University ROTC graduate, was serving as commander of all ground transportation in Frankfurt, Germany in connection with the Berlin airlift *Operation Vittles*. Command opportunities were also available for African American officers in the 7777th Infantry Platoon Honor Guard stationed in Heidelberg and the 7800th Infantry Platoon Honor Guard in Berlin. Both organizations had received high praise from Secretary of Defense James V. Forrestal and Secretary of the Army Royall. By March 1, 1949, African Americans were in National Guard organizations in the District of Columbia and several states were assigned to the Organized Reserve Corps.[90] Indicative of the interest in acquiring an ROTC unit during 1950 to 1953, Alabama AM and N, Alcorn A and M, Arkansas AM and N, Atlanta, Fisk, Fort Valley State, Grambling State, Howard Payne College, Jackson State College, Kentucky State, Lincoln, North Carolina College, Savannah State College, St. Paul's Polytechnic Institute, Texas Southern University, Virginia Union and Xavier submitted requests for ROTC detachments.[91]

Colleges with military science programs had difficulty in having some DMS graduates assigned within the first two branches of their choice. An Army Personnel Board which consisted on MG M. S. White, MG Edward S. Bres and representatives from each combat arm and service convened on

March 21, 1949 to reconsider branch designations for certain DMS students. Although the Finance Department representative had previously stated his department did not recommend the approval of African American regular Army officers for the Finance Department, the reconvened board ruled that LT Lonnie W. Williams and LT William B. Proctor, who anticipated graduating from Hampton in June, were designated to join the Finance Department. The Chief of Finance, MG E. M. Foster, felt it was inadvisable to assign African Americans to the Finance Department for several reasons. He stated that the department did not have any African American detachments, the greater portion of the civilian personnel in the thirty Class II installations were white, and their assignment would not permit well rounded careers in accordance with effective career planning since extreme difficulty was anticipated when African American officers obtained field grade ranks. MG Foster considered that African American officers would be more valuable and receive greater satisfaction in organizations with African American personnel. He emphasized that both candidates had been accepted by their second arm or service.[92]

There were only eleven African American regular Army officers with five assigned to the Transportation Corps, two to the Quartermaster Corps, one to the Chemical Corps and three to the Medical Service Corps. There were twenty-two DMS candidates for commission into the regular Army and the previous actions of the Army Personnel board revealed that the Infantry accepted eight, the Field Artillery accepted five, the Coastal Artillery Corps accepted three and the Quartermaster Corps accepted two. One applicant with training in architectural design, structural engineering and mathematics was undecided but selected Infantry, and the Corps of Engineering withdrew its selection which was the candidate's second choice. One candidate was referred to the Air Force, another was selected for Field Artillery and one was rejected. However, the Director of Personnel and Administration, LTG Edward H. Brooks, referred to Department of the Army policy and concurred with the recommendation of the Army Personnel Board in reference to the assignment of LT Proctor and LT Williams. Although his protest had been considered and the reconvened board ruling was in accordance with Department of the Army policy, MG Foster stated the Finance Department would comply with the policy regardless of the anticipated unfavorable consequences alleged by the department.[93]

The outbreak of hostilities in Korea influenced TAG on July 25, 1950 to notify military commands of possible expansion of the ROTC program during the fiscal year of 1951. Although the need for officers had increased, the lack of personnel and materiel prevented the military from meeting the demands of many deserving institutions. The endeavor to select institutions with the greatest military potential and give priority to those having applications of long standing influenced the denial of a request from Gordon Gray, president of the University of North Carolina, who had interceded on behalf of North Carolina College to obtain an ROTC detachment. North Carolina College with favorable support from the North Carolina Military District during the previous year was also denied a detachment.[94]

J. R. Otis, president of Alcorn A and M, with the support of Governor Fielding L. Wright stressed on September 30, 1950 that African Americans were denied the opportunity to receive military training in Mississippi and that many potential Alcorn A and M students were attending colleges in Louisiana and Tennessee where ROTC detachments were established. He requested the formation of an Infantry, Transportation or Military Police Corps ROTC detachment for the college. COL Stuart C. MacDonald, chief of the Mississippi Military District at Jackson, Mississippi and his deputy for ROTC, LTC Ralph H. Elliot, inspected Alcorn A and M on December 12, 1950 and recommended the establishment of an ROTC detachment.[95] Lincoln in Pennsylvania which requested a Military Police Corps ROTC detachment was similarly inspected and the inspecting officer recommended the allocation of a Military Police Corps ROTC detachment.[96] Unfortunately, requests from Joseph F. Drake of Alabama A and M and William A. Fountain, Jr. of Morris Brown College were denied on January 17, 1951.[97]

Chief of Organization and Training Division, BG D. A. D. Ogden, alleged on May 18, 1950 that Texas College in Tyler, Texas, Texas State University for Negroes in Houston, Texas, Arkansas AM and N, and Langston were no longer interested in ROTC and only recommended the establishment of a Corps of Engineers ROTC detachment at Lincoln, effective April 3, 1950. The commanding general of the Fourth Army on September 29, 1950 concurred with the denial of a detachment to Langston, Bishop College in Marshall, Texas, Howard Payne College in Brownsville, Texas, and Xavier.[98] Two years later, MG William E. Bergin, TAG, denied detachments to Benedict College, Fisk, Howard Payne College, Morris Brown College, North Carolina College, Southern A and M, Tennessee A and I, Texas Southern and Xavier.[99]

COL Samuel S. Graham, Executive Officer of the Arkansas Military District, had surveyed Arkansas AM and N College on October 5, 1950 and concluded the institution, which was the largest in the state for African Americans, not only qualified for a detachment but such a detachment would help to alleviate the critical shortage of African American reserve officers in Arkansas. He supported Lawrence A. Davis, president of Arkansas AM and N, who submitted an ROTC application on June 30, 1952. The Arkansas Legislative Council on April 11, 1952 adopted a resolution urging TAG to establish an ROTC detachment and solicited the assistance of state officials, Arkansas congressmen, Secretary of the Army Frank Pace and the chief of the ROTC Division. Arkansas Governor Sid McGrath was informed by Secretary of the Army Pace that from 500 applicants the Department of the Army was able to select only one in twenty-five applicants. MG Hugh M. Milton, Executive for Reserve and ROTC Affairs, had visited the college in April and advised Davis of the physical plant deficiencies. However, the Department of the Army would consider new applications from Arkansas AM and N College and State Teachers' College at Conway in view of an early consideration for 953 ROTC accessions. Herrin Northcutt, Director of the Arkansas Legislative Council, was informed by MG Harry H. Vaughan, Military Aide to the President, that obtaining highly productive ROTC detachments in the institutions best qualified to conduct the ROTC program was the primary concern of the Department of the Army and no preference was given to land grant colleges. A special study initiated at the request of the Assistant Secretary of the General Staff revealed that Arkansas AM and N possessed the necessary qualifications to accommodate an ROTC detachment. The study also stated that the Department of the Army was only indirectly concerned with the Morrill Act since the administration of that act was vested in the Office of Education, Federal Security Agency. Although the authority given to the president to establish and maintain ROTC detachments was permissive and not mandatory, land grant colleges must offer courses in military science and tactics. This obligation was separate and distinct from maintaining ROTC detachments in such institutions maintained by the Federal government. States were entirely free to determine the branches of military training provided, the content of instruction offered, and the objectives obtained according to the opinion in *Hamilton v. Regents 293 U.S. 245* in 1934. The ROTC program when available merely provided a medium through which land grant colleges were afforded an opportunity to meet their obligations under the Morrill Act. The study also revealed that of 1,398,735 collegiate male students in 1951 only 29,777 or 2.3 percent were African American, of 126,827 enrolled in ROTC only 5,242 or 4.13 percent were African American. There were 551,118 students enrolled in states practicing segregation but only 29,777 or 5.4 percent were African American, and of 65,419 students enrolled in ROTC where segregation was not practiced there were 5,242 students or 8.01 percent African American cadets.[100]

Arkansas Congressman John L. McClellan, displeased with the omission of Arkansas AM and N from the list of institutions granted ROTC detachments in 1952, was keenly interested in when the college would be granted an ROTC detachment and urged Secretary of the Army Pace to personally intercede on behalf of the college. He did not know the reason for the omission and respectfully insisted that when another list was announced it would include the college. Senator McClellan was reluctant and always refrained from urging Secretary of the Army Pace to use his position in favor of Arkansas or its citizens and institutions but he felt that this issue warranted his personal interest and attention, at least to the extent of satisfying himself that the college was not being discriminated against or neglected during the next evaluation of institutions. He emphasized that African American institutions in Alabama, Florida, Louisiana, Maryland, Missouri, North Carolina, South Carolina and Texas had ROTC detachments but apparently Arkansas and Mississippi were the only southern states which had not received favorable consideration. Senator McClellan stressed that George McKinney, president of the Student Government, and 396 other students at Arkansas AM and N had petitioned him to assure military training at their college. He reiterated that the college deserved a detachment, and should have had an organization established during World War II, and had college officials brought the issue to his attention, he was positive that the secretary of war could have been persuaded to grant a detachment. Unfortunately, his assistance was only requested after the quota of organizations was filled. Assured by Secretary of the Army Pace that several ROTC detachments would be discontinued and that Arkansas AM and N would receive preferred consideration, new detachments would not be established until some colleges became ineligible or lost their detachments. Senator McClellan was still confident that the Department of Defense was not discriminatory against Arkansas and was equally confident of the eligibility of Arkansas AM and N. Undersecretary of the Army Karl D. Johnson carefully reexamined the possibility of establishing an ROTC detachment at the college but the situation concerning activating new detachments had worsened. Because of manpower and budgetary limitations, providing the required personnel to existing detachments, and reducing requirements for extra personnel as a result of the Korean armistice affected the establishment of additional detachments. Similar information was given to Senator J. W. Fulbright who expressed interest in a resolution adopted by the American Legion of Arkansas, Congressmen E. C. Gathings, John Slezak, and Senator McClellan on March 9, 1954.[101]

In 1952 African American ROTC detachments received satisfactory ratings except for Wilberforce. The university was the only African American institution included among eight others which had not enrolled the minimum students although with seventy-four cadets it had the highest enrollment of all the unsatisfactory colleges. Since Wilberforce had ended the past academic two years with enrollments below 100 students and was given probationary status by TAG on August 16, 1951, the Second Army Commanding General on July 17, 1952 recommended that the ROTC detachment be withdrawn. The detachment was not withdrawn but after the next annual inspection when the enrollment increased to seventy-seven another recommendation was submitted by Second Army requesting the elimination of the detachment at the termination of the 1953-1954 academic year.[102]

The denial of ROTC detachments did not prevent some African Americans from achieving military training under the sub-detachment and satellite or feeder programs. This enabled Virginia State to establish a JROTC detachment at its branch in Norfolk in September 1948. On April 14, 1953 TAG also requested that the Executive for RROTC have the commanding general of the Fourth Army inform Langston University that it was granted an ROTC detachment for September 1952 as part of the satellite program of Oklahoma A and M at Stillwater, Oklahoma. However, Kentucky State and Atlanta were not offered satellite detachments in 1953.[103] Fort Valley State formed a JROTC detachment with MAJ H. Alonzo Robinson offering all of the basic courses from 1957 to 1960. The expansion of the program with the addition of advanced courses by 1963 increased the ROTC cadre to ten and cadet enrollment to approximately 100 students.[104]

LTC James H. Robinson of the Office of the Civilian Assistant to the Secretary of Defense, COL West A. Hamilton, former PMST at Morgan State, and Joseph H. B. Evans, the Associate Executive Secretary of Fahy Committee, visited the 1949 ROTC encampment at Fort Meade where approximately 1,220 cadets from colleges in the Midwest, southern and eastern seaboards were training. The largest representation of African American cadets was from Howard, Morgan State and Wilberforce and all of the African American cadets were concentrated into Company C commanded by CPT Harlan from Wilberforce. Cadets from Wilberforce State College and Wilberforce were within the summer encampment area of Camp Campbell in Kentucky but according to established policy they were sent to Fort Meade as part of the all-African American company. Cognizant of presidential executive legislation to integrate the Armed Forces and the mission of the Fahy Committee, the delegation was concerned about efforts to desegregate Company C and the integration of personnel billets, messing facilities and other operations pertaining to the encampment of ROTC students, and were informed that, with the exception of its own barracks and mess hall and the consolidation of African American cadets in Company C, segregation did not extend beyond the formation of the company. The service club was integrated but there were separate swimming pools and scheduled dances were segregated.

The delegation dined at the integrated officers' consolidated mess and were guests of Georgetown University PMST who was serving as the ROTC camp commander. They were joined by a delegation from Morgan State which consisted of George C. Grant, Edward N. Wilson, Edward P. Hurt and MAJ Clinton Burke, the PMST at the college. They also met with COL Carnes, who was not African American but was PMST at Howard University and served as camp inspector, and seemed to function as advisor on African American affairs for both the camp commander and LTG L. T. Gerow. The delegation met with LTG Gerow who stated that from a professional and military aspect he supported complete integration and was planning the elimination of the African American company and all cadets would serve in the same detachments during the 1950 encampment. However, he was not convinced of eliminating separate social affairs where women were involved since it could lead to unpleasant incidents that might cause problems. Although suggestions were offered by George C. Grant and others of the civilian delegation, Evans concluded that emphasis regarding desegregation must occur within the military to ensure racial cooperation and it was necessary to follow-up on the plan of integration because of the scheduled retirement of GEN Gerow in July 1950. He further concluded that the general impression from officers who attended previous ROTC camps was that real progress had occurred especially in the process to eliminate the African American company. There was also the impression that Wilberforce State College, Wilberforce, and other colleges similarly situated would be assigned to ROTC camps within their corps area except in the case of African American students living near Fort Meade during the summer months. Changes were also influenced by the specialized branch training other than infantry offered at several African American institutions. Lincoln University with an engineer program was required to send its cadets to Fort Carson in Colorado. Evans also discovered an interesting sidelight on the inequality of treatment of African American officers while questioning COL Hamilton concerning his ROTC summer camp experiences. COL Hamilton explained that he had never served during ROTC summer encampments prior to his retirement because he would have been the senior ranking colonel at camp, and therefore would have been the camp commander.[105]

Legislation providing for the establishment of ROTC did not include female enrollment but females were commissioning as nurses. Authorization was granted for the first time to commission civilian women into the Women's Army Corps. Applicants were required to be college graduates or prospective graduates in their senior year and training was conducted at Fort Lee, Virginia. Vivien Davis and Salome Butler of Howard completed the program in 1951 and LT Butler was assigned to the Adjutant General's Office, Fifth Army Headquarters at Camp Custer, Michigan while LT Davis was retained temporarily at the WAAC School as an instructor. This change in military policy caused some speculation that ROTC would be offered to women since pending legislation before the House Armed Services Committee would authorize their participation in ROTC.[106]

# 4

# Air Force and Navy ROTC

When Congress amended the National Defense Act in 1920, the Army Air Service initially established four Air ROTC detachments and expanded the training to a total of seven by 1923. Postwar demobilization and protests from civilian organizations, which were appalled by the casualties and enormous destruction during the World War, opposed the formation of standing armies and military training and advocated the elimination of 223 Army and Air ROTC detachments. The major world leaders agreed in principle to reduce naval construction and the size of their naval forces after a disarmament conference held in Washington in 1922. Congress did not favor increased funding for national security and drastically reduced allocations for reserve training. Personnel in Air ROTC detachments by 1925 were reduced to seven regular officers and five enlisted men further reductions in the Army budget by 1935 eliminated all Air ROTC detachments. After December 1941, War Department officials considered ROTC inadequate to provide commissioned officers to meet wartime demands and substituted special officer candidate schools to produce qualified commissioned officers. The implementation of GO 124 which was signed on August 22, 1946 by GEN Dwight D. Eisenhower, Army Chief of Staff, established seventy-seven Air ROTC detachments which were initially under the control of the Air Training Command but on November 15, 1946 they were transferred to the Air Defense Command. A reorganization and alignment of the armed forces caused the establishment of the Department of Defense on September 26, 1947 with all Army Air Force detachments and personnel transferred to the United States Air Force. A further realignment within the USAF merged the Air Defense Command and Tactical Air Command to form the Continental Air Command which gained responsibility for training collegiate detachments which were referred to as the Air Force Reserve Officer Corps. The requirements for Air ROTC cadres assigned as PMSTs was field grade rank, a pilot's rating, being between twenty-seven and forty-eight, having three years of active commissioned service, above average efficiency ratings and a bachelor's degree.[1]

Howard and Tuskegee were among the institutions authorized to establish ROTC and Army Air ROTC detachments in 1946 with a summer camp conducted in 1947 at the USMA Preparatory School at Camp Stewart.[2] Patterson desired an African American officer for the Air Force ROTC detachment which was assigned to Tuskegee in 1946. BG Leon W. Johnson selected an officer who was detailed to temporary duty at Perrin Field in Texas to complete the Air ROTC Instructor's Indoctrination Course. Upon the completion of the course on October 7, 1947, he was scheduled for assignment at Tuskegee Institute as PAST.[3] The Air Force was simultaneously expanding pilot training and organized teams that visited major colleges and universities to acquaint interested students with educational and career opportunities and benefits offered by the Air Force. The Air Force had reactivated the Aviation Cadet Pilot Training program and recruited personnel who qualified for the twelve-month training course and an Air Force Reserve commission. Basic training was given at Randolph Field in Texas while advanced single-engine training was offered at Williams Field in Arizona and multi-engine training at Barksdale Field in Louisiana.[4]

Aviation was a major objective of the PNLGC which selected G. L. Washington, general manager of the Division of Aeronautics at Tuskegee Institute, to evaluate post war aviation possibilities in African American land grant colleges. A survey of colleges, which included visitations to state colleges in North Carolina, South Carolina and Virginia in addition to Hampton, revealed that the majority of twelve colleges favored flight and allied ground instruction, aviation education and vocational aviation courses. With the exception of three colleges in the survey, there was not a history of aviation education training, and with the exception of six colleges organized flight training had never been afforded to students, and where flight training was provided instruction had ceased with the conclusion of the Civilian Pilot Training Program. Although an aviation committee existed at one college, twelve colleges were located within a radius of fifteen miles of African American communities with populations between 175,000 and 300,000. Seven colleges were within ten miles of airports where they were denied flight training according to local aviation policies. However, suitable sites for landing fields were available near seven of the colleges, and Washington, during a PNLGC conference held in October 1945 in Chicago, recommended the reinstitution of flight scholarships under the Civilian Aeronautics Administration similar to a previous program under Civilian Pilot Training Program, the formation of an aviation committee by the college presidents, the implementation of a summer aviation program by

PNLGC in 1946 and the extension of any plans involving flight training in connection with ROTC. He stressed that the Tennessee State Bureau of Aeronautics awarded twenty scholarships, consisting of ten hours of flight instruction, to African Americans pursuing aviation education at Fisk.[5]

Charles Wesley attended the conference and was interested in establishing an Army Air Force ROTC for Wilberforce by August 12, 1946. The university which had an airplane mechanics course, appointed a licensed pilot to instruct aeronautics and with the approval of its board of trustees was prepared to establish an airport. Referred by the Second Army commanding general to the commanding general of the Army Training Command in Barksdale, Louisiana, Wesley was informed by MAJ Robert A. Stevens that 1946-1947 War Department AFROTC allotments had been activated and COL Monro MacCloskey, Chief of the Reserve and National Guard Air Corps, considered the low male enrollment at Wilberforce insufficient to ensure the success of an AFROTC detachment in addition to an Infantry detachment already established at the university.[6]

After the reorganization and realignment of armed forces and the recreation of the Department of Defense, Wesley on April 29, 1948 endeavored unsuccessfully to obtain an AFROTC detachment. He stressed to James C. Evans that during the war the university gave instruction to airplane mechanics and provided trained mechanics for employment at Wright Field in Ohio, and with the conclusion of the war, airplane engines and other aviation material were donated to the university for aeronautical instruction to veterans and other civilians on an improvised airfield which was formerly used as one of the university's farms. The university had purchased 250 acres of land about a mile from the campus between Wilberforce and Xenia, Ohio for $31,500 with the intention of building an airport. The Ohio Aviation Board approved the project but Wilberforce University which was unable to fund the construction of an airport was seeking assistance from the Army Air Force through the allocation of an AFROTC detachment.[7]

CPT Howard L. Baugh assigned to Howard AFROTC felt compliance with the Gillem Board report required that African American squadrons on Air Force bases established for predominately white organizations should be commanded by African American officers to ensure some progress toward integration, and that selected officers and enlisted personnel assigned to three or four AFB on a trial basis be African Americans in order to further the process of integration. He recommended that new African American ROTC detachments be limited to colleges willing to accept well-screened white ROTC instructors since he alleged the quantity of qualified African American ROTC Ground and Air instructors was limited.[8] However, Air

Force Deputy Chief of Staff for Personnel and Administration I. H. Edwards reported to Assistant Secretary of the Air Force that on November 1, 1947 there were 237 African American officers and 15,473 enlisted men assigned to major air commands in the Continental United States.[9]

Encouraged by the establishment of Army Air Force ROTC detachments at Howard and Tuskegee, Evans felt that priority should be given to West Virginia State and then Prairie View A and M because of the unlimited aspirations of the students, faculty and administration.[10] The headquarters of the Fifth Service Command in conjunction with the Army Air Force Training Liaison Office at Indianapolis, Indiana had conducted an ROTC survey in April 1946 which determined that West Virginia State was eligible for the establishment of an Army Air Force ROTC detachment. Eligibility was partially based on the military record of the college which included SATC during World War I, the activation of a Field Artillery ROTC detachment in 1942, participation in ASTP and ASTRP from July 20, 1943 to April 30, 1944, and the reactivation of ROTC in February 1946 with an advanced course. West Virginia had also formulated plans for the first African American CAA training course in 1939 which was transferred together with its personnel to Tuskegee. Prior to the transfer the college trained approximately 110 aviators who formed the nucleus of aviation training at Tuskegee Institute and the initial cadre of the 99th Pursuit Squadron. John W. Davis felt the college was capable of providing an excellent opportunity for training a detachment of 150 aviators. However, TAG held all ROTC applications in abeyance until the size and composition of the postwar military was established by congressional legislation.[11]

John W. Davis informed Secretary of War Robert P. Patterson on March 15, 1947 that surveys of the campus facilities had been conducted, and he submitted a list of more than 100 students who desired aviation training. Evans met with MAJ Thomas B. Nichols of Army Air Force operations on March 24, 1947 and was informed that an Air Force ROTC detachment was not feasible at West Virginia State because of budgetary limitations and other circumstances. MAJ Nichols revealed that Air Force ROTC did not have a specific authorization or budgetary allotment since it was appended to regular ROTC detachments which were already operational. On campuses where Air Force ROTC operated concurrently with ROTC organizations, AFROTC was the subordinate command. This procedure was necessary to establish detachments during the fiscal year but it was anticipated that authorization giving equal status to Air Force ROTC detachments would occur during the ensuing years. The allocation for African American participation in the program of 100 Army Air Force ROTC detachments was 1 percent. The allocation was changed with the inclusion of Howard among a total of seventy-eight detachments, and with the addition of Tuskegee the percentage of African American colleges improved to 2.5 percent but the enrollment percentage undoubtedly was lower. When proposals were submitted to bring the overall detachment total to 100 and higher it appeared that West Virginia State would become the third African American college with an Army Air Force ROTC since it was included on the list of fifty new detachments. When it became necessary to reduce the list of new detachments to twenty-five and eventually to twenty-three, West Virginia State was placed in the deferred category for later consideration. Evans was confident that the college would be in the second group of institutions granted an AFROTC detachment.[12]

Difficulties encountered in the establishment of ROTC programs were partially attributed to adjustments necessary to accommodate the characteristics of individual educational institutions. The Civilian Components Policy Board which convened in 1949 reviewed a Secretary of the Army recommendation requiring a Joint Army-Air Force-Navy Advisory Committee on ROTC Affairs. Each service had concurred with the establishment of the committee, and civilian educators recognized the necessity of an organization to deal with ROTC affairs. Since the Department of the Air Force had an Advisory Committee on ROTC Affairs and the Navy Department utilized an Association of Naval ROTC Colleges and Universities in a similar capacity, the Army concluded that a joint advisory committee would provide economy of personnel through the elimination of duplicated efforts by the services and by conformity to Department of Defense policies which required coordination and cooperation between the services. Approval of the Joint Army-Air Force-Navy Advisory Committee on ROTC Affairs extended membership to PNLGC but the Participation of the African American representative did not guarantee the extension of AFROTC to African American colleges and universities but at least their concerns were articulated at the policy level of the Components Policy Board. The advisory committee was under the Civilian Components Policy Board which was responsible to the chairman of the Executive for Reserve and ROTC Affairs.[13]

The Bureau of the Budget in the Executive Office of the President was concerned with the expenditure for ROTC which was estimated to increase from $50 million to $200 million in the future. The bureau also cited that draft ROTC legislation of 1949 appeared to permit the procurement of women officers. Since it was more efficient and economical to procure and train the limited number of required women officers by the services through existing procedures, it was determined that ROTC would be limited to male students. The Bureau of the Budget also suggested a single authorization for college training programs, a reduction in subsidized educational programs involving active duty from four to three years, the elimination of graduate and professional school training, and the extension of Army and Air Force authority comparable to Navy ROTC and Marine Corps platoon leadership training programs.[14]

The Department of the Air Force was delegated the responsibility of presenting to the Bureau of the Budget the views of the Department of Defense on the proposed revisions of ROTC legislation. Secretary of Defense James Forrestal also formed a committee to study all aspects of civilian component activities and appointed Gordon Gray as chairman of the commission. The Gray Committee recommended extensive revisions of ROTC programs especially those operated by the Army and Air Force and concluded that the single problem was the procurement of adequately trained-college reserve and regular officers. It was essential that reserve officers were available for duty in time of national emergency, to serve extended active duty for reasonable lengths of time to supplement military operations, and to serve as career officers in regular establishments. The committee urged that Title I of the proposed revision require advanced ROTC detachments be accredited by a recognized accrediting agency, that common instruction be provided for all ROTC students, that statutory cognizance of the Office of Professor of Air Science and Tactics be established for the senior Air Force officer on duty with an AFROTC detachment on the same basis as their counterparts in the Army and Navy, and that authority be provided for flight instruction to ROTC students by contract with civilian educational institutions or flying schools recognized by the Civil Aeronautics Administration with the possibility of expanding the program into summer training. The committee further urged that provision for Federal payment of hospitalization and burial expenses incurred while participating in military or naval training, be provided for ROTC students, and that students receive National Service Life Insurance in the amount of $10,000 while engaged in hazardous training and a $5,000 death gratuity in place of the insurance. Title II authorized a Reserve Officer Procurement Program similar to Army and Air Force ROTC programs and the contractual Navy ROTC program. Title III provided an Augmentation Officer Procurement Program which required extended active duty immediately after graduation, for three years after completing flying training, in the case of those who attained an aeronautical rating, or for two years for other graduates. Titles IV and V established a Career Officer Procurement Program that was comparable to the Navy Holloway Plan included in Public Law 729 during the 79th Congress.[15]

Implementation of the revised ROTC legislation influenced the Air Force to consider the necessary allocation of officers and enlisted personnel required to maintain all existing AFROTC detachments. With an identical allocation of 556 officers and enlisted men in 1950, an increase to 625 cadres respectively was needed during the next fiscal year to prevent the elimination of some of the less-essential detachments. The continuation of the 556 allocations in 1950 had already set back the program at least one year and prevented the establishment of four ROTC detachments and seventy-eight specialized courses at detachments solely because of the lack of personnel authorization. The production rate was also affected in the technical fields since detachments which were least-essential to the long range program were low producers and incapable of producing in the technical fields. The elimination of low nontechnical detachments would enable the transfer of their production quotas to larger universities already in the program. However, the technical-type detachments with low production rates created a problem because if eliminated their production quotas could not be absorbed by other institutions since it was extremely difficult to find new replacement institutions. There were 147 engineering schools but detachments were already established in ninety-five of them with sixteen institutions planning to obtain detachments. Of the remaining thirty-six, Army or Navy or both had detachments in twenty-eight institutions, leaving little potential for the formation of AFROTC detachments, especially since two of the remaining eight declined invitations to apply for an Air Force detachment. During the 1948 academic year, there were twenty-four detachments at nontechnical institutions below the critical enrollment level of 168 for first-year basic students, although ten of them appeared capable of increasing their enrollment above the critical level at the beginning of the next academic year. Tuskegee was included in the group below the critical level.[16]

The commanding general of ConAC was informed by the Air Force Assistant Vice Chief of Staff on March 17, 1950 that until the establishment of numerical procurement objectives for each AFROTC detachment and specialized options became nonpractical, the minimum production standards would apply. Effective during the 1950 academic year, the graduation of twenty-five commissioned officers was required annually at institutions where the only specialized options were Communications, Aircraft Maintenance Engineering, Air Installations, or Armament. Effective during the 1951 academic year, the minimum production standard of fifty was applied to all other AFROTC detachments except where two or more specialized options were established within an AFROTC detachment. Air Force detachments with the least officer production were given a year prior notification of the elimination of their AFROTC by the Secretary of the Air Force. The procedure allowed for the completion of training for second-year advanced students before the termination of the detachment at the conclusion of the fiscal year.[17]

An unexpected outbreak of hostilities in Korea in June 1950 negated the traditional practice of training personnel for deployment after mobilization. The absence of a trained reservoir of manpower since the termination of World War II in 1945 caused the immediate recall of veterans to reinforce the skeletonized organizations based in the Far East that were deployed in Korea. Because of the lack of full mobilization and because the most significant confrontations were conducted during the first year of combat, the Army and Air Force increased their officer production through ROTC programs rather than expand extensively or significantly their OCS, although short-term OCS systems were maintained to allow diversions of ROTC and AFROTC students and other personnel if battlefield conditions required more officers quicker than the normal four-year programs could provide. The ROTC production goal was increased slightly to more than 23,200 reserve officers and by the 1951 academic year the total of participating institutions had increased from 190 to 228 in order to meet the established goal. The AFROTC production was increased from 6,500 to 27,750 annually. The Army did not envision difficulty with expanding the ROTC program with approximately 250 applications on file, and the response to AFROTC expansion produced applications from 487 institutions of which 62 were selected to bring the total of AFROTC detachments to 187.[18]

Thirty minutes after Secretary of Defense Louis Johnson announced on July 7, 1950 a policy concerning drafting men into the armed services, John W. Davis, president of West Virginia State telephonically notified his office of the availability of men at his college. Although ready for immediate expansion of ROTC with scientific departments able to provide technical support for mobilization toward preserving the nation's democratic form of government, his request was referred to the secretaries of Army, Navy and Air Force. Secretary of Air Force Thomas K. Finletter was gratified to learn that facilities were available but stressed that during critical times, in which planning must consider every eventuality in accomplishing established missions, contingency plans would involve an evaluation of expanding AFROTC. Davis reiterated the excellent military contributions of the college during World War II but Air Force officials did not extend the AFROTC program to West Virginia State.[19]

On July 20, 1950, W. A. Dent of Dillard University in New Orleans offered its facilities for the preparation of personnel to serve during the emergency and to develop a reservoir of manpower through the formation of an AFROTC Detachment since it offered specialized training in chemistry, mathematics and physics. His request was similarly retained and filed for future consideration.[20]

Horace M. Bond, President of Lincoln in Pennsylvania, submitted a request on July 24, 1950 for the extension of military training to his campus. It was supported by Congressman Francis P. Bolton who stressed that the nonsegregated policies at the institution would enhance the development of an Air Force integration policy, and that the existence of an Institute of African Studies at Lincoln University, with the ability to procure students from several African countries, was desirable from his point of view. Congressmen Edward Martin and A. J. G. Priest offering additional support also emphasized the university's distinguished record of graduating a significant portion of African American lawyers, dentists and physicians.[21]

Mary McLeod Bethune, who had expressed her faithfulness to the Democratic party, submitted a request in 1951 for the establishment of an AFROTC detachment at Bethune-Cookman College and sought assistance from Anna M. Rosenberg, the first Assistant Secretary of Defense for Manpower and Personnel. Rosenberg referred the issue to BG R. L. Copsey, the Deputy Special Assistant for Reserve Forces, who stated that only sixty-two of more than 450 applications from colleges and universities would be selected for approval, and Bethune-Cookman was disqualified since its male full-time enrollment did not meet the minimum requirement of 400 students.[22]

In anticipation of providing military training, Kentucky State organized a Reserve Detachment that enrolled staff, students, and community citizens and veterans. On January 8, 1951, a request from Rufus B. Atwood of Kentucky State which gained support from Senator Earle C. Clements was referred by Anna M. Rosenberg to the commandant of the Air Force Institute of Technology at Wright-Patterson AFB in Dayton, Ohio since his command monitored collegiate training in professional, scientific and technical matters, and to the commanding general of Air Training at Scott AFB in Illinois who monitored training commonly given in trade and vocational schools.[23]

Earl S. Hoag, Special Assistant to the Chief of Staff for Reserve Forces, convened a meeting on September 14, 1950 to determine whether the Air Force should take advantage of technically qualified college students by increasing its AFROTC program during the 1951 fiscal year. Advised that the potential of college students in engineering and related fields was not exploited by the AFROTC program, R. M. Thurston, an assistant to the AFROTC Division of the Office of the Special Assistant for Reserve, assisted in the formulation of revisions which were disseminated to the major subordinate commands by senior staff representatives who attended the meeting. The major changes involved the enrollment of an additional 1800 seniors who were qualified to pursue an abbreviated one-year advanced course with four technical options pertaining to aircraft maintenance engineering, communications, armament, or air installation. Completion of the programs and Air Force summer camp qualified graduates for appointment into the Air Force Reserves. These options were also extended to an additional 3,000 first-year advanced course students while an additional 2,000 students who qualified for training in administrative options such as administration-logistics or comptroller duties received reserve commissions after completing their program and summer camp. Cadres required to provide the additional training were authorized through an augmentation of personnel spaces allocated to AFROTC. Although the total was later modified, colleges and universities were notified of the AFROTC revisions and were encouraged to enroll qualified applicants.[24]

The secretary of the Air Force approved a major increase in AFROTC on January 19, 1951 which enabled the commissioning of approximately 22,500 during the summer of 1953 and 27,750 the following summer which became the projected annual production based on mobilization requirements. During hearings on universal military service and training, Carl Vinson expected all students commissioned to serve their obligations to the government and he believed a revision including mandatory enrollment in the AFROTC program objectives was necessary. Personnel end strength requirements of the ninety-five Wing Program on June 30, 1952 called for 51,102 officers in the lieutenant grades and the necessity to absorb 27,750 officers for a mandatory period of two years required 55,550 spaces for junior officers. Achieving this requirement under the allocated force structure was impossible because spaces were reserved for personnel completing pilot schools. Although some ROTC graduates would complete flying training and the number in this group would not materially improve the situation, BG Edmund C. Lynch, director of Manpower and Organization, recommended an immediate reevaluation of the AFROTC program. The amended Universal Military Training and Service Act of 1951 implemented the requirement that reserve officers serve two years of their five-year Reserve commitment on active duty. However, Air Force commanders in Korea wanted more pilots and navigators for combat duty instead of non-rated specialists.[25]

MG Hoag considered that the expansion and reorganization of AFROTC with the establishment of flight operations, general technical, and other necessary career training options in the program would influence a considerable number of liberal arts colleges and engineering institutions to apply for detachments. He also expected the national emergency would influence the majority of educational institutions to adopt year-round accelerated academic programs which would become operational by July 1, 1951. This would enable AFROTC students to complete their degree requirements and accept their commissions in approximately thirty months, making the AFROTC program more flexible and adaptable to changing requirements. MG Hoag expected the establishment of 62 additional detachments by July 1, 1951, with ten of them exclusively located at engineering colleges, at least twenty at liberal arts colleges, and the remainder at either liberal arts colleges or universities offering liberal arts as well as other engineering and technical programs.[26]

There were 125 AFROTC detachments assigned to colleges and universities by March 31, 1951 with 469 others seeking to establish detachments. An Air Force Board composed of BG R. L. Copsey, Deputy Special Assistant for Reserve Forces; BG G. P. Disosway, Director of Training, Deputy Chief of Staff of Personnel; BG A. L. Moore, Deputy Director of Manpower and Organization, Deputy Chief of Staff for Operations; and Edmund P. Learned, professor at the Graduate School of Business Administration at Harvard University, who served as a Special Consultant to the AF Chief of Staff, was assisted by educators selected from a panel nominated by the American Council of Education. The board announced on April 20, 1951 the selection of sixty-two new AFROTC sites which included North Carolina A and T and Tennessee A and I.[27]

W. S. Davis, president of Tennessee State A and I, which did not become a land grant institution until August 8, 1958, with the support of J. A. Barksdale, Tennessee Commissioner of Education and Chairman of the State Board of Education, similarly requested assistance from Representative J. Percy Priest concerning an application submitted to MG Hoag. Congressman Priest urged favorable consideration of the application from Secretary of the Air Force Thomas K. Finletter and when Jack O. Crawford in the Material and Operations Branch of the Congressional Division responded to his office on April 20, 1951, Gladys Clark informed Crawford of a recent notification to Congressman Priest confirming Tennessee A and I inclusion of the list of institutions scheduled to receive AFROTC Detachments.[28]

Davis recognized the responsibility attached to obtaining an AFROTC detachment and informed Secretary of Defense Finletter and COL Cortland S. Johnson at Robins AFB in Georgia of an accelerated program that would be commenced the next academic year at Tennessee A and I State College on June 4, 1951 instead of September. F. D. Bluford similarly expressed confidence in the accelerated freshmen academic curriculum which would influence student participation in AFROTC that began on September 1,

Tennessee State University Air Force ROTC Flight Exercise. (Courtesy of the Tennessee State University Air Force ROTC Detachment, Nashville, TN, 37209)

1951. The successful organization of these detachments increased African American detachments by 100 percent but the Air Force Board disappointed African American college and university officials who contemplated the expansion of an aeroscience program in their institutions. In addition to Bethune-Cookman College, other institutions denied AFROTC included Dillard University, Hampton, Kentucky State, Lincoln, South Carolina State A and M and West Virginia State.[29] Lawrence A. Davis, President of Arkansas AM and N, considered it unfortunate that circumstances were such that African American colleges and universities had slight chances of ever being considered for ROTC detachments. This meant inevitably that African American students in segregated institutions were seldom given the opportunity to enroll in military science courses within their institutions.[30]

John T. Williams in 1947 became the first president of Maryland State College, formerly known as Princess Anne State College, and announced the major objectives of his administration were the development of a successful agricultural program, the formation of ROTC and the implementation of a successful athletic program. An AFROTC detachment was allocated in February 1951 and became operational on September 10, 1951 as the smallest detachment in the AFROTC program.[31] Therefore, the postwar AFROTC detachments located at Howard, North Carolina A and T, Tennessee A and I, Tuskegee, Tennessee State and Maryland State composed the Civilian Pilot Training Program that was operated in eight African

American institutions prior to the wartime Tuskegee Army Air Force Training Center. The presence of African American cadets in others institutions where enrollment was permitted was not discernible and usually the quantity was not pronounced until upperclassmen reported for summer camp. Although cadets were dispersed throughout the camps, it can only be asserted that African American cadets were integrated into other programs and were no longer excluded on the basis of military policies. Equally significant was the assignment of some African American officers to other colleges but their quantity and proportion was less than white officers assigned to African American colleges and university campuses.[32]

Naval ROTC was established in 1926 with detachments initially organized at the University of California, Northwestern University, University of Washington, Harvard, Yale, and Georgia Institute of Technology. After an extensive review by distinguished naval officers, civilian educators, and congressmen, the mission of Naval ROTC was greatly increased after the passage of Public Law 729 on August 13, 1946 and the implementation of a peacetime training plan formulated by Rear Admiral James A. Holloway, Superintendent of the United States Naval Academy. The plan provided for a scholarship program to influence the commissioning of well-trained and educated junior officers to supplement the academic program at the Naval Academy. The original Naval ROTC concept of 1926 continued as a Reserve Officer Procurement Program and was referred to as the Navy-Marine College Program, known as the Contract Program, and was eventually expanded several years later to include fifty-two detachments.[33]

Edward S. Hope in the Department of Engineering and Architecture at Howard University and a reserve naval officer was authorized by the Navy to assist and influence the procurement of personnel for the Navy. With the specific mission of publicizing the Navy and Marine Corps College Training Programs, and giving assurances of equal opportunity and fair treatment to all applicants, Hope visited several colleges and high schools during December 1946. Initially attending the Annual Convention of the Association of Colleges and Secondary Schools which met in Tuskegee and represented fifty colleges and 125 high schools, he publicized NROTC in the *Manuscript*, a newsletter read by many prominent African Americans, which was the first and only notice of the program received by many school officials in southern states. After the completion of his itinerary which involved traveling west to Prairie View A and M, he submitted several recommendations to the Chief of the Bureau of Personnel. He specifically recommended the elimination of racial designations and considerations from all Naval correspondence, forms, assignments and other literature, the reinforcement of new policy directives pertaining to eliminating segregation and discrimination regarding race, creed and national origin, and that commanding officers report all violations of Naval policy and directives, and formulate a plan to secure an immediate African American ratio for officer training schools. Hope further advocated the transfer of African Americans and Filipinos from the steward branch and their advancement in other branches of the Navy, and said that rated stewards should have the same rights, privileges and responsibilities as petty officers. He emphasized the implementation of special measures to secure and retain African American officers, including the promotion and retention of LT Dennis Nelson who was the only African American officer remaining on active duty.

LCDR Hope understood African American disillusion and disgust with discriminatory governmental policies concerning racial minorities. Veterans in particular were resentful of their treatment in the armed forces and found difficulty in accepting announced plans or policies and expected to find a *joker* regarding their future service. They did not expect the implementation of polices without discrimination since racism was so widespread and pervasive and racial conditions had negated opportunities to attract African Americans. Unless announcements specifically were labeled for their attention and since they were often deprived of due consideration, they felt responding to naval and marine programs was a waste of their time. A more critical concern was the possibility of humiliation while applying for certain *rights or benefits* which were arbitrarily denied. LCDR Hope concluded African Americans were not informed of opportunities and progressive Naval measures designed to create a new Naval policy of nondiscrimination. He attributed their adverse responses partially to personnel who deliberately or accidentally withheld information, the lack of interest by African Americans who had become frustrated by past experiences, and the lower educational level of some African Americans who were generally at a disadvantage because they were denied the privileges and benefits of education in southern areas.[34]

The Southern Field Division of the National Urban League was actively involved in an effort to support naval visitations to sixteen cities with more than 8,525 African American youth. LT Dennis Nelson in response to naval orders issued on October 22, 1948 conferred with National Urban League officials and together with LT Samuel Gravely and John W. Reagan planned itineraries to acquaint African Americans with the naval integration policy and to encourage southern communities to administer the naval qualifying examination to African American students. Convinced public relations would achieve their first goal, the National Urban League emphasized conferences with directors of Navy procurement offices in Atlanta and New Orleans and the enforcement of a naval statement issued through Princeton University which stressed that no civilian contracts for NROTC examination centers would be let where examinations were administered on a segregated basis. The naval officers presented information to a combined audience of approximately 2500 African Americans but only 213 participated in the competitive examination process. The National Urban League was displeased with the few candidates who successfully completed the examinations but emphasized that the passing percentage was not necessarily important but the significant issue was the failure rate of the applicants. A conclusion was that the substandard segregated institutions were not equipped with the necessary human and physical resources and lacked course offerings in the fundamentals of basic and physical science to enable students to compete on a competitive basis. Attributing the failures to inferior academic preparation and programs, inadequate educational and vocational guidance and counseling, the National Urban League stressed the integration of examination centers. In New Orleans there were no African American applicants in 1948 but there were more than 100 in 1949 while in Atlanta participation increased from forty-three in 1948 to sixty-five in 1949.[35]

Naval officials considered the NROTC program was superior to ROTC since the government paid the cost of student tuition, fees and textbooks and gave students a retainer fee of $600 for additional college expenses. The Holloway Plan required completing academic curricula leading toward a bachelor's degree or higher and twenty-four semester hours, or the equivalent hours, in Naval science plus requirements in mathematics, physics and English. The Navy also operated a Naval Aviation College Program as a supplement system which provided qualified aviators to the Navy and Marine Corps. With only thirteen detachments in southern states, African Americans complained that excellent opportunities were not available to them since all of the institutions where the programs were operational did not admit African American students and a survey of thirty-eight of the fifty-two colleges revealed that only twelve African Americans were enrolled in NROTC detachments under the Holloway Plan that required annual training for 14,000 midshipmen. All Naval candidates were required to meet standards similar to those established by the Naval Academy. Candidates were compelled to pass an aptitude test administered nationwide, pass a rigid physical examination, be selected by their State or Territorial Selection Committee, and then be assigned to a college of their choice if possible. However, only the best qualified candidates were selected by the committees to fill quotas allocated to states and territories. Assignments were governed by a candidate's rating by his committee, the candidate's choice of colleges, the admission requirements of by the selected colleges, and the number of applicants for each college. Successful applicants signed contracts with the Secretary of the Navy and agreed to accept a commission in the Navy or Marine Corps, if offered, or a commission in the Organized Naval or Marine Corps Reserves. Midshipmen were not permitted to marry until after their commissioning and they were not eligible for resignation until six years after their commissioning.[36]

Twelve African American midshipmen had enrolled under the Holloway plan by 1948 and were attending institutions in northern states.[37] Two midshipmen had served in the armed forces during the previous world war. John E. Rudder of Paducah, Kentucky had enlisted June 1943 and was selected for educational training under the Navy's V-12 Program. Completing training at Montford Point, the African American training site of Parris Island, South Carolina, and serving with the Marine Corps 51st Defense Battalion before his discharge in 1946, Rudder accepted admission to Purdue University and was awarded a regular NROTC midshipmen contract. Commissioned in 1948 and assigned to the Marine Corps Basic School, LT Rudder resigned his commission for religious reasons and on April 1, 1949 he was honorably discharged. William K. Jenkins of Elizabeth City, New Jersey, had served in the Navy prior to his admission to Illinois Polytechnic Institute. Commissioned in 1948 and assigned to the inactive reserve, LT Jenkins later served in the Korean War as a weapons and a rifle platoon leader with Company B, 1st Battalion, 7th Marines and thereby became the first African American Marine officer to lead marines in combat. In 1973, he had attained the rank of LTC in the Marine Corps Reserves. Other African American Marines on inactive duty included LT Frederick C. Branch who was not an NROTC graduate but was accepted into the V- 12 program at Temple University. Graduating in a class of 250 officer candidates on November 10, 1945, he became the first African American commissioned officer in the Marine Corps. In 1946, three others previously in the V-12 program were commissioned and serving on inactive duty. They were LT Charles C. Johnson of Washington, DC who resigned in November 1947 to accept a commission in the U.S. Public Health Service, LT Judd B. Davis of Fuquay Springs, North Carolina who was honorably discharged in 1952, and LT Herbert L. Brewer who later served in the Korean War and when promoted to the rank of COL in 1973 became the highest ranking African American in the Marine Corps Reserve.[38]

The strength of African Americans in NROTC was negligible and African American enrollment at the Naval Academy was not impressive. The Navy had not seriously considered commissioning African Americans and had admitted only three to the Naval Academy during the era of Reconstruction. Midshipmen from South Carolina, John Henry Conyers and

Alonzo C. McClennan were respectively admitted on September 21, 1872 and September 25, 1873 and resigned on March 16, 1874. Midshipman Henry Edwin Baker, Jr., from Mississippi, was appointed on September 24, 1874 and was dismissed on November 5, 1875. The next midshipman, James E. Johnson, from Illinois, who previously had attended the Case School of Applied Science, was enrolled on June 15, 1936 and academically dismissed on February 12, 1937. He returned to the Case School of Applied Science which became Case Western Reserve and completed the requirements for a degree in mechanical engineering before his commissioning in 1941 and service in the 99th Pursuit Squadron. George J. Trivers like Johnson was from Illinois and was appointed on June 16, 1937 and similarly was dismissed on July 7, 1937. The midshipmen admitted on June 30, 1948 were Reeves R. Taylor from Providence, Rhode Island, appointed by Senator Theodore F. Green, and Lawrence Chambers from Dunbar High School in DC who was appointed by Representative William Dawson. However, Wesley Anthony Brown from New York was appointed by Representative Adam C. Powell on June 30, 1945 and became the first African American commissioned by the Naval Academy on June 3, 1949.[39]

The establishment of an NROTC detachment at Hampton was the accepted understanding of African Americans since the Second World War, and they also expected an expansion of Naval ROTC to Southern University. James C. Evans on March 1, 1948 emphasized his major concerns to John W. Davis, the chairperson of PNLGC. He explained that there were Naval ROTC detachments established at inland institutions so that waterfront facilities were not essential considerations, but a competitive naval integration program could not guarantee that the Navy Department would allow the formation of African American ROTC detachments. Although Charles S. Johnson, president of Fisk, Ralph A. Bridgman, president of Hampton Institute, Horace M. Bond of Lincoln in Pennsylvania and Dwight O. W. Holmes of Morgan State had expressed interest in the formation of NROTC detachments, Navy officials stated that few colleges met the requirements of the NROTC program because most did not have facilities to accommodate heavy weapons or other equipment necessary to teach naval courses and few students were able to pass the aptitude test.[40]

Martin D. Jenkins of Morgan State and L. H. Foster of Virginia State did not favor a rigorous campaign to establish NROTC detachments. Cognizant that the Navy program was limited to fifty-two colleges by congressional legislation, Jenkins stressed the naval policy was based on nonsegregation, and HBUCs would extremely weaken their position by insisting on the establishment of a segregated NROTC detachment. He insisted that persuading students to take the examination and concentrating their campaign on assurance that men who passed the examination would be accepted by institutions having NROTC programs were the major objectives. Foster felt that they were fortunate that NROTC was not connected with legislation involving land grant colleges and that participants in NROTC selected on a national competitive basis were permitted to choose their institutions. This selection process enabled African Americans to matriculate at institutions other than those restricted to African American students. Jenkins and Foster supported the establishment of NROTC at Hampton where a large proportion of African Americans would seek admission with their efforts directed toward stimulating and encouraging male students to successfully pass the qualifying examinations for the NROTC program. The accomplishment of these objectives would not deter their efforts to have NROTC established at Hampton Institute and other qualified African American colleges and universities on a nonsegregated basis. Carl Murphy of the Baltimore *Afro-American* emphasized that of 80,030 candidates who had applied to take the competitive examination only thirty candidates were identified as non-white.[41]

President Truman appointed Charles Fahy who convened the President's Committee on Equality of Treatment and Opportunity in the Armed Services. On April 26, 1949, CPT John H. Schultz, Assist Chief of Naval Personnel for Reserve, CPT J. B. Rooney, Director of Training, Bureau of Naval Personnel, and CDR Luther C. Heinz, Head Officer of Candidate Training Section, Bureau of Naval Personnel, appeared before the committee to explain the Naval Reserve Program. CPT Schultz informed the committee that of 1,327 officers and 12,396 enlisted personnel in the Naval Reserve on active duty there was only one officer and 191 enlisted African American personnel. Fahy concluded the Navy's policy of exclusion or discrimination was a policy of absent exclusion which was not intended to procure African Americans for active duty. By affirmation CPT Shultz acknowledged that nothing special was implemented to recruit African Americans. LT Dennis Nelson who had been invited to participate in the hearings affirmed the process to procure African Americans for the Naval Academy in addition to the normal selection of officer personnel through NROTC. LT Nelson stated that NROTC had graduated three midshipmen who were respectively assigned the *USS Helena*, *USS St. Paul* and the Marine Corps in addition to others with inactive duty status. In comparison to Army ROTC graduates, there were thirty, which represented 23.6 percent of the regular Army officers.[42]

CPT Rooney stressed that NROTC contractual students recruited on campus by the Professor of Naval Science were different from those selected by the Navy and tested by the Princeton Educational Testing Service, evaluated by state boards, and interviewed and given physical examinations by the Office of Naval Officer Procurements. Fahy questioned whether the system of procuring African American officers was equitable since thirteen of the NROTC detachments were located at southern colleges where the possibility of recruiting African American cadets was negligible. Although LT Nelson had visited African American institutions in sixteen southern cities and explained the Naval program to approximately 8,500 students, CPT Rooney estimated that only 90 students applied to take the examination. James C. Evans contributed the low response to a statement in the application materials requiring students to indicate whether the applicant was African American was a factor which caused members of state boards and college officials to deny NROTC recommendations for minority students. He further stated that administering examinations at segregated locations affected the decisions of board officials who were familiar with the designation of African Americans schools. CDR Heinz alleged the reason that ETS included the question regarding race was to accommodate states where segregation was legal. The question was discontinued with the issuance of testing materials in December 1948.[43]

Joseph E. B. Evans stressed that 10 percent of the 15,400 allocation under PL 729 of the 79th Congress gave a 15.40 percent representation of African American Naval cadets and the seven which had been admitted to the program was only one-twentieth of 1 percent. He was alarmed that not a single NROTC detachment was organized in the seventeen states with African American land grant colleges. CPT Rooney was unable to ascertain if African American colleges were considered when the program was expanded in 1945 but alleged that other institutions with engineering instruction and required enrollment, facilities and personnel were needed. He also informed John H. Sengstacke, a member of the Fahy committee, that he was unaware of an earlier consideration of establishing NROTC at Hampton.[44]

Another program designed to supplement Naval officer procurement established by 1949 provided for the draft exempted students who qualified for commissions in the Organized Naval Reserve to qualify for reserve commissions. Training centers were established at the Naval Training Station in Newport, Rhode Island and the Naval Training Center at San Diego in California to accommodate a maximum of 2,500 collegiate students. The candidates were required to complete two six-week training courses and graduate from their respective colleges prior to receiving commissions in the Line, Supply or Civil Engineer Corps of the Naval Reserves. Theodore M. Daily and William H. Scott, Jr. who enrolled in the School of Engineering and Architecture at Howard were among the midshipmen commissioned respectively in the Civil Engineer Corps of the Naval Air Reserve and

Line Officer Service. When the program was extended to women, two former students of Howard, Charlotte S. Hutchinson with a degree in sociology and Ida I. Stephens, a Law School graduate, completed the naval requirements and were assigned as Ensigns in the WAVE Naval Reserve.[45]

# 5

# *Aeroscience and Military Science Policies*

The Universal Military Training and Service Act in June 1951 extended provisions of selective service for an additional four years and confirmed acceptance, for the first time in American history, of the principle of peacetime conscription and the establishment of a National Security Training Commission to recommend a plan for implementing universal military training. The legislation provided a special deferment for ROTC cadets who signed contracts during their sophomore year to serve on extended active duty for two years after their commission into the Reserve Corps. Students who refused to sign an agreement were dropped from the program and became eligible for the draft as enlisted men. The Universal Military Training and Service Act also confirmed the principle of compulsory training in peacetime and made eligible men liable for service of two years of active duty and six years of reserve duty.[1]

The Korean War influenced congressional legislation but the Department of the Air Force Director of Legislation and Liaison, BG Robert E. L. Eaton, complained about the lack of interest pertaining to information on recent air battles in Korea that was expressed by Representative Carl Vinson, chairman of the House Armed Services Committee. However, Vinson was more interested in the fear of flying by some airmen, the rationale of incentive pay, the proportion of reserve officers to regular officers in combat crews in Korea, and whether all of the sit-down strikers in the Air Force were part of Strategic Air Command. He considered sixty-five year old general officers and sixty year old LTCs on flying status to be indefensible. Vinson apparently concluded that flying had to be voluntary but emphasized that there was no chance of congressional action on an Air Academy or ROTC. Vinson agreed with Carl Brooks that it was an inopportune time to thoroughly evaluate matters involving ROTC during that session but agreed that the Air Force and the Army should have the benefits of the Holloway provisions contained in the ROTC legislation. He was confident in his ability to obtain favorable congressional action on the issue of ROTC and the Air Academy during the next session.[2]

The Air Force advised collegiate presidents of the necessity to eliminate summer camps for 1951 and the following year since higher priority training requirements for the active Air Force establishment during the emergency augmentation program utilized the entire training structure of the Air Force. Graduates were permitted to enter the Air Force as scheduled and pursue technical or other special training programs because of the cancellation of the summer camp requirement. However, each commissioned officer was given an indoctrination course at the beginning of his active duty period to compensate for the lack of camp training. The waiver was extended to all students graduating between July 1, 1952 and April 30, 1953. The projected cost of training approximately 20,000 students represented a substantial saving for the Department of the Air Force.[3]

An incident affecting the relationship between Army ROTC and Air Force officials occurred on June 3, 1953 at Central State University. Without the permission of the dean of administration, two AF officers representing the Air Force Aviation Cadet Procurement Program visited Central State College and met with approximately 50 students to encourage their enlistment into the Aviation Cadet Training program. Among the students were 14 ROTC students who were allegedly advised to refuse their Army Reserve commissions upon graduation and accept direct commissions in the Air Force. The Central State PMST with assurance from officials at the Ohio Military District located at Fort Hayes met with the students and explained the possible consequences of refusing to accept their commissions. His advice was apparently effective since all of the graduating seniors were commissioned.[4]

African American colleges were concerned that the transition to separate Army and Air Force programs would affect their internal operations. On May 8, 1950, an inspector from the Ninth Air Force Headquarters reported that the Howard AFROTC detachment was still operating under the supervision of the PMST, and the autonomy of the program was only in theory. Every phase of the AFROTC operation was integrated with the Army program, and it was extremely difficult to evaluate the Air Force program. The university had not implemented the commutation system for uniforms upon the advice of the PMST, and Air Force cadets were training with infantry rifles. A separate area was not allocated to AFROTC and both programs jointly utilized the same assigned area. The inspector further stated that the PAST was not considered as a member of the faculty and functioned under the PMST. He recommended an equal division of space, the issuance of blue uniforms to Air Force cadets and a revision of instruction which emphasized the Air Force program in its entirety beginning with the first year of the basic course taught by Air Force personnel. The inspector considered the AFROTC organization to be completely unsatisfactory and believed a revision would ensure the capability of the detachment to meet Air Force standards. Mordecai W. Johnson refuted the conclusion of the inspector and informed the headquarters of the Ninth Air Force regarding its directive issued on February 28, 1949 that the senior ROTC officer may be appointed to coordinate university affairs concerning AFROTC and ROTC detachments. Johnson further emphasized the Statement of Joint ROTC Policies issued by the respective commanding generals of headquarters Second Army and headquarters Ninth Air Force on July 25, 1949 which authorized common use of property in connection with institutional ROTC programs, common utilization of administrative operations to the extent compatible with economy, efficiency, and the requirements peculiar to each department. The policies also permitted collaboration among ROTC officers, the use of instructors for cross-service instruction, common training of cadets in their respective ROTC programs when such action promoted economy and efficiency, and the appointment of a line officer to represent the services and coordinate local ROTC matters of mutual interest. Johnson was confident in the leadership of the PMST and felt that the university was in compliance with the collocation of the detachments because of the lack of space.[5]

Assistant Secretary of the Air Force Harold C. Stuart emphasized the intent of the policies was to promote a spirit and practice of unification and reduce to a minimum the burden for facilities and services universities furnished to detachments while ensuring equal status and importance to each program at every institution where two or more detachments were established. After a special inquiry was conducted and confidence was expressed in the competence and good faith of the inspecting officer, the assistant secretary of the Air Force stated the report as a whole reflected credit upon Howard and the AFROTC detachment. He acknowledged that close integration resulted from the desire of the PMST in his capacity of Coordinator of ROTC Affairs to ensure the operating efficiency of both detachments in an economical manner. However, it was not the intent of the policies to carry integration to the point where an evaluation of any service program became difficult. He also recognized aspects of the policies implemented by the inspecting officer were contrary to the spirit and letter of the Statement of Joint ROTC Policies and he was cognizant of changes within the programs. He regretted the adverse effects of the inspection but hoped that the excellent relations between the detachments were not adversely affected.[6]

It was imperative and in the best interest of national security that the requirements of the Departments of Army and Air Force be fulfilled. MG N. B. Harold, Air Force Director of Personnel Procurement and Training, urged the PMST and the PAST to avoid destructive and unnecessary competition and employ every legitimate means of persuading non-cadets to enroll in the department which had not met its enrollment requirement and to seek assistance from their institutional authorities in this effort. He was cognizant that institutions with specialized ROTC detachments and a comparable AFROTC detachment with a specialized option drew primarily from the same academic field, and an acceptable ratio of recruitment was required. Authority was granted to enable interdepartmental transfers of ROTC students with the approval of the PMST and the PAST. Howard formulated a memorandum of agreement on July 10, 1952 which provided a ratio of 40 percent for ROTC and 60 percent for AFROTC. Assistant Secretary of the Army Fred North and the Assistant Secretary of the Air force for Management approved the reallocation on August 28, 1952 and TAG, MG William E. Bergin on June 2, 1952 advised Howard of the necessity to maintain the minimum freshmen requirement of 100 to ensure the annual graduation requirement. Cognizant that it was unable to maintain the freshmen standard for the Army, Howard requested to maintain ratios with the flexibility to assign maximum enrollment into ROTC or AFROTC. This would allow the university to satisfy the 100 student requirement and permit maximum student choice within the same ratio. MG F. W. Farrell did not support the revision, and based on the previous enrollment of freshmen at Howard he recommended a revised apportionment ratio of 50 percent for each detachment. He further alleged that the lack of interest prevailing at the university concerning the enhancement of ROTC necessitated the new ratio to encourage active support from some of the university officials. Mordecai W. Johnson was notified of the revision by Assistant Secretary of the Army James P. Mitchell on August 12, 1954.[7]

A satisfactory inspection of Tuskegee Institute in 1952 revealed a requirement to establish a more realistic quota between the AFROTC and ROTC detachments. Frederick D. Patterson met with the PMST and the PAST and reapportioned the student ratio to 55 percent AFROTC and 45 percent ROTC from the 67-33 percent ratio of the previous year. This readjustment was accepted by MG William E. Bergin who appreciated the interest of Patterson in the success of the Army ROTC program.[8] The competition between ROTC and AFROTC was particularly influenced by the increased officer production during the Korean War and the commitments to cadets scheduled for commission between 1954 and 1956, with approximately 15,000 cadets scheduled for commission in 1954. The Republican administration had initiated a national expenditure reduction program which required greater reliance on nuclear weapons and Air Force delivery capability and a reduction of active duty forces.[9]

MG Harold concluded that wide fluctuations in procurement objectives and polices caused confusion and lack of public confidence in the AFROTC program. He urged that the Department of the Air Force honor all contracts of students enrolled in advanced courses prior to the announcement of program changes during the summer of 1953. He further advised the introduction of a competitive-quality principle which permitted advanced course enrollment in excess of annual active duty requirements. After students completed the program, the final selection for commissioning was based on a best-qualified basis to fill available active duty spaces. Active duty tours for commissioned graduates were set at three years which included time spent in flying training school, and two years for non-rated commissioned graduates. The annual input of advanced courses was already stabilized at approximately 15,000 to ensure 11,000 commissioned graduates annually for active duty and reserve requirements. MG Harold stressed that economy and efficiency dictated a reduction of the AFROTC program by disestablishing detachments with low production and effectiveness. He proposed the disestablishment of twenty-eight detachments and five subdetachments which were commonly referred to as the Ohio Complex. After the adjustments were accomplished, MG Harold did not envision the establishment of additional detachments. Tuskegee and Howard were included on the list for disestablishment. Staff evaluators alleged that Tuskegee had extremely low production potential and its students were not interested in flight training. The attitude of officials and faculty at Tuskegee was judged to be below standard in regards to AFROTC and the available facilities were substandard. Evaluators also alleged that an extremely low production capability of Howard would produce only eleven, twenty-six, and seventeen flight qualified graduates respectively for the academic years of 1955 through 1957. Support from university officials, faculty and students was below average and the facilities were less than below average when compared to other AFROTC detachments in the same liaison area.[10]

Assistant Chief of Staff for Reserve Forces, MG William E. Hall, concurred with the disestablishment of twenty-eight AFROTC detachments and emphasized that the President direct the formation of a general and flag officer services board to jointly study the Reserve Components of the Armed Forces. Although not opposed to the elimination of detachments which failed to meet established criteria, he considered it more prudent to postpone any action pertaining to disestablishment of AFROTC detachments until the submission of the board's report and the approval of the President since the Air Force may have required a substantial portion of the officer production potential from the ROTC program to meet the officer requirements of the Reserve Forces, instead of meeting solely the requirements of the Active Force Structure.[11]

MG E. S. Wetzel determined the proposed disestablishment represented approximately 6.54 percent of the total enrollment of 188 organized detachments and their elimination was an impressive monetary reduction. The remaining detachments were capable of producing adequate flying applicants needed to maintain the required balance between flying and non-flying officers and fulfilled the needs of the Active and Reserve establishment. He maintained the Air Force would commit a grave error by reverting to a program that permitted AFROTC to produce large quantities of non-flying officers and few flying applicants. The senior class for 1954 had more than 8,800 commissioned officers willing to take flying training while the junior class was expected to produce 8,050 from 11,000 students. BG William S. Stone, Air Force Deputy Director of Personnel Planning, was concerned that the budget for fiscal year 1955 provided for 7,750 commissioned officers with 6,750 entering flying training but only 7,000 seniors were projected for pilot or observer training and some congressmen were interested in ascertaining how the additional officers would be absorbed into the flying program. General Thomas D. White approved the disestablishment proposed but indicated to Assistant Secretary of the Air Force H. Lee White that the timing of the AFROTC closures would probably have an adverse affect on the Air Force Academy bill. General White acknowledged the detrimental effect of immediately approving the elimination of ROTC detachments and retaining the correspondence until the President endorsed the Air Academy bill on April 1, 1954. He recommended the distribution of official notification at the earliest practical date to provide the maximum adjustment period for each institution.[12]

Prospective limitations on Air Force personnel caused Assistant Vice Chief of Staff, MG William F. McKee, to conclude it was essential to exercise greater economy in the utilization of personnel in the AFROTC program. A study of the production of commissioned graduates revealed several programs were below the minimum production standard. The Air Force determined that in order to adequately maintain established AFROTC programs it was necessary to enroll freshmen classes of 250, sophomore classes of 195, junior classes of sixty-five and senior classes of fifty to attain the annual goal of fifty commissioned officers while the Army only required respective enrollments of 146, sixty, fifty and thirty-five in 1950. MG McKee announced minimum production standards, effective during the 1950-1951 academic year, required twenty-five commissioned officers with specialized options in Communications or Armament. All other AFROTC detachments retained their production requirements.[13]

LTC George S. Roberts was informed by the commanding general of the 14th Air Force to withhold diplomas of graduating students pending their successful completion of summer camp. This was an unusual measure that had never been implemented since the formation of the AFROTC Detachment. Tuskegee required all senior cadets to complete summer training following the fourth year of enrollment, and records revealed that no student had defaulted in regards to such training. LTC Roberts and I. A. Derbigny, Vice President of Tuskegee determined the withholding of diplomas would affect morale and the performance of cadets during summer camp. Anticipating actions by the Air Force, efforts were made to identify graduating seniors and establish a procedure to notify Frederick D. Patterson of the results of summer training. LTC Roberts was confident of attaining the minimum since 60 seniors were enrolled on September 26, 1950 and 54 juniors under contract.[14]

The Air Force was attempting to provide allocations for the anticipated increase of AFROTC graduates while eliminating an aging senior core through forced retirement. However, the exodus of younger officers who left the Air Force after the completion of their military obligations was a cause of increased concern. An initiative was begun to streamline ROTC enrollment to a lean core of highly motivated cadets. In 1957 a drastic step toward limiting the quantity of students in nonflying categories was initiated by requiring commissioned cadets in pilot and navigator categories to agree to serve on active duty for five years, therefore, transforming commissioned service for many students into a commitment to join AFROTC for a subsequent career in the Air Force. The Air Force recognized the acceptance by more institutions than were required for the program with many cadets in non-rated categories who had no desire to enter flight training, but the five-year obligation served as a method of eliminating uneconomical AFROTC programs. The Air Force further expected flight instruction would eliminate and attract students to flying careers by detecting in the early stages of AFROTC those who would fail pilot training and it was the best incentive and test for good flight officers.[15]

Army and Air Force policies provided for commissioned service by females, and some students at African American institutions were influenced to join the armed forces. Mordecai Johnson at Howard was informed by the Military District of Washington that women college graduates, regardless of their disciplines, were eligible for military training at FT Lee, Virginia and successful candidates would receive commissions. In 1950 Salome Butler was commissioned through this program and was assigned as an administrative officer in the Adjutant General's Section of 5th Army Headquarters at Camp Custer in Michigan. Vivien Davis was similarly commissioned and was temporarily retained at the Women's Army Corps School as an instructor. Collegiate officials were also cognizant of pending legislation in the U.S. House Armed Services Committee which, if implemented, would provide for the extension of ROTC to women.[16] Charlotte S. Hutchinson in August 1952 was one of 240 candidates selected for a similar Navy Reserve program conducted at the Naval Station in Newport, Rhode Island. Commissioned an ensign in the WAVES, formerly known as Women Accepted for Volunteer Emergency Service, Hutchinson was assigned to the Naval Supply School at Bayonne, New Jersey. Ida I. Stephens completed the naval program in December 1952.[17]

Female graduates who enrolled in Air Force officer programs included Sandra Williams Ortega who graduated from Morgan State in 1957 and became the only African American in her flight of twenty-one. Commissioned on July 4, 1958 and completing the officer basic course, LT Ortega was not invited to the course commissioning party, which was held in a private home in Houston, because allegedly the neighbors would not understand her participation in the affair.[18] Marcelite J. Harris graduated from Spelman College in Atlanta, Georgia in 1964 and in September 1965 entered the Air Force Officer Training School at Lackland AFB. She became the first

Commission Awards Ceremony, Women's Army Corps, for LT Salome Butler and Vivien Davis, at Howard University, May 26, 1950. (Courtesy of the Moorland-Spingarn Research Center, Howard University Archives)

female Air Force African American BG with her promotion on September 8, 1990.[19] Women were obviously interested in more than serving as ROTC queens and at some colleges which included Tennessee State a women's drill team was organized in September 1953 and at South Carolina State a female rifle team was organized in 1954.[20]

The insufficient procurement of officers by AFROTC influenced the Air force to consider the desirability and practicality of expanding the program as a source of procuring women officers and the Air Force urged the Army to join the effort. Army officials expressed several reservations concerning revising ROTC to accommodate the procurement of female officers. The Army alleged the tendency among some institutions to reduce academic credit granted for ROTC toward a bachelor degree, especially in engineering, would be construed by some educational institutions as additional justification for withdrawing all academic credit for ROTC. Since military science emphasized command and leadership training which was perceived as a man's field, the inclusion of women would reduce the attractiveness of ROTC to male students. Assuming that either of the possibilities was proved factual, officials envisioned a reduced production of male commissioned officers at a time when shortages existed within the Reserve Corps. A high attrition factor during the first year of the advanced course would result from any form of WAC ROTC and financially the training would not be cost effective. The Army Chief of Legislation Liaison, BG C. J. Hauck, Jr., did not interpose an objection to Air Force legislation that authorized female enrollment in AFROTC but stressed the Army preferred to procure officers for the Women's Army Corps from colleges through the direct appointment of qualified applicants. Qualified candidates were offered reserve commissions without any prior commitments or additional expense as required by ROTC and by completing an extensive service school course at the WAC Training Center at Fort McClellan in Alabama where college graduates were adequately trained for active duty. LTG Walter L. Weible, Deputy Chief for Personnel stressed the WAC program, compensated by OCS, was sufficient and more economically met the requirements of the Army.[21] However, an Ad Hoc Committee appointed by the chairman of the Reserve Forces Policy Board in July 1955 had recommended the procurement of reserve officers from all sources and established 1960 as the goal for the attainment of reserve officer mobilization requirements. The board urged Department of Defense support of efforts to increase the career attractiveness of the armed services and support legislation providing preliminary flight training during the institutional phase of the AFROTC program, and that the Army and Navy consider the feasibility of providing preliminary flight training for ROTC and NROTC programs.[22]

The Air Force Director of Personnel, Procurement and Training, BG R. H. Carmichael, together with officers from the armed services appeared before the Senate Armed Services Committee on June 8, 1956 in support of congressional legislation designed to encourage flight training for cadets in ROTC programs. Emphasizing the evolution of technology which extended to the utilization of aircraft which was not envisioned under the National Defense Act of 1916, he stressed the expenses that would be incurred providing flight instruction by the legislation, but proclaimed airplanes had become a vital asset in modern warfare. Flight training for AFROTC cadets would achieve the objectives of attracting more qualified students for the advanced course, afford a more inexpensive opportunity for cadet pilot training after their commissioning, and motivate students to pursue careers in the Air Force. A survey of 8,000 cadets in the basic course revealed that only 31 percent who were physically qualified would not enroll in the advanced course without the inclusion of flight training in the curriculum. However, nearly 100 percent of the pilot-qualified cadets surveyed expressed an interest in flight training as an integral part of their collegiate program and approximately 90 percent were confident that their parents would favorably support the program. Screening devices which measured the aptitude and physical qualifications had to be combined with actual flying experience because only then would officials discover that some cadets lacked the most basic aptitudes, some would succumb to airsickness, a fear of flying or pressures from home, and some who originally were enthusiastic about the program would not enjoy flying. The light-plane training offered cadets a unique opportunity for self-selection and motivation but retention was the most urgent problem confronting the Air Force. The same considerations pertained to the Army with its smaller aviation requirement. Therefore, a proposal required the Army to establish educational programs in 40 institutions with an eventual annual production of 800 pilot applicants. The Navy was not initially included in the House of Representatives Bill 5738 but the service requested the inclusion of an amendment to provide permissive NROTC authority for the Navy. The armed services were authorized to provide contracts to institutions to give flight instruction up to thirty-five hours per cadet under the administration and supervision of the Civil Aeronautics Administration. The legislation was also amended to provide compensation for cadets fatally injured, and the House of Representative Bill 7089 proposed that the Servicemen's and Veteran's Survivor Benefits Act extend certain death benefits to ROTC cadets. The power granted was limited to a period of four years after August 1, 1956 and in 1960 Congress extended the time limitation to eight years after August 1, 1956.[23]

Tennessee State University Air Force ROTC Cadre, ca. 1960s. (Courtesy of the Tennessee State University Air Force ROTC Detachment, Nashville, TN, 37209)

Headquarters ConAC with the responsibility of training cadets as officers in the Reserve and Regular components of the Air Force instituted other changes designed to improve morale and the AFROTC program. Cadets were issued Air Force blue uniforms and cadets replaced their instructors by assuming command of the cadet corps, and after the establishment of the Arnold Air Society Honor Society in 1947 which recognized the achievements of outstanding cadets, detachments were encouraged to organized chapters. To improve the selection efficiency of cadets for the advanced program, Headquarters AFROTC began to administer a general aptitude examination, which was later referred to as the Air Force Officer Qualifying Test, to all sophomores. Another change designed to attract cadets to flight school was the implementation of introductory flights aboard C-45 aircraft for sophomores. This voluntary activity eventually became the AFROTC Flying Orientation Program but the shortage of C-45 aircraft and base closures during and after the Korean War made full participation for all detachments impractical. Attempting an expansion of flight opportunities, AFROTC officials proposed a Flight Instruction Program which gained congressional support and was approved by President Dwight D. Eisenhower on August 1, 1956 as Public Law 879. The legislation authorized the Air Force to establish contracts with local flying schools which provided thirty-six and one-half hours of flying instruction for senior cadets that included sixteen and one-half hours of solo flight. Completion of the program and passage of the Federal Aviation Administration examination qualified cadets for their private pilot's license.[24]

The expansion of ROTC during the Korean War produced serious difficulties in the production of officers although the branch material program was not determined by Army requirements but by college and university programs which were randomly established. There were relatively few combat arms detachments consisting of armor, artillery or infantry where the production was most needed. Military assignments under the branch immaterial programs were governed by service requirements and the individual aptitude of cadets. Changing to a general curriculum provided the Army an opportunity to appeal to cadets on a wider basis to meet manpower procurement requirements and to adjust the procurement system to changing officers' requirements while accomplishing the primary objective of training all ROTC cadets in the techniques of combat leadership. A revised ROTC curriculum was reviewed by a joint civilian and military committee that was convened by the Executive for Reserve and ROTC Affairs in 1952. The Army developed a General Military Science curriculum which resembled an infantry training camp course. Major components of the curriculum included a military history course that stressed the history of the Army, military leadership as inspirational, and detailed factual information. Freshmen were also taught individual weapons and marksmanship and sophomores received instruction involving crew-served weapons, and map and aerial photography reading. The first year advanced courses stressed leadership with emphasis on leadership principles, military teaching, and small unit tactics and communications. In the senior year a transition was made to introduce cadets to Army service with instruction in staff procedures and operations, personnel management, logistics, military administration and military justice. The General Military Science program was designed to eliminate a piecemeal and unrelated approach in the former branch curricula, and related this essential military training to considerations external to the armed forces through courses in American military history and the role of the United States in world affairs. Additional recommendations by the American Society for Engineering Education led to a reduction of credit allowed for ROTC toward the first degree in engineering, and although a report of the Humanistic-Social Research Project of the American Society for Engineering Education revealed several critical reservations concerning the substitution of courses in the social sciences for ROTC courses the Army also implemented the revisions. The revision the Army implemented were similar to AFROTC recommendations to have each participating institution establish an AFROTC advisory committee to consider the selection of civilian faculty to teach selected air science courses, to have civilian departments design courses in lieu of air science courses, and to substitute established courses which met the overall objectives of the Air Force curriculum.[25]

MG Bergin informed the major subordinate commanders that the experience of fifty-nine institutions which participated in the GMS Program the previous academic year influenced forty-eight others to inaugurate similar programs in the Fall of 1954. The efficiency of the conversions was realized in cost reductions in addition to reducing officer overproduction in some branches and eliminating officer shortages in other branches. The intention of the Army was not to require all institutions to accept GMS but senior commanding officers were expected to provide positive encouragement so that branch material institutions would voluntarily request conversions. MG Bergin stressed conversions would effectively resolve the issue of branch balance within the Army. However, the conversion transition period had aggravated the underproduction of officers in combat arms without a corresponding alleviation of overproduction in some of the other branches because conversions occurred mainly from former combat arms branch material detachments. Therefore, the conversion objectives were to obtain the maximum practical conversion of branch material detachments to GMS and to achieve an efficient and balanced branch program by the 1954-1955 academic year. The success of these objectives depended on the aggressive support of the major subordinate commanders and the effective dissemination of conversion policies to all institutions with branch material ROTC detachments. Solicitation priority was given to selected institutions with single ROTC branches of Transportation Corps, Military Police Corps and Quartermaster Corps where the overproduction of officers was prevalent, followed by those with multibranch detachments.[26]

MG Hugh M. Milton, II, reinforced the concerns of TAG and the problems which had occurred because of the partial mobilization of military forces that affected the ROTC program. On October 28, 1953, he stressed to the presidents of educational institutions that the flexibility of GMS would permit the assignment of graduates to any arm or service. Each graduate was required to select an arm or service and list several alternatives which were reviewed by a faculty board composed of civilian and military personnel who made recommendations to the Army. To provide equity and give GMS graduates the opportunity to serve in branches of their selection and maintain the maximum flexibility of the Department of the Army in meeting the military demands, a policy was adopted which established a GMS percentage of officers for each service. MG Milton recognized that the existence of branch material detachments encouraged student participation in some institutions while in others, especially small campuses where the academic pattern was broad, the best assignments for students were in branches which were underproducing. He was also cognizant that where GMS programs had been adopted some faculty failed to give credit for general courses, which formerly had been given for technical programs, and such loss of credit particularly in the engineering curricula upon which ordnance, signal and the corps of engineers depended heavily had mitigated against the ROTC program. These factors influenced the decision to submit the issue of conversion to each institution for a decision.[27]

During the consecutive 1953 and 1954 academic years, Antiaircraft ROTC at Hampton, Artillery ROTC at Florida A and M, Infantry ROTC at North Carolina A and T, Central State, Howard, Morgan State, Prairie View, South Carolina State and Tuskegee, Quartermaster Corps at Virginia State, and Transportation ROTC at Southern A and M were converted to GMS detachments. They were among 181 GMS detachments but there were fifty-four branch material detachments which offered Signal Corps, Corps of Engineering, Chemical Corps or Ordnance Corps instruction. The acceptance of the program at Oklahoma A and M College probably extended to Langston.[28]

William J. L. Wallace of West Virginia State met with Dean Harrison H. Ferrell and the PMST at West Virginia State College to inform them of the military's attempts to influence the adoption of the GMS program, but he had not received a satisfactory response to the question of whether or not there was an overproduction of artillery officers. There was not an assurance that African American officers would have adequate opportunities to enter services other than those where African Americans were traditionally assigned. He favored the retention of the Field Artillery until college officials had more time to study the two programs. The inclination of the collegiate officials was that there was little likelihood of an overproduction of artillery officers and that the record of West Virginia State ROTC indicated that their graduates met the competitive standards of Field Artillery. Wallace emphasized the increased interest in ROTC and felt a conversion to GMS would have the same effect.[29] The Reserve Forces Act of 1955 also required those ROTC graduates, who did not serve two years of active duty, to complete six months of specialized branch training with the balance of their seven and half year requirements completed in the organized reserves. The total ROTC students deferred from induction during the 1955-1956 academic year were 140,800.[30]

The PNLGC was concerned about announced policy changes regarding the ROTC program and several college presidents were especially interested in regulations pertaining to eligibility test scores for student participation and the minimum cadet enrollment requirement. Robert P. Daniel, the

Morgan State College cadets at a Howitzer briefing by personnel of the 2nd Armored Cavalry, April 10, 1956. (Courtesy of Morganiana Collection, Prints and Photographs Collection, Beulah M. Davis Special Collections Department, Morgan State University)

President of Virginia State and the PNLGC, was accompanied by Martin D. Jenkins of Morgan State, who served as a special consultant to the conference, when he met with James C. Evans and other Army officials on May 14, 1954 to discuss their concerns. Daniel stressed the Department of Health, Education and Welfare had notified certain states that Federal funding would be withheld from some land grant institutions not offering military science as required by the Morrill Act. The delegation emphasized that ROTC policies initiated on June 2, 1953 appeared to be sound but collectively they militated against African American institutions and prevented land grant colleges from obtaining ROTC detachments. There were seventeen African American land grant colleges but only in Florida, Louisiana, Missouri, North Carolina, Oklahoma, South Carolina, Texas, Virginia and West Virginia were ROTC detachments organized. Maryland and Tennessee had AFROTC detachments but there were no detachments at African American land grant colleges in Alabama, Arkansas, Delaware, Georgia, Kentucky or Mississippi, or at other state institutions in these states that did not permit the enrollment of African Americans who were economically unable to attend institutions in other states where ROTC detachments were organized. Therefore, in six states with large African American populations,

African Americans by state law, Federal policy or economics were prevented from participating in ROTC programs. If additional separate detachments were not authorized, they recommended the extension of the satellite system which permitted colleges to enroll students from neighboring non-ROTC institutions as freshmen in their programs and organize satellite detachments on subsidiary campuses and other institutions. Implementation of this procedure allowed Langston to operate as a satellite detachment of Oklahoma A and M. The Army officials responded that the problem of segregation and the attendant nonavailability of ROTC was a state issue and that the Morrill Act did not require ROTC instruction but merely military instruction which was available under Section C of the National Defense Act. Although ROTC was a convenient method of fulfilling Morrill Act obligations, ROTC detachments were granted only at institutions where the production of officers was justified. The decreasing strength of the Army did not merit an increase in detachments or satellites since the assignment of ROTC personnel was based on student enrollment. The officials stated that whenever ROTC was expanded all applicants would be considered and detachments would be assigned based on the individual merit of each institution. Evans stressed that African American students should have the opportunity to enroll into ROTC programs especially in states where they resided. Fourteen ROTC detachments enrolled 4,709 cadets which represented 3.3 percent of the 140,026 national enrollment. Graduating seniors received only 383 of the 14,230 commissions which represented 2.7 percent. African American enrollment in AFROTC was 1,385 but only 64 or 0.6 percent of the national total commissioned.[31]

The established minimum score of 115 on the RQ-3 was considered inappropriate by Daniel and Jenkins who felt that many outstanding students and potentially good officers would be denied the opportunity to receive a commission. Students with high academic averages who scored 112 would be excluded from an advanced course solely because of the failure to obtain the minimum score of 115. The position of the PNLGC was that PMST should be permitted to accept on a limited basis outstanding students who scored lower that 115. The RQ-3 requirement also jeopardized the retention of the detachments which were unable to produce twenty-five graduates. The PNLGC requested that twenty-five graduates should not be a definite rule, but only used as guide. The Army officials recognized that no test would adequately determine essential leadership qualifications but the RQ-3 test was only a screening device used to assist in selecting students capable of completing their ROTC requirements, competing successfully with other officers at service schools and performing military duties that would make them eligible for promotions and increase their value to the

Morgan State College Commissioning Ceremony, June 1961 (Willigean Harvin, 2LT Charles Johnson, Jr., and Rosetta Johnson). (Author's collection)

Army. They concluded that any relaxation of the requirements would pave the way for increasing collegiate protests and viewed the annual production rate of twenty-five as an economical measure which applied to all colleges.[32]

After the departure of Daniel and Jenkins, the officials concluded that the Army should not become involved with state problems and that ROTC policies regarding criteria for establishing detachments were valid. Approval of satellite detachments was obtainable but to do so solely for African American colleges would place the Army in an untenable position of discriminating for a small group of colleges regardless of how worthy the cause. Granting satellites would encourage requests from other institutions which were denied detachments because of their failure to meet the required standards. Delegating authority to major subordinate commanders or PMST to accept a fixed percentage of students scoring between 100 and 115 would not increase officer production unless there was need to increase the Reserve Corps or respond to a mobilization. The long range policy demand for quality exceeded the demand for quantity and no exceptions should be made to reach the requirement. They anticipated the possibility of losing some institutions which failed to commission twenty-five annual graduates. It was only feasible to retain economical detachments and most were expected to produce more than the minimum requirement. During the 1952-1953 academic year approximately 250 ROTC detachments produced 15,000 commissions for an approximate average of an 80 per detachment. The established minimum only provided an opportunity for selected small institutions to participate in the program and to widen the base for future increased production. However, a change of ROTC policy on June 1, 1954 gave eligibility to selected outstanding students who scored from 110 to 114 on the RQ-3 test.[33]

Assistant Secretary of the Army Hugh M. Milton informed Daniel that additional detachments or branches of existing detachments would not be considered since ROTC detachments were producing officers in excess of the requirements. The ROTC qualification test was the nationwide standard and was comparable to the examination required for admission to OCS. The test in addition to leadership, motivation and other qualities desired of officers was designed to evaluate candidates but the revision of June 1, 1954 allowed some flexibility of the minimum required score. Colleges furnishing less than twenty-five graduates would be placed on probation and retained, provided the minimum was attained the following year. Daniel assured Milton that the African American land grant colleges were not seeking any preferred racial differential treatment with respect to test scores but Army policies made it impossible for qualified African American students in several southern states to enroll in an ROTC program. Milton emphasized that this matter should be given serious consideration when an activation program for additional detachments was implemented.[34]

Secretary of the Army Milton was cognizant that other institutions failed to meet the minimum of entering students in Military Science I (MS I) and were automatically placed on probation for the 1954 academic year. Similarly deactivation of the detachments would occur if the deficiencies were not remedied. Although Military Science was a requirement at Langston University which enrolled ninety of its ninety-nine freshmen and Lincoln University which enrolled seventy-eight of its 111 freshmen, the list included Harvard, Dartmouth and Princeton Universities which respectively enrolled sixty, ninety-three and ninety-five of their 1,278, 728 and 754 freshmen where ROTC was an elective. He supported the student requirement since it influenced the annual graduation of twenty-five commissioned officers at most institutions and stressed that Harvard never attained the minimum freshmen allocation but its attrition rate was low and Harvard always satisfied the graduation requirement. Milton deemed it unwise to apply the policy to such an institution and would have supported the elimination of other detachments to increase the advanced enrollment of universities such as Harvard.[35] Cognizant that 10 percent of the participating institutions enrolled fewer than 100 freshmen, past enrollment for many of the institutions revealed that once enrolled, fewer students dropped the program, that the application of quantitative standards exclusively negatively affected graduates from many institutions of high academic standing, while policies were initiated to attract and retain skilled and talented personnel, and that despite their low enrollment most institutions provided the minimum quantity of commissioned graduates. Therefore, the freshmen enrollment of 100 was eliminated for the continuance of ROTC but the requirement of twenty-five commissioned graduates was retained.[36]

MG Ralph A. Palladino, Chief of the Army Reserve and ROTC Affairs, on November 14, 1957 attempted to improve the production at several institutions which included Lincoln University and North Carolina A and T by reiterating the ROTC requirements.[37] MG Frederick M. Warren as Chief of the Army Reserve and ROTC Affairs in 1960 reviewed a staff study entitled Methods for the Improvement of the ROTC Program which evaluated the implementation of plans to maintain the quantitative enrollment of ROTC while increasing the qualitative production of commissioned officers to meet the annual requirement of 14,000. Implementation of the plan required the elimination, adjustment, and realignment of ROTC detachments. In determining the best methods of achieving the objectives, the plan required the elimination of marginal detachments at institutions which failed to meet the minimum MS I enrollment of 100 during each academic year and produced fewer than twenty-five commissioned officers, the withdrawal by the Army from certain institutions which maintained AFROTC and ROTC programs, the realignment and adjustment of MS III quotas among the institutions conducting the ROTC program with officer production above the annual twenty-five minimum, and establishment of new detachments at selected colleges and universities, if necessary, to maintain the annual requirement of 14,000 commissioned officers. In the implementation of the revisions, the Army designated eight institutions where ROTC and AFROTC detachments were established and selected three colleges where detachments were to be withdrawn. Howard and North Carolina A and T were designated to lose their ROTC detachments, and Tuskegee would lose its AFROTC detachment. In the event the Air Force adhered to the policy that detachments would not be withdrawn unless requested by colleges, the Army would unilaterally pursue its plan. With the elimination of marginal detachments, the MS III quota would be increased at institutions which demonstrated the need for additional allocations for their program. Therefore, the realignment and reallocation of quotas among proven quality producing ROTC detachments would improve the quantity and quality of the program. The Chief of the Army Reserve and ROTC Affairs was ready to establish new ROTC detachments whenever necessary in order to maintain its 14,000 officer requirement. The staff study was approved by MG Warren in September 1960.[38]

Further analysis of the plan revealed that of the 38 marginal detachments, the quality of the graduate record for thirty was inadequate with six failing the production criteria, and the remaining 8 failing only to meet the production criteria. Fifty-six other detachments rated in the upper level of quality and production did not include any of the African American institutions and they required a total increase of 832 MS III allocations. The CRROTC reported that the six continental commands had received 177 applications for ROTC detachments which included nine for two-year satellite detachments. The Army realized that even with a plan and required probationary periods the elimination of a substantial number of marginal detachments at one time was unlikely. Planning the establishment of ROTC detachments had to be flexible and capable of progressive development to provide the most practical and feasible means to sustain production requirements as each marginal detachment was withdrawn. Ranking qualitatively detachments from 1955 to 1959, the statistics revealed that 30 detachments were consistently in the lower third of their class at the officers' basic course, or in the failure category. This was considered as a valid factor in determining the quality of the officers produced by ROTC detachments. The Air Force did not employ a quality criterion for the evaluation of its marginal detachments and until a qualitative factor was developed, the Air Force employed a cost per graduate factor at each institution in determining marginal status. Although the Air force had indicated its desire to withdraw eight detachments considered marginal to both services or to the Air Force, a small number of ROTC detachments were marginal producers for the Army and Air Force and both were competing for the same marginal product. At other institutions where the same competition existed, ROTC was not marginal by Army criteria, but was marginal according to Air Force standards due to the cost per graduate at these schools. The production for fiscal years 1958 and 1959 respectively was 12,901 and 12,333, and the estimated production for fiscal year 1960 was 12,110. The Army recognized the general unattractiveness of ROTC to outstanding students in terms of management and inadequate credit for required courses. These significant factors influenced a reduction of military contact hours from 180 to 150 in the basic course. The elimination of the thirty-eight marginal detachments was estimated to cause a quantitative reduction of approximately 265 cadets but, with the transfer of allocations to the fifty-six detachments in the upper 25 percent would have immediately improved quality production by exploiting the existing base of quality producing ROTC detachments.[39]

African Americans benefited from the revisions and although some were concerned with compulsory or elective ROTC participation an overriding issue was still the extension of programs to African American colleges. A compilation of the Advisory Panel on ROTC Affairs of the Reserve Forces Policy Board revealed the status of 68 land grant colleges in 1962. Forty-seven or 70 percent had compulsory programs and 14 or 30 percent had elective programs, and seven colleges did not have programs. Land grant colleges comprised 30 percent of the compulsory programs and 9 percent of the elective programs. Ironically, all programs at African American institutions were compulsory and of the seven land grant colleges which did not have programs all were African American colleges which included Arkansas AM&N, Alabama A and M College, Alcorn A and M, Delaware State, Fort Valley State, Kentucky State and Langston. The only African American land grant colleges with programs were Southern A and M, Lincoln, Prairie View A and M, South Carolina State, Howard and North Carolina A and T, the latter two having both had ROTC and AFROTC detachments. Although the land grant colleges submitted numerous requests for the extension of ROTC to all of the land grant institutions, Army officials maintained that an interpretation of the Morrill Act by the United States Attorney General in 1930 stated that the statute only required the inclusion of military science as elective courses but military training was not mandatory.[40]

Howard was placed on probation for failing to attain production standards for 1955-1956 but the commissioning of twenty-five officers in 1958 removed the ROTC detachment from probation. An evaluation of academic and military records of cadets selected for advanced training revealed the quality of the students selected for commission from 1959 to 1961 manifestly low. Howard was notified by the commanding general of Second Army on September 29, 1961 of a report by the Twenty-First Army Corps that indicated 63.1 percent of the graduates attending service school orientation courses during 1959 and 1960 had failed or were ranked in the lower third of their classes which placed the university in the lower ten percent of all ROTC detachments. An attempt to prevent this issue was made when the president appointed to an ROTC committee to investigate the circumstances which caused the earlier probation. On June 30, 1956 the committee recommended the establishment of a University Military Committee, the publication of a brochure stressing the advantages of the program especially to veterans, and that remedial instruction in vocabulary building and elementary algebra be provided to MS II cadets. The first and third recommendations were approved and implemented by the President. Undersecretary of the Army Milton offered assistance to the university but stressed that in addition to the qualitative issue the university needed to improve the ROTC facilities to ensure retention of the program.

Although PMSTs were authorized under Army Regulations 145-350 to enroll students in the advanced course with scores less then 115 on the ROTC qualifying examination but who had scored at least 110 on the examination and possessed exceptional qualifications, aptitude, motivation and had demonstrated outstanding abilities, Second Army Deputy Commanding General Rinaldo Van Brunt on January 14, 1960 informed Howard that some officers who had performed poorly at service schools were those selected below the 115 score and consequently this authority was withdrawn from those institutions, which included Howard, whose graduates failed to meet acceptable performance standards. Howard stressed that the PMST had not implemented the authority previously granted under Army Regulations 145-350 and that by February 10, 1960 the screening process of potential MS III cadets was improved especially after the graduation of poor performers. More significantly, the criteria used in selecting the best qualified students during 1959 to 1960 should have resulted in more efficient graduates entering service schools from 1960 to 1962.[41]

A similar evaluation of ROTC at North Carolina A and T revealed most science and engineering freshmen were assigned to AFROTC since college officials felt that the Air Force offered better opportunities but this practice was not initiated until 1958. The evaluation alleged the poor performance of graduates at Army service orientation courses was attributed to lack of academic preparation, comprehension and self-confidence in addition to the inability to express ideas in writing or verbally. Corrective measures instituted by the PMS and the administration involved English and mathematical tutorial programs and a compulsory program initiated in 1960 that required MS III and MS IV cadets to enroll in their respective precommissioned extension courses administered by the Army service schools. To eliminate the probationary status caused by the inability of cadets to complete their academic requirements for commission, a revised counseling program was instituted to assist cadets in their efforts to select required courses.[42]

Tennessee State AFROTC had experienced problems with officer production and was confronted with the loss of its detachment. A major factor for the difficulty was the failure of some cadets to pass the Air Force Officer Qualifying Test for selection and admission into the advanced program which was implemented in 1953 that was a revision of the Air Crew Classification Battery examination used during World War II. The morale of students, faculty and administrators remained positive and cadet enrollment under LTC Howard L. Baugh increased to 1,152 by 1961 with forty-eight in

MSGT Richard Robinson with Morgan State College Pershing Rifles, 1959. (Booker, Peters, MSGT Robinson, Johnson, PR Pledge, Willis). (Author's collection)

advanced Air Science.[43] Influenced by a proposal to abolish compulsory ROTC by the Council on Instruction at Ohio State University, students at Tennessee State University recognized the advantages of military science but concluded that those who opposed ROTC would more than likely become arrogant and uncooperative and would not learn the concepts necessary for further military training. CPT Arthur L. Fox concurred that an elective program would definitely improve the detachment since cadet performance was related to motivation and interest in AFROTC. Estimating that nine of ten students would not enroll in an elective program, the remaining students would receive better training and advanced students would be granted an increased stipend under a proposed Department of Defense plan. The operational costs of the program would be less expensive since the cost was determined by the annual production of officers as compared to the quantity of enrolled cadets.[44]

The implementation of the plan would have devastated the African American ROTC programs. In addition to Howard and North Carolina A and T, the Army's marginal list included South Carolina State, Tuskegee, Central State, Prairie View A and M, Morgan State, Florida A and M, Lincoln, Virginia State, Hampton, West Virginia State, and Southern A and M. The Air Force marginal list included North Carolina A and T, Tuskegee and

Howard. Of these colleges only North Carolina A and T, Lincoln, West Virginia State and Southern A and M were in a probationary status. With the planned inactivation of Central State, Morgan State, Virginia State, West Virginia State, Howard and Hampton in the Second Army area, the Army did not plan the activation of any new detachments at African American institutions. In the Third Army area, South Carolina State, and Florida A and M would have been inactivated but detachments would have been activated at Alabama A and M College and Atlanta University. In the Fourth Army area, Southern A and M and Prairie View A and M would have been eliminated but ROTC detachments would be activated at Texas Southern, Grambling College, Xavier in New Orleans and Arkansas A and M. In the Fifth Army area, Lincoln would have been inactivated without another African American detachment organized in the area. The military commanders were also cognizant of African American institutions which had applied for ROTC detachments. In the Second Army area, Virginia Union University in Richmond, VA, Lincoln in Pennsylvania, Kentucky State and St. Paul's Polytechnic Institute in Lawrenceville, VA had applied for senior ROTC, Maryland State had applied for a satellite detachment, and Bluefield

Morgan State College Cadet Colonel David Adderley and his staff, 1960. (Courtesy of the Morganiana Collection, Prints and Photographs Collection, Beulah M. Davis Special Collections Department, Morgan State University)

State College had shown interest in sponsoring a ROTC detachment. In the Third Army area, Alabama A and M, Atlanta, Fort Valley State, Savannah State, Alcorn A and M, Jackson State, North Carolina College and Fisk had submitted applications. In the Fourth Army area, Arkansas A and M, Grambling, Howard Payne College, Texas Southern and Xavier had filed applications.[45]

The Army envisioned the elimination of thirty-eight detachments, which would have caused certain political implications especially since three of the eight institutions with Army and Air Force detachments were located at African American institutions. The withdrawal of the ROTC detachment from North Carolina A and T was proposed in January 1960 but General G. H. Decker, Army Vice Chief of Staff, viewed it unwise to withdraw the detachment unless similar action could be taken against Centenary College. After the Assistant Chief of Staff for Reserve Components advised CRROTC of his desire to accelerate the withdrawal of marginal detachments on June 23, 1960, the withdrawal of the ROTC at North Carolina A and T was reconsidered by MG Frederick M. Warren on July 29, 1960 since the commanding general of the US Continental Command indicated that the college commissioned only fourteen officers during the 1959-1960 academic year with 86.3 percent in either the lower third of the officer basic classes or failing. This was slightly higher than the 82.4 percent of the previous year. The Twelfth Army Corps commanding general recommended an extension of the detachment to permit the college to accomplish the necessary adjustment to meet its production quota. The Third Army commanding general noticed the enrollment of MS II and IV students had increased and the level of graduates receiving commissions had remained static, ranging from ten to nineteen, and he recommended probationary status for the detachment. However, the commanding general of CONARC recommended the withdrawal at the end of the 1960-1961 academic year because for the seventh consecutive year the college had failed to meet the minimum production and since 1955 over 80 percent of its ROTC graduates attending the officers' basic course were in the lower third or failed their courses. Samuel Dewitt Proctor, President of North Carolina A and T, was notified on August 16, 1960 that after careful consideration of all the factors pertaining to the ROTC detachment a decision was made to withdraw the detachment at the completion of the 1960-1961 academic year. This action did not preclude students who had completed MS I and MS III from completing their respective basic and advanced courses.[46]

Without having the opportunity to assess the program to ascertain the cause of the disparity in the quality of students in the ROTC and AFROTC detachments and having assumed the presidency of North Carolina A and

Morgan State College Pershing Rifles Drill Team, 1959. (Author's collection)

T on July 1, 1960, Samuel M. Proctor was dismayed to learn of the decision to withdraw ROTC. He appealed to Undersecretary Hugh M. Milton to extend the 1962 withdrawal to permit him the opportunity to admit new freshmen and evaluate the quality of the 1962 graduates and their performance in the officer basic courses. He assured Undersecretary Milton that if graduates in the classes of 1961 and 1962 had not shown remarkable improvement, North Carolina A and T would voluntarily terminate Army ROTC on August 15, 1962. Proctor further explained that before 1958, science and engineering students were guided inadvertently into the Air Force ROTC because it was felt that opportunities were broader in that branch of service. When the PMST, MAJ Lawrence D. Spencer, arrived in 1958 this trend was corrected and a dramatic increase occurred in the quality and quantity of cadets passing the RQ 5 between 1958 to 1960 with the passing percentage moving from 20.4 to over 50 percent. The PMST also considered it more advantageous to have a firm production of well-trained candidates than to dilute the program to meet the quota of twenty-five. The college had produced 383 officer candidates since 1948 and with the exception of the significant increase in the quantity of graduates during the Korean War, the production since his arrival was increasing and the quantity of failures in the basic officer course was declining. Proctor maintained that the college could have easily met its quota by utilizing the earlier standard of 1954. The college had self-imposed higher standards to ensure that students who completed ROTC were also completing their other collegiate requirements. Students failing to meeting their academic requirements were denied graduation and this was reflected in the inability of the institution to maintain its quota. In view of the progress since 1958 and the quality of the MS IV cadets, his confidence in the success of the self-imposed program to maintain efficiency with a balance of exceptional students in the AFROTC and ROTC detachments was increased. Proctor emphasized that North Carolina A and T was the only African American institution in North Carolina offering military science and aeroscience to African American students. The institution was not oblivious to its weaknesses nor did the college make excuses for them. Proctor only requested consideration for the progress accomplished when other impediments were removed.[47]

In justification of its actions and responding to a request from the Commission on Civil Rights concerning discontinuance of ROTC detachments at African American institutions, Duncan Hodges, serving as the Deputy Assistant Secretary of the Army, provided a response for the Assistant Secretary of Defense. Hodges stated in December 1960 that there were fourteen ROTC detachments on probation during the previous academic year. Six of the detachments which included Lincoln University had met the production minimum and were removed from their probationary status. Seven others which included West Virginia State, Southern A and M, and North Carolina A and T failed the production standards and were continued in a probationary status. The ROTC unit at Centenary College in Shreveport, Louisiana would be withdrawn at the end of the 1960-1961 academic year. He further stated that effective in January 1961 the Department of the Army would notify institutions that beginning with each March collegiate officials would know whether their detachments were scheduled for elimination at the end of the academic year.[48] A major factor for this revision was the angry protest from college presidents who were notified near the beginning of the academic year of the withdrawal of their detachments. William J. L. Wallace of West Virginia State complained that when suddenly informed that the discontinuance of the ROTC was imminent, students were preparing to enroll and registration materials and catalogs, printed during the summer, included the ROTC program. The college was obligated to the contractual agreement with students and to discontinue the program at such a late date would damage the integrity of the college, causing the loss of numerous man hours and thousands of dollars of material. Additionally, many students had selected the college because of the presence of military science.[49]

Felton G. Clark of Southern A and M raised similar issues and was especially disturbed since the university raised its standards for advanced military science cadets and organized its admission procedures in an effort to improve the quality of commissioned officers. The seriousness of the issues impelled him to request a conference with Undersecretary of the Army Milton to present relevant facts supporting the continuation of the program since ROTC was tremendously important to the total educational program at Southern A and M as a land grant institution. Felton agreed with the urgency of having African American detachments meet the same exacting standards of the ROTC complex but he reminded Undersecretary Milton of the thwarting circumstances engendered by a culturally diverse and deprived environment which was thrust upon African Americans. However, he envisioned a future environment where all Americans would be permitted, encouraged and stimulated to achieve their best.[50]

Governor Luther Hodges of North Carolina and Congressional Senator Sam J. Ervin made inquiries concerning the extension of the ROTC at North Carolina A and T, which prompted a reiteration of Army policies and issues pertaining to the college by Undersecretary Milton. As a result of their inquiries and the concern of the Commission on Civil Rights about the discontinuance of ROTC detachments at four historically African American colleges, Undersecretary Milton deferred withdrawal for another year and stated that this decision was influenced by the aggressiveness and interest in the ROTC program by Proctor who subsequently assigned 60 of his best students to ROTC and 40 to the AFROTC. Proctor was grateful for the extension and stressed that the college should be judged on the performance of the 1961 graduates. North Carolina A and T did not only want to keep ROTC for institutional pride but to serve the nation and carry its share of the national defense burden. The college would have been disgraced if it failed in the accomplishment of its mission and Proctor anticipated that with the conclusion of the 1961 summer camp North Carolina A and T would graduate thirty-eight commissioned officers.[51] The extension of ROTC to Southern A and M caused Felton G. Clark to express the gratitude of the university community which felt the elimination of the detachment would have imposed an incredible hardship on the institution and damage morale in many areas of the state. Similar to Proctor at North Carolina A and T, he was confident that the candidates in the 1961 class would exceed twenty-eight and meet the desired qualitative criteria.[52]

Relieved by the retention of West Virginia State ROTC and satisfied that Army officials planned to notify colleges of their standings by March 1, 1961, William J. L. Wallace requested that midyear inspections be conducted in February to permit the accumulation of the progress by MS III and MS IV cadets. He realized that colleges were below the minimum production standards and discovered discrepancies in the Army production calculations during the past two academic years. Instead of graduating thirteen commissioned officers in 1958, the college had actually commissioned eighteen, and during the following academic year nineteen were commissioned instead of the seventeen recorded by the Army. Wallace did not have any objections to the officers' basic course ranking system except that there would always be a lower 10 percent and the comparisons of colleges implied that the conditions were approximately the same in all institutions with ROTC detachments. He felt that this was contradictory in the case of West Virginia State since it had only thirty allocations for MS II in 1958 and it was impossible to produce twenty-five commissioned officers two years later with all of the obstacles and difficulties students encountered, including financial and academic scheduling problems. However, he was grateful for an additional allotment in 1959.

Wallace concluded that before adequate and fair comparisons of the quality of production could be assessed, the leadership and instruction at institutions had to be of comparable quality. He was shocked when the Second Army planned to assign only African American officers and enlisted personnel to the college. Although white officers were assigned to the college from nearby locations at their request, he notified Second Army officials of the racial transition at the college and requested staffing based on quality and ability instead of membership in a particular racial group. Cognizant that African Americans composed 10 percent of the Army, Felton reasoned that the college had not received top quality staff personnel and most of the assigned staff personnel were non-college graduates although four officers had received their bachelor's degrees from West Virginia State within the last three years. Informed that the cadre included some of the best available African American enlisted men, Wallace inferred that it was impossible to receive the best instructional personnel when the Army was selecting only from 10 percent of the personnel in the Army. In his judgment, some of the enlisted personnel were obnoxious and he was surprised that personnel officers would assign them as instructors of college students. He assured Undersecretary Milton that the standing of the institution was based upon the comparative standing of the graduates' performances at service schools. West Virginia State would have accepted some of the previously assigned personnel. Wallace did not imply that some officers who possessed quality leadership and performed excellent work should not have been assigned to the college, but on a comparative basis he advocated that the college should have had officers of the same quality that served at other institutions with ROTC programs. Wallace was grateful that his protest on the selection of enlisted men was promptly acknowledged and a change of policy was inaugurated.

Wallace was further perturbed by the abrupt removal of two officers. One officer removed at the beginning of the academic year had earned his degree at West Virginia State and was reassigned to the District Office at South Charleston and the officer removed during midterm was the PMST. The transfers caused morale problems and decreased *esprit de corps*. Wallace was astounded by the insensitivity of the military and vigorously protested the actions when he only received threats of discontinuing ROTC. The only tangible result of the assignment of non-college graduate officers was the tremendous difference of opinion between the military and the academic staffs regarding the quality of student accomplishment. Faculty members were concerned about the DMS designation given to cadets who had completed their ROTC requirements but failed to complete their academic requirements for graduation. Wallace inferred that military cadres were incapable of recognizing the difference and their views contributed to the comparative standing of the ROTC detachment. He would not recommend students as DMS cadets when their academic records did not indicate such distinction. Although MAJ Edward D. Hinkson articulated Army policy and procedures which influenced the deputy commander of the 1960 ROTC Camp at Fort Knox, Kentucky to tentatively designate ten students as DMS students, he insisted that students who were designated as distinguished should have at least an academic average of 2.5 or higher. After refusing to recommend four students for the designation, Wallace on September 23, 1960 recommended Douglas W. Cooper, Charles E. Evans, Thomas A. Marks, Alonzo B. Methods, George L. Rich and Charles E. Stokes, Jr. as DMS cadets. He surmised that students below an acceptable level of achievement would be encouraged to feel that they were outstanding candidates and would be lulled into a false sense of accomplishment and fail to achieve an acceptable level in the basic officer course. Wallace also did not comprehend the failure of excellent students who were disqualified for military service at the end of their summer camp training. The physical condition of the cadets did not hinder their military participation and academically they were outstanding.[53]

On October 3, 1960, the Reserve Forces Policy Board deliberated recommendations made by the Advisory Panel on ROTC affairs and formulated a policy providing military officials with the initiative to determine when ROTC detachments were to be established or disestablished with final approval reserved for the Secretary of Defense. The Undersecretary of the Army directed the Inspector General on October 13, 1960 to inquire when the Army notified institutions regarding their probationary status or withdrawal of ROTC detachments. The inquiry contained significant issues which had been evaluated by several Army officials. It reiterated that by the direction of the Undersecretary of the Army on September 7, 1960 the Chief of Staff developed a plan that was approved on October 4, 1960 and became effective by CONARC on October 10, 1960. The Inspector General also included in his inquiry a staff study entitled Plans for the Elimination, Adjustment, and Realignment of Detachments within the Senior Division of ROTC Program that was prepared by CRROTC and approved by the Army Vice Chief of Staff on August 5, 1960. From information received on October 10, 1960 from PMST whose detachments failed to meet the minimum production during the 1960 fiscal year, ten were granted waivers and ten were placed on probation. Proctor of North Carolina A and T was notified that the decision to withdraw the detachments was deferred for a year. Charles W. Wesley of Central State, George W. Gore of Florida A and M, E. B. Evans of Prairie View A and M and Benner C. Turner of South Carolina State were notified that in September 1961 the ROTC detachment was on probation with possible withdrawal of the detachment by 1963.[54]

Wesley recognized Central State ROTC deficiencies and implemented corrective action by emphasizing that a major vulnerability area was the performance of graduates at their respective service schools. Although the percentage of candidates in the lower third and failing courses had declined significantly since 1958, remedial programs in mathematics and reading were developed, counseling was conducted by faculty and psychological staff provided motivational instruction. LTC Roy W. Sorrell as PMST carefully selected students with a minimum score of 115 RQ 3 for the advanced course. He emphasized to Undersecretary Milton that the overall standing of the college had improved, that twenty-three officers were commissioned with another scheduled to complete his academic program during the summer. The program also had a cadet who was attempting to lose weight to receive his commission on June 30, 1960. Wesley further stressed that the college was sincerely interested in commissioning quality officers.[55]

Benner C. Turner was alarmed by the statistics presented by his PMST which reflected the poor performance of South Carolina State's graduates and the low production rate. However, an earlier inspection by LTC Rieder W. Schell of the ROTC Affairs Division had revealed several problems. LTC Schell met with Turner and MAJ Anthony C. Turner on February 8, 1957 and emphasized that the enrollments from 1951 to 1957 were significantly above the requirement except for the academic years from fall 1952 to spring 1954 when the MS III respective enrollments were 68 and 11 as a result of student difficulty with the RQ-3 test. This caused a decline in the officer production for the next two years although increases in the basic course were expected to improve production above the minimum requirement in 1957.[56] Turner assured Undersecretary Milton of the voluntary release of thirty-two advanced students in a sincere effort to improve the quality of the graduates. The faculty council also determined that it was mandatory for all students accepted by the ROTC program, regardless of RQ-3 scores, to have acceptable academic averages. Having discussed the ROTC program with the commander of the South Carolina Military District and the commanding general of the XII Army Corps and implemented corrective action, Turner did not believe that the desired qualitative and quantitative improvements would be attained within the short span of two years.[57]

Collegiate officials were cognizant of the Army's 1960-1961 mid-year evaluations to determine the withdrawal of substandard Army ROTC detachments from the total of twenty-eight which had failed the inspection the previous academic year. Although twenty were granted waivers of the minimum standards and one was withdrawn, North Carolina A and T, Southern A and M and West Virginia State Colleges were among the seven institutions evaluated in January 1961 at the direction of the Undersecretary of the Army. The evaluation of North Carolina A and T revealed that approximately thirty-eight candidates would graduate that year but past unsatisfactory graduate performances at service schools and low production influenced the Army staff concurrence with the recommendations of the Second Army commander and CONARC to withdraw the ROTC detachment. A graduate production of twenty-seven was estimated for Southern University but by July 1960, 50 percent were in the lower third or failed their class. The Fourth Army commander recommended indefinite probation to observe the results of the methodology instituted to improve the ROTC detachment but CONARC, doubtful of any meaningful improvement, recommendation of withdrawal was approved by the Department of Army. West Virginia State with 75 percent of its graduates in the lower third or failing expected to produce thirty-five officers. Although CONARC emphasized the quality of its graduates at service schools was still unsatisfactory, the Army recommended the continuation of probation for the next academic year. In view of the quantity of detachments recommended for withdrawal and the presidents of most probationary detachments expressing their desire to maintain the ROTC programs, MG Warren expected pressure from congressmen, private organizations and the media concerning the planned elimination of seven ROTC detachments. On February 23, 1961, he recommended to the Assistant Chief of Staff for Reserve Components, Army Chief of Staff, and Undersecretary of the Army the withdrawal of ROTC at North Carolina A and T, Southern A and M and the Universities of Chattanooga and Wichita at the end of the 1961-1962 academic year. However, he recommended the continuation of ROTC at West Virginia State as well as detachments at Arkansas Polytechnic College and the Georgia College of Business Administration.[58]

Lincoln recognized that the performance of commissioned officers at branch schools and annual officer production influenced the continuation of ROTC detachments. An analysis of the 160 commissioned graduates since 1954 who attended their appropriate branch schools was a matter of close scrutiny by the university and especially the Military Science Department. However, the low performance of some graduates from 1959 to 1963 which had placed Lincoln in the lower 10 percent category of effectiveness prompted the PMS to present his findings to the faculty.` The analysis revealed that eighty-four attended branch schools and only five or 5.95 percent were ranked in the upper third of their classes, fifteen or 17.92 percent in the middle third, and fifty-one or 60.7 percent in the lower third. Thirteen were in the failed category from 1961 and 1963 which represented respectively failed percentages of 21.4, 20.8 and 13.3 and the combined lower third and failed categories was 76.19 percent which alarmed the cadre. In comparison to the entire Eleventh Army Corps which consisted of Illinois and Missouri, the combined failure percentage for all institutions excluding Lincoln annually for the same years were 0.3, 1.0 and 0.9. Further analysis of the branch school standings and ROTC records revealed the same total of two for students with grade point achievement of 3.5 or higher but in the ranking in averages from 3.4 and below decreased significantly in the branch schools with two placed below the grade point average of 2.0. Therefore, ROTC and collegiate performances were clear indications of expected ability performance in branch schools. Recommendations by the PMS included further study to determine the cause of the excessive placement of grades in the lower third category and the implementation of measures to prevent low student achievement and increase a desire for excellence.[59]

Commissioned graduates of Hampton fell below minimum standards at officer basic courses but LTG John S. Upham, Commanding General of the Second Army, waived the failures during 1962 and 1963 since Jerome H. Holland, President of Hampton, had initiated measures to improve the performance of future graduates. The quality and amount of cadets passing the qualifying examination was increased under the leadership of LTC Osceola T. Thornton who was provided an opportunity to select students with the potential to receive their commissions and score high in their appropriate service school. The acting Dean of Faulty established a committee of mathematics and communications faculties to assist ROTC students and the faculty in general recognized the importance of the military science program as essential to the overall development of students. Students responded positively toward the program and were enthusiastic in supporting extracurricular activities sponsored by the military science department. More impressive was that the leading students in ROTC were also leaders in campus-wide organizations and activities. To eliminate difficulties and maintain a successful detachment, the PMST improved the records screening process and all selectees for the advanced program were required to have a 2.5 grade point average with a 3.0 in Military Science. Cadets in the advanced program were encouraged to participate in campus activities that enabled them to develop their oral and written expression. However, extra-curricular activity required acceptable passing grades in all courses. A minimum of two field exercises were conducted annually and MS IV students were required to participate in Service School Extension courses. Administrators and faculty supported the efforts of the Military Science Department and encouraged conferences with cadets.[60]

An evaluation of ROTC and AFROTC in relation to Federal resources by the United States Comptroller General revealed that many institutions affiliated with AFROTC were producing appreciably fewer commissioned officers each year and their retention was not justified. Citing several lowest producing colleges of which Maryland State was the lowest, a report issued on October 30, 1964 stated that for three consecutive years, from 1961 to 1963, Maryland State commissioned two, three, and one student respectively, at a respective cost of $19,000, $12,600 and $38,000 for assigned cadre officer. The national average of all colleges was $6,500. The comptroller general concluded inadequate expenditures were caused by the lack of a Defense Department policy to disestablish ineffective programs to save approximately two million dollars without reducing the quantity of commissioned officers. Although Army and Air Force officials were knowledgeable of the situation, contractual agreements provided that collegiate officials or military services had the authority to unilaterally discontinue detachments but officials had failed to terminate uneconomical detachments and college officials were reluctant to eliminate their programs. The Department of Defense was reviewing the status of detachments at institutions where more than one service was represented and would make changes after the enactment of legislation in October 1964 that was designed to make the programs more attractive to students during 1964. The comptroller general planned to review the effectiveness of the corrective measures implemented by the Department of Defense.[61]

Requiring military training as an elective or two-year obligation for all qualified freshman had always been an issue for many college officials. An Army staff study in 1960 revealed that in programs where colleges change from required to elective military training the participation in the basic courses declined by 50 percent and there was a significant decline of cadets in the advanced program and in commissions granted. Agitation for changing the requirement to elective at seventeen major universities was a concern of the CRROTC, MG Frederick M. Warren, and the Deputy Assistant Chief of Staff for Reserve Components, BG M. W. Schewe.[62] The Army considered that compulsory training offered for two years assisted in evaluating the performance and potential of cadets and sought the best qualified students. Opponents argued that the system repelled rather than attracted students toward the armed services and that the best officers were developed from students who volunteered for the program. The attrition rate in the compulsory institutions was high and the programs were compelled to train a large quantity of disinterested freshmen and sophomores to procure a proportionately small quantity of commissioned officers. They also stressed that on campuses where more than one program existed, indoctrination not only separated military service from higher education, but the intensity influenced students to further the process of separation.[63]

MG Frederick M. Warren, CARROTC, was also cognizant that the ROTC program had failed to meet the annual requirement of producing 14,000 officers and under the supervision of the Assistant Chief of Staff for Reserve Components conducted a revision of ROTC policies. Major revisions pertained to increasing college enrollments, curriculum changes, required versus elective basic ROTC, equitable Federal support to institutions, increased pay to cadets, provisions for accommodating junior college and transfer students from non-ROTC institutions, competition and compatibility among all ROTC programs, and variations of the four-year program. On April 7, 1961, MG Warren recommended to CONARC the formation of a two-year program with a ten-week summer camp preceding the junior year but CONARC preferred a three-year program with an eight-week summer camp but supported the two-year program and the feasibility of using the Army Training Centers to train approximately 25,000 cadets. Undersecretary of the Army Stephen Ailes also announced that Army reservists who volunteered for the Peace Corps and other similar federally sponsored overseas programs would be transferred to the Standby Reserve at the time of their departure and would not be obligated to participate in any reserve training while overseas. Upon their return to the United States they would be assigned to the Ready Reserve.[64]

Second Army Deputy Commanding General Rinaldo Van Brunt on January 14, 1960 emphasized that the low achievement of several officers at service schools were former cadets who had attained grades below the 115 score and consequently this authority was withdrawn from those institutions, which included Howard, whose graduates failed to meet acceptable performance standards. Howard stressed that the PMST had not implemented the authority previously granted under AR 145-350 and that by February 10, 1960 the screening process of potential MS III cadets was improved especially after the graduation of poor performers. More important, the criteria used in selecting the best qualified students during 1959 to 1960 should have resulted in more efficient graduates for entering service schools from 1960 to 1962. The successful selection process negated probation by the Second Army which on December 26, 1962 indefinitely waived the annual production of twenty-five for institutions in the lower 10 percent to allow the detachments to concentrate on the quality rather than the quantity of the programs.[65]

Analysis of the Howard program revealed administrative officers, faculty and cadets concurred with the value of military and air science. Although cadets disagreed with the compulsory aspect of the programs, first year cadets had a more positive attitude and intensity toward the programs but during their second year their attitudes began to change. Some factors that influenced change were the failure of students to qualify for the advanced course, opposition to regimentation during leadership laboratory, and the determination that military service was not desirable and consequently was a waste of time. Administrators and faculty favored compulsory programs but faculty were concerned that they were competing for students since the military and air science programs diminished the participation of cadets in their academic curricula. The analysis also revealed the programs were viable and provided excellent public relations and publicity for the university. Emphasizing that there was absolutely no tolerance for cadet abuse, disrespect and arrogance in the programs, and stressing that the Department of Defense announced that ROTC programs were the primary source of officer procurement, the legislation enacted on October 13, 1964 provided several options but recommended that Howard retain compulsory programs since there were dangers of an insufficient number of student volunteers to support both programs on a voluntary basis.[66]

From an analysis of the ROTC conducted by the LTC Osceola T. Thornton in 1964, the PMS concluded that nationwide a serious problem existed in the ROTC program. With approximately 63 percent of the officers' cadre commissioned through ROTC, it was imperative to maintain a standard of discipline and training that was comparable with the active Army since ROTC graduates affected the quality of the service. He was gratified to report the high standard obtained at Hampton but emphasized two critical issues in the career of students. Freshman had to enroll into the program or the opportunity to enter ROTC with its long-range advantages of commissioned service was lost. Sophomores had to successfully complete their applications and qualify for the advanced program. However, it was essential that cadets receive wise counseling and correct information concerning the advanced program. LTC Thornton stressed that ROTC would not interfere or detract from their concentrations since only two and a half academic credit were allowed during each semester. The acceptance of a commission would not preclude graduate study, and past experiences revealed that the same quantity of students commissioned attended graduate school as those not in the program. The Army had a deferment policy to permit the completion of graduate study and many officers attended graduate school during the off-duty hours. Commissioned service satisfied the military obligation and further planning was facilitated with a definite date of service after graduation. Cadets received a stipend during the academic year and for attending a summer camp. The diversity of branch assignment in many instances related to the academic training received at Hampton but an assignment in an unrelated field also was advantageous for commissioned officers who acquired additional skills.[67] These counseling initiatives were significant but many students were influenced by current events or preferred to utilize all of their credits for courses in the disciplines.

On October 16, 1963, Hampton was informed of the low achievement of its commissioned graduates but on April 5, 1964 LTG John S. Upham, commanding general of the Second Army stated that the Department of the Army had waived the failure to meet minimum quality standards during 1962 and 1963 in anticipation that efforts would be implemented to improve the quality of service school performance of the ROTC graduates. An assessment of the ROTC Qualifying Examination (RQ7) results from 1960 to 1964 revealed that the total of MSII cadets who completed the RQ7 had increased from eighty-nine to 129 and those passing the examination increased from fifty to ninety-eight which represented a decrease in the failure percentage from 43.9 to 25 percent. Conferences with Hugh M. Gloster, the acting Dean of Men, who was an ardent supporter of ROTC, constantly counseled advanced cadets and established a committee of mathematics and communications faculties to assist students with difficulty in those areas. The faculty recognized the importance of the program which was essential to the development of students and the enthusiasm and participation of students in extra curricular activities was indicative of the attractiveness of the ROTC. Leading campus students were also enrolled in the advanced course. Measures specifically implemented to alleviate difficulties and maintain a viable detachment consisted of screening MSII records and selecting only cadets with a cumulative academic average of 2.5 or higher and 3.0 averages in military science. MS III and IV cadets with passing accumulative grades were encouraged to participate in extra curricular activities and all cadets were urged to join campus activities which improved their written and verbal skills, and various contests were developed to improve their competitive spirit. A reading laboratory was organized and the faculty formed a book-of-the-month program which increased cognitive comprehension and study skills. A minimum of two field exercises was conducted and MS IV cadets were required to participate in the Service School Extension program pertaining to their branch assignment. The cadre served as mentors and encouraged cadets scheduled for extended active duty to report to the military science department for orientation and counseling.[68]

# 6

# Revisions and Extensions of Military Science, Aeroscience and Naval Science

Successful Russian space missions prompted an announcement by President John F. Kennedy of plans to send a manned spacecraft into space and to the moon. Kennedy's dramatic statements influenced James C. Evans in October 1961 to ascertain the quantity of African Americans available for the space program and indirectly established the past procurement of officers from African American colleges and universities with ROTC and AFROTC detachments. Information was gathered from individuals and other organizations which included ROTC detachments concerning the participation of African Americans in the Astronaut program through the Air Force Aero-Space Research Pilot School, with the exception of Howard, Tuskegee and North Carolina A and T AFROTC programs. The records of the Professors of Air Science caused pessimism and revealed little hope of selecting officers for the astronaut program. Professors of Military Science stated that their ROTC programs seldom commissioned graduates who pursued aviation careers and those with aviation experience had relatively little or no opportunity to become jet-qualified. They emphasized that their colleges had few non-ROTC graduate students with Air Force experience in fixed-wing aircraft. LTC James A. Hurd provided a personnel roster of Howard graduates who had qualified for pilot training with bachelor degrees in civil, electrical or mechanical engineering in addition to chemistry, physical science, or mathematics. LTC Howard L. Baugh of Tennessee A and I considered the quantity of aviation officers commissioned through

AFROTC was probably small or nonexistent but advised Evans that the Air Force Experimental Test Pilot School at Edwards AFB in California was a possible source of information.[1]Evans also endeavored to establish a list of senior officers for consideration as nominees for appointment to ambassador posts, and Louis Martin reviewed the list of candidates, active and reserve officers, that constituted a ready reserve of screened experienced and competent personnel. Evans recommended to Ralph Dungan, Special Assistant to the President for Appointments, several distinguished military officers. COL Edward O. Gourdin, a 1924 Olympian who graduated from Harvard and commanded the 372nd Infantry Regiment during WWII, was serving as a municipal judge in Boston. COL James H. Robinson, retired, a Howard graduate with a University of Pennsylvania graduate degree in physics, was serving as a staff executive with the Howard School of Engineering and Architecture. LTC John T. Martin, another Howard University graduate called to active duty in 1940, who served on extended active duty after the war as a Public Information Officer with the Department of the Army and the Department of Defense, was serving as Executive of the Office of the Counselor of the Assistant Secretary of Defense for Manpower. LTC Dennis D. Nelson, a Fisk graduate who became the senior African American line officer in the Navy with previous staff duty with the Navy Office of the Chief of Information and with the Department of Defense, was assigned to the Armed Forces Radio and Television Service in Los Angeles, California. Veteran George Holland had served as a civil advisor on Taiwan and was serving as head of the District of Columbia Veterans Benefits Office.

The recommendations for military and cultural attache assignments were equally impressive. LTC Allen R. Anderson, a Howard graduate who had served as a Tuskegee PMS&T, was a staff officer at Fort Clayton, Canal Zone in Panama and was fluent in French, German, Italian and Spanish. LTC Reuben Horner was a graduate of the University of Arizona and a recipient of the Silver Star with service in the Central Intelligence Agency prior to his assignment with the Turkish Army. LTC James R. Hillard was a Wilberforce graduate, who became the senior African American in the Armor branch, had served as a military advisor to the Vietnamese army and was assigned as chief of the Publications Branch in the Office of the Chief of Military History. LTC Ronald W. Mordecai was a special weapons ammunition expert who had served in the Korean War. COL Hubert L. Jones graduated from West Virginia State and performed combat duty in Korean as an Intelligence Officer with the 5th Air Force where he received an *on the spot* promotion for outstanding service. LTC Frederic E. Davison with bachelor and master of science degrees from Howard was selected as the first African American regular Army officer to attend the Army War College course at Carlisle Barracks in Pennsylvania which began in August 1962. CPT Edward Brooke, with a degree from Howard, served in the 366th Infantry Regiment during WWII and received a law degree from Boston University, campaigned unsuccessfully for the office of Massachusetts Secretary of State but in 1967 was sworn in as the junior U.S. Senator from Massachusetts. LTC David A. Lane, a graduate of Bowdoin College and Harvard, was assigned to the Historical Section of Headquarters US Army in Europe before retiring from military service. MAJ Edward D. Hinkson graduated from the University of Omaha with combat experience in the Pacific during WWII. He was extremely knowledgeable in the area of geopolitics and was assigned as the West Virginia State PMST. LTC Joseph L. Bailey, a graduate of West Virginia State, was the senior African American officer in the Judge Advocate General's Corps. Although a certified attorney prior to entering the military, his more than thirty years were performed in the Infantry branch. LTC Merle J. Smith was a West Virginia State ROTC graduate who had served as PMS at Howard University and was assigned to the faculty of the Ordnance School at Fort Holabird in Baltimore, Maryland. LTC Daniel James, Jr., with a commendable combat record in Korea and one of the outstanding Air Force jet pilots, was appointed squadron commander of the 81st Fighter Wing at Bentwaters, England. COL Clarence M. Davenport was a 1943 USMA graduate who served with the 366th Regiment during WWII. He also graduated with honors from the University of California with a Master's degree in bioradiology. He was assigned to the National Guard Bureau in the Pentagon and was selected for an assignment in the Office of the Director of Defense Research Engineering. COL Hyman Y. Chase graduated from Howard and Stanford Universities and had earned a Ph.D. degree in zoology. He taught at Howard before entering the Army in 1940 and serving in combat in Italy. Prior to retiring, COL Chase served as the chief of the US Military Mission in Liberia. The majority of the officers had received their commissions through the ROTC programs.[2]

LTC John T. Martin, Executive to the Counselor in the Office of the Assistant Secretary of Defense, recognized the significance of maintaining a roster of senior African American officers which he compiled. On September 25, 1962, he emphasized that with the promotion of COL James D. Fowler, a 1941 USMA graduate, the quantity of senior field grade officers in the Army was increased to six. MG Benjamin O. Davis, Jr., assigned as Director of Manpower and Organization, Office Deputy Chief of Staff for Operations, Headquarters, USAF in the Pentagon, was the senior Air Force officer. There were eight Air Force colonels which included COL Vance H.

Marchbanks, a medical officer serving with Project MERCURY. LCDR Samuel L. Gravely became the first African American commanding a Naval ship in modern times, but the senior Naval officer was CDR John H. Jackson, a reservist and physician serving at the US Naval Hospital in St. Albans, New York. There were no field grade officers in the United States Marine Corps although Navy CDR Thomas D. Parham was serving as a Chaplain with the Marines Corps at San Diego. The United States Coast Guard had three officers and an aviator with LT Bobby C. Wilks serving as the senior officer.[3] LTC Martin envisioned that changes that reflected the variety of occupations and skills of active duty and retired officers in addition to those with less than the required years for retirement would influence ROTC cadets. He and Evans thought the presence of African Americans as Army field grade commanders and staff officers and Air Force B-52 and tactical air wing commanders as well as civilian leaders in significant assignments would also inspire the cadets.[4]

LTC Edward D. Hinkson of West Virginia State considered the roster distributed in 1962 as a valuable reference concerning the substantial progress accomplished in the armed forces and rendered a unique service to military college officials. Emphasizing the character of enrollment at the colleges which was becoming more representative of the state population, communication with the African American students and staff concerning certain matters had become more difficult. The problem which existed pertained to preserving the identity of African Americans in a critical area where they had not accepted their minority status and where the most identifiable reaction to this change was resignation. The roster was an inspirational instrument especially with the inclusion of military science and aeroscience graduates whose exemplary performances had encouraged cadets. LTC Hinkson was gratified with the 6.48 percent increase in the graduation of commissioned officers attending service schools during the previous fiscal year but he requested that TAG implement specific measures to increase the procurement and training of qualified African American candidates. He urged the inclusion of African American recipients of the Medal of Honor in future rosters because little information was disseminated and the roster would have immeasurable value to interested citizens.[5]

LTC L. W. Cracken with the Maryland State AFROTC, a sub-detachment of the division of the University of Maryland, was equally interested in the roster which had a favorable effect on students and faculty. Many faculty members who served as officers during WWII expressed their surprise at the wide range of officer assignments. LTC Cracken felt the roster was an extremely motivational document and its distribution in the Princess Anne area would have positive results.[6]

Requiring military training as an elective or two-year obligation for all qualified freshman had always been an issue for many college officials. An Army staff study in 1960 revealed that in programs where colleges changed from required to elective military training the participation in the basic courses declined by 50 percent and there was a significant decline of cadets in the advanced program and commissions granted. Agitation for changing the requirement to an elective at seventeen major universities was a concern of the CRROTC, MG Frederick M. Warren, and the Deputy Assistant Chief of Staff for Reserve Components, BG M. W. Schewe.[7]

The ROTC Vitalization Act of 1964, Public Law 88-647, called for extensive changes in agreements between the Department of the Army and educational institutions with ROTC detachments. Rather than attempting to modify existing agreements, the parties developed a new agreement, which incorporated Department of the Army policies and requirements for the establishment and retention of ROTC detachments.

Enacted on October 13, 1964, the ROTC Vitalization Act enabled more flexibility for ROTC programs designed to challenge students. Institutions were permitted to retain their four-year programs with a summer camp after the junior year, change to a two-year program with two summer camps, or provide both programs of instruction. The addition of the two-year program allowed training of students transferring from junior colleges and did not rely on decisions by freshmen concerning their participation in ROTC programs. The revision also enabled some students engaged in curricula where academic pressure was unusually severe to pursue ROTC. However, scholarship assistance was available only to students participating in four-year programs.

Decisions to maintain elective or compulsory ROTC programs were the responsibility of colleges. All participants in the advanced course were required to enlist in a Reserve Component for a specified period. This provision by Congress was to ensure students' compliance with the spirit of their contracts and to outline the appropriate action against cadets who refused to accept commissions upon the completion of the course. The Department of Army policy required active duty prior to graduation only if there were evidence of a willful breach of contracts. However, cadets who dropped the ROTC program or withdrew from college for academic, physical or other bona fide reasons were discharged from the Army Reserve. Cadets refusing to accept a commission were normally scheduled for the draft within two years. Plans were formulated for the completion of the agreements by each educational institution by April 1, 1965.[8]

An assessment by LTC Samuel F. Sampson revealed that the most critical problem at Florida A and M evaluated by the president and the academic Dean was the lack of a planned program for entering freshmen. The major student deficiencies were in basic English and mathematics and an apparent lack of interest or apathy among the academic leadership in providing solutions to eliminate inequities at the freshmen and sophomore levels. He alleged there was a noticeable absence of a professional academic atmosphere with the ROTC problem becoming his personal problem. LTC Sampson informed COL Willard C. Stewart, Executive to the Deputy Assistant Secretary of Defense, on November 24, 1964 that standards in the ROTC program must be raised to produce commissioned officers capable of competing nationally with ROTC graduates from other universities. He revised the advanced program in accordance with military classes, increased the pace of instruction, testing and classroom participation, and cadet responsibilities. Implementation of the revisions was scheduled to commence with the next MS III class but the effectiveness of the program would not statistically appear until three years later.[9]

LTC Reginald E. Crocker was equally concerned with the standing of Tuskegee ROTC in comparison with other detachments. A guest speakers program was initiated in 1964 with dynamic African American officers informing cadets of issues pertaining to their future military careers. He criticized Department of Defense films that were designed to motivate ROTC cadets and attract high school students but failed to emphasize African American achievements within the military which adversely affected students' morale and negated the efforts of his cadre. LTC Crocker recommended that the Third Army Information Officer develop a film patterned after *Army ROTC, The Decision Is Yours*, depicting Tuskegee ROTC graduates. With a competent officer serving as technical advisor and graduates serving in a variety of capacities, he was confident that a new film would become a successful recruiting and motivational asset. The Third Army commanding general who had referred the recommendation to the Chief of the Office of Reserve Components at the Department of Army informed LTC Crocker that a localized film pertaining only to Tuskegee Institute was of little value to most of the 247 ROTC detachments and rejected the project. Adamant in having ROTC revise its film program which systematically excluded African Americans, LTC Crocker conveyed his recommendations to LTC John T. Martin, explaining that he had pursued the issue to the extent of his capability, and emphasized that by the failure to include African Americans in forthcoming films the Army would fail to capitalize on an available source of needed of manpower.[10]

LTC Crocker also conveyed his enthusiasm to LTC Martin concerning an *Army Times* announcement reporting the transfer of COL Frederic Davison to Fort Bliss, Texas to the 199th Infantry Brigade and surmised the mil-

Tuskegee Institute PMS&T with cadre and cadets. (Courtesy of Tuskegee University Archives, Tuskegee, AL)

itary was grooming him for something special.[11] African Americans realized the significance of the nomination was symbolic because COL Davison became the first ROTC graduate from a historically African American institution to receive an assignment with a potential of promotion to flag rank, thereby giving impetus to the ROTC program. James C. Evans on August 20, 1968 did not restrain his admiration when he notified COL Davison of his great pleasure in coordinating with COL Hyman Y. Chase and numerous other senior sponsors who had supported him and were expressing their pride over his achievement. Elated with the success and avoiding the necessity of dwelling upon details, Evans considered the eventual promotion of COL Davison to brigadier general was a source of pride, and joined with others in offering congratulations and saying *"we knew he could do it."* He informed COL Chase of the advancement of his protégé Freddy Davison and congratulated him on the hundreds of other young officers commissioned while he served as the Howard PMS. The achievements of the ROTC graduates revealed the strength and validity of the ROTC program.[12]

Upgrading minority participation in the advanced program had become a pressing issue by June 1968 and a twofold plan was developed by the Army. The twin objectives were increasing minority enrollment and enhancing the attractiveness of the program for highly qualified minority students without lowering the enrollment standards. The adjutant general of Headquarters, U.S. Continental Command at Fort Monroe, Virginia stressed that the military was competing with business firms which were attempting to attract highly qualified minority personnel since the enactment of the Civil Rights Act of 1964 and the formation of the Equal Employment Opportunity Commission. He emphasized that corporate training programs, attractive salaries and opportunities of advancement must not deter ROTC recruiting which offered similar advantages involving financial assistance, leadership training, and a commission with opportunities to contribute significantly to national defense and national welfare. The major requirements implemented included soliciting support from the Army Advisory Panel on ROTC Affairs in obtaining support from educators and their organizations, from the Department of Health, Education, and Welfare and other appropriate agencies within the District of Columbia area, and from leaders of national minority organizations. The requirements also involved assistance from senior military and civilian officials with the Department of the Army, Department of Defense and other governmental agencies to give speeches and provide articles and manuscripts that were useful in recruiting undergraduate students.[13]

Problems relating to ROTC matters caused Evans to confide in COL Chase concerning the interest of the Secretary of the Army in the revitalization of ROTC at African American colleges and universities. Students nationwide in 1969 were showing their disaffection but the Department of the Army had not removed quota limitations and instead had mounted a

MG Frederic E. Davison, the first African American cadet commissioned from an historically African American institution to attain the rank of brigadier general, returned to Howard and participated in an awards ceremony. (Courtesy of the Moorland-Spingarn Research Center, Howard University Archives)

massive effort to increase minority ROTC input, particularly at MS I and MS II levels. Evans only hoped that it was not too little too late, minority-wise or otherwise. He praised COL Chase for the leadership he had given to the Howard ROTC detachment and similarly recognized the tremendous contribution of COL West A. Hamilton when he commanded the Prairie View A and M ROTC detachment.[14] When Evans spoke during Howard University's ROTC Awards Day Assembly, the event provided a reassuring affirmation, and a contrast to the general college scenes as portrayed by the media.[15]

An analysis of a major factor that affected officer production was the enrollment of students in African American institutions which had increased slower than at other institutions. The male enrollment at 12 host ROTC institutions for 1965-1966 was 18,258 and by 1969-1970 there was an enrollment of 21,761 or an increase of 12 percent. ROTC programs nationwide experienced a decline from 117,422 in 1966 to 73,705 in 1971 with detachments at African American colleges and universities decreasing from 7,288 to 3,981, representing a 45 percent decrease compared to the nationwide decline of 59 percent. However, the establishment of three additional detachments which increased the total from thirteen to sixteen in 1970 caused an increase in the percentage of enrollment and a ratio of student participation that was higher than other institutions. African American enrollment had increased from 234,000 in 1964 to 492,000 in 1970 which represented a 110 percent increase which probably would have been higher with the inclusion of two other institutions, Lincoln and West Virginia State, which traditionally were considered as African American colleges.[16]

Ironically, West Virginia State which joined Lincoln, Howard and Morgan as a fully accredited institution had encouraged integrated cadres, and after World War II John W. Davis had fostered integration with the admission of white students in several vocational and civil defense training programs and summer courses. Efforts to integrate the faculty was initiated before 1954. The West Virginia Council of State College and University Presidents submitted a draft resolution to the State Board of Education supporting the admission of African American students to state colleges to pursue undergraduate programs not offered at West Virginia State or Bluefield State College. Student enrollment which peaked at 1,791 in 1947 because of the high enrollment of veterans had fallen nearly 50 percent in 1953 to 837 students and threatened the reduction of faculty and staff. Private corporations further threatened to purchase property planned for the expansion of athletic activities. President William J. L. Wallace fearing the college might become a dying institution was cognizant of the significance of the Brown decision, and the closing of the first African American institution in 1955,

Storer College, because of integration and the transfer of students to other colleges. He was acutely aware of statements by the editor of the Charleston *Gazette* who stressed the existence of too many state colleges and questioned the presence of West Virginia State and Bluefield State since the majority of higher learning institutions were open to African American students. When the state withdrew land grant status from West Virginia State in 1957 it became the only African American college to lose land grant status although the state committed funding to maintain positions partially funded by Federal appropriations which included support of ROTC. The enrollment of 983 students in 1954 including 182 white students had increased by 1972 to 2,269 that included 769 African American students in addition to the 210 who composed the part-time student enrollment of 1,259 in 1972.[17]

Although African American enrollment was higher at non–African American colleges where enrollment into ROTC programs was not encouraged, the major factors affecting their commissioning were their failure to enter advanced programs, their difficulty in qualifying for admission, and the inequity in the distribution of ROTC scholarships. The Directorate of Individual Training, Deputy Chief of Staff for Personnel in 1970 stressed an increase in the procurement effort of disadvantaged minority groups and authorized a study to determine methods of increasing the procurement and retention of African American officers in the active Army. A preliminary study recommended the participation of African American officers in the Army Speakers Program, nominating officers to ROTC detachments without regard to ethnicity, renewed emphasis on command counseling of potential OCS candidates from African American enlisted personnel and reemphasis on recruiting for USMA, ROTC and OCS. After approval of the preliminary study by DCSPER, another analysis exclusively devoted to officer procurement through ROTC was conducted and specific recommendations were submitted. In addition to scholarships awarded on a nationwide competitive basis, a four-year ROTC scholarship was allocated to each JROTC/National Defense Cadet Corps high school within communities designated by the Office of Equal Opportunity as a poverty area beginning with the 1972-1973 academic year. There were also seventy-five three-year ROTC scholarships awarded to 3 percent of the host institutions with the highest percentage of students with annual family incomes less than $6,000, and this provision pertained to fourteen colleges of which ten were African American colleges. A continual review of seven institutions concerning their ability to host ROTC detachments was conducted, and they were encouraged to implement cross-enrollment with emphasis on junior colleges. A methodology was developed by the Behavior and Science Research Laboratory to assess aptitude, and the military potential of ROTC applicants, and minority recruiting offices were established at Department of Army. CONARC and CONUS were established with the specific missions of developing and executing specialized minority recruiting programs. In addition, Congress increased ROTC scholarships from 5,500 to 6,500 with 20 percent available for two-year scholarships with the expectation that minority groups would benefit from the revision.[18]

The PMS acknowledged their difficulty in recruiting for the advanced program and specifically cited three primary factors concerning student opposition to advanced ROTC. The most significant was the inability of students to qualify because of failure to pass the RQ Test or meet their academic standards. There was nearly unanimous PMS agreement that the RQ Test adversely affected advance enrollment although the role of the test as a screening device had been minimized. They considered the test a culturally biased measurement and many students who were otherwise qualified failed to attain a satisfactory score. Previously PMS had complained about the procedure, especially COL Clarence M. Hurtt of Morgan State who obtained permission to initiate a pilot program to enroll nine students on a probationary basis into advanced ROTC who had failed the test. Jackson State on June 9, 1970 received similar authorization and by 1972 there were eleven participating institutions in the Expanded ROTC Opportunities Program, eight of which were African American colleges. Approximately 50 percent of the PMS did not endorse the program. They adhered to the maintenance of established standards and some referred to the Expanded ROTC Opportunities Program as a counterpart to Project 100,000 which implied the acceptance of substandard performance of African Americans. However, most objected to the application of the RQ Test as a screening device and considered grade point average, the Scholastic Aptitude Test, and PMS evaluations were more effective predictors of potential than the RQ Test. They also felt that ROTC recruiters had high expectations of results gained from efforts directed toward high school principals, counselors and African American organizations but they eventually realized that these groups were more interested in their own goals than those of the Army and determined the most effective recruiting efforts were directly toward prospective students and their families.[19]

Other factors that affected student enrollment into advanced ROTC programs were the incompatibility of the Army with career goals and opportunities, an unfavorable image of the Army in Vietnam, opposition to mandatory ROTC participation for freshmen and sophomore students and an increasing disrespect of racial ethnicity. In an era when ROTC enrollment was increasing because of more students attending colleges and when African Americans serving in Southeast Asia were regarded as unsung heroes, students had formed the Student Nonviolent Coordinating Committee to protest civil rights injustices and denounce the war in Vietnam as well as military service under the selective service system. The NAACP Youth and College Division in 1967 proposed that the draft be eliminated and replaced with a system of voluntary service to fight poverty and discrimination within the United States. Michael Mitchell who served as chairman of the NAACP special committee that reviewed the selective service system and Isaac Williams serving as President of the Youth Work Committee denounced the practice of granting deferments to the educational elite of college students at the expense of those, particularly African Americans, who were economically and educationally disadvantaged by circumstances beyond their control.[20]

Discriminatory legislation and segregationist activities that affected the student performance, especially in southern states where the majority of African American colleges and universities were enrolled, were deployed by African Americans. The violence against the Freedom Riders was condemned, as were a series of bombings that reached an apogee with the damage to a church in Birmingham that caused the death of four children. Students understood the anger and frustrations of their parents who were denied suffrage and realized that the Voting Rights Act of 1965 would not alleviate the problems which persisted during the Civil Rights movement. Many students concurred with the efforts of Robert Williams in North Carolina and the Deacons for Defense and Justice in Alabama in their attempts to protect African American citizens. They were cognizant of police brutality in incidents which involved Fannie Lou Hamer and other African American females. Students assessed the value of the Black Panther movement and the exhortations expressions of Bobby Seale who urged the necessity of African Americans to "seize the time" for justice, equality and freedom. The surveillance activities of the Federal Bureau of Investigation and the horrendous death of Fred Hampton influenced African American students to despise the FBI and conclude that the struggle for democracy was within the United States instead of volunteer service in Vietnam. They were aware that while Dr. Martin L. King endeavored through the Southern Christian Leadership Conference to gain full equality for African Americans he opposed the war in Vietnam until his assassination in Memphis, Tennessee on April 4, 1968. The civil unrest that occurred after his death only contributed to their adverse experiences and encouraged many students to oppose the draft and resist mandatory enrollment into ROTC programs.[21]

The sit-in demonstrations had heightened the attention of African Americans throughout the nation and the "Freedom" songs and musicians associated with the movement increased musically the knowledge of students. The Greensboro sit-ins, the Freedom Rides of 1961 and the confrontations in Mississippi inspired musicians to financially support the Congress of Racial Equality, the National Association for the Advancement of Colored People, and the Student Nonviolent Coordinating Committee, which enabled them to fund the tremendous cost of bail for students and legal fees. With concerts sponsored by SNCC and their friends from June 1962 to December 1963, approximately $359,000 were raised that enabled the establishment of voter registration projects in Alabama, Georgia, Mississippi and Danville, Virginia. CORE sponsored concerts in New York at the Village Gate on August 7, 1960 and at Goodson's Town Cabaret on November 17, 1963 while SNCC on February 1, 1963 sponsored "A Salute to Southern Students" at Carnegie Hall in recognition of their courage, dedication and persistent struggle for humanity and dignity. In support of the SCLC and A. Philip Randolph, musicians performed at the Apollo Theater on August 23, 1963 in recognition of the "Emancipation March on Washington for Jobs and Freedom." Art Blakey and the Jazz Messengers' dynamic album, *The Freedom Rider*, is indicative of their commitment to equality and justice. Julian "Cannonball" Adderley's Quintet's *The Price You Got to Pay To Be Free* is also an astounding tribute to the Civil Rights movement. The frustration of the adverse racial situations, therefore, is clearly understood when Nina Simone recorded *Mississippi God Damn*. The contributions of musicians and the Freedom Songs affected the career aspirations of many cadets and influenced their decisions against volunteer enrollment into advanced ROTC programs.[22]

Many students were influenced by the *Autobiography of Malcolm X* and the direct approach which Malcolm X who became El-Hajj Malik El-Shabazz articulated to problems confronting African American advancement and proposed possible solutions. They began to inculcate his views that African Americans must own their communities, which included the resources and institutions within their communities. He also stressed that they must not hesitate to utilize any means necessary to accomplish their goals, must develop a sense of Black Nationalism to unify and prevent outside forces from controlling their movements and communities. In addition, he emphasized they must recognize that their primary enemy had always been the legalized established institutions and national government and anyone, regardless of ethnicity, who supported those institutions and government. They accepted the premise that all authority not appointed, controlled or elected by African Americans should be ejected by force or any means necessary. Stokely Carmichael, who became the prime minister of the Black Panther Party and later became Kwame Ture a proponent of Pan Africanism, agreed with El-Hajj Malik El-Shabazz's assessment of the central problem in the United States which was institutionalized racism that caused an *American Dilemma* in the summer of 1966 during the Freedom March through Mississippi that influenced Carmichael to formulate and express his concept of Black Power.[23]

African American colleges were a primary focus of Stokely Carmichael and SNCC because at these schools students were not demanding integrated facilities and instruction and the presence of white faculty, administrators and students was extremely small. However, the African American student revolts in 1967 and 1968 shifted from emphasizing confrontations on separate areas of student life on college campuses and campuses were no longer considered as merely bases of operations and recruitment. The campus became the main battleground of the struggle because of the need for students to establish their objectives and responsibilities which were traditionally assumed by oppressive individuals, black or white, in their communities. Students realized for the first time that the educational system was not the shining ideal as expressed by white apologists, and they regarded themselves as constituting an elite vanguard in the struggle of Black liberation. Therefore, students returned to the campuses where they channeled their political activities into the struggle for liberation because of their unreadiness to engage in activities which had either augmented or replaced nonviolent action, such as violently engaging police, national guardsmen and state troopers in armed resistance, as legitimate means of achieving liberation.[24]

Carmichael visited Morgan State on January 28, 1967 and criticized Martin D. Jenkins for denying an earlier campus appearance. He denounced accusations that his visitation influenced the gubernatorial election where Spiro T. Agnew was opposed by segregationist George P. Mahoney. Carmichael was appalled by Jenkins' support of compulsory ROTC which encouraged institutionalized violence and claimed that Black Power was about violence. Demonstrating students requested the elimination of ROTC, a reduction of chaperons required for social affairs, the teaching of African American education for African Americans, a revision of dormitory regulations, the elimination of physical education especially for veterans, revisions in registration procedures, the elimination of provisions concerning missed classes, a more liberal cultural program, and dismissal of classes for special programs. Jenkins referred to student power as the catalyst for change at Morgan State. He denounced efforts to close the university and advised students to submit their grievances through the Student Government Association. However, Jenkins acquiesced and agreed to meet with a group of protest leaders that included Tama Myers, president of the Student Government Association, Paulette Holtsclaw, vice president of the Student Government

Association, Cheryl Dorsey, editor of the *Spokesman*, Fred Mason, vice president of the Afro-American Society, John Clark, vice president of the Social Science Club, Clarence Davis, president of the Social Science Club, John Lanier and Bassard Jordan. Jenkins announced that among the revisions of university policies was the elimination of compulsory ROTC in the fall of 1968. He cautioned and reminded students that ROTC was the chief source of African American officers and a decline of student enrollment into the voluntary ROTC program that caused a reduction of required commissioned officers would place the college in jeopardy of losing ROTC to another institution. He urged the majority of freshmen and sophomores to continue their participation in the basic ROTC program. LTC Grady A. Culpepper was confident that the achievements of the ROTC brigade would continue and supporters of military science felt that students who were subject to the draft would base their decision on whether to enter military service as commissioned officers or enlisted personnel. The annual ROTC celebration terminated the twenty-year history of compulsory two-year military training at Morgan State. However, the effects of the anticipated reduction were lessened with the expansion of the program to Coppin State College. Cadet morale and *esprit de corps* were improved when nine of 27 cadets finished in the top 10 percent of 6,500 cadets attending the summer camp at Indiantown Gap Military Reservation in Annville, Pennsylvania.[25]

Other effects of the concessions were the elimination of several varsity programs, the weakening of intramural programs and reductions of faculty and staff because of reduced participation in physical education activities and a change in student attitudes and class attendance especially in courses which were not directly related to their curricula majors. These conditions in part contributed to the entrenchment of the faculty in other disciplines, as administrators and staff during the next decade. More significantly, many African American colleges and universities experienced similar changes during this era of student demonstrations. The elimination of mandatory ROTC was an objective of a campus group called DISSENT which was formed in September 1964 by a group of students who had participated in the summer 1964 Civil Rights movement. Demonstrations at the White House called for Federal intervention in Selma, Alabama in support of voter registration and participation, and in Washington on April 17, 1965 to endorse the Students for a Democratic Society protest of American involvement in Vietnam. DISSENT on March 9, 1965 also opposed a faculty decision to continue compulsory basic ROTC. On December 15, 1965, DISSENT held a panel on Vietnam and the American Conscience. The participants were Father Philip Berrigan of St. Peter Claver Catholic Church, Sam Legg in the Counseling Office of Morgan State, Clifford Duran of the

Philosophy Department, Reverend Howard Cornish, Director of the Morgan State Christian Center, and Morgan student Robert Hinton. Students further criticized ROTC revisions in the *Spokesman* with statements allegedly by Befor A. Battle that referred to military science as the Reserve Officers Trivia Group (ROTG) under the leadership of the new Civilian Professor of Militant Science, the Honorable Butcher U. Quick.[26]

In 1967 Carmichael attended the SNCC national organizational meeting in Nashville and appeared on the campus of Tennessee A and I where he was denounced by university administrators who refused to grant an official appearance and accused Carmichael of trespassing, although permission to speak at Vanderbilt University's Impact Symposium was granted.[27] SNCC reorganized some of its local organizations to ensure that policy decisions were not formulated by white participants and planned to increase civil rights activities and student demonstrations in several cities that included Houston where approximately 488 Texas Southern University students were arrested on campus by local policemen.[28]

South Carolina student grievances were primarily influenced by the policies of Benner C. Turner who was dean of the law school, which was disestablished in 1966, prior to assuming the presidency of the college. They denounced the erection of a fence topped with barbed wire, which was known as the "Berlin Wall," that separated the campus from that of Claflin College, the non-renewal of contracts for three teaching fellows, especially Thomas Wirth, who was appalled by the limiting and inferior segregated public school system that affected students prior to their admission to South Carolina State, and the suspension of three students who demonstrated in front of the President's home. The class Presidents organized approximately 80 percent of the students in a two-week protest that demanded quality education and appropriations for the college by state officials. The senior class President, Isaac Williams, was the leader of the protest. Matthew J. Perry, the chief legal counsel for the state NAACP, Isaac McGraw of the state Department of Education, and other officials' negotiations with the students resulted in the readmission of the suspended students, and a court order from U.S. District Judge Robert Hemphill which stressed that the college regulation authorizing suspensions placed restraint on free speech and the right of assembly and therefore violated the First Amendment. Williams gained authority to form a campus NAACP chapter and M. Maceo Nance, who replaced Turner after his retirement, accepted students to all college standing committees, eliminated compulsory chapel attendance and eliminated dress requirements during student meals. Students also formed the Black Awareness Coordinating Committee and joined local SNCC activities in Orangeburg. Evidently, ROTC was not a major issue since Williams was commissioned and served in Vietnam. In 1969, he returned to South Carolina and became the NAACP field secretary.[29]

Students also supported Muhammad Ali who was indicted in Houston, Texas, for refusing induction into the military because of his ministry in the Nation of Islam and moral opposition to warfare in Vietnam. The boxing commission withdrew his heavyweight championship and suspended his participation in boxing for three years. These actions became more significant when many athletes in other sports were not selected by their draft boards or were assigned to National Guard detachments which required participation during the months which did not interfere with their athletic careers. Muhammad Ali had also gained support from Africans who protested his scheduled trial on April 11, 1967 and emphasized he was more beneficial to the United States government in the ring than on the battlefield.[30]

Rudolph F. Pierce, President of the Hampton Student Government Association, and Kenneth A. Murphy, chairman of the Coordinating Committee, after a meeting held in Harkness Hall on May 1, 1967, submitted a petition from 416 male students to the faculty dean, Hugh M. Gloster, requesting the termination of compulsory ROTC. The petition emphasized that military science was not consistent with their graduation program unless students completed the advanced program and that all of the total quality points obtained from basic ROTC were not among the quality points required for graduation. The students considered the inclusion of the military science program incongruent with their career goals and regarded the training as an exercise in futility for those not desiring enrollment into the advanced program. They had conducted a survey and alleged that 120 of approximately 200 sophomores were interested in the program which was eighty-five more than the required 35 required to maintain the program. They urged Jerome H. Holland, President of Hampton, to call a special faculty meeting and convey their sentiments to the Board of Trustees during its next session. A minor problem occurred when cadets attempted to turn in their ROTC uniforms a week earlier than authorized and some dissatisfaction with the quality of their education caused them to refuse to discuss their grievances with President Holland, and threatened to close the institution. Informed that uniforms would be accepted the following week approximately 100 demonstrated at the ROTC facility before the group dispersed.[31]

In preparation for a meeting with the Executive Committee of the Board of Trustees on June 18, 1967, Holland surmised the student protest was sensitized by a campus presentation by Carmichael and by the Vietnam War. A vote during a special faculty meeting approved a recommendation to eliminate compulsory ROTC and make the program an elective. He stressed the issue affected the role of African American soldiers in the conflict, the contractual obligation of the Federal government and the military tradition established by the institute which was a matter of alumni interest. Holland stressed the program required further analysis and recommended completion of a compulsory program for freshmen and enrollment on a voluntary basis for sophomores. He was further aware of the Army's dependence on a successful ROTC program which in 1965 produced 45 percent of the 100,000 commissioned officers in the active Army which included 85 percent of all 2LTs and 67 percent of 1LTs. More significantly, ROTC annually produced approximately twenty-two times more officers than the USMA. The Hampton PMS emphasized that freshmen were not familiar with ROTC or the Reserve Forces Act of 1955, and therefore unable to determine whether they should enroll in the program, that sophomores were inclined to view only the relevance of the immediate future and considered the small credit allowed for ROTC as not important, and that many were influenced by the anti-militarism prevalent on many campuses during peacetime. LTC Ernest B. Johnson concluded that the decision should be made for freshmen and that in the First Army area 50 percent of the ninety-one colleges with ROTC programs required the completion of the basic course. Students learned a greater appreciation of American military history and benefited from the acquisition of skills pertaining to leadership, self-discipline, teamwork, responsibility, self esteem and appearance. Considering that approximately fifteen percent or less would enroll in the basic course, the smaller potential officers production would cause the termination of the program. However, the forced retention of sophomores who were not interested and who probably would not become suitable officers would have adversely influenced freshmen who were considering a commissioned service.

The elimination of unwilling students with negative attitudes permitted the department of military science to evaluate the viability of the advanced program and simultaneously provide a better selection than a completely volunteer program. The reduced enrollment would automatically reduce instructor requirements and financial costs in maintaining ROTC. The revision was recommended for implementation at the beginning of the Fall 1967 semester to allow further analysis of the military science program. The Hampton Board of Trustees on April 26, 1968 approved a recommendation which provided for voluntary ROTC effective with the commencement of the 1968-1969 academic year. A Faculty-Administration Advisory Committee was also established to advise Holland on matters pertaining to ROTC, to develop and propose programs for the maintenance of a viable program, to review the curriculum and recommend revisions, to revise the curriculum, to evaluate and change academic credit allocated for ROTC courses, to represent the interests of the ROTC program at the Administrative Council and to faculty committees, to serve on a joint military-faculty board to hear appeals and consider admission into the advanced courses as well as select cadets for scholarships, branch selection and disenrollment.[32] *Esprit de corps* was maintained through an aggressive program relating to the leadership training offered by the military science department and with cadet participation in the Pershing Rifles, the ROTC band, a reorganized Counter Guerilla Company and a reactivated Scabbard and Blade Society. On June 21, 1968, the executive committee of the board of trustees also approved eighteen academic credit hours for the four-year ROTC program. However, Howard V. Young, Chairmen of the Department of History and Political Science urged that students be given the opportunity to learn more about the accomplishments of African Americans to foster a greater consciousness of racial identity and proposed African and African American courses as social science alternatives for cadets.[33]

Compulsory AFROTC at Tennessee A and I was terminated in the fall of 1967 and enrollment decreased from 1219 in 1966 to 363 in 1967 with a gradual decline to 262 in 1970. The policy revision simultaneously decreased emotional discontentment toward the Vietnam War with the elimination of perceived military regimentation but cadets were disturbed by the assassinations of Reverend Martin L. King of the Southern Christian Leadership Conference, who demonstrated against racism, war and poverty, and Senator Robert Kennedy. The AFROTC building which was really a reconverted field house containing Air Science records was destroyed by fire. Many students deplored the demonstrations and the loss of the AFROTC building, and AFROTC was relocated to the library while the university was given an opportunity to plan and design a modern AFROTC.[34]

In May 1967, Tennessee State A and I Cadet COL Willie Greer commanded a joint review of AFROTC, NROTC and ROTC detachments from Tennessee State University and Vanderbilt University in honor of Assistant Secretary Thomas Morris who visited Nashville. Assistant Secretary Morris emphasized the participation of approximately 45,000 African American personnel serving in Vietnam who volunteered more frequently than others for hazardous duty and represented 10 percent of the deployed force. He praised the contributions of Tennessee State AFROTC which annually commissioned approximately twenty officers.[35]

Student unrest at Delaware State College ignited by protests on May 10, 1968 over the designation of a residence hall in honor of Medger Evers contributed to the reduction of the ROTC program to a one semester voluntary course requirement by 1969.[36] G. Leon Netterville met with several

Southern A and M administrators on October 18, 1968 to consider student senate proposals which included the feasibility of voluntary ROTC that was approved by the faculty. Similar to other institutions the enrollment of a brigade of three battalions with approximately 1400 was reduced to a battalion of approximately 400 cadets. LTC Warren Rhodes was confident that the revision would improve the quality of the program and the forty-nine students who entered the advanced program, the largest in the history of the institution, was significant. The ROTC objective was an enrollment of between sixty and seventy cadets in the advanced program while maintaining its traditional leadership as the major producer of qualified African American officers.[37]

Students empathized with African American athletes and their planned boycott of the 1968 International Olympic games in Mexico City. They were cognizant of a meeting held in New York on December 15, 1967 where African Americans, including Louis Lomax and Floyd McKissick, concurred with Dr. Martin L. King's view that perhaps the condition of race relations in the nation demanded a total boycott of the International Olympics by black people as a means of nonviolent protest. Harry Edwards released demands which requested the restoration of the heavyweight title to Muhammad Ali and his right to compete in the sport of boxing in the United States, the removal of Avery Brundage as chairman of the International Olympic Committee, curtailment and elimination of an all-white team from the Union of South Africa and Southern Rhodesia from Olympic competition, the addition of at least two African American coaches to the men's track and field coaching staff and two others to the policy committee prior to the 1968 competition, and a complete desegregation of the New York Athletic Club. Achieving success with the banning of South Africa from the Olympics, African Americans with the Olympic Committee for Human Rights dedicated African American participation in the 1968 Olympics as a memorial to Dr. Martin L. King. The exceptional performances and reactions of Lee Evans and John Carlos against the racial attitudes of some of the international Olympic officials were inspirational to African American students. Their achievements and the contributions of others influenced the imitation of the black power salute, evoked students' expressions of James Brown's *I'm Black and I'm Proud*, and provoked proud and forceful affirmations of *Right On*.[38]

The divisiveness caused by the war in Vietnam affected American society and continued increased student unrest and rejection of authority. African Americans agreed with Edwin Starr's protest song "War" and participated in a nationwide demonstration in opposition to the draft and declared the Vietnam War unjust and immoral. Wiley College students were displeased with the inaction of President T. W. Cole and his failure to implement agreements reached during their protest earlier in February of 1969. Alleging the administration of President Richard M. Nixon had implemented a policy of black genocide in Vietnam, some Morgan State faculty and students joined the Vietnam Moratorium Day demonstration held on October 15, 1969 in Washington. Students demanded the immediate and total withdrawal of African American armed forces personnel from Vietnam and the acceptance of nothing less than self-determination and liberation for African Americans rather than the suppression of Vietnamese. Jenkins stressed that Morgan State as a state institution was not permitted to participate in social action demonstrations and emphasized policy statements concerning the dismissal of classes by faculty and student absences.[39] Herman H. Long of Talladega College during the decade of student unrest was flexible, progressive, sympathized with students and their grievances, and was regarded as a students' president.[40]

Howard students were affected by reactions to the war in Vietnam and some urged more aggressive participation in several events which protested African American involvement. They acknowledged the concern of Senator Ted Kennedy who concluded that the Armed Forces Improvement Act of 1967 would create a completely voluntary professional army with African Americans disproportionally represented in the Army and would give the false impression that the military offered the best opportunities for advancement in the American society. Major emphasis was placed on the elimination of the mandatory draft system since it infringed on constitutional liberties and other freedoms associated with a free democratic system. They further acknowledged that if a draft was necessary there should have been special exclusion provisions for oppressed minorities which included African Americans, Puerto Ricans, Native Americans, and citizens located in the regions of Appalachia and the Ozarks. A protest by approximately 300 students in April 1967 led by professor Nathaniel Hare was conducted during a campus appearance by LTG Lewis B. Hershey, and several students denounced the actions of professor Frank Snowden and president James M. Nabrit, Jr. Some students also supported the Mobilization for Peace in Vietnam protest held at the United Nations headquarters in New York City during May 1967.[41]

Howard's faculty was disunited on the issue of mandatory ROTC and several deans expressed their concern over the viability of the program. The elimination of a mandatory program would result in the loss of officer production and weaken the major attributes involving character, discipline and citizenship. A student boycott adopted demands that urged the dismissal of charges against demonstrators during the Hershey appearance, the elimination of senior comprehension examinations, the non-dismissal of faculty or denial of promotion because of their political activism or political nonconformity, the elimination of compulsory ROTC, and the repeal of the policy statement on student protest issued by President Nabrit. The student protest was renewed in the fall of 1967 and Michael Harris, president of the freshmen class, and several other freshmen refused to sign a loyalty oath for induction into ROTC. Harris maintained that he was not a conscientious objector nor a radical but had reservations concerning the oath which referred to defending the nation against domestic enemies. With increased activity against African Americans in urban and rural areas during the civil rights movement, he felt that an obligation for ROTC training would involve military activities against African Americans. However, all freshmen were not opposed to military training and expressed the view that if ROTC were eliminated from the university program, there was no legitimate method of knowing what would be the demand for discontinuing other courses since many students opposed the completion of required core courses which they considered irrelevant to their major concentrations.[42]

MAJ Pierre, Acting PMS, supported any measure which enabled the successful commissioning of officers for military service but he questioned whether the goal was attainable under a voluntary program. LTC Lehman felt the issue of voluntary ROTC should have been discussed within the context of the African American experience and within the environment of Howard University. Ernest Goodman, who had served as Director of the Public Relations Office since August 1964 and had announced his resignation and accepted an assignment with the U.S. Foreign Service, stated after a demonstration in front of Douglass Hall by university students, led by the student government with support from such organizations as the Ad Hoc Committee to Abolish Compulsory ROTC and the United Black Peoples Party, that Nabrit would call an emergency meeting of the Board of Trustees and consult with the University Council composed of tenured faculty before responding to student demands in fifteen days. On November 22, 1967, Howard University announced the elimination of compulsory ROTC beginning in September 1967 but continued student demonstrations against the war in Vietnam resulted in fire damage to a wooden temporary building where the ROTC office and English department were located in 1969.[43]

Virginia State students were active in the protest against the war in Vietnam as well as compulsory ROTC. In April 1968 a spontaneous boycott influenced the drafting of a lengthy document with sixteen grievances that included the elimination of compulsory assemblies, the elimination of compulsory class attendance and noncompulsory ROTC. These issues became concerns for James F. Tucker who assumed the leadership of the college.[44]

Headquarters AFROTC at Maxwell AFB stressed that the increased anti-ROTC activities affected approximately forty-five AFROTC detachments during FY 1968. Incidents involved no violence against staff or cadets and were confined primarily to verbal abuse, sit-ins with placards and pamphlets, and articles published in official and unofficial campus newspapers. AFROTC was discussed by student and faculty groups and the essence of their discussions pertained to training which taught the art of warfare having no place on the college campus, AFROTC instructors, curricula and textbooks being of inferior quality, instructors and classes not permitting academic freedom, and institution-ROTC contracts violating faculty prerogatives concerning hiring and firing of faculty and faculty approval of courses. An analysis of the anti-ROTC activities concluded that students from the "new left" were responsible for the revolts on college campuses and that the basic issue was the presence of AFROTC on campus.[45]

The unprecedented destruction inflicted on AFROTC facilities which began in March and climaxed in May 1970 was confined primarily to non-African American institutions. Regarding the disturbance that occurred at Jackson State where two students were killed and twelve were wounded, the President's Commission on Campus Unrest reported that the tragedy could have been avoided if officers who responded to unconfirmed firings had permitted the local anti-sniper squads to cover the incident instead of firing a lethal barrage of buckshot and armor piercing ammunition into Alexander Hall crowded with students. The ROTC building was damaged by individuals who threw objects and Molotov cocktails at the building. A Federal panel headed by former Pennsylvania Governor William W. Scranton cited that the failure of law enforcement officers involved the lack of a mobilization plan which should have included a coordinated tactical plan, a unified chain of command, a dedicated radio channel for use during the disorder, a clear sense of their objective, and adequate coordination with college officials. African American colleges and universities held memorial services for the tragic events that occurred at Jackson State University and Kent State University in Ohio.[46] The opposition to social equality throughout the nation and the horrendous loss of life in Vietnam was clearly enunciated in musical selections in Marvin Gaye's album, *What's Going On?*

With African American colleges serving as the primary source of officers, the Gesell Committee was concerned with the low percent of African American officers in the armed forces but there was little optimism for immediate improvement. Excluding the large increase of procurement through the five AFROTC programs, the percentage of officers entering the Air Force

remained essentially unchanged in spite of new equal opportunity programs implemented during the civil rights era. The PNLGC had urged the
expansion of programs to their institutions and other predominantly
African American colleges but some civil rights leaders argued the establishment of detachments in African American colleges would merely per-
petuate the national segregated collegiate system. Albert B. Fitt as the first
civil rights deputy for the Department of Defense agreed, allegedly, that
with integration education would become more commonplace and the
quantity of African American graduates would increase in predominately
white colleges. However, Fitt considered African American institutions
were essential and that among the 140 without ROTC, AFROTC and
NROTC affiliation it was conceivable that some would qualify for detachments. Stephen N. Shulman, who succeeded Fitt, in February 1965 requested
the formation of ROTC detachments as an equal opportunity measure[47]
based upon the officers procurement from ROTC and AFROTC. The charts
reflect the officers commissioned at African American institutions that
influenced Shulman.

## Army Commissions

|                                     | 1964 | 1965 | 1966 | 1967 |
|-------------------------------------|------|------|------|------|
| North Carolina A and T              | 24   | 22   | 10   | 17   |
| Central State                       | 29   | 14   | 26   | 25   |
| Florida A and M                     | 29   | 15   | 23   | 15   |
| Hampton                             | 29   | 34   | 20   | 19   |
| Lincoln                             | 19   | 14   | 16   | 19   |
| Morgan State                        | 21   | 27   | 12   | 16   |
| Prairie View                        | 20   | 27   | 31   | 38   |
| South Carolina State                | 16   | 23   | 24   | 24   |
| Southern                            | 23   | 37   | 19   | 21   |
| Tuskegee                            | 14   | 14   | 20   | 26   |
| Virginia State                      | 21   | 14   | 18   | 21   |
| West Virginia State                 | 22   | 19   | 15   | 14   |
| Howard                              | 19   | 37   | 30   | 23   |
| Total                               | 286  | 297  | 264  | 278  |
| Percentage of total granted commissions | 2.4  | 2.7  | 2.5  | 2.6  |

## Air Force Commissions

|                         | 1964 | 1965 | 1966 |
|-------------------------|------|------|------|
| North Carolina A and T  | 12   | 10   | 33   |
| Howard                  | 24   | 31   | 23   |
| Maryland State          | 2    | 4    | 4    |
| Tennessee A and I       | 13   | 26   | 32   |

|          | *1964* | *1965* | *1966* |
|----------|--------|--------|--------|
| Tuskegee | 14     | 33     | 41     |
| Total    | 65     | 104    | 133    |

Source: Morris J. Mac Gregor, *Integration of the Armed Forces, 1940-1965* (Washington: Center of Military History, 1981), 570.

Arkansas A and M Normal College at Pine Bluff became the first recipient of the Defense Department's thrust to influence African American enrollment. Authorization for the establishment of ROTC at the University of Arkansas at Pine Bluff was granted in November 1967. When students enrolled in the detachment in September 1968, James C. Evans emphasized its formation culminated many years of effort by Butler T. Henderson, Chairperson of the Department of Business and Economics, who had joined the United Board for College Development in Atlanta, Georgia, university President Lawrence A. Davis and Dean Wilson who had transferred to Florida Memorial College.[48] Denmark Technical College and Orangeburg-Calhoun Technical College.[49]

Jackson State established an ROTC through the efforts of President John A. Peoples, Jr. on December 17, 1968. James C. Evans expressed his pleasure that Lawrence A. Oxley was present during the installation ceremony and stated that this historic event represented an untiring effort of having a military unit in each of the seventeen states where African American land grant colleges were formed. The program was extended to Hinds Junior College in 1973, Mary Holmes College in 1975, and to Tougaloo College.[50]

LTG William F. Train, Commander of First Army Headquarters at Fort George G. Meade, announced to Holland at Hampton on May 9, 1967 that the Department of the Army was planning the establishment of a limited quantity of new detachments during the next two years. Colleges were requested to send representatives to a meeting where an optional GMS curriculum was discussed that would augment the Regular and Modified GMS curriculum. An increased MS III enrollment was distributed among the ninety-one institutions in the First Army area. Assistant Secretary of Defense for Manpower and Reserve Affairs, Roger T. Kelly, on April 29, 1969 expressed the unique mission of ROTC in relationship to 350 colleges and universities throughout the nation where 21,000 cadets were commissioned in 1968. The total ROTC enrollment at institutions where most of the demonstrations had occurred represented only a small portion of the estimated 200,000 enroll into ROTC programs. The resolutions of protests involving curriculum content, teaching methods and faculty status were obtained through joint cooperation with universities where student disruption had occurred.

Thirteen graduates of the Howard University Army Reserve Officers Training Corps program commissioned on June 18, 1965. They are (first row, from left to right) 2LT Wallace O. Peace, Raleigh, NC; Thomas N. Malone, Montgomery, AL; Walter L. Evans, Memphis, TN; Harold L. Brooks, Philadelphia, PA; Togo D. West, Winston-Salem, NC; Charles Williams, Washington, DC; Frank N. Schubert, Washington, DC; and Taft Broome, Hickory, NC; (second row) 2LT Ernest Withers, Memphis, TN; Michael A. House, Cleveland, OH; LeRoy Randolph, Chicago, IL; Donald A. Haynes, Philadelphia, PA; and McKenzie Whitaker, Suffolk, VA. In addition to these commissioned officers, 14 graduates of the Howard University Air Force ROTC Detachment were commissioned into the U.S. Air Force. (Courtesy of the Moorland-Spingarn Research Center, Howard University Archives)

The Department of Defense was prepared to consider revisions to improve ROTC at individual colleges that would not degrade the program. Demonstrations threatened the opportunity to provide a portion of the potential national leadership to gain commissions and the nation and the military services would suffer a loss if any civilian academic community declined that opportunity. However, he was confident that the administration, faculty and students at institutions where ROTC programs were maintained shared his viewpoint.[51]

African American officer production at African American colleges and retention of officers on active duty appeared to be the only viable solution. Excluding Lincoln and West Virginia State, African American cadets comprised 1.1 percent of the advanced ROTC programs in predominately white institutions and composed approximately 1 percent of the commissioned officers although the average enrollments were 6.8 percent. At Lincoln and West Virginia State, participation in ROTC and the percentage of African American commissioned officers slightly exceeded the proportion of enrolled African American students. Procurement of African American officers through OCS was correlated with the reduction of Army personnel. In fiscal year 1969, 223 cadets were commissioned which represented 2.8 percent of the total commissioned officers and in fiscal year 1970 there were 116 commissioned or 1.5 percent of the commissioned officers. During fiscal year 1971 the total was fifty-eight or 2.6 percent, however, an increase was experienced during calendar year 1971 because of a special in-service program initiated by the Department of the Army which screened the files of SSGT and SFC that produced a potential 1,100 NCOs who were counseled by battalion commanders on opportunities as commissioned officers. Procurement through the USMA was not very promising since the 1968 graduating class commissioned only nine of the 706 commissioned officers and eight of the 800 the following year. The 1970 class was encouraging only because all eight cadets graduated in the class of 749. Three of seven cadets were commissioned in the 1971 class of 729 and although the projection for the following year was seven the class of 1973 had twenty-eight cadets.[52]

A special program designed for the retention of African American officers was not developed and all officers were managed in an overall retention program. Army projections called for a greater quantity of African American officers but as Army requirements decreased with a reduction of the armed forces, approximately 5,200 officers of 12,000 commissioned through ROTC in June 1972 were expected to receive active duty assignments with the remainder receiving training for active duty assignments. African American graduates commissioned in fiscal year 1972 were offered extended duty with the more qualified integrated into the regular Army and the others applying for indefinite active duty status. However, a serious concern was that the percentage of African American field grade officers in the ranks of MAJ and LTC in 1970 was higher than the combined percentage of company grade officers. There were 1120 and 586 respectively in the grades of MAJ and LTC but only 338 2LTs, 480 1LTs and 1,360 CPTs.[53] This alarming trend undoubtedly contributed to the extension of detachments to other qualified institutions and the enrollment of females into detachments.

Expansion of African American detachments had been implemented prior to 1970 with the establishment of Norfolk State as a branch of Virginia State. A twofold program was available and cadets were required to transfer to Virginia State College to complete their advanced course until

September 1964 when a four-year ROTC program was offered at Norfolk State. On July 1, 1969, Norfolk State was officially separated from Virginia State and in August 1987 established an extension at Elizabeth City State in North Carolina.[54] Fort Valley State organized a military science department in the fall of 1956 which offered basic ROTC for cadets. Implementing a cross-enrollment program with Mercer University in Macon in September 1969, the Department of the Army on January 25, 1962 authorized the establishment of an independent ROTC program at the college that became operational at the beginning of the 1972 academic year. The program was expanded in January 1976 to Albany State College under a cross-enrollment agreement.[55] South Carolina State in 1969 established cross-enrollment programs at Claflin College and Voorhees College.

The Army on January 28, 1971 authorized additional detachments beginning with the 1971-1972 academic year at Alabama A and M in Normal, Alabama, Alcorn A and M in Lorman, Mississippi, and Grambling College in Louisiana.[56] Alabama A and M had not offered ROTC training since the disbanding of the SATC, commanded by LT William H. Thompson, on December 20, 1918, and the establishment of a JROTC under LT William R. Small, similarity discontinued because of an Army reduction of military detachments.[57] The PNLGC supported the efforts of the presidents at Kentucky State, Langston, Lincoln, Arkansas A and M at Pine Bluff and Morris Brown in 1948 but it was not until spring of 1970 when MAJ Philip T. Blanton of Third Army met informally with students and submitted a favorable report recommending the formation of an ROTC detachment at Alabama A and M. Secretary of the Army Stanley R. Resor informed Richard D. Morrison of the selection and an examination was administered on February 25, 1971 to students interested in joining the ROTC detachment.[58]

The organization of ROTC did not occur without some student resistance to mandatory military training. Alabama A and M students in October 1971 submitted nineteen grievances to administration, faculty and staff and refused to attend classes until a response was received. A major demand was the elimination of mandatory ROTC for freshmen and sophomores and the curfew for female students. Freshmen students were cognizant of congressional legislation that continued the military draft until July 1, 1973. With the assistance of the Student Government Association they met with Vice President Henry Ponder to discuss the relevance of military training to career goals. Students organized a hunger strike, and a peaceful demonstration near Bibb Graves Hall influenced Morrison to announce on October 13, 1971 the indefinite closing of Alabama A and M which did not affect the graduate school program. Not clear about how the protest began, Morrison stated that a student who was involved in several issues was expelled and readmitted under the provision that he remained out of trouble. The student together with others attempted to submit withdrawal slips to the registrar's office and was automatically expelled. A statement was issued that closed the university after five days of protest. Morrison also stated that ROTC requirements would continue for the remainder of the academic year but agreed to reconsider the merit of compulsory ROTC. He urged students to terminate their boycott of classes, sit-in demonstrations and their refusal to eat in the dining hall. Morrison held conferences with the faculty who were attempting to keep the university open and with student leaders to resolve the issues affecting the academic schedule. He agreed to three student requests which included the establishment of a committee to review the compulsory ROTC program. Morrison stated that compulsory ROTC for freshmen and sophomores would remain in effect for the academic year but the policy would be reviewed for the next academic year. Alabama A and M instituted a voluntary ROTC system at the beginning of the next academic year.[59]

The majority of the students were not aware or were disinterested in the relentless effort of Joseph F. Drake, former president of Alabama A and M, to obtain all of the programs common to the land grant philosophy of education. He endeavored to maintain faculty members, who were loyal and dedicated to the mission of the institution, who had opportunities to seek positions elsewhere with higher salaries. However, the major objectives of Drake were establishing a military science program, instituting an engineering program, expanding research opportunities and providing cooperative extension supervision for students and faculty. He denounced the difficulty of African American colleges in securing permission to organize ROTC detachments and coordinated with Carl Murphy and the PNLGC in urging President Harry S. Truman to expand military science to their colleges and universities. Informed by Murphy that the application of Alabama A and M was ranked 177 among the colleges seeking ROTC detachments, Drake knew that the approval of the application was in the category of a miracle for acceptance. African American colleges were also informed by TAG that ROTC was not mandatory under the provisions of the Morrill Act of 1862 and 1890. Drake resubmitted his application in 1950 and was informed by James C. Evans on May 15, 1952 that the additional nineteen colleges approved for ROTC did not include Alabama A and M or any African American institution. The denial of ROTC, together with the lack of equitable funding under the Morrill legislation and subsequent federal land grant programs, hindered the advancement of Alabama A and M, and Drake was extremely perturbed by correspondence from the Birmingham Ordnance Corps District which stressed that the expansion of its activities necessitated the employment of additional personnel in engineering, physics, electronics, optics and instrumentation. The invitation which may have been sent with good intentions, when viewed by an institution that had been systematically denied opportunities to train students in these disciplines became an unintelligent backhanded slap at an oppressed institution. Therefore, Drake simply replied that the college did not have the faculty nor students available for the employment positions. The frustrated process of obtaining an ROTC detachment was relegated to his successor who fortunately accomplished the mission.[60] The success of Morrison was undoubtedly attached to the expected reduction of officer procurement caused by anti-war demonstrations, the transition from compulsory to volunteer programs at most colleges, the elimination of programs by some institutions and complaints from enlisted men who experienced their only service under the leadership of African American officers during combat operations.

Alcorn A and M officials were persistent in their efforts to obtain ROTC from January 1942 when the War Department denied the college a unit. Nine additional applications were submitted before a detachment was granted and organized by LTC Charles D. Randall who arrived on April 5, 1971 together with SGT Deloy Wade, and enrolled 203 cadets. The first students were commissioned in May 1973 when BG Edward Greer, who had served as a MSGT in the 777th Field Artillery during World War II and later was commissioned at West Virginia State in 1948, conducted the ceremony. In May 1973 the unit was expanded when Utica Junior College began a satellite unit. The Military Science Department was reorganized on July 1, 1973 and assigned to the Third ROTC Region located at Fort Riley, Kansas.[61]

The extension of ROTC enabled the formation of additional detachments at several African American colleges and universities. Virginia State in August 1974 established cross-enrollment agreements with African American institutions, Virginia Union and St. Paul's College, and Richard Bland College and John Tyler Community. Informal agreements were negotiated with J. Sergeant Reynolds Community College, Randolph Macon Community College, Southside Virginia Community College and Virginia Commonwealth University.[62] Grambling State established a Military Science Department in May 1980. The ROTC became a host unit on September 1, 1994.[63] Saint Augustine's College officials contemplated the establishment of ROTC in 1962 and after considerable deliberations an application was submitted in 1967 with approval granted to implement the program during the 1972 academic year. However, the college delayed action until April 1974 when the initial ROTC cadre arrived to commence the program in August 1974 with 140 cadets which were more than twice the anticipated enrollment. Cross-enrollment agreements with Shaw University in

Raleigh and North Carolina Wesleyan College in Rocky Mount increased the corps of cadets.[64] Morris Brown College accepted ROTC and commissioned its first Army candidates in 1980.[65] By 1995 extension centers were established at Benedict College, Bethune-Cookman College, Bowie State College, Chicago State College, which became a host institution, and Dillard University.

The same issues that influenced revisions and expansion of ROTC affected Naval decisions to expand NROTC. The request of Alvin I. Thomas, president of Prairie View A and M College, for NROTC was submitted to the Chief of Naval Personnel on November 6, 1967. Secretary of Defense Robert S. McNamara announced on December 15, 1967 that the Navy had selected Prairie View A and M to receive a detachment. This announcement was significant because it culminated the efforts of African Americans to obtain an NROTC unit. Operations Naval Notice 5450 promulgated on March 12, 1967 officially established the detachment which became the first NROTC unit organized on an African American campus and the first NROTC unit organized since 1946. CPT Francis X. Brady was reassigned from Harvard University to command NROTC and he received generous support, supplies and services from LTC Lloyd J. Stark, PMS of the Prairie View A and M ROTC. CDR Thomas had served as acting commanding officer since April 2, 1969 but with transfer of CPT Brady to the Naval District in Boston, Massachusetts he became the first African American commanding officer on July 14, 1969. The NROTC Flight Indoctrination Program began on October 11, 1969.[66]

Prairie View A and M NROTC held its first commissioning ceremony on May 17, 1970 when ten Ensigns and three LTs were administered the oath by Secretary of the Navy John Chaffee. The SECNAV recognized the valuable service that the university would render in augmenting the quantity of African American officers commissioned by the Naval Academy to the Navy and Marine Corps. LCDR Robert Anthony and CPT Thomas explained to Carl Rowan, a graduate of the Navy V-12 program during World War II, that the Navy was attempting to improve the quantity of commissioned African Americans and that LCDR Anthony was assigned as a special assistant to the Navy Director of Recruiting to manage the Minority Officer Recruiting Effort referred to as MORE. Rowan was also informed that the Navy would probably authorize the organization of NROTC detachments at other African American colleges. On September 21, 1970, Charles Washington became first student to receive a regular appointment in the detachment as a result of national competition in the NROTC Scholarship Program and was sworn into the Naval Reserve as a midshipman by CPT Warren H. Lowans who had succeeded CDR Thomas on July 1, 1970.[67]

ADM Elmo R. Zumwalt announced a plan to increase the African American officer and enlisted strength, unparalleled in naval history since the integration of armed forces under President Harry S. Truman. LT CDR William Norman, his special assistant for minority groups, together with five other naval officers, drafted and supervised a program which improved education, job training, promotions and recruitment of African Americans. LCDR Norman was cognizant of the limited number of African Americans volunteering for Naval service and that the acknowledged Naval reputation for limited opportunities for minorities reduced the percentage of African Americans in the Navy. Although the armed forces enlisted strength was 10.8 percent and the officers' strength was 1.9 percent, African Americans represented 5.5 percent of the Navy enlisted strength and 0.6 percent of officer strength. LT CDR Norman acknowledged that the majority of African Americans assigned to aircraft carriers were employed in laundries and other service areas or assigned to deck crews. Objectives of ADM Zumwalt involved the elimination of bias in personnel assignments, advanced training for selected personnel, reviewing promotion policies and developing new basic skills tests to determine positions for new recruits and to reflect more accurately the abilities of minority personnel from urban and rural areas. To obtain an unofficial goal of doubling the size of African American sailors and increasing the officers' strength tenfold by 1976, the Navy planned an aggressive recruitment campaign which included the expansion of NROTC and increasing the African American enrollment at the Naval Academy.[68]

The expansion of NROTC to Savannah State and Southern A and M was announced in March 1971, but SECNAV Chafee on June 1, 1971 authorized the formation of NROTC at Southern A and M. CDR Donald A. Griffin arrived on July 16, 1971 and on August 30, 1971 the detachment became operational with 59 midshipmen accepted for training after a screening of 60 applicants. Assisting CDR Griffin in the operation of the unit was LCDR Harold A. Walton. The formal commissioning of the unit was held on October 7, 1971 with RADM Samuel L. Gravely, Director of Naval Communications, as the guest speaker. In August 1972 the detachment was one of four detachments selected to admit females and by 1984 it had more female midshipwomen than any other NROTC detachment.[69]

President Jackson of Savannah State College was concerned about the formation of an NROTC detachment since there was significant student hostility toward military training on campus and antiwar feelings toward the American involvement in the Vietnam War. Together with several influential student campus leaders, he convinced the student body that an NROTC detachment would strengthen the institutional programs and enhance the image of the Savannah State College. The Board of Regents on March 10, 1971 authorized the immediate formation of a detachment and the Naval Science curriculum was approved by the Savannah State Curriculum Committee on August 6, 1971. A Division of Naval Science was organized and CDR Virgil V. McGee, a graduate of Tennessee A and I, was assigned to Savannah State when the program became operational on September 22, 1971. A dedication ceremony was held on October 27, 1971 and by December 31, 1971 there were 41 midshipmen in the program. The Flight Indoctrination Program became operational on September 1971 with two midshipmen enrolled.[70]

CDR McGee was the ideal leader and catalyst for the embryonic NROTC program, providing the necessary nurturing and guidance to midshipmen, and preparing students for successful careers in the Navy or the Marine Corps. The NROTC cadre became an integral component of the faculty and in June 1974. The program commissioned Ensigns Larry D. Carr, Larry Hall and Marshall Pollard in addition to Marine Lieutenant Walter E. Gaston. All of the first graduates reached senior field rank and probably the most distinguished graduate was LT CDR Donnie L. Cochran of Pelham, Georgia who graduated with a degree in civil engineering in 1976. He was the first African American aviator to fly with the prestigious Blue Angels and in 1988 he was recognized as the Black Engineer of the Year.[71]

SECNAV John W. Warner on June 1, 1972 approved NROTC for North Carolina Central which became operational under Commander Raymond A. Lambert on September 1, 1972 with twelve scholarship midshipmen. SECNAV Warner attended the dedication ceremony where he emphasized support of equal opportunity, and in response to racial incidents aboard naval vessels he stressed that fleet commanders were instructed to establish training cycle sessions designed to detect racial problems before they developed into incidents. However, the detachment was subsequently decommissioned.[72]

NROTC representatives consisting of CPT Rex Warner, PNS at the University of North Carolina, Elman Morrow, Special Assistant for the Officer Education Program of the Bureau of Naval Personnel, LCDR Reeves Ramsey Taylor, and Preston Valien, Deputy Associate Commissioner of the U.S. Office of Education, met with the Florida A and M Academic Council and George W. Gore, Jr., President of FAMU, on October 9, 1967 to determine the feasibility of establishing an NROTC detachment. The FAMU Director of Admissions and Records, Edwin M. Thorpe, was designated to provide the initial organizational leadership at Florida State for a detachment which was commissioned on August 1, 1972 which became operational September 1, 1972 with a dedication ceremony held on November 8,

1972. Assigned to the College of Arts and Sciences, a reorganization of the university in 1978 transferred NROTC to the College of Engineering Sciences, Technology and Agriculture since NROTC students were required to complete exceptionally heavy concentrations in sciences, engineering and technology. CDR Benjamin Hacker began the program with ten midshipmen but in 1980 enrollment reached its zenith with 122 midshipmen. The program was extended to serve students enrolled at Florida State University and later Tallahassee Community College in 1986. CPT Richard Williams succeeded CDR Hacker and with the commissioning of first midshipman Ensign Robert Conrad of Mount Mora, Florida, the detachment established an excellent reputation in the fleet through the commissioning of graduates who have consistently maintained a high standard of performance on summer cruises and active duty.[73]

African American students were offered naval training at other institutions after 1973 when a detachment was formed at Atlanta University Center which included Clark College, Morehouse College, Morris Brown College, and Spelman College. Initially established in 1980 on the campus of Morris Brown as a branch of the Georgia Institute of Technology organization, the NROTC branch was relocated from Morris Brown to Morehouse and on September 27, 1984 was officially detached from Georgia Tech and became an independent organization.[74] NROTC also was established at Hampton University and expanded to Old Dominion University where the detachment headquarters was relocated, and to Norfolk State University.

Special interest was devoted to the procurement of African American officers during FY 1968 when two previous Air Force studies revealed that only 3.5 percent were commissioned through AFROTC. Although the 1968 fiscal year total had decreased to 2.1 percent and many officials considered the percentage was in line with the number of African Americans graduating from colleges and universities, the Secretary of the Air Force requested an increase in the production. Recommendations included the disestablishment of non-economical detachments and the transfer of available enrollment quotas to other institutions, the establishment of new AFROTC detachments in African American centers such as Atlanta University, increasing the quotas of established African American AFROTC detachments, seeking support of African American leaders in the recruitment of cadets, assigning more African American officers as PAS at predominately white schools, and emphasizing African American recruitment at predominately white schools.[75]

North Carolina A and T AFROTC was mandatory until 1968 and the detachment experienced a decline from approximately 400 to 160 during the 1970s and gradually increased during the 1980s to 258 by 1986. The detachment also served five consortium institutions which were the University of North Carolina at Greensboro, Bennett College, High Point College, Guildford College and Elon College.[76]

Mississippi Valley State College Board of Trustees approved an AFROTC program in January 1971 which began to receive the cadre by the following April to inaugurate the establishment of the detachment.[77]

Alabama State gained an AFROTC detachment during the administration of Levi Watkins who refused to accept an Air Force proposal to organize a segregated cadre. The Division of Aerospace Studies was formed and LTC Clarence W. Holloway organized the detachment which also served students at Auburn University in Montgomery and Huntington College. An incident which perturbed Watkins occurred when the commandant of AFROTC at the Air University, GEN Benjamin B. Cassidy, notified him that officials at Auburn University in Montgomery had approached Congress seeking to transfer the AFROTC detachment to the Auburn campus. GEN Cassidy supported the retention of the detachment at Alabama State and stressed that if Montgomery ever required two senior AFROTC programs Auburn campus would be considered, however, as long as Montgomery required one program to provide AFROTC training the detachment would remain at Alabama State. GEN Cassidy supported cross-enrollment and informed LTC Holloway to expect communication from AUM. William Cook, assistant vice president for development, invited LTC Holloway and CPT David Bass to meet with him and two AFROTC officers from the main campus of Auburn University. The Auburn representatives proposed that Auburn students in Montgomery train at Alabama State but be commissioned at Auburn University. LTC Holloway rejected their proposal which he viewed was motivated by blatant racism. He emphasized Alabama State AFROTC was an officially approved Air Force program which followed the prescribed AFROTC curriculum. The program was properly staffed and supervised by authorized Air University officers. The Auburn representatives were compelled to acquiescence and agree to a policy of cross-enrollment with their students trained and commissioned at Alabama State.[78]

Cheyney State University in Pennsylvania had a minority recruiting program that was initiated on August 6, 1971. CPT Hudson W. Griffin assumed command of the program and attempted to increase the selection base of qualified students and the orientation program was extended to nearby colleges and universities with an apparent focus of attracting African American students at predominately white institutions.[79]

Grambling State through an agreement with its host institution, Louisiana Technical University, organized an AFROTC detachment on August

27, 1971 under the command of LTC Henry L. Frederick. The initial enrollment of 32 was attributed to the lack of publicity during registration and
students were unaware of the program. Although the cadet corps increased,
COL Frederick extended recruiting to the Shreveport-Bossier City campus
of Southern University and attended high school career days in addition to
publicizing AFROTC in the press and including brochures in student correspondence. Presentations were also given by cadets from Louisiana Tech
but this procedure was terminated during the next academic year. Recruitment of students at the Shreveport-Bossier campus was similarly discontinued primarily because of the difficulty encountered in scheduling the Air
Force Officer Qualification Test and physical examinations at Barksdale
AFB and because most students declined to transfer to Grambling State
because the possible reduction of their credits in the transfer process. The
success of the program was measured in the commissioning of its first
cadet, Billy Aiken, in 1973.[80]

Fayetteville State University in Fayetteville, North Carolina, initiated
its program with the formation of a department of Aerospace Studies with
CPT Walter E. Davis serving as the acting director. Seven students who
completed their summer encampments were admitted into the AFROTC
detachment in September 1972. Among the cadets who entered the
AFROTC program were Franklin Melvin, Ronnie Smith and Bobby H.
Washington who became the first FSU commissioned officers.[81]

The Department of Defense considered the most inexpensive method
of producing officers was through the established ROTC programs but
increased efforts for admission of African Americans into the service academies. On July 1, 1969, the academies accepted eighty-seven as compared to
the previous year of forty-seven. The USMA enrolled forty-five, the USNA
seventeen, and the USAF had twenty-five. The USMA commissioned eight
in 1969 which brought the total of commissioned African Americans to sev-
enty-three of the 136 admitted into the Military Academy since 1870. Two
years earlier, Bobby G. Whaley and James D. Fowler, Jr. were commissioned, and more significantly, LT Fowler's father, COL James D. Fowler,
had graduated from the Military Academy in 1941. There were forty-two
who did not graduate, and twenty-nine or 22 percent of the total admitted
were completing the four-year program. The Naval Academy since 1949 had
commissioned sixty-eight midshipmen by 1972 with an additional twelve
commissioned in 1973. Some midshipmen accepted commissions in the
Marine Corps, which was gratified that members of the Montfort Point
Marine Association, composed primarily of former and active duty African
American marines, supported the assignment of six African American
officers, whom LTC Kenneth H. Berthoud detailed to visit colleges and

speak to veterans', civic and fraternal organizations. This program encouraged the recruitment and commission of LT Sharon Holley who graduated from Lincoln University in Missouri in 1970 and LT Johnnie Calhoun who returned to Prairie View College for graduate study but accepted a commission into the Marine Corps. Relatively few had been admitted into the United States Merchant Marine Academy at Kings Point, New York but in 1969 three were commissioned.[82]

Violent reactions followed the assassination of Dr. Martin Luther King in 1968 and continued opposition to the draft and warfare in Vietnam caused several states to seek additional enlisted and commissioned African Americans. Delaware officials were severely criticized after civil disturbances in Newark for recruiting only fifty-one minority candidates under a plan which provided for 850. Previously, the more than 17,000 member National Guard organization was composed of 17 percent African Americans in the Army National guard and less than 2 percent in the Air National Guard. The absence of African Americans during the crisis in New Jersey was attributed to increased tension when guardsmen were ordered to control urban disorder. In an effort to correct the imbalance and obtain personnel sensitive to urban conditions, Delaware commissioned five African Americans in 1967. Obviously, this was an excellent opportunity to recruit ROTC commissioned officers into their National Guard. The nationwide African American strength in the Army National Guard was 1.15 percent and minus 1 percent in the Air National Guard.[83]

ROTC programs provided students with an opportunity to experience a variety of leadership challenges and to excel through a variety of formal

Morgan State College Pershing Rifles at Fall Dance, 1959. (Author's collection)

organizations and a summer camp. Bands were an integral part of some ROTC organizations and at Howard the band pursued the prescribed instruction, except in marching and drilling, which averaged one hour per week, and they were ineligible for the advanced course. Durkee protested after an inspection on December 15, 1925 when the inspecting officer complained of the unauthorized issuance of uniforms to the band. Since the band was established with the formation military detachments and had won acclaim under SGT Dorcey Rhodes who had been assigned to Howard especially to train the unit which had been formed with members of the Howard University Symphony Orchestra, Durkee emphasized that it would have been an embarrassment to withdraw their uniforms. He also considered the 3rd Corps Area policy of denying uniforms to band members as an interference in his ROTC policies and that it affected the college regulations concerning compulsory training. Durkee informed COL Howard that the band would not be considered as part of ROTC and the uniforms in the possession of band members would be returned pending the implementation of other arrangements. The Third Corps Area commanding general considered it a violation to permit Howard to enroll students in ROTC who did not qualify for reserve commissions. If concessions were granted to Howard, MG S. D. Sturgis requested that the War Department regulations be amended to extend the same privileges to all ROTC detachments. The

Watson's Rangers, Morgan State University. (Courtesy of the Morganiana Collection, Prints and Photographs Collection, Beulah M. Davis Special Collections Department, Morgan State University)

fact that Howard had a compulsory military training policy for undergraduates for the first three years did not mean that ROTC was mandatory for all male students, and that all of them were required to complete the basic training. The secretary of war stressed that the mission of ROTC was to provide replacements for the Officers Reserve Corps and any diversion of funds and personnel to other objectives not pertaining to this mission could not be approved. Although the strength fluctuated, Howard maintained its band which was composed of 50 cadets by April 1926. Howard University ROTC Band performances also included annual concerts in the Rankin Chapel.[84]

Alabama A and M rendered valuable service to LTC Thomas W. Downes at Missile Command at Redstone Arsenal, when he found that an Army policy which enabled the early release of personnel had left the 55th Army Band with eight soldiers. With a drum major and other vital positions unfilled, LTC Downes and the band director, Warrant Officer Burton Lydic, requested that LTC John H. Redd, Alabama A and M PMS, provide cadet bandsmen and Morrison respectfully agreed to provide the necessary cadets.[85]

Bands performed during drills, retreats and accompanied cadets who participated in parades and other official ceremonies. Howard cadets performed in an inaugural parade on March 4, 1929. The Howard Band under SGT Brice and two companies participated in the inaugural on March 4, 1933. The Virginia State ROTC Band joined the National ROTC Band Association and in 1967 won the first place award during the ROTC Band Association Musical Festival. Performing with ROTC bands did not negate the assignments of commissioned officers and indicative of the success of cadets is Thomas Prather, a fine arts major at Morgan State, who was commissioned into the Ordnance Corps and served as the commanding general of the United States Army Troop Command in St. Louis, Missouri and served as a MG prior to his retirement.[86]

Drill teams, rifle teams, glee clubs, marching detachments and rangers organizations performed at events and other campus activities in addition to participating in local, state and national events which included Armed Forces Day parades and the National Cherry Blossom Festival parades. Many drill teams became affiliated with the National Pershing Rifles and some of the AFROTC detachments joined the Arnold Air Society. Howard formed the Turner Squadron of the AF Arnold Air Society in honor of MAJ Andrew D. Turner, a Howard University graduate who served in the 100th Fighter Squadron during WWII and was later killed in an aircraft crash at Lochbourne AFB. Howard AFROTC also established the George F. Welch Memorial Honor Guard in recognition of CPT George F. Welch who was killed in action in Italy in 1945. Among the awards presented to Howard

*Top:* Pershing Angels, Morgan State College. (Courtesy of the Morganiana Collection, Prints and Photographs Collection, Beulah M. Davis Special Collections Department, Morgan State University)

*Bottom:* Company A, Morgan State University, 1975. (Courtesy of the Morganiana Collection, Prints and Photographs Collection, Beulah M. Davis Special Collections Department, Morgan State University)

ROTC cadets was the memorial trophy honoring CPT William R. Spencer who commanded African American guardsmen in the Maryland Monumental Guards that was redesignated as the First Separate Company.[87] Tennessee State University formed the Tiger Jets drill team and an AF Arnold Air Society in May 1954 in honor of Vance H. Marchbanks who

Tuskegee Institute ROTC Auxiliary Drill Team with the Tuskegee Drill Team in the background. (Courtesy of Tuskegee University Archives, Tuskegee, AL)

became the first African American to serve as a COL in the Air Force Medical Service when he departed the university to become a staff surgeon of the 313th Air Division on Okinawa.[88] On October 7, 1947, Howard ROTC initiated efforts to establish the first African American chapter of the National Society of Scabbard and Blade which was initiated as Company D, 9th Regiment on January 28, 1950.[89] Alcorn A and M also formed a Utility Police Platoon with the primary mission of performing as an honor guard, escort detail, traffic control, color guard or flag detail.[90]

The acceptance of females into the ROTC, AFROTC and NROTC programs was long overdue. Women had served in the armed forces during World War II when the nation was in need of personnel to perform various duties to relieve soldiers for combat and combat support duties. African American women were interested in commissioned service and formed informal participation at many institutions. With the enactment of Selective Service legislation that drastically reduced male student enrollment at Prairie View A and M, female students participated in the ROTC band and marched in military formations. They also formed a jazz band that played in Texas as well as cities in other states.[91] In addition to serving as queen or members of the female court, Wilberforce women were appointed as honorary officers of the battalion staff, and South Carolina State in 1954 organized a female rifle team. Tennessee State formed a women's drill team in September 1954, Lincoln had organized an ROTC Auxiliary Drill Team by October 1961 and Prairie View A and M organized an NROTC Women's

Auxiliary, which was called the Anchorettes, on October 4, 1971 to provide female students an opportunity to participate in social and naval functions.[92] Morgan State organized the Persherettes in 1960 which was reorganized into the Pershing Angels in 1965. Alabama A and M formed the Drillets that was superseded by Pershing Rifles Coed Affiliates to promote understanding and improvement between ROTC and the college community, to foster morale, and create awareness of the mission and importance of ROTC among female students.[93]

South Carolina State ROTC, which organized a female rifle team in 1954, was selected as one of ten institutions to participate in a pilot program to extend military training to females in 1972. Virginia State enrolled female students in 1972 which contributed to making the institution one of the top three detachments in the First ROTC Region, and made Virginia State ROTC the only detachment which had an increase in cadet enrollment. LT Irene Fitzgerald was commissioned in 1976 with LT Pattie L. Scott graduating the following year. However, approximately 44 percent of cadets in 1979 graduated with regular Army commissions that included Denise Jones, who had served as the first female battalion commander, and Debra Mountcastle. Hampton accepted female cadets in 1973 and of the first fifteen to register and qualify for the advanced course was Rhonda J. Scott. Women joined the Jackson State College ROTC and organized a drill team in 1972 that was commanded by Dorothy Fortune who formerly had served in the regular Army. Jackson State established a national record with the commissioning of ten women in 1976.[94]

Patricia Gilner and Earlene Shelly joined the Alcorn A and M ROTC detachment when it was formed in 1971 and by March 1972 the female enrollment had increased to twenty-nine cadets. They formed the Women's Affiliate Platoon of the battalion with the intention of becoming the best female ROTC drill team in the southern states.[95] Fayetteville State University urged the enrollment of female cadets while Alcorn A and M College in August 1973 had the largest enrollment of women in Mississippi.[96] Hazel Young at Southern A and M was the first commissioned female together with others in the class of 1976.[97] Velma LaVonne of Bennettsville, South Carolina was commissioned at Livingstone College in Salisbury, North Carolina in 1973 with the ceremony conducted by her aunt, LTC Vashti V. Jeffries, a former Livingstone student who became the first African American WAC to attend the Command and General Staff School in 1963 and was assigned to Fort Lee, VA.[98]

COL Ruth Lucas was the highest ranking African American when the secretary of the Air Force authorized the enrollment of females in AFROTC detachments in two programs. One option was a two-year program that included a six-week summer camp and passage of the AFROTC Qualifying Test and the other option was the regular four-year program. Female cadets

Morgan State Miss ROTC, 1962–1963. (Courtesy of the Morganiana Collection, Prints and Photographs Collection, Beulah M. Davis Special Collections Department, Morgan State University)

were enrolled at Tennessee State University.[99] Jacqueline Pattishall was the only female cadet who remained in the North Carolina A and T AFROTC program and became the first female to complete the program in the nation with her commissioning on May 13, 1973.[100] The success of the program at Grambling A and M enabled COL Rosetta Armour-Lightner to become the female PAS of the Grambling AFROTC detachment.[101]

A Mariners Woman's Auxiliary was organized with twenty students on September 10, 1971 at Southern A and M and in August 1972 the NROTC detachment was one of four detachments selected to admit females. The Southern A and M detachment by 1984 had more female midshipwomen than any other NROTC detachment.[102] The first female midshipwomen commissioned at Savannah State in June 1977 were Martha L. Hall and Cynthia Miller. In that same year the extension program established at Armstrong State College graduated its first ensign. The NROTC program by December 1989 had commissioned eighty-one ensigns and twenty-nine LT which included eighteen female ensigns and six lieutenants. The Navy also conducted a Nurse Corps Candidate Scholarship program and Valerie

McKay of Florida State was one of six candidates from fifty applicants accepted into the program. She was inducted into the Naval Reserve by LCDR Hattie Elam, one of the senior ranking African American women in the Navy.[103] Doris A. Daniels who graduated from Kentucky State and began her service career in 1974 was employed by the Bureau of International Narcotics in the State Department and became the first African American female in the Marine Corps to reach the rank of COL.[104] The enrollment achieved through the recruitment of African American women in the armed service programs enabled many colleges to retain their organizations and meet their procurement production. Similar enrollment at the service academies influenced the graduation of the first African American Ensigns, Angela Dennis and Daphne Reese, from the U.S. Coast Guard Academy in New London in 1983. Ensign Andrea Parker became the first African American female to complete the Coast Guard Academy's engineering program with a degree in civil engineering in 2001. Ensign Parker after her commissioning was assigned duty as an intelligence officer aboard the *CGC Tahoma* stationed at New Bedford, Massachusetts.[105]

Many commissioned officers have joined their respective organizations to assist in the mentoring, training and orientation of cadets and assisting cadres in their missions. Significant contributions have been rendered by the ROCKS, an organization initially formed by African American officers assigned to the Command and General Staff College at Fort Leavenworth in Kansas. Their common goal was the survival and successful completed of the Fort Leavenworth program and they referred to themselves as the BLUE GEESE, a term which was frequently used at the CGSC. The reassignment of many of the BLUE GEESE to the Pentagon and the Military District of Washington influenced a formal revision of the group on October 9, 1974, which was referred to as the "No Name Club." In December 1974, a prominent member of the organization. BG Roscoe C. Cartwright, who was known as Rock, and his wife, Gloria, were aboard an airplane en route to Dulles Airport in Virginia when the aircraft crashed. All of the passengers were killed. In recognition of the achievements of BG Cartwright the "No Name Club" established the Roscoe C. Cartwright Scholarship Fund and changed its name to the ROCKS. The organization is dedicated to mentoring and enhancing the professional development of members in the ROCKS and their contemporaries in addition to providing support to cadets attending African American colleges and universities.

The objective to establish detachments in qualified African American institutions, especially the land grant colleges and universities, during the decades of segregation was a difficult task. However, the transition toward integration had a detrimental effect on programs at African American colleges and universities since some students who would have qualified for ROTC were attending other institutions where military training was not viewed as a viable option. Many students who qualified for admission to ROTC programs at African Americans colleges were similarly not encouraged to pursue military training. The Department of Defense recognized the concerns of African American institutions, but the expectation of graduating an acceptable quantity of qualified commissioned officers who finished in the upper third of their officers' basic orientation schools was not diminished. Indeed, changing strategic demands and technological advancements required an increased commitment from collegiate institutions and the emphasis to commission the established quantity was compounded by the mission of African American colleges which admitted excellent students in addition to some students who were denied admission by other institutions and excelled beyond the expectations of college administrators. The majority of the students with marginal entrance scores were eligible for military training although their subsequent records indicated their high levels of achievement. Collegiate officials were cognizant of the civil rights movement to eliminate discrimination and afforded the right of all students to matriculate at institutions of their choice, but they appealed to the students to maintain their interest and attendance in African American institutions.

The advancement of many graduates to rank of flag officers is indicative of the success of ROTC programs at historically African American colleges and universities. Although Howard commissioned the majority of officers promoted to the highest officer ranks, Morgan State in 2000 claimed the highest, commissioning more general officers than any other public African American institution. The achievements of LTG Larry R. Ellis have enhanced the legacy of Morgan State and the quality of leadership of its commissioned officers. LTG Ellis became the first African American to become the Army Deputy Chief of Staff for Operations and Plans and in 2001 President George W. Bush nominated LTG Ellis to receive the highest peacetime four-star medal. LTG Ellis became the commanding general of the U.S. Army Forces Command at Fort McPherson in Georgia and was promoted to the rank of GEN at the Pentagon on November 13, 2001.[106] However, the achievements of all commissioned officers are significant and symbolize the efforts of collegiate personnel, especially the staffs of ROTC programs, and the perseverance of the commissioned officers. The tradition of aeroscience, military science and naval science training in historically African American colleges and universities exists because cadets commissioned prior to 1974 effectively met the challenges of leadership. Their performance of duty and the legacy they established are excellent models for other cadets and midshipmen to emulate.

# Notes

## Chapter 1

1. Henry O. Flipper, *The Colored Cadet at West Point* (New York: Arno Press, 1969), passim; John F. Marszalek, *Assault at West Point: The Court-Martial of Johnson Whittaker* (New York: Collier Books, 1972), passim.

2. David A. Lane, Jr., "The Development of the Present Relationship of the Federal Government to Negro Education," *Journal of Negro Education* 7 (July 1938): 276; Walter Milan Davis, *Pushing Forward: A History of Alcorn A. & M. College and Portraits of Some of its Successful Graduates* (Okolona, MS: Okolona Industrial School, 1938), 11.

3. Rayford W. Logan, *Howard University: The First Hundred Years, 1867–1967* (New York: New York University Press, 1969), 53–54.

4. Donal F. Lindsey, *Indians at Hampton Institute, 1877–1923* (Chicago: University of Illinois Press, 1995), 35–36, 39, 47, 126–27, 259; Keith L. Schall, *Stony the Road: Chapters in the History of Hampton Institute* (Charlottesville: University Press of Virginia, 1977), 31. Hereafter, BG will be used for brigadier general, CPT for captain, Howard for Howard University and Wilberforce for Wilberforce University.

5. Latharhus Goggins, *Central State University: The First One hundred Years, 1887–1987* (Wilberforce: Central State University, 1987), 5, 8–15; Willis L. Brown and Janie M. McNeal-Brown, "Langston University: The Early Years," *Chronicles of Oklahoma* 74 (Spring 1996): 34.

6. LT John H. Alexander Service Record, LT John H. Alexander Pension File, Records of the Veterans Administration, Record Group 15, National Archives, Washington, DC; Executive Board Minutes, Wilberforce University, March 6, April 3, 1894, Archives and Special Collections, Rembert E. Stokes Learning Center, Wilberforce University, Wilberforce, OH; Cleveland *Gazette*, March 31, May 26, July 7, 1894, *Tawawa Remembrances* (Wilberforce: Wilberforce Class of 1914, 1914), 38; Wilberforce University *Forcean*, 1939, 88; Robert E. Greene, *Black Defenders of America* (Chicago: Johnson Publishing Co., 1974, 109, 158; Charles Johnson, Jr., *African American Soldiers in the National Guard* (Westport: Greenwood Press, 1992), 60, 63, 67; Frederick A. McGinnis, *A History and an Interpretation of Wilberforce University* (Blanchester: Brown Publishing Company, 1941), 60–61, 81. The other officers who commanded the cadets were CPT J. S. Coage, LT W. P. Welsh, A. A. Brown, C. M. Gaines and A. W. Asbury. Hereafter, LT will be used for the ranks of first and second lieutenant, PMST for professor of military science and tactics, USMA for United States Military Academy, RG will be used for record group, NA for the National Archives and RG 15 for Records of the Veterans Administration, Record Group 15, National Archives, Washington, DC.

7. John C. Harlan, *History of West Virginia State College, 1891–1965* (Dubuque: William C. Brown Book Company, 1969), 15–16, 23, 29, 41, 63, 148–151, 155–156, 158–160; West Virginia State College, *The History of the Military Science Department: West Virginia State College* (Institute: West Virginia State College, 1968), 7–12. The early official designation of the Institute was the West Virginia Colored Institute but on February 27, 1929 the Institute became West Virginia State College.

8. Walter J. Satneck, The History of the Origins and the Development of the Delaware State college and its Role in Higher Education for Negroes in Delaware, Unpublished EdD dissertation, New York University, New York, NY, 1962, 29, 74.

9. John Potts, *A History of South Carolina State College, 1896–1987* (Orangeburg: South Carolina State College, 1978), 11–15, 54–55.

10. Zella J. Black, *Langston University: A History* (Norman: University of Oklahoma Press, 1979), 13–15; Willis L. Brown and Janie M. McNeal-Brown, "Langston University: The Early Years," 36–46; Donald Spivey, "Crisis on a Black Campus: Langston University and its Struggle for Survival," *Chronicles of Oklahoma* 59 (Winter 1981–1982 ): 441. Although generally referred to as Langston University, the passage of House Bill 447 on May 1, 1941 officially changed the Colored Agricultural and Normal University of Oklahoma to Langston University.

11. Edward Wilson, *The History of Morgan State College: A Century of Purpose in Action, 1867–1967* (New York: Vantage Press, 196 , 59–60, 87; Ruth E. Wennersten, "The Historical Evolution of a Black Land Grant College: The University of Maryland Eastern Shore," Unpublished Thesis, University of Maryland, College Park, MD, 1976, 83.

12. Johnson, *African American Soldiers in the National Guard*, 1–96; Gene M. Lyons and John W. Masland, "The Origins of ROTC," *Military Affairs* 23 (Spring 1959): 1–12. Benjamin O. Davis, Sr. had served as a LT in the 8th (Immune) Volunteer Regiment during the Spanish-American-Cuban-Filipino War and after the war he enlisted into the 9th Cavalry Regiment as a Sergeant Major before becoming a commissioned officer in the 10th Cavalry Regiment. He was the first African American to successfully pass an examination for a regular Army commission while assigned to Fort Leavenworth, KS. LT John E. Green was recruited while attending Walden University in Nashville, TN by Chaplain Allen Allensworth in 1898 and later retired as a LTC. A total of 300 enlisted men were commissioned from the ranks between 1898 and 1902 but LT Davis and LT John E. Green, assigned to the 25th Infantry Regiment, were the two Infantry African American officers. See Robert E. Greene, *Who were the Real Buffalo Soldiers?* (Fort Washington, MD: R. E. Greene, 1994), 138, 366; Frank N. Schubert, *On the Trail of the Buffalo Soldiers, 1866–1917* (Wilmington, DE: Scholarly Resources, 1995), 114, 171. Hereafter, SATC will be used for Student Army (and Navy) Training Corps and SMAJ for sergeant major.

13. General Orders 1, Headquarters, Students Army Training Corps, War Department, Washington, DC, September 15, 1918, in Records of the SATC Units, Records of the War Department General and Special Staffs, RG165, National Archives II, College Park, MD; Chief Warrant Officer Hartley S. Newman, "A Study on Students' Army Training Corps, World War I," Historical Section, Army War College, September 1942, Executive for Reserve and ROTC Affairs, Records of the Army Staff, Record Group 319, National Archives II, College Park, MD; Emmett J. Scott, *Scott's Official History of the American Negro in the World War* (New York: Arno Press, 1969), 328–30; *Report of the Chief of Staff, 1918*, 160; *Report of the Adjutant General, 1918*, 187; *Report of the Chief of Staff, 1919*, 320. The members of the Committee on Education and Special Training were Colonel Robert I. Rees of the General Staff Corps, Colonel John H. Wigmore of the Provost Marshal General's Department, Lieutenant Colonel Grenville Clark of the Adjutant General's Department, and Major William H. Morton of the War Plans

Division. An Advisory Board Representing Educational Interests was composed of James R. Angell, Samuel P. Capen, J. W. Dietz, Hugh Fratne, Charles R. Mann, Raymond H. Pearson and Herman Schneider. Hereafter, GO will be used for general orders, HQ for headquarters, CEST for Committee of Education and Special Training, SATC for Students' Army Training Corps, WD for War Department, NA II for National Archives at College Park, COL for colonel, LTC for lieutenant colonel, MAJ for major and CWO for chief warrant officer, Atlanta for Atlanta University, Florida A and M for Florida Agricultural and Mechanical College, and South Carolina State A and M for State Agricultural and Mechanical College of South Carolina. Hereafter NA II will be used for National Archives II, College Park, MD.

14. COL Robert I. Rees to Commanding Officers of SATC, September 20, 1918, SATC Units, RG 165, NAII; CWO Hartley S. Newman, A Study on Students' Army Training Corps, World War I, Records of the Army Staff, RG 319, NA II; Scott, *Scott's Official History of the American Negro in the World War*, 335–36; Gene M. Lyons and John W. Masland, *Education and Military Leadership* (Princeton: Princeton University Press, 1959), 42; Pine Bluff *Commercial*, September 20, 1918. Although the Branch Normal School detachment was commanded by CPT Alfred V. Ednie, the only African American officer was LT John Montgomery Gill who was assigned to the Medical Corps. CPT Ednie later recommended the appointment of LT Gill into Officers Reserve Corps. See Evaluation of LT John M. Gill, SATC Units, 1918–1919, RG 165, NA II. Hereafter, RG 165 will be used for Records of the War Department General and Special Staffs, NA II and RG 319 will be used for Records of the Army Staff, NA II.

15. Scott, *Scott's Official History of the American Negro in the World War*, 335–37, Memorandum 15, Headquarters, U.S. Army Training Detachment, Howard University, Washington, DC, September 25, 1918, Records of Committee on Education and Special Training, Records of the War Department General and Special Staffs, Record Group 165, NA II; Tuskegee *Student*, March 1, 1919. Other institutions which applied for SATC detachments included Allen College in Columbia, SC, Arkansas Baptist and Philander Smith Colleges in Little Rock, AR, Benedict College in Columbia, SC, Biddle University in Charlotte, NC, Colored Agricultural and Mechanical University in Langston, OK, Fort Valley High & Industrial School in Fort Valley, GA, Morris Brown University in Atlanta, GA. See SATC Investigations, Committee on Education and Special Training, RG 165, NA. Hereafter, Lincoln in Pennsylvania will be used for Lincoln University in Chester County, Pennsylvania, Alabama State A and M for Alabama State College, Wiley for Wiley University and Bishop for Bishop College.

16. Administrative Memorandum 39, MAJ Chesleigh H. Briscoe for the CEST, WD, Washington, DC, October 29, 1918, SATC Memoranda, RG 165, NA II; W. E. Bigglestone, "Oberlin College and the Negro Student, 1865–1940," *Journal of Negro History* 56 (July 1971): 207; Scott, *Scott's Official History of the Negro in the World War*, 338–40.

17. *Report of the Chief of Staff, 1919*, 320–322; LT Leonard L. McLeod, Report of the Department of Military Discipline and Physical Instruction, Hampton Institute, Virginia, January 1919, ROTC File, Hampton University Archives, Harvey Library, Hampton, VA; Scott, *Scott's Official History of the Negro in the World War*, 338–40, 471–81; George M. Lightfoot, Alaine Locke, and Martha MacLear, "Howard University in the War: A Record of Patriotic Service," *Howard University Record* 13 (April 1919): 15–19; Logan, *Howard University,*180–81; Joe M. Richardson, *A History of Fisk University, 1865–1946* (University, AL: University of Alabama Press, 1980), 76; Walter Dyson, *Howard University: The Capstone of Negro Education, A History, 1867–1940* (Washington: Howard University Graduate School, 1941), 71; U. S. War Department, *Training Camps for Reserve Officers' Training Corps* (Washington: Government Printing Office, 1918),

2–3. Among the colleges invited to attend the camp were Howard University, Atlanta University, Lincoln University in Chester County, Pennsylvania, Lincoln University in Jefferson City, Missouri, Raleigh University, Shaw University, Wilberforce University, Virginia Union, Straight University, Morehouse College, Talledega College, Bishop College, Benedict College, Allen University, New Orleans University, Florida A and M for Negro Youth, Biddle University, Livingston College, Tuskegee N and I Institute and Hampton N and A Institute. Wilberforce also selected several faculty and students to attend the training and later personnel from the university were commissioned at Camp Hancock, GA where machine gun instruction was offered. Others were commissioned at Camp Pike, AR where artillery training was conducted. See McGinnis, *A History and an Interpretation of Wilberforce University*, 81–81. The staff officers in Battalion B, commanded by LT Russell Smith, were Adjutant Fisher Pride, Assistant Adjutant Harry J. Mack and LT Joseph H. Scott. LT Charles M. Thompson, Thomas Gregory, John H. Purnell and Ernest Johnson were assigned to Company 1, while LT Campbell C. Johnson, John Love, Joseph Copper and Harry J. Mack were assigned to Company 2.

Among the students who joined the efforts of the Central Committee of Negro College Men were Wilfrid W. Lawson of Syracuse University and Rayford W. Logan of Williams College. Among the initial officers commissioned at Camp Des Moines who had attended Howard University: CPT Louis Mehlinger and William E. Davis; LT William I. Barnes, Oscar C. Brown, Frank Coleman, Clarence B. Curley, Merrill H. Curtis, Thomas M. Dent, Joshua W. Clifford, Clayborne George, Jesse J. Green, Montgomery Gregory, Charles H. Houston, John R. Hunt, Maxey Jackson, Campbell C. Johnson, Linwood G. Koger, Charles E. Lane, Benton R. Latimer, Howard H. Long, Alfred E. Marshall, Louis A. Middleton, Walter H. Mazyck, William S. Nelson, Robert R. Penn, Percy (Percival) R. Piper, John W. Rowe, Percy H. Steele, James H. N. Waring, and Christopher C. Wimbish; and LT Elbert L. Booker, Clifford Bruen, Nathan O. Goodloe, Ernest C. Johnson, George Hollomand, Cyrus W. Marshall, Humphrey C. Patton, and Louis H. Russell. See Central Committee of Negro Men Petitions in Thomas M. Gregory Papers, Manuscript Division, Moorland-Spingarn Research Center, Howard University, Washington, DC; *"Commissions for Howard Men as Reported at Time of Going to Press," Howard University Journal* 15 (October 19, 1917): 1. For a list of the 639 officers commissioned on October 15, 1917, see Scott, *Scott's Official History of the American Negro in the World War*, 471–81.

Rayford W. Logan was among students denied admission to the Des Moines Officer Training Camp because of the minimum age requirement of twenty-five. He concluded the age requirement was instituted to eliminate college students and recent college graduates who were more independent and possessed more initiative. Logan enlisted into the 1st Separate District of Columbia National Guard on July 10, 1917 as a private and after several promotions he was commissioned a LT. See Kenneth R. Janken, *Rayford W. Logan and the Dilemma of the African-American Intellectual* (Amherst: University of Massachusetts Press, 1993), 35–36.

18. Lightfoot, Locke and MacLear, *Howard University in the War*, 18–19.

19. Lightfoot, Locke and MacLear, *Howard University in the War*, p. 12; COL Campbell C. Johnson Charter Day Address, Howard University, Washington, DC, March 1943, in Campbell C. Johnson Papers, Manuscript Division, Moorland-Spingarn Research Center, Howard University, Washington, DC.

20. Walter S. Buchanan to TAG, October 10, 1918, Emmett J. Scott to C. R. Dooley, October 1918, C. R. Dooley to W. S. Buchanan, October 9, 1918, Walter S. Buchanan to L. R. Roy, October 18, 1918, RG 165, NA II.

21. *Catalogue of State Agricultural and Mechanical College of South Carolina, 1917–1918*, 55–57.

22. West Virginia State College, *The History of the Military Science Department, West Virginia State College* (Institute: West Virginia State College, 1968), 16, 18. The detachment also included QM Walter R. St. Clair and Surgeon M. T. Sinclair. The personnel who qualified as SATC instructors during the summer camp at Howard were Albert C. Spurlock, Dennis Smith, George Fowler, Albert G. Brown, Christopher Morgan, Willis E. Lewis and Walter E. Clarkson. Other students who had responded to a call for volunteers from Governor John H. Cornwell included Charles L. Adams, Matthew Ballard, Robert L. Black, Bernard Brown, Soloman Brown, William P. Ferguson, Herman Few, William Houston, James McHenry Jones, Jr., F. Hurt Marshall, George Patterson, Wilbert Peters, Ivory Reid and William Vaughn.

23. Reports of Discharge of Officer at Wiley University and Bishop College, December 5–6, 1918, LT Elijah H. Goodwin to Southern Department Commanding General, December 6, 12, 1918, LT John R. Finley to District Military Inspector, December 11, 1918, SATC Units, CEST, RG 165, NA II.

24. Special Orders 34, Headquarters Training Detachment, Hampton Institute, VA, September 26, 1918, Special Orders 36, Headquarters SATC Corps, Hampton Institute, VA, September 26, 1918, CEST, RG 165, NA II. Hereafter, SO will be used for Special Orders.

25. CPT Joseph H. Scott to District Inspecting Officers of District 4, November 18, December 2, 1918, CEST, RG 165, NA II; Clarence A. Bacote, *The Story of Atlanta University: A Century of Service, 1865–1965* (Atlanta: Atlanta University, 1969), 161.

26. SO 263, Headquarters Southeastern Department, Charleston, SC, October 18, 1918, LT Joseph H. Cooper to District Military Inspector 5, March 5, 1919, CEST, RG 165, NA II.

27. Edward A. Jones, *A Candle in the Dark* (Valley Forge: Judson Press, 1967), 98–101. Atlanta University organized an Army School for Mechanics that was commanded by MAJ Raymond P. Cook with George K. Howe serving as educational advisor. When the SATC detachment was formed on October 1, 1918 the same officers served at Atlanta University and Morehouse College. However, CPT Joseph H. Scott became the commander under the policy of assigning African American officers in charge of the SATC detachments until demobilization on December 11, 1919. See Clarence A. Bacote, *The Study of Atlanta University*, 160–162.

28. Lightfoot, Locke and MacLear, *Howard University in the War*, pp. 22, 27.

29. CPT James R. Walsh to Atlanta University SATC Commanding Officer, November 21, 1918, CEST, 65, NA II. Among the detachments in the Southeastern Department ordered on November 21, 1918 to discharge personnel inducted into the military for potential commissioning were Atlanta, Branch Normal School at Pine Bluff, Fisk University, Meharry Medical College, Morehouse, North Carolina A and T, Shaw University, South Carolina State Agricultural and Mechanical, Talledaga College, Tuskegee Hereafter Talledaga will be used for Talledage College.

30. Scott, *Scott's Official History of the American Negro in the World War*, 341. African American officers assigned to SATC detachments included: LT W. H. Thompson and LT William R. Smalls at Alabama A and M; LT James Gordon and LT Samuel Lawson at Talladega; LT Joseph H. Scott at Atlanta; LT R. C. Thompson at Morehouse; LT Alfred E. Marshall at Savannah College in Savannah, GA; LT Ernest C. Johnson at Louisiana A and M in Baton Rouge, LA, LT Jefferson Grigsby and LT F. S. Upshur at North Carolina A and T; LT Henry Morrow at Biddle University in Charlotte, NC; LT Percival R. Piper and LT Merrill Curtis at Wilberforce; LT John Sims and LT Ernest Smith at Lincoln in Pennsylvania; LT Samuel Hull at South Carolina State A and M; LT Grant Stewart at and LT George L. Vaughn at Tennessee Agricultural and Mechanical; LT Scott Moyer at Fisk; LT Cecil Howard and Joseph Cooper at Virginia Union and LT

Walter St. Clair at West Virginia Collegiate Institute. See Officer List, WVA, RG 165, NA II. LT William R. Smalls was the son of South Carolina Militia Major General Robert Smalls and Hannah Jones Smalls. He was educated at Armstrong Manual Training High School in Washington, DC, and at the University of Pittsburgh. After a brief teaching career in Kentucky, Virginia and Austin, Texas, he served in World War I and later migrated to Toledo, Ohio where he became affiliated with the National Urban League. See Edward A. Miller, Jr., *Gullah Statesman: Robert Smalls from Slavery to Congress, 1839–1915* (Columbia: University of South Carolina Press, 1995), 245. Okon E. Uya, *From Slavery to Public Service: Robert Smalls, 1839–1915* (New York: Oxford University Press, 1971, 161.

## *Chapter 2*

1. *Report of the Secretary of War, 1919,* 21; *Report of the Chief of Staff, 1919,* 322; *Report of the Adjutant General, 1920,* 260; Gene Lyons and John W. Masland, *Education and Military Leadership* (Princeton: Princeton University Press, 1959), 42–44; Emmett J. Scott, *Scott's Official History of The American Negro in the World War* (New York: Arno Press, 1969), 342. Hereafter, TAG will be used for The Adjutant General.

2. TAG to President of Straight College, September 24, 1919, TAG to President of West Virginia Collegiate Institute, September 24, 1919, TAG to Chief of Staff, November 20, 1919, COL William Lassiter, Memorandum for TAG, December 17, 1919, TAG to President of Prairie View N and I, December 22, 1919, TAG to President of South Carolina A and M, December 22, 1919, TAG to President of Branch Normal School at Pine Bluff, December 22, 1919, President of Tennessee A and I, December 22, 1919, Records of the Adjutant General's Office, 1917, RG 407, NAII. Prior to the withdrawal of the detachments, the strength of the JROTC was 114 at South Carolina State A and M, 68 at Alabama State A and M, 101 Tennessee A and I, 107 at Branch Normal School, and 137 at Prairie View N and I. By April 1, 1919, the officers assigned to ROTC detachments were: MAJ Milton T. Dean and 1LT James H. Love at Howard, CPT Russell Smith, 1LT James C. Pinkston, and 2LT Harry J. Mack at Tuskegee, 1LT Percival R. Piper at Wilberforce; 2LT Horace G. Wilder at A and T College of North Carolina, 1LT Samuel Hull at South Carolina A and M; 1LT William Leonard L. McLeod at Hampton, 1LT Walter A. Giles at Prairie View A and M; 1LT Grant Stuart at Tennessee A&I, 1LT John H. Purnell at West Virginia Collegiate Institute, and 1LT Elijah H. Goodwin at Branch Normal School at Pine Bluff. See Scott, *Scott's Official History of The American Negro in the World War,* 341–42. TAG reported an enrollment of 104,651 in October 1919 was reduced to 88,375 with 43,598 in ROTC and 44,777 in JROTC. See the *Report of the Adjutant General, 1920,* 260. Hereafter. Alabama A and M will be used for Alabama State A and M College and Tennessee State A and I is used for Tennessee Agricultural and Industrial State Normal School. Hereafter, RG 407 will be used for Records of the Adjutant General's Office, 1917, NA II.

3. J. G. Ish, Jr. to COL A. S. Williams, December 4, 1919, COL A. S. Williams to TAG, December 13, 1919, RG 407, NA II; Debra Newman Ham, ed., The African Odyssey (Washington DC: Library of Congress, 1998), 90.

4. Memorandum, COL William Lassiter for TAG, December 17, 1919, AG G. M. Holley to TAG, May 27, 1920, RG 407, NA II; *Catalogue of State Agricultural and Mechanical College of South Carolina, 1918–1919,* 61–62; *Catalogue of State Agricultural and Mechanical College of South Carolina, 1920–1921,* 8; *Catalogue of State Agricultural and Mechanical College of South Carolina 1922–23,* 10. Hereafter, SGT will be used for sergeant.

5. Inspection Report of South Carolina A and M, 1921–1922, Fourth Corps Area

HQ, July 22, 1921, GR 407; Record of Government Aided Schools under Section 55c, National Defense Act and Section 1225, Revised Statues, May 18, 1027, Records of the Adjutant General's Office, 1780's to 1917, RG 94, NA II. Hereafter RG 94 will be used for Records of the Adjutant General's Office.

6. James B. Dudley to COL F. J. Morrow, August 6, 1919, Memorandum, COL F. J. Morrow for TAG, September 8, 1919, TAG to James B. Dudley, September 13, 1919, James B. Dudley to TAG, September 18, 1919, RG 407, NA II.

7. TAG to James B. Dudley, September 24, October 4, 11, 1919, James B. Dudley to TAG, September 27, October 8, 1919, Memorandum for TAG, October 3, 1919, Memorandum, MAJ Person Mencher for TAG, October 4, 1919, James B. Dudley to MG W. G. Haan, October 6, 1919, Memoranda, COL William Lassiter for TAG, October 3, 10, 1919, RG 407, NA II. CPT Robert L. Campbell born in Athens, GA and had taught machine shop and engineering at A and T College of North Carolina from 1913 until he entered the Army in 1917. Although he enlisted in the military during the Spanish American War and was discharged as a SGT, Campbell was commissioned a 1LT and served in France with the 368th Infantry Regiment, 92nd Infantry Division. Assigned the duties of adjutant, liaison and munitions officer, LT Campbell displayed extraordinary courage in action near Benarville by crossing an open field which was swept by heavy enemy machine gun fire and shelling to rescue a wounded soldier. For his bravery under fire, he was award the Distinguished Service Cross and the Croix de Guerre and promoted to the rank of CPT. Discharged from the regiment after the war, he was detailed as PMST in 1919 at A and T College of North Carolina and Alabama A and M. After his release from ROTC duty, he reassumed his teaching responsibilities and taught until 1931. CPT Campbell was also the recipient of a Bronze Star medal which he earned at the Atlanta Exposition in 1895 for construction of a model locomotive. He also issued a patent for the invention of gear valve for a steam engine and passed a civil service steam electric engineer examination with a rating of 89.2 percent. See the North Carolina A and T *Register*, November 1947.

8. Senator F. M. Simmons to MG P. C. Harris, October 1, 1919, TAG to Honorable F. M. Simmons, October 11, 1919, RG 407, NA; Record of Government Aided Schools under Section 55c, National Defense Act and Section 1225, Revised Statues, May 18, 1927, RG 94, NA II.

9. MG Edward L. King to TAG, March 17, 1933, RG 94, NA II.

10. TAG to Chief of Infantry, April 4, 1935, Agricultural and Technical College of North Carolina ROTC Application, April 30, 1935, MG George Van Horn Moseley to TAG, July 2, 1935, LTC Bernard Lentz, Memorandum for Assistant Chief of Staff for Operations, July 18, 1935, Chief of Infantry to TAG, July 18, 1935, TAG to Fourth Corps Area Commanding General, August 16, 1935, Ferdinand D. Bluford to Commissioner of Education, July 27, 1936, Acting TAG to Ferdinand D. Bluford, August 10, 1936, RG 94, NA II; History of the ROTC at A and T State University, ROTC Records, A and T University, Greensboro, NC. In addition to Agricultural and Technical College of North Carolina and St. Michael's College in Santa Fe, NM, one junior college and eight high schools were rejected by TAG. Hereafter, North Carolina A and T will be used for Agricultural and Technical College of North Carolina.

11. W. B. Bizzell to TAG, December 17, 1920, MG J. T. Dickman to TAG, December 27, 1920, Memorandum, COL William M. Cruikshank for TAG, January 6, 1920, TAG to W. B. Bizzell, January 8, 1921, TAG to 8th Corps Commanding General, January 8, 1921, RG 407, NA II; Gaston, O. Sanders, *The Prairie, 1926* (Prairie View: Senior Class of Prairie View State Normal and Industrial College, 1926), 160–164; Prairie View *Purple and Gold*, 66; Prairie View College *Panther*, May 1949.

12. COL G. S. Goodale to TAG, December 23, 1919, William J. Hale to Secretary of

War Newton D. Baker, January 17, 1920, Albert Williams to Secretary of War Baker, January 20, 1920, Albert Williams to Senator K. D. McKellar, January 26, 1920, TAG to Senator K. D. McKellar, January 27, 1920, RG 407, NA II. Hereafter, Tennessee A and I will be used for Tennessee A and I State Normal School.

13. Memorandum, COL F. E. Lacey, Jr. for TAG, January 24, 1920, TAG to W. J. Hale, January 27, 1920, TAG to Albert Williams, January 27, 1920, RG 407, NA II.

14. Tennessee A&I State Normal School *Bulletin* 8 (July 1919): 37, William J. Hale to Secretary of War, January 20, 1920, William J. Hale to TAG, January 20, 1920, TAG to Southeastern Department Commanding General, February 2, 1920, COL G. M. Holley to CPT Glenn P. Anderson, February 10, 1920, MAJ C. W. Elliott to William J. Hale, February 10, 1920, COL G. S. Goodale to MAJ C. W. Elliott, February 12, 1920, CPT Glenn P. Anderson to Headquarters, Southeastern Department, February 18, 1920, COL E. H. De Armond to TAG, February 21, 1920, William J. Hale to Southeastern Department Commanding General, February 21, 1920, Memorandum, COL F. E. Lacey for TAG, March 8, 1920, TAG Michael J. Lenihan to President of Tennessee A and I, March 11, 1920, William J. Hale to TAG, March 23, 1920, William J. Hale to Secretary of War, March 23, 1920, RG 407, NA II.

15. Inspection Report of Tennessee A & I State Normal School, 1921–1922, RG 407, NA; Record of Government Aided Schools under Section 55c, National Defense Act and Section 1225, Revised Statutes, May 18, 1927, RG 94, NA II.

16. R. Grant Lloyd, *Tennessee Agricultural and Industrial State University, 1912–1962: Fifty Years of Leadership Through Excellence* (Nashville: Tennessee A&I State University Press, 1962), 19–20. Also see *Nashville Tennessean*, February 5, 16, 17, 19, March 1, 2, 1922.

17. MAJ J. E. Ardrey to 2nd Corps Area Commanding General, June 5, 1924, RG 407, NA II; MAJ J. E. Ardrey to 2nd Corps Area Commanding General, July 10, 1926, Record of Government Aided Schools under Section 55c, National Defense Act and Section 1225, Revised Statues, May 18, 1927, Fourth Corps Area Assistant Adjutant Alfred J. Booth to TAG, June 23, 1927, RG 94, NA II. Hereafter, Delaware State will be used for Delaware State College.

18. Rufus L. Logan to U.S. Army Commanding General, August 18, 1923, N. B. Young to TAG, September 6, 1923, LTC Fred V. S. Chamberlain to 7th Corps Area Commanding General, September 7, 1923, MG George B. Duncan to TAG, September 21, 1923, Memorandum, COL William M. Cruikshank for TAG, September 29, 1923, TAG to 7th Corps Area Commanding General, October 1, 1923, MG George B. Duncan to TAG, June 17, 1924, Memorandum, N. B. Young to Harvey W. Miller, June 13, 1924, BG H. A. Drum for TAG, July 3, 1924, TAG to 7th Corps Area Commanding General, July 5, 1924, RG 407, NA II; Record of Government Aided Schools under Section 55c, National Defense Act and Section 1225, Revised Statutes, May 18, 1927, RG 94, NA II; Lincoln University *Quill, 1925*, 63, 69–70; ROTC History, Lincoln University Collection, Ethnic Studies Department, Lincoln University Library, Lincoln, MO. SGT Arthur P. Hayes with previous commissioned experience during WWI commanded the detachment when it was formed. The Military Department emphasized that the detachment was the only African American unit wearing the officially prescribed military uniform and the band of twenty-six musicians, one of the largest of its type in the state, was an ensemble of syncopation that was cherished by radio listeners. See W. Sherman Savage, *The History of Lincoln University* (Jefferson City: Lincoln University, 1939), 186; Lincoln University *Quill, 1926*, 91–94.

19. Lincoln University President to 7th Corps Area Commanding General, September 2, 1929, MG Harry A. Smith to TAG, September 8, 1927, TAG to 7th Corps Area Commanding General, September 22, 1926, 7th Corps AG Harvey W. Miller, June

10, 1927, RG 94, NA II. There were 99 of 138 students receiving military training as of June 1, 1927.

20. Memorandum, COL Edward Croft for Chief of Staff, April 8, 1929, Memorandum, Chief of Staff Charles P. Summeral for Assistant Chief of Staff for Operations, Secretary of War James W. Good to Congressman Daniel R. Anthony, Jr., April 20, 1929, John S, Dean to Congressman D. R. Anthony, May 3, 1929, Congressman D. R. Anthony to Secretary of War Good, May 10, 1929, Memorandum, TAG for Assistant Chief of Staff for Operations, July 14, 1930, March 23, 1931, Senator Arthur Capper to Secretary of War P. J. Hurley, May 6, 1931, Secretary of War P. J. Hurley to Senator A. Capper, May 11, 1931, RG 94, NA II; Thomas C. Cox, *Blacks in Topeka, Kansas, 1865–1915* (Baton Rouge: Louisiana State University Press, 1982), 155.

21. John W. Davis to War Department, January 27, 1936, WD to Fifth Corps Area Commanding General, February 8, April 18, 1936, Fifth Corps Area Commanding General to WD, March 25, 1936, RG 94, NA II; West Virginia State College, *The History of the Military Science Department, West Virginia State College* (Institute: West Virginia State College, 1968), 20–21. Hereafter, West Virginia State will be used for West Virginia State College.

22. John W. Davis to TAG, March 21, June 12, 1936, Congressman Joe L. Smith to TAG, March 27, May 19, 1936, Senator M. M. Neely to Secretary of War George H. Dern, March 27, May 7, 9, April 1, June 1, 1936, Secretary of War to Senator M. M. Neely, April 7, May 15, June 9, 1936, I. J. K. Wells to Congressman Joe L. Smith, April 7, 1936, Edward McGrail to President F. D. Roosevelt, April 30, 1936, Edward McGrail to Secretary of War, May 1, 1936, TAG to Edward McGrail, Memorandum, Assistant Secretary to the President, May 4, 1936, May 7, 1936, TAG to D. L. Ferguson, May 7, 1936, Congressman Joe L. Smith to David A Lane, Jr., May 19, 1936, Congressman Joe L. Smith to TAG, May 19, 1936, John W. Davis to Secretary of War, May 22, 25, 1936, Senator Ruch D. Holt to WD, May 1936, TAG to Senator R. D. Holt, May 25, 1936, John W. Davis to President Franklin D. Roosevelt, May 25, 1936, Congressman Andrew Edmiston to BG John H. Hughes, May 27, 1936, I. J. K. Wells to Congressman John Kee, May 27, 1936, I. J. K. Wells to President F. D. Roosevelt, May 28, 1936, I. J. K. Wells to TAG, May 28, 1936, Congressman John Kee to MG E. T. Conley, June 6, 1936, TAG to I. J. K. Wells, June 9, 1936, TAG to John W. Davis, June 9, 1936, TAG to Congressman John Kee, June 10, 1936, I. J. K. Wells to TAG, June 12, 1936, RG 94, NA II. The West Virginia State Congress of Parents and Teachers approved its resolution during its annual meeting that was held in Gary on April 15–16, 1936. The executive committee of the West Virginia American Legion passed it resolution during its meeting at Morgantown that was held on April 25–26, 1936. The West Virginia High School Principals' Conference approved its resolution on May 11, 1936.

23. Memorandum, COL Robert L. Collins for Publications Division, February 20, 1936, Congressman A. Edmiston to MG Edgar T. Conley, February 10, 1937, TAG to Congressman A. Edmiston, February 17, 1937, John W. Davis to President F. D. Roosevelt, February 19, 1937, Senator M. M. Neely to Secretary of War Harry H. Woodring, February 23, March 6, 1937, Secretary of War to Senator M. M. Neely, February 26, March 11, 23, 1937, Senator M. M. Neely to Assistant Secretary of War Louis A. Johnson, March 18, 22, 1937, April 7, 12, 1938, Memorandum, BG L. D. Gasser for Chief of Staff Malin Craig, March 18, 1937, Congressman A. Edmiston to Assistant Secretary of War Louis Johnson, March 21, 1937, Assistant Secretary of War Louis Johnson to Senator M. M. Neely, March 22, 24, 26, 1937, April 8, 1938, Assistant Secretary of War Louis Johnson, March 23, 25, 1937, Congressman Joe L. Smith to Secretary of War Louis A. Johnson, March 1938, Assistant Secretary of War Louis A. Johnson, March 21, 24, 1938, RG 94, NA II; *Report of the Secretary of War, 1937,* 32.

24. David A. Lane, Jr. to Assistant Secretary of War Louis A. Johnson, July 15, 1937, Assistant Secretary of War Louis A. Johnson, July 19, 1937, Daniel L. Ferguson to Secretary of War Harry H. Woodring, August 6, 1937, MG E. T. Conley to Daniel L. Ferguson, [month?] 14, 1937, Daniel W. Ambrose, Jr. to Assistant Secretary of War Louis A. Johnson, April 4, 1938, Assistant Secretary of War Louis A. Johnson to Daniel W. Ambrose, April 8, 1938, RG 94, NA II.

25. D. T. Murray to Assistant Secretary of War Louis Johnson, March 19, 1939, June 17, 1940 Honorable Louis Johnson to D. T. Murray, March 25, 1938, June 21, 1940, RG 94, NA II. For information concerning the operation and participation of African Americans in the CCC, see Glen Cole, Jr., *The African-American Experience in the Civilian Conservation Corps* (Gainesville: University Press of Florida, 1999), passim; Charles Johnson, "The Army, the Negro and the Civilian Conservation Corp: 1933–1942," *Military Affairs* 26 (October 1972): 82–88.

26. Charles E. Hodges to Secretary of War Harry H. Woodring, March 30, 1938, Fred D. Cobb to Franklin D. Roosevelt, March 23, 1938, Charles E. Hodges TAG, March 30, 1938, TAG to Charles E. Hodges, April 2, 4, 1938, TAG to Fred D. Cobb, April 4, 1938, H. D. Hazelwood to President Franklin D. Roosevelt, April 11, 1938, H. H. Hazelwood to Senator M. M. Neely, April 11, 1938, Senator M. M. Neely to Assistant Secretary of War Louis Johnson, April 14, 1939, Assistant Secretary of War Louis Johnson to Senator M. M. Neely, April 19, 1938, TAG to H. D. Hazelwood, April 23, 1938, RG 94, NA II. The special committee of the Frederick Douglass Luncheon Club consisted of H. D. Hazelwood, J. J. Huguly, Reverend B. J. Nolan, S. E. Wade, Gillie Radford, A. L. Williams and two African American Women, B. J Nolan and G. A. Wright.

27. John W. Davis to Honorable Harry H. Woodring, January 18, September 28, 1938, January 3, 1939, Secretary of War Harry H. Woodring to J. W. Davis, January 19, 1938, TAG to John W. Davis, October 1, 1938, Memorandum, D. L. Ferguson to President Franklin D. Roosevelt, February 25, 1939, D. L. Ferguson to Assistant Secretary of War Louis Johnson, February 25, 1939, Secretary M. H. McIntyre for President Roosevelt, March 4, 1939, John W. Davis to Honorable George W. Johnson, March 4, September 29, 1939, June 4, 1940, Assistant Secretary of War Louis Johnson to D. L. Ferguson, March 6, 1939, George W. Johnson to Assistant Secretary of War Louis Johnson, March 7, October 10, 1939, TAG to D. L. Ferguson, March 9, 1939, Assistant Secretary of War Johnson to Honorable George W. Johnson, March 13, October 13, 16, 1939, John W. Davis to Congressman A. C. Shiffler, September 29, 1939, Congressman Schiffler to Assistant Secretary of War Louis Johnson, October 2, 1939, Congressman John Kee to Secretary of War Harry H. Woodring, October 7, 1939, Assistant Secretary of War Louis Johnson to Congressman A. C. Schiffler, October 10, 1939, Secretary of War Harry H. Woodring to Congressman John Kee, October 11, 1939, Assistant Secretary of War Louis A. Johnson to John W. Davis, June 8, 1940, Congressman Andrew Edmiston to Assistant Secretary of War Louis Johnson, March 5, 1939 Assistant Secretary of War Louis A. Johnson to Congressman Andrew Edmiston, March 15, 1940, Howard P. Jeter to President Franklin D. Roosevelt, June 1940, John W. Davis to President Franklin D. Roosevelt, June 4, 1940, TAG to John W. Davis, June 15, 1940, TAG to Howard P. Jeter, June 25, 1940, RG 94, NA II.

28. John W. Davis to President Franklin D. Roosevelt, October 21, 1940, John W. Davis to Secretary of War Stimson, October 21, 1940, John W. Davis to Congressman George W. Johnson, October 21, 1940, John W. Davis to Congressman John Kee, October 21, 1940, John W. Davis to David Kirby, October 21, 1940, John W. Davis to Congressman M. M. Neely, October 21, 1940, Governor Homer A. Holt to Secretary of War Stimson, October 23, 1940, Congressman A. C. Schiffler to Secretary of War Stimson, October 25, 1940, L. A. Toney to President Franklin D. Roosevelt, October 23,

24, 1940, L. A. Toney to Secretary of War Stimson, October 24, 1940, L. A. Toney to Congressman George W. Johnson, October 24, 1940, David Kirby to Secretary of War Stimson, October 25, 1940, I. J. K. Wells to President F. D. Roosevelt, October 26, 1940, I. J. K. Wells to Secretary of War Stimson, 26, 1940, Congressman George W. Johnson to General George C. Marshall, October 28, 1940, Congressman John Kee to Secretary of War Stimson, October 29, 1940, Secretary of War Stimson to Congressman Schiffler, October 30, 1940, Secretary of War Stimson to Governor Holt, October 30, 1940, Walter R. Thurmond to Secretary of War Stimson, October 30, 1940, M. M. Neely to Secretary of War Stimson, October 28, 31, 1940, Secretary of War Stimson to M. M. Neely, October 31, 1940, Secretary of War Stimson to I. J. K. Wells, November 4, 1940, Acting Secretary of War William Bryden to Congressmen Kee, November 5, 1940, TAG to L. A. Toney, November 2, 5, 18, 1940, TAG to John W. Davis, November 4, 1940, Acting Secretary of War William Bryden to Congressmen Neely, November 5, 1940, TAG to Walter R. Thurmond, November 8, 1940, S. S. Gordon to President F. D. Roosevelt, November 24, 1940, TAG to S. S. Gordon, December 19, 1940, RG 94, NA II.

29. Chief of Staff George Marshall to Congressman George W. Johnson, RG 94 NA II. The list of applications submitted to the congressman did not include West Virginia State. The only African American institution was Tuskegee and it was listed as a 55c organization.

30. Daniel W. Ambrose to TAG, April 4, 1941, TAG to D. W. Ambrose, April 5, 1941, Senator Harley M. Kilgore to GEN George C. Marshall, December 30, 1941, GEN Marshall to Senator Kilgore, January 2, 1942, RG 94, NA II.

31. TAG to James E. Gregg, September 24, 1919, William H. Scoville to TAG, September 26, 30, October 13, 1919, TAG to W. H. Scoville, October 8, 1919, JAG E. H. Crowder, Memorandum for Chief of Staff, November 8, 1919, COL William Lassiter, Memorandum for TAG, November 24,1919, TAG to Judge Advocate General of the Army, October 4, 30, 1919, Judge Advocate General of the Army to TAG, October 6, November 1, 1919, TAG to W. H. Scoville, October 9, November 5, 1919, RG 407, NA II; Report of the Department of Military Discipline and Physical Training, Hampton Institute, VA, January 1919, Hampton University Archives, Harvey Library, Hampton, VA. The formal designation of Hampton was Hampton Normal and Agricultural Institute. Hereafter, Hampton University Archives will be used for Hampton University Archives, Harvey Library, Hampton, VA and JAG for Judge Advocate General of the Army.

32. Secretary of War Baker to James E. Gregg, May 8, 13, 27, 1920, J. E. Gregg to Secretary of War Baker, May 4, 11, June 4, 1920, Memorandum, Secretary of War for GEN [Peyton C.], March 13, 1920, Memorandum, COL F. E. Lacey, Jr. for TAG, May 19, June 29, 1920, TAG to Eastern Department Commanding General, May 19, 1920, Memorandum, MG W. G. Haan for TAG, June 9, 1920, TAG to J. E. Gregg, June 23, 1920, RG 407, NA II.

33. 1LT Leonard L. McCleod to James E. Gregg, July 8, 1920, Adelbert Cronkite to James E. Gregg, September 29, 1920, Military Science File, Hampton University Archives.

34. J. E. Gregg to TAG, September 24, October 16, 1920, Third Corps Area HQ to TAG, October 5, 1920, AG P. C. Harris to J. E. Gregg, October, October 11, 16, 1920, Memorandum, COL F. E. Lacey, Jr. for TAG, Memorandum, Chief of Staff Third Corps Area HQ to TAG, October 21, 1920, November 2, 1920, AG C. H. Danielson to Third Corps Area Commanding General, November 5, 1920 RG 407, NA II. LT Leonard L. McLeod had served with 1LT John A. Love in the 350th Field Artillery and upon their arrival in September 1918 at Hampton Institute were respectively assigned to be commanders of Companies A and B. CPT Charles W. Fairfax was relieved of his duties as commander of Company A and became the battalion commander. LT Love was trans-

ferred to Howard University and 2LT Lee J. Purnell assumed command of Company B on October 5, 1918. See SO 34, Headquarters Training Detachment, Hampton Institute, VA, September 26, 1918, SO 36, Headquarters SATC Corps, Hampton Institute, VA, September 26, 1918, CEST, RG 165, NA; TAG to J. E. Gregg, October 11, November 5, 1920, J. E. Gregg to TAG, October 16, 1920, J. E. Gregg to MG Adelbert Cronkhite, October 19, 1920, MG A. Cronkhite to J. E. Gregg, October 23, 1920, Report of the Department of Discipline and Military Training, Hampton Institute, March 1921, Military Science File, Hampton University Archives; Hampton Normal and Agricultural Institute, *Act of Incorporation By-Laws, Extracts from the Code of Virginia, etc. for the use of the Trustees* (Hampton: Hampton N&I Institute Press, 1922), 9.

35. MAJ John Green to James E. Gregg, October 3, 1920, James E. Gregg to TAG, November 3, 1920, May 9, 23, 1921, James E. Gregg to COL Hall, November 4, 1920, SO 267–0, War Department, Washington, DC, November 12, 1920, TAG to James E. Gregg, November 8, 1920, James E. Gregg to MAJ C. R. Norton, November 27, 1920, James E. Gregg to COL F. J. Morrow, December 17, 1920, MG Cronkite to James E. Gregg, May 31, 1921, COL E. J. Morrow to James E. Gregg, December 30, 1921, Military File, Hampton University Archives. Retired Army noncommissioned officers assigned to Hampton Institute included 1SGT Edward Madison from Camp Stephen D. Little, Nogales, Arizona, MSGT George A. Holland and SSGT Baxter W. Watson. See SO 12–E, War Department, Washington, DC, January 15, 1921, SO 262–E, War Department, Washington, DC, November 15, 1921, SO 257–E, War Department, Washington, DC, November 8, 1921, Military File, Hampton University Archives. Hereafter, WO will be used for warrant officer.

36. J. E. Gregg to TAG, September 30, December 20, 1921, January 28, 1922, Memorandum, BG W. Lassiter for TAG, October 18, 1921, January 24, February 11, 1922, TAG to Third Corps Area Commanding General, October 18, 1921, Third Corps Area HQ to TAG, January 3, 16, 1922, Memorandum, BG W. Lassiter for Chief of Staff, January 11, 1922, TAG to J. E. Gregg, January 13, 24, 1922, Memorandum, TAG for Assistant Chief of Staff for Operations, February 6, 1922, RG 407, NA II; Report of the Department of Discipline and Military Instruction, Hampton Institute, VA, March 1921, Military Program File, Hampton University Archives.

37. COL N. M. Cartmell (retired) to Third Corps Area Commanding General, February 4, 8, 1926, Third Corps Area HQ to J. E. Gregg, February 5, 1926, Third Corps Area Commanding General to TAG, February 16, 1926, TAG to Third Corps Area Commanding General, March 2, 1926, WD Bulletin 1, Washington, DC, March 21, 1926, RG 94, NA II; 1SGT Edward Madison, retired, of Phoebus was assigned to Hampton on October 1, 1925. See Special Order 125, Headquarters, War Department, Washington, DC, June 26, 1925.

38. Robert H. Brisbane, *The Black Vanguard* (Valley Forge: Judson Press, 1970), 107–09; Joe M. Richardson, *A History of Fisk University, 1865–1946* (University, AL: University of Alabama Press, 1980), 84–100.

39. Tuskegee Institute Newspaper Release, January 11, 1919, CPT Russell Smith to Robert R. Moton, July 14, 1919, TAG To Robert R. Moton, July 21, 1919, Robert R. Moton to CPT Russell C. Smith, July 29, 1919, Robert R. Moton to TAG, n.d., TAG to Robert Moton, July 23, 1919, Robert R. Moton Papers, Hollis Burke Frissell Library, Tuskegee University, Tuskegee, AL. Hereafter cited as Robert R. Moton Papers. Other African American officers assigned to ROTC detachments were: MAJ Milton Dean and CPT Charles C. Johnson at Howard; CPT John H. Purnell at West Virginia Collegiate Institute; and 1LT Leonard McLeod and 2LT Ernest C. Johnson at Hampton; 1LT Robert L. Campbell at North Carolina State A and T; 1LT Samuel Hull at South Carolina State A and M; 1LT William R. Smalls at Alabama A and M; 1LT Grant Stewart at Tennessee

State A and I; 1LT Percival R. Piper at Wilberforce University; 1LT Elijah H. Goodwin at Branch Normal School at Pine Bluff, Arkansas; CPT Cooper at Straight College; and 1LT Walter Giles at Prairie View N&I College.

40. Robert R. Moton to MAJ W. H. Loving, May 26, 1919, COL G. S. Goodale to Robert R. Moton, August 4, 1919, Secretary of War Newton D. Baker to Robert R. Moton, October 23, 1919, Robert R. Moton to Secretary of War Newton D. Baker, October 27, August 12, 1919, November 4, 1920, TAG to Robert R. Moton, July 31, 1920, Robert R. Moton Papers; Tuskegee *Student*, October 19, 1918, March 11, 1922. 1LT James C. Pinkston was discharged, reenlisted as a SSGT and assigned to Tuskegee together with MSGT Charles Ecton. MSGT Ecton and SGT Pinkston who was severely wounded in action in France had eighteen and nineteen months respectively until they were eligible for retirement. Therefore, LTC Davis requested that Russell Smith who was similarly discharged, reenlisted and detailed to Tuskegee Institute be commissioned a CPT similar to the other military instructors. The procedure was continued when SGT Arthur P. Hayes, assigned to the Detached Enlisted Men's List (DEML), was relieved from duty with the Cavalry Detachment at the USMA and reassigned to the institute. See Minutes of the Meeting of the Military Committee, September 10, 1922, Robert R. Moton to Honorable Newton D. Baker, October 1, 1920, LTC Benjamin O. Davis to Robert R. Moton, December 2, 1920, February 14, 1922, SO, War Department, Washington, DC, January 31, 1922, Robert R. Moton Papers.

41. LTC Benjamin O. Davis to TAG, February 22, 1922, Garnet C. Wilkinson to LTC Benjamin O. Davis, June 28, 1922, LTC Benjamin O. Davis to COL Harrison Hill, July 2, 1922, LTC Davis to MAJ Edgar W. Burr, June 1923, BG Benjamin O. Davis Papers, Manuscript Division, Military History Institute, Carlisle Barracks, PA. Hereafter, BOD will be used for Benjamin O. Davis, MHI for Military History Institute, and CBPA for Carlisle Barracks, PA; Robert R. Moton to COL Harrison Hall, July 7, 1922, TAG to Robert R. Moton, July 10, 1922, Fourth Corps Area Chief of Staff to Robert R. Moton, July 10, 1922, MG David C. Shanks to Robert R. Moton, July 25, 1922, Robert R. Moton Papers.

42. Robert R. Moton to Fourth Corps Area ADJ R. B. Parrott, March 13, 1922, Robert R. Moton to Fourth Corps Area ADJ R. B. Parrot, April 27, 1922, Fourth Corps Area Chief of Staff H. G. Bishop to Robert R. Moton, May 29, July 10, 1922, TAG to Robert R. Moton, July 10, 1922, Robert R. Moton to LTC Benjamin O. Davis, July 12, 1922, COL TAG to LTC Benjamin O. Davis, July 19, 1922, MG David C. Shanks to LTC Benjamin O. Davis, July 25, 1922, Wilkinson to LTC Benjamin O. Davis, September 1, 1922, BOD Papers, MHI, CBPA.

43. Emmett J. Scott to LTC Benjamin O. Davis, September 14, 1922, LTC Benjamin O. Davis to Emmett J. Scott, September 14, 1922, BOD Papers, MHI, CBPA.

44. Robert R. Moton to Fourth Corps Area Commanding General, April 17, 1923, MG David C. Shanks to TAG, May 24, 1923, MG J. H. McRae to TAG, June 25, 1923, RG 94, NA II.

45. TAG to Fourth Corps Area Commanding General, April 17, 1923, February 29, July 3, 1924, Memorandum, COL W. R. Smedberg for Assistant Chief of Staff (G-1), July 5, 1923, Memorandum, BG C. H. Martin for TAG, July 23, 1923, Memorandum, COL J. E. Woodward for Promotion and Assignments Section, July 23, 1923, MG David C. Shanks to Robert R. Moton, March 3, 18, 1924, A. L. Holsey to GEN Shanks, March 21, 1924, Robert R. Moton to GEN Shanks, March 29, April 21, June 16, 1924, Fourth Corps Area Chief of Staff George H. McManus to TAG, April 5, 1924, Memorandum, TAG for Assistant Chief of Staff (G-1), April 10, 1924, MG Shanks to TAG, April 26, 1924, Fourth Corps Area Chief of Staff George H. McManus to TAG, June 24, 1924, Memorandum, BG Hugh A. Drum for TAG, July 1, 1924, RG 94, NA II.

46. Robert R. Moton to Secretary of War James W. Good, June 6, 1929, Robert R. Moton to President Herbert Hoover, June 6, 1929, Secretary of the President Lawrence Richey to Secretary of War Good, June 10, 1929, Memorandum, COL E. G. Peyton for Chief of Staff, June 18, 1929, Secretary of War Good to Robert R. Moton, June 20, 1029, RG 94, NA.

47. Robert R. Moton to Secretary of War Patrick J. Hurley, October 1, 1929, Secretary of War Hurley to Robert R. Moton, October 3, 1929, Robert R. Moton to President H. Hoover, October 18, 1929, Robert R. Moton to Walter H. Newton, November 7, 1929, RG 94, NA II.

48. Lawrence Richey to Secretary of War, October 22, 1930, Secretary of War to L. Richey, October 23, 1930, Memoranda, Walter H. Newton for Secretary Hurley, October 29, November,1930, Secretary of War Hurley to W. H. Newton, November 15, 26, December 8, 1930, Undersecretary of State to W. H. Newton, November 21, 1930, Memorandum, COL R. C. Foy for Chief of Staff, December 4, 1930, Acting Secretary of War to Secretary of State, December 5, 1930, Memorandum for SO 286, War Department, December 8, 1930, TAG to MG Frank R. McCoy, December 10, 1930, RG 94, NA II.

49. LTC Davis to Dean of the College, February 11, 1931, LTC Benjamin O. Davis to Robert R. Moton, April 20, 1931, BOD Papers, MHI, CBPA.

50. Robert R. Moton to Secretary of War, August 26, 1931, TAG to Robert R. Moton, September 3, 21, 1931, Robert R. Moton to TAG, September 17, 1931, Fourth Corps Area commanding general to TAG, November 30, 1931, Chief of Infantry to TAG, December 10, 1931, Memorandum, MG Edward L. King for Chief of Staff, December 21, 1931, Chief of Staff Douglas MacArthur to Robert R. Moton, December 29, 1931, Robert R. Moton to Chief of Staff MacArthur, January 7, 1932, Memorandum, MAJ John F. Davis for TAG, August 14, 1933, Memorandum for SO 195, WD, August 22, 1933, RG 94, NA II.

51. Fred D. Patterson to Senator Hugo L. Black, September 1, 1936, Senator H. L. Black to TAG, September 2, 1936, TAG to Senator H. L. Black, September 10, 1936, CPT C. C. Cavender to TAG, November 24, 1936, COL J. B. Woolnough, December 2, 1936, RG 94, NA II.

52. Fred D. Patterson to Chief of Staff Malin Craig, June 28, 1937, Chief of Staff M. Craig to Fred D. Patterson, July 2, 1937, Memorandum BG George P. Tyner for TAG, July 6, 1937, MG George Van Horn Moseley to TAG, July 29, 1937, Memorandum, COL G. W. Cocheu for Chief of Staff, July 30, 1937, Memorandum, BG Frank C. Burnett for Assistant Chief of Staff, July 30, 1937, Tuskegee Dean of Men to TAG, September 18, 1937, RG 94, NA II; Tuskegee Institute *Crimson and Gold, 1938*, 29. CPT Charles Ecton together with CPTs George W. Winston, Walter J. Love, Hugh F. Barrington and Conrad Hutchinson had served as assistant PMSTs under COL Davis in 1935. The clerical staff included A. D. long and M. L. Golden. See COL B. O. Davis to Robert R. Moton, April 20, 1935, Fred D. Patterson Papers, Hollis Burke Frissell Library, Tuskegee University, Tuskegee, AL.

53. Frederick D. Patterson to Secretary of War H. H. Woodring, September 19, October 4, 1939, TAG to Frederick D. Patterson, September 26, 1939, RG 94, NA II.

54. George M. Lightfoot, Alaine Locke, and Martha MacLear," Howard University in the War: A Record of Patriotic Service," *Howard University Record* 13 (February 1919): 89; *Howard University Record* 13 (April 1919): 23; Rayford W. Logan, *Howard University: The First Hundred Years, 1867–1967* (New York: New York University Press, 1969), 183; COL Campbell C. Johnson Address, Charter Day Exercises, Howard University, Washington, DC, March 1943, COL Campbell C. Johnson Papers, Moorland-Spingarn Research Center, Manuscript Division, Howard University, Washington, DC.

55. COL A. Thayer to Eastern Department Commanding General, May 3, 1920, RG 407, NA II.

56. Emmett J. Scott to Secretary of War Baker, December 22, 1919, January 7, 12, 23, 1920, Secretary of War Baker to E. M. Scott, January 2, 10, 14, 1920, Secretary of War to Secretary of the Interior Franklin K. Lane, January 10, 1920, Secretary of the Interior Lane to Secretary of War Baker, January 12, 1920, RG 407, NA II; Public Law 245, 68th Congress, 2nd Session, June 7, 1924; Logan, *Howard University*, 195, 207. The estimate of the athletic field and drill ground was $47,500 and the estimate for the gymnasium and armory was $150,000. The Howard University Executive committee gave the administration and control of Spaulding Hall where the gymnasium and armory were located to ROTC in 1926. Other appropriations requested by Durkee were for an agricultural building at $75,000, engineering building at $150,000, home economics building at $85,000, administration building at $80,000, university hall at $200,000, enlargement of conservatory of music at $60,000, medical buildings at $370,000, and dormitories for men and women at $100,000 respectively.

57. MAJ Harry L. Jordan to Third Corps Area HQ, June 1, 1921, Third Corps Area Chief of Staff to J. S. Durkee, June 2, 1920, J. S. Durkee to Third Corps Area Chief of Staff, June 9, 1920, RG 407, NA II.

58. Third Corps Area Chief of Staff to TAG, June 16, 1921, Memorandum, COL William M. Cruikshank for TAG, June 27, 1921, TAG to Durkee, June 29, 1921, Durkee to TAG, August 9, September 15, 1921, RG 407, NA II. Durkee was also angered by the delayed correspondence from TAG because he referred to C. H. Daniels as D. H. Daniels.

59. E. J. Scott to Theodore Roosevelt, July 11, 1921, T. Roosevelt to J. Matthew Wainwright, July 19, 1921, J. M. Wainwright to T. Roosevelt, August 1, 1921, J. S. Durkee to Third Corps Area Assistant AG E. H. Metzer, August 24, 1921, Third Corps Area Commanding General to TAG, September 1, 1921 TAG to Third Corps Area Commanding General, September 8, 1921, RG 407, NA II.

60. BG H. F. Hodges to TAG, September 30, 1921, RG 407, NA II.

61. J. S. Durkee to TAG, October 1, 18, 1921, Durkee to Third Corps Area Commanding General, October 18, 1921, Assistant Adjutant E. H. Metzer to J. S. Durkee, October 21, 1921, Memorandum, BG W. Lassiter for TAG, October 21, November 2, 1921, TAG to Third Corps Area Commanding General, November 5, 1921, RG 407, NA II.

62. CPT Julian De Court to TAG, July 6, 13, 1922, J. S. Durkee to Assistant Secretary of War Wainwright, July 10, August 22, 1922, E. M. Scott to Ernest Lyon, July 11, 1922, LTC Louis J. Van Schick, July 18, 1922, Third Corps Area Commanding General to TAG, July 25, 1922, TAG to CPT De Court, August 5, 1922, Assistant Secretary of War Wainwright to J. S. Durkee, August 5, September 8, 1922, Secretary of War John W. Weeks to Congressman Sydney E. Mudd, August 5, 1922, TAG to Third Corps Area Commanding General, August 5, September 1, 1922, Memorandum, MG J. H. McRae for TAG, August 24, 1922, Memorandum, MG J. G. Harbord for Assistant Chief of Staff for Personnel, September 6, 1922, Memorandum for SO 211, WD, September 8, 1922, Memorandum for SO 217, WD, September 15, 1922, RG 407, NA II; Howard University *Hilltop*, February 4, 1924, November 4, 1925, March 11, 1926, November 10, 1926, November 22, 1927, October 24, 1928, February 26, 1929; Logan, *Howard University*, 113. The officers commissioned in 1922 were Julian B. Allen, Benjamin Bell, Alston W. Burleigh, Leonard H. B. Foote, Julius M. Gardner, William I. Gough, William B. Greene, Peyton R. Higginbotham, King Solomon Jones, J. Wycliffe Keller, Crumwell H. McDonald, Joseph W. Nicholson, Claude A. Riley, George H. Sembly, Arthur H. Simmons, Julius T. A. Smith and Charles S. Walker.

63. Howard University *Hilltop*, June 5, October 2, 1935, October 19, 1936. Other personnel who served in the Military Science Department included CPT Frank E. Linnell (DOL) whose transfer was announced in March 1929. LT H. F. G. Matthews

served in the ROTC department for several years until assigned to the Philadelphia Quartermaster School in 1934. He was replaced by LT Samuel S. Conley who was transferred from Fort Meade to Howard University. LT Conley was reassigned after the summer camp at Fort Howard in 1935 to Fort Leavenworth and was replaced by CPT William B. Miller. CPT Edward A. Kimball was also reassigned to Fort Davis in the Canal Zone after the 1935 summer encampment. In 1939, CPT Henry J. Boettcher was assigned to the ROTC detachment and was promoted to the rank of MAJ on November 10, 1939. See Howard University *Hilltop*, December 20, 1928, March 18, 1929 September 26, 1934, March 6, 1935, Thanksgiving 1939.

 64. LTC D. Y. Beckham to Howard PMST, December 20, 1924, COL P. T. Hayne to COL Howard, January 7, 1925, Durkee to COL Howard, January 25, 1925, RG 407, NA II.

 65. Howard University *Hilltop*, March 29, April 29, May 8, 1925; Logan, *Howard University*, 213, 220–22, 231, 239–40, 242–44, 277–278; Raymond Wolters, *The New Negro on Campus: Black College Rebellions of the 1920s* (Princeton: Princeton University Press, 1975), 112–118; Clipping File, J. Stanley Durkee Papers, Manuscript Division, Howard University Library, Washington, DC; COL W. W. McCammon to Third Corps Area Commanding General, November 28, 1934, NA. For regulations concerning delinquency and demerits for failure to attend classes, see Howard University, *Reserve Officers' Training Corps Regulations, Howard University Unit 331*, Washington, DC, November 31, 1919. The author is grateful to MAJ Robert Greene, ret., who provided a copy of Howard University's regulations.

 66. Operations and Training Division for Operations, Memorandum for the Chief of Staff, December 30, 1929, RG 94, NA II.

 67. Fletcher, Marvin E. *America's First Black General: Benjamin O. Davis, Sr., 1880–1970*, (Lawrence: University of Kansas Press, 1989), 70.

 68. COL A. L. Fuller to Wilberforce PMST, February 20, 1936, MAJ Joseph W. Whitney to Fifth Corps Area Commanding General, February 21, 1936, Fifth Corps Area Commanding General to TAG, February 24, May 12, 1936, TAG to Fifth Corps Area Commanding General, February 28, 1928, TAG, Memorandum for SO 118, May 18, 1936, TAG, Memorandum for SO, July 29, 1936, RG 94, NA II; Fletcher, *America' First Black General*, 79.

 69. David A. Blake to Secretary of War, February 13, 1939, TAG to D. A. Blake, February 17, 1939, RG 94, NA II.

 70. LT Leonard L. McLeod, Report of the Instruction of Military Science and Tactics, March 1, 1920, Military Science File, Hampton University Archives.

 71. LTC A. F. Dannemiller to Third Corps Area Commanding General, July 24, 1928, RG 94, NA.

 72. Third Corps Area HQ to TAG, July 28, 1928, RG 94, NA.

 73. TAG to Third Corps Commanding General, August 1, 1928, HQ Fifth Corps Area to Third Corps Area Commanding General, November 10, 1928, MAJ Spaulding to TAG, November 20, 1928, Memorandum, BG Frank Parker for TAG, January 30, 1928, TAG to Third Corps Commanding General, December 1, 1928, Third Corps Area Commanding General to TAG, December 13, 1928, Memorandum, BG Frank Parker for Chief of Staff, December 22, 1928, RG 94, NA II. The Third Corps Area had estimated the cost to train 43 Howard students and 7 Wilberforce students during the summer of 1929 was $3,463.41 at Camp Knox, $538.48 at Fort Wood, and $2,633,02 at Wilberforce University. The cost of maintaining the summer ROTC camp at Fort Wood was a major factor which prevented the establishment of a separate camp in the Fifth Corps Area. Hereafter, CMTC will be used for Citizens' Military Training Camp.

 74. Howard University *Hilltop*, September 26, 1934.

75. LTC Benjamin O. Davis to Robert R. Moton, May 7, 1921, Fourth Corps Area Assistant AG Robert Whitfield to LTC Benjamin O. Davis, March 18, 1923, Fourth Corps Area Commanding General to Fifth Corps Area Commanding General, April 16, 1929, TAG to Fifth Corps Area Commanding General, April 25, 1929, BOD Paper, CBPA. Training at CMTC was divided into three courses. The red course was designed to teach new citizens the responsibilities of American citizenship, the white course provided training for selected privates in the organized reserves to qualify as noncommissioned officers, and the blue course provided advance training to WO and selected noncommissioned officers of the regular Army, National Guard, Enlisted Reserve Corps, and civilians seeking commissions in the Officers Reserve Corps.

LTC Davis also served as advisor to ORC personnel attached to the Ohio National Guard Battalion and officers affiliated with the Wilberforce Chapter of the Reserve Officers' Association. Officers in the 449th Infantry, ORC, included CPT Charles C. Buford, James E. Bush, Amos A. Carter, Charles T. Isom and Joseph T. Jackson, 1LT John W. Rowe, 2LT Holley Cooley, C. H. Harrison, Harry Lueber, and W. H. Motley. Officers in the Wilberforce Chapter of the Reserve Officers Association met at the residence of 2LT Charles F. Points on March 16, 1930 and passed a resolution in recognition of Davis being the first African American while on active duty in the regular Army to reach the rank of COL. Other officers at the meeting were CPT Orestus J. Kincaid and James Nichols, 1LT Grover Harden and William Madison, and 2LT J. Aubrey Lane.

76. Supplemental Report of the War Department Special Board on Negro Manpower: Discussion of Specific Comments as to the Recommendation made by the Board in tis Original Report dated November 17, 1945, RG 165, NA II; Bernard C. Nalty, *Strength for the Fight* (New York: Free Press, 1986), 133.

## Chapter 3

1. *Report of the Secretary of War, 1941*, 74–75; W. B. Hatcher to President Franklin D. Roosevelt, October 1940, TAG to W. B. Hatcher, November 5, 1940, COL James T. Watson to 93rd Division Signal Officer, July 10, 1942, COL Campbell C. Johnson Papers, Manuscript Division, Moorland-Spingarn Research Center, Howard University, Washington, DC. Hereafter, COL Campbell C. Johnson Papers will be referred to as the C.C. Johnson Papers.

2. Memorandum, MAJ Campbell C. Johnson for COL William H. Draper, Jr., March 41, 1941, C. C. Johnson Papers.

3. MAJ C. C. Hill to Hyacinth Holmes, January 15, 1942, Robert B. Hill to MAJ C. C. Johnson, March 27, 1942, C. C. Johnson to Robert B. Hill, April 2, 1942, C. C. Johnson Papers. The physicians were James E. Bowman, C. P. Carmichael, Theodore R. George, Albert R. Hughes, William C. Goines, D. McCarthy Harper, Isaiah B. Horn, Ulysses L. Houston, K. Albert Harden, Edward S. Jones, Ulysses B. Martin, J. O. Miles, G. Frazier Miller, Kline Price, William T. Randall, Henry S. Robinson, Walter S. Savoy, O. N. Simmons, Herbert L. Stevens, Frank Turner and Ira Warf. See the Washington *Afro-American*, November 14, 1942.

4. Memorandum, William H. Hastie for the Assistant Secretary of War, April 4, 1941, C. C. Johnson Papers.

5. Memorandum, Hastie for Under Secretary of War, February 5, 1942, C. C. Johnson Papers. The 1941 Troop List for African Americans revealed that 99th Pursuit Squadron was assigned to the Tuskegee but the other nine Air Force Aviation Separate Squadrons were based at Langley Field, Al, Barksdale Field, LA, Savannah, GA, Maxwell Field, AL, Dale Mabry Airport in Tallahassee, FL, Jackson, MS, Daniels Field in Augusta, GA, MacDill Field, FL, and New Orleans, LA. The Air Corps Services which

consisted of the 31st, 34th, 35th Quartermaster Truck Regiments, and the 810th Engineer Battalion (An) were similarly dispersed from air fields along the east coast to bases in California. The 78th Tank Battalion was training at Camp Claiborne, LA, while the 4th Cavalry Brigade with the 9th and 10th Cavalry Regiment, located at Fort Riley, KS. The 76th and 77th Coastal Antiaircraft Artillery (Mobile) Regiments trained at Fort Bragg, NC and the 99th and 100th Coastal Antiaircraft Artillery (Semi-Mobile) Regiments were located at Camp Davis, NC. The 54th Coastal Artillery (155 mm Howitzer) Regiment was stationed at Camp Wallace, TX but performed some training with detachments stationed at Camp Davis. Headquarters and Headquarters Battery, 46th Field Artillery Brigade together with the 350th (155mm Howitzer), 351st (155mm Howitzer), 353rd Field Artillery (155mm Gun) Regiments were at Camp Livingston, LA but the 349th (155mm Gun) Regiment was located at Fort Sill, OK. The 24th Infantry Regiment was assigned to Fort Benning, GA, 25th and 368th Infantry Regiments to Fort Huachuca, AR, 366th to Fort Devens, MS and the 367th to Camp Claiborne, LA. The 1st and 2nd Chemical (Decontamination) companies were at Edgewood Arsenal, MD. The 41st and 45th Engineer Regiment (General Service), 91st, 92nd, 93rd, 94th, 95th, 96th, 97th, 98th Engineer Separate Battalions, 76th and 77th Engineer Companies (L Pon), and 576th and 585th Engineer Companies (Dp Trk) were scattered at different locations. The 55th, 57th, 60th 64th, 65th Ordnance Company (Am) Companies were at Fort Lewis, WA, but the 69th, 621st 630th, 632 and 636 Ordnance Companies (Am) were stationed at the Savannah Ordnance Depot in Illinois. Detachments and companies of the 22nd, 28th, 29th, 47th 48th Quartermaster (Truck) Regiments, 393rd Quartermaster Port Battalion, 67th and 68th Quartermaster Truck (Pk), 87th, 91st, 92nd, 93rd Quartermaster Companies (Rhd), 226th, 227th, 228th, 229th Quartermaster Companies (Salv Coll), and the 240th Quartermaster Service Battalions were scattered among many military locations. The 76th Signal Separate Construction Company was assigned to Fort Leonard Wood, MO. The National Guard organizations, which consisted of the 369th Coastal Antiaircraft Artillery, 184th Field Artillery (155mm Howitzer), and 372nd Infantry Regiments, were respectively assigned to Fort Ontario, NY, Fort Custer, MI, and Fort Dix, NJ.

COL Benjamin O. Davis was notified by the Deputy Chief of Staff, MG William Bryan, on November 27, 1940 of the scheduled federal induction of the 369th Antiaircraft Artillery Regiment in January 1941. With this activation, he would be transferred to command the 9th and 10th Cavalry Regiments which were scheduled to form the 4th Cavalry Brigade. The 9th and 10th Cavalry Regiments were stationed at Ft. Riley and Ft Leavenworth, Kansas respectively, with detachments of the latter stationed at the U.S. Military Academy and Fort Myer, Virginia. Each regiment had lost cadres and functioned at a peacetime strength of 450 and 650 respectively. The reason for the lower strength of the 9th Cavalry was due to the reassignment of approximately 150 troopers who served as cadre for the Colored Cavalry School Detachment. MG J. K. Herr, Chief of Cavalry stated that construction at Fort Riley would cause the brigade to billet at Fort Function which adjoined Fort Riley. Serving as part of the 3rd Cavalry Division until October 10, 1940 when transferred to the 4th Brigade, 2nd Cavalry Division at Ft. Leavenworth, the brigade completed training in a maneuver area in Arkansas from August 26, 1941 to October 1, 1941. Both regiments returned to Ft. Riley and later were assigned to Camp Funston, Kansas until the 9th Cavalry was transferred to Ft. Clark, Texas on July 3–4, 1942 and the 10th Cavalry to Camp Lockett, CA on June 30, 1942. Before his transfer, BG Davis had attempted to have his son, CPT Benjamin O. Davis, Jr., transferred to the brigade as his aide-de-camp but the employment of African Americans as aviators at Tuskegee involved his son in a leadership role which determined his future service in the Army.

The 9th and 10th Cavalry Regiments of the 4th Brigade were transferred to a staging area at Patrick Henry, VA where they departed Hampton Roads, VA and arrived in Assi-Ben-Okba, Algeria respectively on March 5 and 12, 1944. By March 20, 1944, the 10th Cavalry was converted into the 6486 Engineer Construction Battalion and nine days later it was disbanded with its personnel reassigned to the 1334th Engineer Construction Battalion. The 9th Cavalry was also disbanded and its assets were transferred to provisional port battalions. When the regiments were transferred to North Africa on March 1944 and inactivated at Assi-Ben-Okba, Algeria by March 31, 1944, personnel in the 27th Cavalry were transferred to form the 6404th Port Battalion and those in the 28th Cavalry formed the 6487th Engineer Battalion. The 3rd Signal Troop which was not transferred to Algeria converted into a signal construction unit. It is understandable that the historical report for the 1334th Engineer Construction Battalion revealed morale and discipline within the battalion very unsatisfactory. The elimination of 27th and 28th Cavalry Regiments in the 5th Brigade was completed with the conversion of the 2nd Cavalry Division.

Ironically, the decision to disband the last remaining cavalry division was discussed during a conference GEN Henry L. Stimson had with Generals McNarney, Somervell, Miller, White, Porter, Handy and Jack McCloy on January 27, 1944. Staff recommendations concerning the shortage of manpower, particularly with reference to African American soldiers, included the transformation of the 2nd Division which was the only remaining cavalry organization into a service corps. Staff personnel were convinced that the manpower shortage required immediate emergency attention and the deployment of a trained divisional organization. This planned conversion of the Buffalo Soldiers terminated the linage of the only African American cavalry regiments which were authorized under congressional legislation enacted on July 23, 1866. Although Army officials had earlier sought the elimination of the 9th and 10th Cavalry Regiments, it is ironic that when combat manpower was desired to complete combat missions their deactivation was the only solution military officials were willing to implement. See MG William Bryden to BG Benjamin O. Davis, November 27, 1940, January 1941, MG J. K. Herr to BG Benjamin O. Davis, January 16, 1941, TAG to BG Benjamin O. Davis, C. A. Franklin to BG Benjamin O. Davis, May 19, 1941, June 28, 1941, July 30, 1943, Benjamin O. Davis Papers, Manuscript Division, Military History Institute, Carlisle Barracks, Carlisle, Pennsylvania; Activation of the 2nd Cavalry Division, USA, at Ft. Clark, Texas, February 25, 1943, HQ, 1334th Engineer Construction Battalion to Historian, PBS, USA, June 6, 1944, CPT Samuel A. Gustavson to Commanding Officer of Peninsular Base Section, September 4, 1944, Records of The Adjutant General's Office, 1917–, RG 407, WNRC; Diaries of Henry L. Stimson, January 27, 1944, Papers of Henry L. Stimson, Manuscript and Archives, Yale University Library, New Haven, Connecticut; Charles Johnson, Jr., *African American Soldiers in the National Guard: Recruitment and Deployment during Peacetime and War* (Westport: Greenwood Press, 1992) pp. 145–46.

6. Robert J. Jakeman, *The Divided Skies: Establishing Flight Training at Tuskegee, Alabama, 1934–1942* (Tuscaloosa: University of Alabama Press, 1992), passim; Stanley Sandler, *Segregated Skies: All-Black Combat Squadrons of WWII* (Washington: Smithsonian Institution Press, 1992), passim; Lawrence P. Scott and William M. Womack, Sr., *Double V: The Civil Rights Struggle of the Tuskegee Airmen* (East Lansing: Michigan State University, 1994), passim; Howard University *Hilltop*, February 27, October 23, 1940, April 21, November 7, 1941; BG Davis to C. Alfred Anderson, August 12, 1941, BOD Papers, CBPA. .

7. *Report of the Secretary of War, 1941*, 75; General Administrative Inspection of Tuskegee ROTC, Headquarters Fourth Army Service Command, Army Service Forces, Atlanta, GA, January 12, April 23, 1943, November 29, 1944, MAJ John A. Welch to

Fourth Service Command Commanding General, November 29, 1944, MAJ John A. Welch to F. D. Patterson, March 8, December 9, 1944, F. D. Patterson Papers, Hollis Burke Frissel Library, Tuskegee, Tuskegee, AL; *Tuskeanna, 1941*, 67, *Tuskeanna, 1942*, 62. LT John H. Hurd was also assigned to the ROTC detachment.

8. Truman K. Gibson to LTC Lester S. Ostrander, February 24, 1941, TAG to Commanding Generals of Third Corps and Fifth Corps Areas, February 26, 1941, Third Corps Area Commanding General to TAG, August 27, 1941, RG 407, NA II.

9. Memorandum, COL W. B. Smith for Chief of Staff G-3, December 6, 1941, Memorandum, BG Harry L. Twaddle for TAG, December 10, 1941, TAG to Third Corps Area Commanding General, December 17, 1941, TAG to Fourth Corps Area Commanding General, December 17, 1941, TAG to Fourth Corps Area Commanding General, December 17, 1941, TAG to Eighth Corps Area Commanding General, December 17, 1941, RG 407, NA II.

10. TAG to President William H. Bell of Alcorn A and M College, December 17, 1941, TAG to B. F. Hubert of Georgia State University, December 17, 1941, TAG to Malcolm S. MacLean of Hampton Institute, December 17, 1941, TAG to Ferdinand D. Bluford of A and T College, December 17, 1941, TAG to G. L. Harrison of Langston University, December 17, 1941, TAG to J. W. Janey of Paul Quinn College, December 17, 1941, TAG to John W. Gandy of Virginia State College, December 17, 1941, TAG to Dominion R. Glass of Texas College, December 17, 1941, TAG to M. W. Dogan of Wiley College, December 17, 1941, TAG to John W. Davis of West Virginia State College, December 17, 1941, TAG to Mother M. Agatha of Xavier University, December 17, 1941, W. L. Wright of Lincoln University (PA) to Chief of Staff Marshall, December 18, 1941, G. L. Harrison to TAG, December 27, 1941, TAG to Eighth Corps Area Commanding General, January 5, 1942, William H. Bell to TAG, January 6, 1942, Kentucky State College to TAG, February 2, 1942, RG 407, NA II.

11. MAJ Jesse H. Ruder to D. R. Glass, February 28, 1942, Senator Walter F. George to TAG, March 28, 1942, Thomas E. Jones to TAG, April 4, 1942, Memorandum COL B. W. Venable for TAG, April 8, 1942, TAG to Senator Walter F. George, April 10, 1942, Memorandum, COL Walter L. Weible for TAG, April 14, 1942, Representative Lindley Beckworth to Secretary of War Stimson, January 30, 1943, TAG to Representative Lindley Beckworth, February 4, 1943, RG 407, NA.

12. TAG to Eighth Corps Area Commanding General, December 17, 1941, W. L. Wright to GEN Marshall, December 18, 1941, TAG to W. L. Wright, December 24, 1941, TAG to Third Corps Area Commanding General, December 24, 1941, Mother M. Agatha to TAG, January 8, 1942, MAJ Frank Milani to TAG, January 12, 1942, MAJ Jesse H. Ruder to TAG, February 28, 1942, Malcolm S. MacLean to Third Corps Area Commanding General, January 13, 1942, COL F. G. Kellond to TAG, January 13, 1942, LTC G. Causey to TAG, January 15, 1942, MAJ E. W. Dennis to TAG, February 2, 1942, COL Walter L. Weible to TAG, April 1942, RG 407, NA; H. Liston to MAJ Campbell C. Johnson, C. C. Johnson Papers. Hereafter, OCS will be used for Officer Candidate Schools.

13. Among the colleges which sought his assistance were Kentucky State, Lincoln in Pennsylvania, South Carolina A and M, Southern A and M and Virginia State. See M. F. Whittaker to William H. Hastie, December 6, 19, 1941, John P. Burgess to Judge William H. Hastie, December 8, 1941, Memorandum, William H. Hastie for Assistant Chief of Staff, G-3, December 10, 1941, Memorandum, COL W. B. Smith for William H. Hastie, December, 1941, William H. Hastie to M. F. Whittaker, December 18, 1941, W. L. Wright to GEN George C. Marshall, December 18, 1941, W. L. Wright to William H. Hastie, December 19, 1941, William H. Hastie to W. L. Wright, December 22, 1941, J. R. E. Lee to William Hastie, January 7, 10, 1942, William Hastie to J. R. E, Lee, January 8, 1942, John

B. Gandy to Judge William H. Hastie, January 10, William H. Hastie to John M. Gandy, January 14, 1942, R. B. Atwood to William H. Hastie, February 10, 1942, William H. Hastie to R. B. Atwood, February 12, 1942, R. B. Atwood to Senator Alben W. Barkley, Senator A. B. Chandler and Congressmen Noble J. Gregory, Emmett O'Neal, E. W. Creal, Brent Spencer, Virgil Chapman, A. J. May, Joe E. Bates, John M. Robison, and Beverly M. Vincent, February 17, 1942, R. B. Atwood to TAG, February 17, 25, 1942, Records of the Office of the Secretary of the Army, RG 107, NA II. John P. Burgess, President of the Palmetto State Teachers' Association and an avid supporter of South Carolina State A and M College, was commissioned a LT at Fort Des Moines during WWI and served in France with the 365th Infantry Regiment, 92nd Infantry Division. Hereafter, RG 107 will be used for Records of the Office of the Secretary of the Army, RG 107, NA II.

14. MAJ Frank Milani to Malcolm S. MacLean, December 18, 1940, Walter R. Brown to MAJ Campbell C. Johnson, July 24, 1941, Walter R. Brown to William H. Hastie, July 24, August 1, 1941, MAJ Campbell C. Johnson to MAJ Walter R. Brown, July 29, 1941, Civilian Aide to the Secretary of War to Walter R. Brown, July 30, 1941, Malcolm S. MacLean to William H. Hastie, December 11, 1941, Malcolm S. MacLean to GEN George C. Marshall, September 18, December 11, 1941, Civilian Aide to the Secretary of War to Malcolm S. MacLean, December 15, 1941, Memorandum, BG Harry L. Twaddle for Judge William H. Hastie, December 18, 1941, RG 107, NA II.

15. Secretary of War Henry L. Stimson to I. J. K. Wells, March 2, 1941, BG C. A. Pratt to Governor Matthew M. Neely, March 25, 1941, Secretary of War Henry L. Stimson to William Sanders, March 26, 1941, TAG to S. S. Gordon, March 27, 1941, TAG to Mary L. Williams, March 28, 1941, Howard P. Jeter to William H. Hastie, May 16, October 27, 1941, William H. Hastie to Howard P. Jeter, May 22, October 29, 1941, William H. Hastie to John W. Davis, May 15, 27, December 13, 15, 1941, February 18, 1942, John W. Davis to William H. Hastie, April 23, 29, 26, May 7, 19, December 11, 15, 16, 17, 1941, February 13, March 3, 1942, GEN George C. Marshall to Representative George W. Johnson, November 7, 1941, Howard P. Jeter to GEN George C. Marshall, December 16, 1941, RG 107, NA II. Officers of the West Virginia State College Student Council were Sherman W. Smith, president, Louise Williams, Vice President, George H. Kydd, III, secretary, Carl D. Hughes, treasurer, and Howard P. Jeter, publicity director; the members were Juanita Shaw, Leon Sullivan, Henrietta Rivers, Albert C. Johnson and Amy M. Jackson. Six student representatives conferred with GEN George C. Marshall and presented a petition signed by 326 male students.

16. TAG to Eighth Corps Area Commanding General, February 24, March 4, April 29, 1942. Memorandum, COL Walter L. Weible for TAG, April 22, 1942, TAG to Fourth Corps Area Commanding General, April 29, 1942, TAG to Third Corps Area Commanding General, April 29, June 8, 1942, TAG to Fourth Corps Area Commanding General, April 29, May 26, 1942, COL Ralph C. Holliday to TAG, June 6, 1942, COL Ralph C. Holliday to Commanding General of Replacement and School Command, May 5, 27, 1942, MAJ Arnold A. Altman to Army Ground Forces Commanding General, May 8, 1942, LTC E. W. Dennis to TAG, May 17, 1942, Assistant Adjutant General of Third Corps Area to Army Ground Forces Headquarters, May 19, 1942, TAG to Fifth Corps Area Commanding General, May 28, 29, 1942, MAJ R. Hippelheuaser to Services of Supply Commanding General, June 9, 1942, MAJ James D. Tanner to Army Ground Forces Headquarters, June 11, 1942, TAG to Fourth Corps Area Commanding General, June 15, 1942, RG 407, NA II. The African American cadre consisted of LT Napoleon Johnson and LT William S. Rice, both of whom were assigned to Camp Davis, NC. The enlisted men, 1st SGT Walter Robinson and SGT Lewis Gilbert, were selected from Fort Eustis in Virginia. Quartermaster equipment and other supplies were provided to ensure the installation of these ROTC detachments.

17. William H. Hastie to Willette R. Banks, August 1, 6, 1942, January 25, 1943, Willette R. Banks to William H. Hastie, August 3, 1942, Memorandum, William H. Hastie for LTC John W. Childs, August 6, 1942, January 19, 1943, S. B. Taylor to Judge William Hastie, August 12, 1942, Truman K. Gibson, Jr. to S. B. Taylor, August 18, 1942, RG 107, NA II; John C. Harlan, *History of West Virginia State College, 1891–1965* (Dubuque: William C. Brown, 1968), p. 81.

18. West Virginia State College News Release, Institute, West Virginia, June 25, 1942, John W. Davis to Judge William H. Hastie, August 6, October 2, 1942, William H. Hastie to John W. Davis, May 1, August 12, 15, September 30, 1942, Memorandum, Civilian Aide to the Secretary of War for LTC Richard T. Goiner, September 18, 1942, Memorandum, LTC Richard T. Goiner, Jr. for Civilian Aide to the Secretary of War, September 29, 1942, John W. Davis to Charles I. Stanton, October 2, 1942, RG 407, NA II. The other personnel in the cadre were LT Samuel J. Evans, William J. Gray, T/SGT William Ferguson, and SGT Willis W. Jackson. See Harlan, *History of West Virginia State College*, 81.

19. Felton G. Clark to William H. Hastie, May 25, 1942, William H. Hastie to Felton G. Clark, June 1, 1942, RG 107, NA II.

20. Memorandum, John W. Martin for Secretary of War, March 19, 1941, Charles H. Thompson to Mordecai W. Johnson, March 22, 1941, William H. Hastie to Mordecai W. Johnson, May 10, 23, 1941, Mordecai W. Johnson, May 19, 1941, bx 244, RG 107, NA. ROTC enrollment for Howard University from 1936–1937 to 1940–1941 was 47, 40, 45, 37 and 34 while Wilberforce was 16, 14, 15, 15, and 16. See Memorandum, LTC W. A. Burgess for Truman K. Gibson, February 21, 1941, RG 107, NA. LTC Zuppann arrived at Howard University in 1936 as a MAJ and was subsequently replaced by LTC Henry J. Beottcher in 1943. See the Howard University *Hilltop*, February 5, 1943. Hereafter, PNLGC will be used for the Presidents of Negro Land Grant Colleges.

21. G. Samuel Darrell to Secretary of War Henry L. Stimson, May 14, 1942, Memorandum, COL Walter L. Weible for TAG, May 26, 1942, TAG to G. Samuel Darrell, May 29, 1942, RG 407, NA II.

22. Memorandum, BG I. H. Edwards for Chief of Staff, June 23, 1942, RG 407, NA II.

23. Memorandum, COL Walter L. Weible for TAG, April 4, September 12, 1942, Memorandum, BG C. R. Huebner for Assistant Chief of Staff G-3, July 7, 1942, RG 407, NA II. The recommended increase for North Carolina A and T was 10, Tuskegee ten and Wilberforce twelve. The allotment contracts for Tuskegee during the 1942–1943 academic year was seventy.

24. TAG to Commanding Generals of All Corps Areas and Puerto Rican Department, April 21, 1942, C. C. Johnson Papers.

25. Memorandum W 150–1–43, TAG, Washington, DC, January 27, 1943, in C. C. Johnson Papers; Press Branch Release, Bureau of Public Relations, War Department, April 30, 1942, RG 107, NA II; Howard University *Hilltop*, February 5, 1943. Howard University had commissioned approximately 440 officers since the establishment of its ROTC program and more than 150 were in active duty detachments by 1942. The majority were assigned to the 366 Infantry Regiment at FT Devens, MA and undoubtedly this regiment had the most educated cadre in the military. Among the commissioned officers serving at FT Devens were MAJ Robert L. Pollard, Ernest R. Welch, assistant professor of electrical engineering at Howard University, Alston Burleigh, Raymond C. Contee, William H. Bowers, and Hyman H. Chase, assistant professor of zoology at Howard University; CPTs Clinton C[?]ke, Jr., Walter Dabney, James Robinson, Frederick O. Peti[?], Robert W. Hainsworth, Herbert Orr, Willis D. Polk, Raymond Diggs and Hermon D. Rich[?]; LT Arthur W. Ferguson, Emerson W. Browne, Penrose E. Goodall,

Richard H. Irving, James W. Jones, Jesse O. Dedmon, John Green, Charles A. Pratt, Llody R. Riley, Fred L. Allen, Rutherford B. Stevens, Clarence B. Wheat, Lucius E. Young, Samuel W. Tucker, Robert S. Armstead, Cyrus Honesty, Nathaniel King, Charles H. Overhall, Harry R. Peersawl, Tunis D. Randolph, George F. Welch, Emmett W. Willis, Weejay S. Bundara, James H. Carr, Fred D. Durrah, William W. Ford, Nathaniel P. King, Harold A. Kyles, Roger B. Kyles, George P. Lawrence, Howard P. Locksley, William A. Pierce, James L. Thompson, Osceola T. Thornton, James T. Toliver, Leroy R. Weekes, Emmett W. Willis, Mervin O. Parker, and Roy W. Sorrell, Allen R. Anderson, James T. Beason, Herman L. Bell, Edward W. Brooke, Frederick E. Davidson, Harry S. Davis, William C. English, Charles M. Bragg, Dennette A. Harrod, John H. Hurd, Samuel C. Jackson, Samuel R. McCottry, Jr., Walter L. Macklin, James I. Minor, John T. Martin, Jasper Ross, Willard C. Stewart, Yancey Williams, Roy F. Greenwood, Clifton E. Davis, Robert A. Brown, Ralph L. McKinney, John H. Euell and James Fowler who completed the ROTC program and later received his commission from the U.S. Military Academy at West Point. Other officers at assigned to FT Dix, NJ included MAJ Joseph A. Holmes, CPT Lorenzo R. Berry, LT Rufus Johnson and Leroy A. Wallace, and LT Millard Williams. CPT John A. Welch, CPT Maurice E. Johnson and LT Hayden Johnson were located at Tuskegee; LT Harold J. Nickens at FT Bragg, NC; and LT Robert W. Wilson at Howard.

COL Llody Zuppann was replaced by LTC Henry J. Boettcher in 1943. The ROTC cadre also included MAJ Raymond E. Contee, CPT Robert W. Wilson, and SGT Amos C. Robinson and Earl E. Spruell. See Howard University *Hilltop*, February 11, 1942, February 5, 1943. Hereafter, ASTP will be used for Army Specialized Training Program.

26. Memorandum W 150–1–43, TAG, Washington, DC, January 27, 1943, in C. C. Johnson Papers; Press Branch Release, Bureau of Public Relations, War Department, April 30, 1942, RG 107, NA II; Howard University *Hilltop*, February 5, 11, 1943.

27. Morgan State College *Spokesman*, December 1942, January, February 1943. Among the students inducted from Morgan State were Parren J. Mitchell, Harry A. Cole, Joseph Gibbs, Milton Shepherd and Robert Watts.

28. U.S. War Department, *ARMY Specialized Training Bulletin* 9 (December 1944): 1–12; Prairie View University *Purple and Gold, 1946.*

29. Third Corps Commanding General to TAG, August 27, 1941, Military District of Washington Adjutant General to TAG, December 9, 1942, TAG to Commanding General of Replacement and School Command, January 14, 1943, Memorandum for TAG, January 15, 1943, TAG to Military District of Washington Commanding General, April 6, 1943, Memorandum, BG Russell B. Reynolds for TAG, May 6, 1943, RG 407, NA II.

30. "Professional News," *Journal of the National Medical Association* 35 (November 1943):206; Hampton Institute Press Service, April 5, 1944, Army Specialized Training Program, Hampton University Archives. PVT Charles V. Cooper was to pursue the dental program and PVT Kennesaw Manning and Jesse Barber were to enter the medicine program.

31. COL Robert S. Walsh to TAG, October 1943, Executive for Reserve and ROTC Affairs, Records of the Army Staff, RG 407, NA; Fourth Corps Area Adjutant General to TAG, November 10, 1941, COL LeRoy W. Nichols to TAG, March 10, 1944, COL W. G. Johnston to TAG, June 29, 1944, MAJ William P. Layton to Army Service Forces Commanding General, December 2, 1944, COL LeRoy W. Nichols to Army Service Forces Commanding General, April 28, May 30, 1945, MAJ R. L. Humbert to TAG, June 12, 1945, LTC James M. Morris to TAG, June 30, 1945, RG 407, NA II.

32. MAJ Wilfred I. Freel to ASF Commanding General, June 4, 1945, Charles H. Wesley to ASF Commanding General, June 13, 1945, LTC Gene A. Robens to TAG, June 21, 1945, RG 407, NA II.

33. 79th Congress, 1st Session, Senate Report 203, Reserve Officers' Training Corps Credit for Military Training While on Active Duty, April 24, 1945; TAG to Commanding Generals of All Service Commands, Military District of Washington, and Antilles Department, RG 407, NA II.

34. Press Branch, Bureau of Public Relations, War Department, Washington, DC, October 7, 1945, Willette R. Banks to Truman K. Gibson, James C. Evans to Ralph P. Bridgman, Ferdinand D. Bluford, Mordecai W. Johnson, F. Patterson, and Charles Wesley, October 8, 1945 October 10, 1945, James C. Evans to Willette R. Banks, October 12, 1945, F. D. Clark to James C. Evans, November 17, 1945, RG 107, NA II; MAJ John A. Welch to D. F. Patterson, October 19, 1945, F. D. Patterson Papers, Hollis Burke Frisell Library, Tuskegee University, Tuskegee, AL. Veterans enrolled in the revised ROTC advance course were scheduled to receive liberal financial inducements during the two-year period. They were to be paid an allowance of $370 in addition to approximately $75 while attending a six-week summer camp. Inducements under the provisions of the GI Bill of Rights authorized a monthly subsistence of $50 for single men and $75 for married men plus the cost of tuition and other college fees up to $500. Veterans with a minimum of a year's service were exempt from the ROTC basic course and those with six months of service were exempt for the first year of the basic course. The minimum age for entrance into the advance course was 19 while the maximum age limit was 26. These provisions immediately affected colleges and universities which had advance courses on March 31, 1943 with the exception of colleges having Medical detachments. For additional information, see Press Branch Release, Bureau of Public Relations, War Department, Washington, DC, May 28, 1946, RG 107, NA II; Circular 300, War Department, Washington, DC, October 7, 1945.

35. BG Benjamin O. Davis to Willette R. Banks, April 29, 1946, BOD Papers.

36. MAJ H. Montaque to TAG, March 29, 1946, TAG to AGF Commanding General, April 5, 1946, Headquarters AGF to TAG, April 16, 1946, TAG to Eighth Service Commanding General, April 20, 1946, Deputy Director of Organization and Training to AGF Commanding General, July 11, 1946, RG 407, NA II; James C. Evans to Thomas L. Holly, December 29, 1945, James C. Evans to Willette R. Banks, January 2, May 1, August 26, September 4, November 6, 1946, Memorandum, LTC Jay W. Doverspike for James C. Evans, January 17, 1946, Memorandum, Marcus H. Ray for Acting Executive Officer for Reserve and ROTC Affairs, January 23, 1946, Memorandum, BG Edward S. Bres to Willette R. Banks, January 23, 1946, Memorandum, Charles W. McCarthy for Commanding General of Army Air Force, January 30, 1946, Willette R. Banks to Marcus H. Ray, April 9, May 20, 1946, Marcus H. Ray to Willette R. Banks, April 15, 1946, Lee E. Perkins to James C. Evans, May 12, 1946, James C. Evans to Lee E. Perkins, May 1, 20, 1946, W. B. Banks to BG Benjamin O. Davis, August 20, 1946, W. B. Banks to James C. Evans, August 30, 1946, RG 107, NA II; "Special 'G.I.' Bulletin," Prairie View University 37 (February 1946): passim. The noncommissioned officers were MSGT James Allen, SGT Robert R. Watson and CPL Eugene Gardner. On September 19, 1946, Marcus H. Ray informed Joseph A. Snead that a recommendation assigning him to Prairie View University had been forwarded to Willette R. Banks for his approval. See CPT Joseph A. Snead to Marcus H. Ray, September 6, 1946, Marcus H. Ray to CPT Joseph A. Snead, September 19, 1946, RG 107, NA II. Although expressing objections and reservation to the assignment of CPT Claude, he was willing to accept the officer in the expectation that his assignment would prove satisfactory for the detachment. Assistant PMST, LT Tolbert Harris, also remained with the detachment.

37. Bureau of Naval Personnel to College President, March 14, 1945, Ralph P. Bridgman to Lester G. Granger, April 28, 1945, Benson to R. P. Bridgman, May 12, 1945, Ralph P. Bridgman to SECNAV James Forrestal, May 1945, Lester B. Granger to SEC-

NAV James Forrestal, June 2, 1945, SECNAV James Forrestal to Lester B. Granger, n.d., Speech, Walter R. Brown, Secretary and Dean of Men of Hampton Institute at the Closing Exercises of the Last Graduating Class of the U.S. Naval Training School, August 8, 1945, Ralph P. Bridgman Papers, Hampton University Archives, Hampton, VA; LT C. H. Miner, Jr. to Ralph P. Bridgman, September 27, 1945, Hampton University Archives. New detachments were established at Alabama Polytechnic Institute, Vanderbilt University and the University of Mississippi. The correspondence received by Granger for the Navy stated that four new detachments were allocated. Hereafter, SECNAV will be used for Secretary of the Navy.

38. Committee on Navy and Army Air Corps ROTCs to Administrative Council, August 28, 1945, Ralph R. Bridgman to Board of Trustees of Hampton Institute, October 15, 1946, Military Science File, Hampton Institute Archives, Hampton VA; Memorandum, COL Russell M. King for TAG, February 7, 1946, COL J. E. Daly to Assistant Chief of Staff for Personnel, February 9, 1946, COL Earl P. Hall to TAG, March 5, 1946, CPT John Mocnik, Jr. to TAG, March 5, 1946, TAG to Third Service Commanding General, February 15, March 1, 1946, SO 58, War Department, Washington, DC, March 11, 1946, RG 407, NA II; Memorandum, MG Edward F. Witsell for Acting Civilian Aide to the Secretary of the Army, January 28, 1948, James C. Evans to MAJ Clarence M. Davenport, February 14, 1948, RG 107, NA II.

39. LTC Arthur H. Black to TAG, February 8, 1946, TAG to Assistant Chief of Staff for Personnel, February 15, 1946, TAG to Infantry ROTC, Fort McClellan, Alabama, February 21, 1946, RG 407, NA II; Charles H. Wesley to James C. Evans, December 31, 1945, February 10, 1948, Marcus H. Ray to Charles H. Wesley, August 5, 1946, MG John T. Lewis to Charles H. Wesley, n.d., RG 107, NA II. Another issue which later caused a problem for Wesley was uniforms for the ROTC band. See Charles H. Wesley to James C. Evans, April 20, May 19, June 11, 1948, LTG L. T. Gerow to Charles H. Wesley, May 10, 26, 1948, James C. Evans to Charles H. Wesley, June 8, 1948, Charles H. Wesley to LTG L. T. Gerow, May 18, 1948, James C. Wesley to TAG, May 19, 1948, MG Edward F. Witsell to James C. Evans, May 25, 1948, RG 107, NA II; Latharus Goggins, *Central State University: The First One Hundred Years, 1887–1987* (Wilberforce: Central State University, 1987), 17–18, 28–31.

40. Baltimore *Afro-American*, September 30. 1947.

41. TAG to Chief Signal Officer, August 23, 1946, Chief Signal Officer to TAG, August 26, 1946, Headquarters, Military District of Washington to TAG, August 7, September 23, 1946, TAG to Assignment Branch, August 22, 1946, RG 407, NA II; Baltimore *Afro-American*, November 29, 1947. MSGT A. S. Robinson, 1SGT M. C. Branch, 1SGT R. L. Chinn and SSGT C. E. Williams formed the noncommissioned cadre.

42. Ferdinand D. Bluford to COL LeRoy Nichols, March 20, 1946, TAG to Fort George G. Meade Commanding General, May 6, 1946, LT Otis O. Zachary to COL Marcus Ray, August 5, 1946, CPT Roger B. Kyles to TAG, August 8, 1946, CPT Roger B. Kyles to James C. Evans, August 8, 9, 1946, James C. Evans to CPT Roger B. Kyles, August 15, 1946, James C. Evans to LT Otis O. Zachary, September 3, October 7, 1946, bx 244, RG 107, NA; LTC H. B. Frederick to AGF Commanding General, June 25, 1946, LTC Russell M. King to TAG, July 17, 1946, MAJ G. R. Long to TAG, August 7, September 3, 1936, LTC T. L. Poole to TAG, July 22, September 3, 1946, TAG to Seventh Army Commanding General, September 10, 1946, RG 407, NA II. LTC Raymond F. Edwards was scheduled to remain at North Carolina A and T until January 1, 1947.

43. F. D. Patterson to Army Service Forces Commanding General, November 14, 1945, COL LeRoy W. Nichols to Army Service Forces Commanding General, November 24, 1945, Memorandum, COL S. M. Prout for Executive for Reserve and

ROTC Affairs, December 1, 1945, COL C. M. Boyer to TAG, December 3, 1945, RG 407, NA II; Memorandum, LTC Jay W. Doverspike for Marcus H. Ray, July 31, 1946, RG 107, NA.

In response to a request from Marcus H. Ray, the Office of the Executive for Reserve and ROTC Affairs reported that the list of officers at the reactivated detachments on July 29, 1946 were: LTC Raymond F. Edwards, PMST, MAJ Edward C. Johnson, and CPT Arthur W. Ferguson at A and T College of North Carolina; CPT Claud[e] C. Clark, Acting PMST, and CPT William J. Gray at West Virginia State College; CPT John R. Reaves, PMST, and LT Tolbert Harris at Prairie University; COL Trevor W. Swett, PMST, CPT Benjamin L. Hunton and LT Darwin E. Smith at Howard University; COL Richard H. Grinder, PMST, LTC Warren E. Cleveland, LTC Harry B. Reubel, MAJ Clarence M. Davenport and LT Leroy S. Gaillard at Hampton Institute; MAJ John A. Welch, PMST, and LT Cecil W. White at Tuskegee; and MAJ Robert C. Johnson at Wilberforce. All of the officers were African American except LTC Edwards, COL Grinder, COL Swett, LTC Cleveland and CPT Reaves. Hampton Institute was over strength by two officers while A and T College of North Carolina and Howard University had one vacancy, and Tuskegee had two. See Memorandum Marcus H. Ray for Chief of Reserve and ROTC Affairs, July 28, 1946, Memorandum, LTC Jay W. Doverspike for Marcus H. Ray, July 31, 1946, RG 107, NA II.

To qualify for PMST, officers were required to be in the regular Army, not older than 55, have field grade rank and have served at least 12 months overseas since December 7, 1941. Completion of Command General Staff School or its equivalent was mandatory and wherever possible, all officers assigned to ROTC were college graduates. The same requirements pertained to Assistant PMSTs with at least three years of commissioned service. Appointments were also open to officers not in the Regular Army if they agreed to remain on extended duty for an indefinite length of time or remain on extended duty until June 30, 1947 and apply for commissions in the Regular Army. In 1944 the PMST was COL John F. Waterman who was assisted by MAJ John A. Welch as Assistant PMST, and CPT John H. Hurd. See Press Branch Release, Bureau of Public Relations, War Department, March 9, 1946, RG 107, NA II.

44. R. B. Atwood to James C. Evans, September 20, 1945, James C. Evans to R. B. Atwood, November 7, December 14, 1945, January 2, 1946, William H. Gray to James C. Evans, November 19, 1945, James C. Evans to William H. Gray, December 12, 1945, R. B. Atwood to War Department, January 10, 1946, Howard D. Gregg to James C. Evans, January 17, 30, 1946, James C. Evans to Howard D. Gregg, January 21, February 5, 1946, William H. Gray to James C. Evans, March 25, 1946, Joseph F. Drake to James C. Evans, August 9, 1947, Thomas Harris to Marcus Ray, September 24, 1946, Marcus H. Ray to Thomas Harris, October 2, 1946, Felton G. Clark to James C. Evans, May 7, 1946, James C. Evans to Felton G. Clark, May 1, 16, 1946, RG 107, NA II.

By June 1946 War Department indicated applications were filed by Delaware State on January 17, 1946, Florida A and M on January 7, 1942 and November 19, 1945, Kentucky State on February 25, 1945 and October 24, 1945, Southern University and A and M on May 25, 1942 and May 7, 1946, North Carolina A and T applied on October 15, 1945, Langston on April 16, 1946, South Carolina State A and M on December 6, 1941, Prairie View A and M on April 9, 1946, Virginia State on January 10, 1941 and April 16, 1946, West Virginia State on March 3, 1942, Hampton on September 18, 1941, Howard October 9, 1945, Lincoln in Pennsylvania on December 19, 1941, Tuskegee on November 17, 1945, and Wilberforce on January 27, 1941. Of the land grant colleges North Carolina A and T and Prairie View A and M had reactivated Infantry ROTC and West Virginia State Artillery ROTC. Tuskegee, Howard and Wilberforce as private institutions had reactivated their Infantry ROTC, and Hampton Coastal Artillery ROTC. All of the colleges and universities seeking ROTC detachment met the enrollment qualification with only Arkansas AM and N, Clark College in Atlanta, Georgia State College, Morris Brown, Kentucky State, Xavier, Morgan State, Lincoln, Johnson C. Smith in Charlotte, NC, North Carolina College, Langston, Lincoln in Pennsylvania, Allen University in SC, Fisk, Bishop, Texas College, Wiley, and Virginia Union having male enrollments less than 200. See James C. Evans, Reserve Officers' Training Corps: Data pertinent to the participation of Negro Colleges in the ROTC Program, Office of the Civilian Aide to the Secretary of War, Washington, DC, June 4, 1946, F. G. Clark to James C. Evans to MAJ Jay W. Doverspike, January 27, 1948, James C. Evans to Felton G. Clark, February 12, 1948, RG 107, NA II; James C. Evans, "Adult Education for Negroes in the Armed Forces," *Journal of Negro Education* 14 (Summer 1945): 439; Martin D. Jenkins, "Current Trends and Events of National Importance in Negro Education: Enrollment in Institutions of Higher Education for Negroes, 1944–1945," *Journal of Negro Education* 14 (Spring 1945): 238–244; Martin D. Jenkins, "Current Trends and Events of National Importance in Negro Education: Enrollment in Institutions of Higher Education for Negroes, 1944–1946," *Journal of Negro Education* 15 (Summer, 1946): 231–239; Martin D. Jenkins, "Current Trends and Events of National Importance in Negro Education: Enrollment in Institutions of Higher Education for Negroes, 1947–1948," *Journal of Negro Education* 17 (Spring 1948): 206–215.

Several presidents of African American land colleges formed an organization in 1913 which was formerly designated at Tuskegee during a meeting of the Southern Conference on Education in Negro Land Grant Colleges on January 15, 1923 as an Association of Negro Land-Grant Colleges. The association met in March 1924 at Hampton Institute and changed the designation to the Conference of Presidents of Negro Land-Grant College. See Richard D. Morrison, *History of Alabama Agricultural and Mechanical University, 1875 — 1992* (Huntsville: Liberal Arts Press, 1994), 244.

45. James C. Evans, Reserve Officers' Training Corps: Data pertinent to the participation of Negro colleges in the ROTC Program, Office of the Assistant Civilian Aide to the Secretary of War, Washington, DC, June 4, 1946, RG 107, NA II.

46. CPT John L. Pfeiffer to War Department Director of Organization and Training, March 17, 1947, D/OT to TAG, April 1, 1947, TAG to Second Army Commanding General, April 16, 1947, TAG to Third Army Commanding General, April 16, 1947, GO 41, War Department, Washington, DC, April 25, 1947, RG 407, NA II; Press Section Release, Public Relation Division, War Department, Washington, DC, April 26, 1947, RG 107, NA II. After the activation of the ROTC detachment at South Carolina State A and M College, LT William E. White of Florence, SC inquired about a position on the ROTC staff. He stated that he was one of the few African Americans eligible in the state. Evans advised him that the cadre was complete but inquiries were to be directed to Whittaker or COL Robinson. Cadre selected for SC State A and M College included LTCs James H. Robinson and Raymond E. Contee, CPTs Frederic E. Davison and Frank T. Talley, MSGT Edwin T. Redding, T/SGTs Thomas J. Simmons, Burt A. Mayberry, Jr., and Jesse C. Scott, T/4 John Evans and property custodians William D. Daniels and Jessie Coulter. See James C. Evans to M. F. Whittaker, August 8, 1947, RG 107, NA II; *SC State Agricultural and Mechanical College Bulletin, 1947–1948*, 11; *SC State Agricultural and Mechanical College Bulletin, 1948–1949*, 11.

47. Senator William B. Umstead to TAG, June 19, 1947, TAG to Senator William B. Umstead, June 30, 1947, RG 407, NA II.

The PMST Robert M. Hendricks and his cadre consisted of LT Lawrence W. Jones, MSGT Floyd K. Bryant, MSGT J. E. Pankey, 1SGT B. B. Simmons, 1SGT Acie Singleton, T/SGT (Technical Sergeant) Haywood Davis. See *Afro-American*, August 30, 1947.

48. Felton G. Clark to Chief of Staff of Executive and Reserve and ROTC Affairs

Edward S. Bres, July 10, 1947, Felton G. Clark to COL West A. Hamilton, April 19, 1948, RG 107, NA II.

49. Press Section Release, Public Relations Division, War Department, July 21, 1947, Ambrose Caliver to James C. Evans, July 29, 1947, James C. Evans to John W. Davis, March 1, 1948, RG 107, NA II.

ROTC cadre attending the regional conferences from the Third and Fourth Army Service areas were COL West A. Hamilton of Prairie View A and M, LTC James H. Robinson of South Carolina State, LTC Herbert A. Barrow and LTC George S. Roberts of Tuskegee and MAJ Edward C. Johnson of North Carolina A and T. George L. Washington represented Fred D. Patterson of Tuskegee. In the Second Army Service Area, cadre which met in Baltimore included COL Trevor Swett of Howard University and CPT Howard Baugh who represented MAJ Lee Rayford.

M. F. Whittaker of South Carolina State was unable to attend his respective conference but planned to send Professor Crawford. Ralph P. Bridgman of Hampton Institute was also unable to attend because of the Hazen conference meeting at the same time, but he planned to send a deputy. The other presidents where scheduled to attend their regional conferences. See Special Orders 145, Headquarters, 14th Air Force, ADC, Orlando, FL, July 28, 1947, M. F. Whittaker to James C. Evans, August 4, 1947, Ralph P. Bridgman to James C. Evans, August 11, 1947, Bluford to Evans, August 5, 1947, L. H. Foster to James C. Evans, August 6, 1947, RG 107. NA II; Baltimore *Afro-American*, August 14, 1947.

50. Carl Murphy to James H. Evans, February 12, March 1, 4, 1948, James C. Evans to TAG, February 17, 1948, James C. Evans to Carl Murphy, February 18, 26, March 1, 3, 8, 1948, James C. Evans to William I. Gibson, February 19, 1948, William I. Gibson to Carl Murphy, February 26, 1948, Memorandum to James C. Evans, February 24, 1948, James C. Evans to William H. Gray, Horace M. Bond, L. A. Davis, H. D. Gregg, Joseph F. Drake, F. D. Patterson, R. E. Clement, C. V. Troup and Charles H. Wesley, February 26, 1948, James C. Evans to R. B. Atwood, J. W, Davis, L. H. Foster, L. B. Evans, W. S. Davis, M. F. Whittaker, G. l. Harrison, Ferdinand D. Bluford, S. D. Scruggs, W. H. Pipes, J. T. Williams and F. D. Clark, February 27, 1948, W. H. Pipes to James C. Evans, March 1, 1948, Ferdinand D. Bluford to James C. Evans, March 1, 1948, William H. Gray to James C. Evans, March 2, 1948, Lawrence H. Foster to James C. Evans, March 2, 1948, Charles H. Wesley to James C. Evans, March 3, 1948, Howard D. Gregg to James C. Evans, March 3, 1948, Lawrence A. Davis to James C. Evans, March 4, 1948, John W. Davis to James C. Evans, March 6, 1948, M. F. Whittaker to James C. Evans, March 9, 1948, James C. Evans to Horace M. Bond, March 18, 1948, James C. Evans to H. Council Trenholm, March 22, 1948, RG 107, NA II; Memorandum, Civilian Aide James C. Evans for TAG, February 17, 1948, Memorandum, MG Edward F. Witsell for Civilian Aide James C. Evans, February 24, 1948, RG 407, NA II. Similar correspondence was also sent to Ambrose Caliver, Senior Specialist in the Education of Negroes, U.S. Office of Education, and Charles H. Thompson, editor of the *Journal of Negro Education*.

51. Baltimore *Afro-American*, February 21, 28, 1948. The twelve colleges were Alabama A and M College, Arkansas AM and N, Delaware State, Florida A and M, Georgia State Industrial College, Kentucky State, Southern A and M, Maryland Princess Ann College, Alcorn A and M, Lincoln, Langston, Tennessee A and I.

52. Ferdinand D. Bluford to James C. Evans, March 1, 1948, RG 107, NA II; Baltimore *Afro-American*, February 28, 1948. Evans was born in Gallatin, Tennessee on July 1, 1900 and joined the Army in 1918 where he served as a SATC instructor. He graduated from Roger Williams University with a BA degree in 1921 and fours years later was awarded a BS degree in Electrical Engineering from Massachusetts Institute of Technology. He also earned a MS degree from MIT in 1926. From 1928 to 1941, Evans

served in several capacities at West Virginia State before becoming a civilian employee with the federal government.

53. Joseph F. Drake to James C. Evans, March 3, 8, 1948, Joseph F. Drake to Executive for Reserve and ROTC Affairs, March 8, 1948, RG 107, NA II.

54. C. F. Troup to James C. Evans, March 1, 26, 1948, James C. Evans to C. F. Troup, March 4, 1948, RG 107, NA II.

55. James C. Evans to Executive Secretary of the Civilian Components Committee, March 3, 1948, James C. Evans Office Memorandum, March 22, 1948, RG 107, NA II.

56. Memorandum, L. Eugene Hedburg for Deputy Director of Public Relations, March 2, 1948, RG 107, NA II; Baltimore *Afro-American*, February 17, 24, 1948.

57. W. A. Fountain, Jr. to James C. Evans, February 11, March 23, 1948, James C. Evans to W. A. Fountain, March 23, 1948, RG 107, NA II.

58. J. T. Williams to James C. Evans, March 1, 1948, J. T. Williams to Executive for Reserve and ROTC Affairs, March 30, 1948, J. T. Williams to Second Army Commanding General, May 4, 1948, RG 107, NA II.

59. Dwight O. W. Holmes to Secretary of War, February 3, 1948, BG Wendell Westover to Dwight O. W. Holmes, February 9, 1948, MAJ R. E. Lines to TAG, March 16, 1948, Chief of Army Field Forces to Provost Marshal General, March 26, 1948, Provost Marshal General to TAG, March 31, 1948, Chief of Army Field Forces to Quartermaster General, April 2, 1948, COL W. R. Ellis to Chief of Army Field Forces, April 8, 1948, Chief of Army Field Forces to TAG, April 15, 1948, TAG to Second Army Commanding General, April 20, 1948, Senator Herbert R. O'Conor, May 11, 1948, MG H. B. Lewis to Senator Herbert R. O'Conor, May 13, 1948, RG 407; James C. Evans to Dwight O. W. Holmes, February 10, 1948, RG 107, NA II.

60. William H. Gray to Senator Claude Pepper, March 19, 1948, William H. Gray to Senator Spessard L. Holland, March 19, 1948, COL S. P. Walker to Senator Claude Pepper, April 16, 1948, Third Army Headquarters to TAG, April 15, 1948, Chief of Army Field Forces to Third Army Commanding General, April 20, 1948, CPT W. D. Spicer to Florida Military District Commanding General, April 23, 1948, William H. Gray, Jr. to TAG, May 6, 1948, MAJ Mark J. Leonardi to Florida Military District Commanding General, May 17, 1948, COL R. G. Howie to Florida Military District Commanding General, May 18, 1948, CPT William C. Wilford to Chief of Army Field Forces, May 20, 1948, Chief of Army Field Forces to The Quartermaster General, May 26, 1948, Chief of Army Field Forces to The Quartermaster General, June 1, 1948, Chief of Army Field Forces to TAG, June 7, 1948, TAG to Third Army Commanding General, June 10, 1948, RG 407, NA II; Memorandum, MG T. B. Larkin for Secretary of the Army, June 8, 1948, RG 107, NA II.

William H. Gray, Jr., president of Florida A and M College for Negroes, submitted an application on May 6, 1948 providing for a Quartermaster Corps ROTC or Transportation Corps ROTC detachment with a two-year mandatory course.

61. William H. Gray, Jr. to John W. Davis, March 31, 1948, Senator Claude Pepper, April 28, 1948, RG 107, NA II.

62. William H. Gray to James C. Evans, March 11, 23, 24, April 28, 1948, John W. Davis to Ferdinand D. Bluford, March 16, 1948, James C. Evans to William H. Gray, March 19, 22, 30, May 4, 1948, James C. Evans to Sherman D. Scruggs, March 22, 1948, L. H. Foster to James C. Evans, March 23, 31, May 4, 1948, James C. Evans to R. B. Atwood, Ferdinand D. Bluford, John W. Davis, L. H. Foster, March 30, 1948, James C. Evans to Charles H. Wesley, April 9, 1948, RG 107, NA II.

63. COL Herbert A. Barrow to James C. Evans, March 2, 30, 1948, G. L. Washington to James C. Evans, March 3, 1948, James C. Evans to LTC Herbert A. Barrow, March 4, April 6, 1948, RG 107, NA II. LTC Barrow also advised Evans to coordinate his plans with MAJ James Fowler, LTC Pollard and LTC George S. Roberts.

The Triple Nickles experienced several changes while civilians fought for enlistment and the existence of African American detachments. The battalion had been designated as one of the few African American organizations included in the composition concept which assigned companies and battalions respectively to battalions and regiments. However, BG G. L. Eberle, AGF Assistant Chief of Staff for Operations, questioned the feasibility of assigning the 555th Parachute Infantry Battalion to the 82nd Airborne Division while temporarily maintaining over-strength white battalions to prevent integration. The AGF assistant adjutant general considered the assignment of the Triple Nickles did not conceptually conform to policies enunciated in Circular 124 since the 555th Parachute Infantry Battalion would become an organic unit instead of an attached organization. He stressed that the battalion had never reached its full strength due to the absence of qualified volunteers, and this deficiency would reduce the potential combat effectiveness and efficiency of the division. He advocated a feasibility study to determine whether a combat parachute regiment composed of two white battalions and a battalion for African Americans should be organized, and whether an African American battalion should assume the history of an organic white battalion in the 82nd Airborne Division. LTG C. P. Hall, the Chief of Staff's Director of Organization and Training recognized the feasibility of not replacing an organic unit with the 555th Parachute Infantry Battalion and suggested to the AGF commanding general the issuance of a special table of organization and equipment which would grant an additional battalion over the authorized strength of the 82nd Airborne Division. This would permit the assignment of the Triple Nickles without eliminating an organic battalion.

The AGF commanding general was opposed to the publication of special tables of organization and equipment unless such special tables were required to enable the completion of the 82nd Airborne Division combat mission. From a tactical and organizational viewpoint, he felt the inclusion of the Triple Nickles as a separate infantry battalion was unsound and it was undesirable to organize divisions differently solely for the purpose of assigning an African American battalion. The AGF commanding general also doubted any change in the attached status of battalion would improve the training of African American paratroopers. His adamant opposition influenced LTG Hall to inform Secretary of War Robert Patterson that the mission of the 82nd Airborne Division necessitated the maintenance of the highest possible degree of training. Although the Triple Nickles were attached to the division for administration and training, the battalion was not at full strength but attempts were being made to eliminate this condition. Since the War Department did not intend to have detachments assume the designation or history of other detachments, the 555th Parachute Infantry Battalion would retain its attached status to the 82nd Airborne Division.

However, the 82nd Airborne Division was reorganized and its parachute infantry regiments were realigned as airborne infantry. All personnel in the 3rd Battalion, 505th Airborne Infantry Regiment were reassigned to the regiment's 1st and 2nd Battalions. The 555th Parachute Infantry Battalion, having served in an attached status with both the 504th and 505th Parachute Infantry Regiments for administration, discipline and training, was inactivated on December 9, 1947 and according to the 82nd Airborne Division General Order 83 the Triple Nickles became the 3rd Battalion, 505th Airborne Regiment. This reorganization, realignment and symbolic integration under the composite unit concept had a profound affect on the Triple Nickles. It was a total disregard of the limited but valuable service rendered by the Triple Nickles. Military officials did not consider the significance of their history and linage and were willing to eliminate the battalion without any thought of its brief but interesting tradition of military service. Initially, the battalion lost some of its African American leadership when former 555th Battalion cadre was replaced by white officers. CPT Joseph Gates, the battalion commander, was relieved and assigned the duty of assistant division training officer. CPT Theodore Owens was reassigned to the 505th Regimental Headquarters and Headquarters Company as a regimental chaplain. First Lieutenant Spurgeon A. Moore was transferred from Company I to the divisional intelligence section, and LT Raymond L. Fleming in Company M became the assistant divisional public relations officer. LT James R. Warrick, Jr., the battalion intelligence officer, was reassigned to the divisional athletics section, and LT John C. Cannon became the assistant medical officer. CWO James Hall was reassigned to the divisional supply office. See Memorandum, BG G. L. Eberle, Assistant Chief of Staff, G-3, AGF Commanding General, June 3, 1946, RG 165, NA; GO 3, HQ, 82nd Airborne Division, FT Bragg, NC, January 20, 1947; GO 55, HQ, 82nd Airborne Division, FT Bragg, NC, July 31, 1947; GO 29, HQ, 82nd Airborne Division, FT Bragg, NC, October 29, 1947; GO 83, HQ, 82nd Airborne Division, FT Bragg, NC, December 9, 1947; GO 1, HQ, 505th Airborne Infantry Regiment, FT Bragg, NC, December 15, 1947, GO 16, HQ, 555th Parachute Infantry Battalion, FT Bragg, NC, December 9, 1947, GO 83, 82nd ABN Division, FT Bragg, NC, December 9, 1947, GO 1, HQ, 505th ABN Infantry Regiment, FT Bragg, NC, December 15, 1947, GO 3, HQ, 505th ABN Infantry Regiment, FT Bragg, NC, December 15, 1947, RG 407, NA II; Bernard C. Nalty and Morris J. MacGregor, ed., *Blacks in the Military: Essential Documents* (Wilmington, DE: Scholarly Resources, Inc., 1981), 41, 115, 214–16. Bradley Biggs, *The Triple Nickles* (Hamden, CT: Archon Books), 80, 86–87.

64. COL S. Z. Abelow to COL West A. Hamilton, February 25, 1948, COL West A. Hamilton to Fourth Army Commanding General, February 28, 1948, COL West A. Hamilton to James C. Evans, March 9, 18, May 18, 1948, Ezra L. Henderson to James C. Evans, March 23, 1948, James C. Evans to COL West A. Hamilton, March 23, April 7, 9, 1948, RG 107, NA II.

Roland A. Laird, Secretary of the Military Affairs Committee of the Chamber of Commerce in Houston, Texas, reported that LTC Sam W. Becker had attended the Army Day at Prairie View A and M College. COL Becker praised and congratulated the State of Texas for the existence of the Prairie View ROTC and he was convinced of the future contributions of cadets. Laird stated that the report which was submitted praised the organization and the deportment of the cadets during their parade. "He described in terms of highest commendation the neatness and soldierly appearance of the cadet corps and referred in flattering terms to the steadiness of the troops on the field and the evidence of a high degree of *esprit de corps.*" See Roland A. Laird to COL West A. Hamilton, May 17, 1948, RG 107, NA II.

65. F. M. Dearborn to John W. Davis, March 18, 1948, John W. Davis to James C. Evans, March 19, 1948, John W. Davis to Executive Secretary of the Committee on Civilian Components, March 19, 1948, RG 107, NA II. An urgent engagement at Florida A and M College prevented William R. Gray, Jr. from attending the hearing. See William R. Gray, Jr. to John W. Davis, April 1, 1948, RG 107, NA II. Evans invited Ambrose Caliver to a conference which preceded the appearance of the delegation of the PNLGC before the Gray Board. See James C. Evans to Ambrose Caliver, March 30, 1948, RG 107, NA II. Davis remembered best his association and accomplishments of the Conference of the Presidents of Land Grant Colleges for Negroes which not only involved the expansion of ROTC but other achievements. See John C. Harlan, *History of West Virginia State College, 1891–1965* (Dubuque: William C. Brown, 1968), 95–96.

66. Statement of the Executive Committee of the Conference of Presidents of Land-Grant Colleges for Negroes as made before the Committee on Civilian Components of the Armed Forces, April 2, 1948, President's Commission on the Equality of Treatment and Opportunity in the Armed forces, Harry S. Truman Library, Independence, MO.

The Arkansas AM and N Board had deferred a decision until June 1948, Delaware State, Fort Valley State, and Maryland State Boards had granted approval, and plans for filing an application were being contemplated. Morgan State College had filed an application. Georgia State with an application filed since 1942 was 97th on the ROTC list. Alabama A and M and Kentucky State, Lincoln in Pennsylvania, Lincoln, Southern A and M College had applications pending before the War Department. The respective boards of Tennessee A and I and Alcorn A and M had similarly not approved the submission of ROTC applications.

67. James C. Evans to The Chief of the Chemical Corps, The Chief of Engineers, The Chief of Finance, The Chief of Ordnance, The Provost Marshal General, The Quartermaster General, The Chief Signal Officer, The Surgeon General, and Chief of Transportation, May 20, 1948, RG 107, NA II.

68. Memorandum, COL Henry F. Hannis for Civilian Aide to the Secretary of the Army, June 3, 1948, RG 107, NA II.

69. Memorandum, MG W. H. Kasten for James C. Evans, June 3, 1948, RG 107, NA II.

70. COL G. C. Bunting to Secretary of the Army, June 1, 1948, RG 107, NA II.

71. Memorandum, MG T. B. Larkin for Secretary of the Army, June 8, 1948, RG 107, NA II.

72. Felton G. Clark to James C. Evans, May 12, 1948, James C. Evans to William H. Gray, May 19, 1948, James C. Evans to Felton Clark, May 19, 1948, William H. Gray to James C. Evans, May 28, 1948, Memorandum, COL H. O. Paxson for Deputy Chief of Staff, June 2, 1948, RG 107, NA II.

73. James C. Evans to L. H. Foster, April 12, August 20, 1948, James C. Evans to John W. Davis, April 12, August 20, 1948, James C. Evans to Ambrose Caliver, August 20, 1948, RG 107, NA II; Charleston *Gazette*, April 6, 1948,

74. Memorandum for the Record, June 10, 1948, RG 107, NAII.

75. Memorandum, Organization and Training Division for Deputy Chief of Staff, n.d, Report of Tour of European Installations by Marcus H. Ray to Secretary of War, n.d., Memorandum, BG J. J. O'Hare for Secretary of the Army, March 9, 1948, Memorandum, Deputy Chief of Staff for Director of Personnel and Administration, May 14, 1948, MG H. R. Bull to Chief of Staff, July 14, 1948, Chief of Staff to European Commanding General, May 14, 1948, LTG W. S. Paul to Secretary of War, June 21, 1948, Memorandum, LTG W. S. Paul for Deputy Chief of Staff, July 21, LTG W. S. Paul to TAG, July 30, 1948, MG Edward F. Witsell to European Commander-in-Chief, August 4, 1948, Memorandum, MG John E. Dahlquist for Deputy Chief of Staff, August 19, 1948, RG 407, NA II.

The recommendations of the Dowdal H. Davis of the Kansas City *Call*, Clifford Mackay of the *Afro-American*, Louis E. Martin of the Michigan *Chronicle*, Frank L. Stanley of the Louisville *Defender*, Carter Wesley of the Houston *Informer*, and Thomas W. Young of the Norfolk *Journal and Guide*, also influenced significant changes in the European Theater. See Memorandum, COL J. H. Phillips for Deputy Chief of Staff, July 8, 1948, RG 407, NA II; *Army Times*, July 3, 1948.

However, it is significant to note that MG F. L. Anderson recommended that the Army Air Force reduce the number of African American personnel assigned to the European Theater since the projected total strength on March 15, 1946 was 63,283 or 18.8 percent of the troop basis. He recommended that all further enlistments and induction be discontinued and that the AAF be authorized to discharge for the convenience of the government all African American enlistees who selected service in the European Theater and were in excess of the AAF requirement for African American troop lists or who indicated their desire for discharge in preference to service in a theater other than the European Theater. MG Willard S. Paul, Assistant Chief of Staff for Personnel, informed the Army Air Forces commanding General that War Department policy regarding three-year overseas assignments permitted personnel to choose their theater. If vacancies did not exist, personnel were offered a choice of service in another theater to fill a vacancy. [Personnel who did not select another theater any attempts to discharge personnel would establish an undesirable precedent and policy.] "In addition, to discharge a volunteer soldier for the convenience of the Government solely because it is impractical to assign him to his theater of choice and at the same time continue to accept enlistments in the Regular Army would be inconsistent and would subject the Army Air Forces and the War Department to justifiable criticism on the grounds of waste of public funds." He assured MG Anderson that other commanding generals were confronted with similar situations but he would carefully scrutinize the matter and take expeditious action whenever possible to reduce the strength of African American troops to the 10 percent level contemplated by the Gillem Committee. See MG F. L. Anderson to Chief of Staff for Personnel, March 1946, Memoranda, MG W. S. Paul for Army Air Forces Commanding General, March 11, 21, May 13, 1946, RG 407, NA II.

76. Acting Director of Organization and Training Division to Secretary of the Army June 16, 22, 1948, Martin D. Jenkins to TAG, June 22, 1948, TAG to Martin D. Jenkins, June 24, 1948, COL C. R. Bathurst to TAG, June 24, 1948, GO 48, Department of the Army, Washington, DC, July 12, 1948, June 22, August 24, 1948, TAG to Commanding Generals of Second, Third and Fourth Armies, June 28, 1948, NA II; Martin D. Jenkins to TAG, June 22, 1948, LTC L. M. Scarborough to Civilian aide to the Secretary of the Army, June 25, 1948, William H. Gray, Jr. to Career Management Branch, June 28, 1948, James C. Evans to Felton G. Clark, William H. Gray, Jr., Martin D. Jenkins, June 29, 30, 1948, July 8, 1948, William H. Gray, Jr. to James C. Evans, June 25, July 2, 1948, 244, RG 107, NA II; GO 48, Department of the Army, Washington, DC, July 12, 1948, RG 407, NAII.

On June 28, 1948, Clark accepted CPT Benjamin W. Johnson and LT William T. Briscoe as part of ROTC cadre. See Felton G. Clark to Career Management Branch, June 28, 1948, RG 107, NA II. MAJ Clarence M. Davenport was selected as PMST at Florida A and M College and his Assistant PMST was CPT Luther Evans, Jr. Davenport understood the significance of his appointment but LTC James H. Robinson emphasized that he had an opportunity which was rarely given to African American officers. COL Robinson stated it reminded him of efforts by Evans to activate ROTC detachments which permitted an increase in the commissioning of African American officers. Interested in getting qualified personnel to assist him, CPT Luther Evans, Jr. was selected as his Assistant PMST and he highly recommended the selection of MSGT Tabron who was highly recommended as his administrative assistant. See COL James H. Robinson to MAJ Clarence H. Davenport, June 30, 1948, RG 107, NA II.

77. Statement of Judge Morris A. Soper to Commission to Study the Question of Negro Higher Education in Maryland, December 6, 1949, Office File of Ambrose Caliver, 1946–1962, Records of the Office of Education, RG 12, NA II. Other issues discussed by the commission was the transfer of the Coppin Teachers College program to Morgan State, the impact of integration at the University of Maryland, Bowie State College and Towson College, and collegiate integration in other states. Also see an Abstract of Remarks of Martin D. Jenkins, president of Morgan State College, before the Commission to Study the Question of Higher Negro Education in Maryland, October 17, 1949, RG 12, NA II; Edward N. Wilson, *The History of Morgan State College: A Century of Purpose in Action, 1867–1967* (New York: Vantage Press), 59–60, 87. For a list of the African American land grant colleges, and the disproportional distribution of federal funds by states, see James A. Atkins, "Negro Educational Institutions and the Veterans' Educational Facilities Program," *Journal of Negro Education* 17 (Summer 1948):141–152;

R[ufus] B. Atwood, "The Future of the Negro Land-Grant College," *Journal of Negro Education* 27 (Summer 1958):381–391; Rufus B. Atwood, "The Origin and Development of the Negro Land Public College, with Especial Reference to the Land-Grant College," *Journal of Negro Education* 31 (Summer 1962):240–250; John W. Davis, "The Participation of Negro Land-Grant Colleges in Permanent Federal Education Funds," 7 (July 1938):282–291; William H. Martin, "The Land-Grant Functions of the Negro Public College," *Journal of Negro Education* 31 (Summer 1962):396; Herbert O. Reid and James N. Nabrit, "Remedies Under Statutes Granting Federal Aid to Land Grant Colleges," *Journal of Negro Education* 17 (Summer 1947):410–425. Hereafter, RG 12 will be used for Records of the Office of Education, RG 12, NA II; Ruth E. Wennersten, "The Historical Evolution of a Black Land Grant College: The University of Maryland Eastern Shore," Unpublished Thesis, University of Maryland, College Park, MD, 1976, 83. A previous attempt to transfer the land grant status from Morgan College's Industrial Branch of Princess Anne Academy to the Maryland Normal and Industrial School was successfully challenged by James O. Spencer, president of Morgan College. For additional information concerning Princess Anne Academy, see Martha S. Putney, "The Formative Years of Maryland's First Black Postsecondary School," *Maryland Historical Magazine* 73 (June 1975): 168–179; John R. and Ruth Ellen Wennersten, "Separate and Unequal: The Evolution of a Black Land Grant College, 1890–1930," *Maryland Historical Magazine* 72 (Spring 1977): 110–117; Edward J. Kuebler, "The Desegregation of the University of Maryland," *Maryland Historical Magazine* 71 (Spring 1976): 37–49.

78. Director of Personnel and Administration to TAG, May 24, July 2, 1948, LTG W. S. Paul to Secretary of the Army, August 6, 1948, Memorandum, Organization and Training Division for Deputy Chief of Staff, Records of the Adjutant General's Office, 1917, RG 407, NA II. Of the thirty-two officers integrated into Army organizations, thirteen were assigned to Infantry detachments, nine to Chaplain Corps, one to Pharmacy Corps although later transferred to Medical Service Corps, one to Army Nurse Corps, one to Field Artillery, and seven to Quartermaster Corps although 4 were later transferred to Transportation Corps. With only one retired BG serving on active duty on April 30, 1948, there were two COL, ten LTC, twenty-six MAJ, 221 CPT, 512 LT, 118 LT, 33 CWO, and 24 WO serving in all branches except Finance and Judge Advocate Corps.

79. COL West A. Hamilton to James C. Evans, May 18, 1948, James C. Evans to COL West A. Hamilton, May 21, 1948, RG 107, NA II.

80. James C. Evans to E. B. Evans, June 30, 1948, LTC L. M. Scarborough to Civilian Aide to the Secretary of the Army, June 25, 1948, Martin D. Jenkins to Career Management Branch, July 1, 1948, RG 107, NA II.

COL Hamilton was the senior African American officer serving with ROTC detachments. COL Hamilton graduated from the M Street School and Minor Normal School in Washington, DC and received bachelor and master's degrees from American University. Teaching in the District of Columbia Pubic School System and publishing the Washington *Tribune*, he began his military career in 1905 by enlisting as a private in the 1st Separate Battalion, District of Columbia National Guard. Having served in every grade to CPT by the beginning of the Mexican border campaign of 1916, CPT Hamilton served in France with the 372nd Infantry Regiment, 93rd Infantry Division during WWI. In 1920 he received an Army Reserve and commanded the 428th Infantry Officer Reserve Regiment in the Third Corps Area. Promoted to COL on August 1, 1933, he also commanded a CMTC at Fort Howard, MD, from 1936 until the program was discontinued in 1940. COL Hamilton became the executive officer of the 366th Infantry Regiment at Fort Devens, Massachusetts prior to his service as administrative inspector with the Eighth Service Command in Dallas, Texas. He was reassigned to Prairie View

A and M in 1942 at PMST and he also served with the Discharge Review Board in Washington prior to returning to Prairie View State College. See Charles Johnson, Jr., *African American Soldiers in the National Guard* (Westport: Greenwood Press, 1992): pp. 106–07, 117, 130, 132, Philadelphia *Tribune*, March 4, 1947, Chicago *Defender*, March 8, 1947, Houston *Informer*, March 8, 1947.

81. Governor Earl C. Clements to LTG L. T. Gerow, July 19, 1948, LTC Gerow to Governor Earl C. Clements, August 3, 1948, LTG L. T. Gerow to H. C. Byrd, August 6, 1948, RG 407, NA II.

82. Governor Earl C. Clements to LTG L. T. Gerow, July 19, 1948, LTC Gerow to Governor Earl C. Clements, August 3, 1948, LTG L. T. Gerow to H. C. Byrd, August 6, 1948, MG H. R. Bull to Chief of Staff, June 22, August 24, 1948, TAG to Commanding Generals of Second, Third and Fourth Armies, June 28, 1948, RG 407, NA II.

83. James C. Evans to Luther H. Foster, June 30, 1948, James C. Evans to George Streater, June 30, 1930, RG 107, NA II.

84. BG Pearson to TAG, November 22, 1947, TAG to LTC James H. Robinson, June 10, September 7, 1948, Memorandum, James C. Evans for COL Frederick J. Munson, August 17, 1948, Memorandum, James C. Evans for LTC T. N. Dupuy, August 31, 1948, Memorandum, James C. Evans for MAJ A. N. Shimkus, November 1948, James C. Evans to LTC James H. Robinson, November 10, 1948, LTC James H. Robinson to James C. Evans, June 16, September 18, November 19, 1948, SO 233, Headquarter, Department of the Army, Washington, DC, November 22, 1948, Press Section Release, Public Information Division, Department of the Army, June 28, 1948, RG 107, NA II.

85. James C. Evans to R. S. Atwood, Rufus Clement, John W. Davis, G. L. Harrison, S. D. Scruggs, June 30, 1948, RG 107, NA II.

86. Conference of Land-Grant Colleges for Negroes to President, August 17, 1947, Records of the Secretary of the Army, RG 335, NA II. College presidents who attended the conference were Joseph F. Drake of Alabama A and M, Ferdinand D. Bluford of North Carolina A and T, R. B. Atwood of Kentucky State, L. H. Foster of Virginia State, John W. Davis of West Virginia State, S. D. Scruggs of Lincoln, and G. L. Harrison of Langston. Davis served as president of the conference, Scruggs; was chairman of the executive committee and Atwood was the conference secretary. Hereafter, RG 335 will be used for Records of the Secretary of the Army, RG 335, NA II.

87. John W. Davis to James C. Evans, July 13, 1948, RG 107, NA II; R. B. Atwood to Carl Murphy, August 4, 1948, Carl Murphy to President Harry S. Truman, August 21, 1948, TAG to Director of Organization and Training Division, September 8, 1928, BG L.W. Cunningham to TAG, September 20, 1948, TAG to Carl Murphy, September 21, 1948, RG 407, NA II; Baltimore *Afro-American*, July 3, 1948.

88. LTG L. T. Gerow to John W. Davis, May 17, 1948, John W. Davis to LTG L. T. Gerow, June 5, 1948, John W. Davis to James C. Evans, June 19, 1948, James C. Evans to John W. Davis, June 14, 1948, RG 107, NA II. CPT Claude, an artillery officer had been assigned to West Virginia State College to assist MAJ Barnette. See John W. Davis to COL Marcus H. Ray, September 24, 1946, Marcus H. Ray to John W. Davis, October 14, 1946, RG 107, NA II.

89. COL John R. Monnett to MG Clift Andrus, September 22, 1949, COL John R. Monnett to Director of Personnel and Administration, September 22, 1949, MG Clift Andrus to LTC Turner, September 22, 1949, Records of the Army Staff, RG 319, NA II. Enrollments for the other institutions were 425 for Alabama A and M, 569 for Arkansas AM and N, 380 for Kentucky State, 219 for Maryland's Princess Anne Academy, 325 for Alcorn A and M, 523 for Lincoln, 403 for Langston, 1214 for Tennessee A and I and 600 for Georgia State. The established ROTC detachments were located at Florida A and M, Southern A and M, North Carolina A and T, South Carolina State, Prairie View A and

M, Virginia State and West Virginia State. Hereafter, RROTC will be used for Reserve and ROTC Affairs.

90. Memorandum, LT John Thomas Martin for COL George S. Ryster, January 18, 1949, Memoranda, COL B. M. McFadyen for Executive Secretary of The President's Commission on the Equality of Treatment and Opportunity in the Armed Forces, April 27, 29, 1949, Memorandum, LTC James H. Robinson for Executive Secretary of Fahy Committee, May 4, 1949, The Presidents Commission on the Equality of Treatment and Opportunity in the Armed Forces, Harry S. Truman Liberty, Independence, MO. African Americans were assigned to the 1st Battalion, 25th Infantry Regiment (Attached), 3rd Battalion, 9th Infantry Regiment, and 503rd Field Artillery Battalion in 2nd Division; 3rd Battalion, 15th Infantry Regiment in the 3rd Infantry Division; 364th and 365th Infantry Regiments in the 9th Infantry Division; 1st Battalion, 86th Infantry Regiment and 571st Field Artillery Battalion (Attached) in the 10th Infantry Division; 24th Infantry Regiment, 159th Field Artillery Battalion, 36th Medical Collecting Company, and 77th Engineer Combat Company; 73rd Engineer Battalion (Attached) in the 2nd Armored Division; 367th Armored Infantry Battalion (Attached) in the 3rd Armored Division; and 3rd Battalion, 505th Airborne Infantry Regiment, 503rd Antiaircraft Artillery (AW) Battalion, 758th Heavy Tank Battalion (Attached), and 589th Quartermaster Field Service Company. In addition to LTC Chase, there were forty-nine other field grade Regular Army officers which included 2 COL and 12 LTC.

91. CPT James V. Hood to CARROTC, May 11, 1960, CPT V. M. St. Peter to CAR-ROTC, May 19, 1960, CWO William A. Brewer GA to CARROTC, May 12, 1960 Memorandum, MG Ned D. Moore for ASA (MP&RF), November 21, 1960, RG 335, NA II. The specific dates when applications were received for each institution are: Lincoln in Pennsylvania, 1950; Virginia Union, 1951; St. Paul's Polytechnic Institute, 1951; Kentucky State, 1952; Atlanta, May 26, 1952; Fort Valley State, June 12, 1952; Alcorn A and M, July 15, 1952 with a resubmission on June 18, 1955; Jackson State, June 30, 1952; North Carolina College, July 24, 1952; Arkansas AM and N College, August 10,1952 with a resubmission on November 18, 1959; Fisk, August 14, 1952; Albany State and Savannah State, September 24, 1952; Arkansas AM and Normal, November 14, 1953; Grambling State, Howard Payne, Texas Southern and Xavier University, March 13, 1953. In 1959 Bluefield State College expressed interest in ROTC. CPT V. M. St. Peter reported for HQ 2nd Army, Fort Meade, MD, CWO William A. Brewer for HQ 3rd Army, Fort McPherson, GA, and CPT James V. Hood reported for HQ 4th Army, Fort Sam Houston, TX.

92. MG E. M. Foster to Director of Personnel and Administration, March 25, 1949, Records of the Army Staff, RG 319, NA II.

93. Memorandum, LTC H. C. McKinley for GEN Kenner, March 8, 1949, MG E. M. Foster to Director of Personnel and Administration, March 25, 1949, LTG Edward H. Brooks to MG E. M. Foster, April 4, 1949, Records of the Army Staff, RG 319, NA II.

94. COL R. F. Perry to Third Army Commanding General, May 17, 1949, MAJ L. P. Sullivan to TAG, May 20, 1949, LTC Neil M. Matzger to TAG, May 25, 1949, TAG to Third Army Commanding General, May 31, 1949, Assistant Chief of Staff for Operations and Training to Secretary of the Army, December 18, 1950, LTC R. W. Bowden to TAG, December 19, 1950, Assistant Secretary of the Army Karl R. Bendetsen to Gordon Gray, December 28, 1950, RG 407, NA II.

95. J. R. Otis to LTG John R. Hodge, October 30, 1950, LTC J. J. Hamlin to Chief of Mississippi Military District, November 27, 1950, COL Stuart C. MacDonald to Third Army Commanding General, December 27, 1950, RG 407, NA II.

96. COL F. A. Hause to TAG, October 18, 1950, RG 407, NA II.

97. COL F. Nowakowski to TAG, December 2, 1950, TAG to Joseph F. Drake, January 17, 1951, TAG to William A. Fountain, January 17, 1951, RG 407, NA II.

98. COL A. P. Thayer to TAG, April 4, 1950, COL Charles A. Worthington to Chief of Army Publications Branch, April 7, 1950, GO 13, Department of the Army, Washington, DC, April 20, 1950, Director of Organization and Training to Chief of Army Field Forces, February 13, 1950, Chief of Organization and Training Division to TAG, May 18, 1950, MAJ H. O. Beeth to TAG, September 29, 1950, RG 407, NA II; Albert P. Marshall, *Soldiers Dream: A Centennial History of Lincoln University of Missouri, 1866–1966* (Marceline, MO: Walsworth, 1966), 30; Lincoln University, *ROTC Handbook* (Jefferson City: Lincoln University, 1962), passim. Assistant Adjutant of the Fifth Army had decided that Lincoln was not eligible for an Engineer ROTC detachment and TAG recommended to the Chief of Army Field Forces that Langston should be considered in the future for a ROTC detachment. See TAG to Chief of Army Field Forces, January 4, 1950, Assistant Adjutant of Fifth Army Command to Assistant Chief of Staff for Operations and Training, March 10, 1950, RG 407, NA II.

99. Mother M. Agatha to TAG, July 8, 21, 1952, TAG to Walter S. Davis, July 15, 1952, TAG to Fulton G. Clark, July 15, 1952, TAG to George W. Gore, Jr., July 15, 1952, TAG to Alonzo Moron, July 15, 1952, TAG to F. D. Patterson, July 15, 1952, TAG to A. Elder, July 16, 1952, TAG to William A. Fountain, Jr., July 16, 1952, TAG to J. A. Bacoats, July 17, 1952, TAG to Mother M. Agatha, July 17, 1952, TAG to R. O'Hara Lanier, July 17, 1952, TAG to Thomas H. Taylor, July 17, 1952, TAG to Fourth Army Commanding General, July 18, 1952, R. O'Hara Lanier to TAG, July 22, 1952, Chief of Army Field Forces to TAG, July 29, 1952, RG 407, NA II. Xavier had previously submitted applications for a detachment in 1942, 1948, 1950 and 1951. Sherman D. Scruggs was notified in July 1948 of a decision by the Office of the Chief of Engineers to send an inspection team to the campus to determine the feasibility of establishing an Engineering ROTC detachment at Lincoln. See LTC James H. Robinson to Sherman D. Scruggs, July 9, 1948, RG 107, NA II.

100. COL Samuel S. Graham to Fourth Army Commanding General, October 31, 1950, LTC M. J. Bartosk to TAG, November 29, 1950, Lawrence A. Davis to Fourth Army Chief of Staff, February 25, 1952, Fourth Army Chief of Staff to Lawrence A. Davis, March 7, 1952, CPT H. O. Beeth to TAG, March 7, 1952, Memorandum, Assistant Secretary of the Army Fred North for Secretary of the Army, March 28, 1952, Secretary of the Army Frank Pace, Jr. to Governor Sid McGrath, June 2, 1952, Lawrence A. Davis to TAG, June 30, 1952, Herrin Northcutt to TAG, July 15, 1952, TAG to Fourth Army Commanding General, July 21, 1952, BG William E. Bergin to Lawrence A. Davis, July 22, 1952, MG Reuben E. Jenkins to Chief of Staff, July 24, 1952 Memorandum, Assistant Secretary of the General Staff for MG Vaughan, July 29, 1952, MG Harry H. Vaughan to Herrin Northcutt, July 29, 1952. MG Fourth Army Adjutant General to TAG, July 30, 1952, TAG to Herrin Northcutt, August 27, 1952, file 000.8, boxes 993 and 1044, RG 407, NA.

101. Senator John L. McClellan to Secretary of the Army Pace, July 17, September 22, 1952, LTC John Lockett to Senator J. W. Fulbright, February 11, 1953, Senator John L. McClellan to Secretary of the Army Robert T. B. Stevens, March 30, October 28, 1953, March 9, 1954, Secretary of the Army Stevens to Senator John L. McClellan, April 14, November 5, 1953, Memorandum, COL C. L. Heitman, Jr. for COL Frank C. Norvell, August 10, 1953, MG C. D. Edeleman to Chief of Staff, Army, August 13, 1953, Undersecretary of the Army Karl D. Johnson, August 18, 1953, George McKinney to Senator John L. McClellan, October 27, 1953, TAG to George McKinney, November 24, 1953, Representative E. C. Gathings to Undersecretary John Slezak, February 17, 1954, Assistant Secretary of the Army Hugh M. Milton, March 3, 1954, Memorandum, T. A.

Young for Secretary of the Army, March 8, 1954, LTC L. W. Smith to Senator J. W. Fulbrigth, February, 19, 1954, RG 407, NA II.

102. CWO O.F. Kindilen to Chief of Army Field Forces, July 17, 1952, MAJ Jack L. Paxton to Chief of Army Field Forces, July 17, 1952, MAJ L. E. Ingram to Chief of Army Field Forces, June 3, 1953, MAJ L. C. Estes to Chief of Army Field Forces, July 14, 1953, RG 407, NA II. Wilberforce was the only unsatisfactory institution in the Second Army with an Infantry ROTC detachment in 1952. All of the others had Medical detachments which included Georgetown University, George Washington University, Johns Hopkins University, University of Louisville, Ohio State University, University of Pennsylvania, Temple University, and the Medical College of Virginia.

103. GO 108, Second Army Headquarters, July 1, 1948, TAG to Executive for RROTC, April 14, 1952, COL George E. Butler to Senator Richard B. Russell, March 6, 1953, GO 44 Department of the Army, Washington, DC, May 22, 1953, RG 407, NA. Langston which was organized by territorial legislation signed by Governor William G. Renfrow on March 2, 1897, and was originally designated as the Colored Agricultural and Normal University of Oklahoma joined Connors State Agricultural College at Warner, Cameron State Agricultural College at Lawton and Panhandle A and M College at Goodwell in the Oklahoma satellite system.

104. Fort Valley State College *Peachite*, March 1963. MAJ Robinson was commissioned a LT in the Army on December 30, 1940 and entered active duty as a chaplain on January 20, 1941. He was promoted to the rank of CPT on February 1, 1942 and to MAJ on June 20, 1946. See MAJ Robinson to Students, Staff and Faculty, February 28, 1973, H. Alonzo Robinson Papers, Fort Valley State College, GA.

105. Memorandum, Joseph H. B. Evans for Fahy Committee, August 1, 1949, The President's Committee on Equality of Treatment and Opportunity in the Armed Services, Harry S. Truman Library, Independence, MO. Lincoln University with Engineer ROTC was required to send cadets to FT Carson, Colorado. MAJ Robert E. Greene, ret., interview with the author, Department of History and Geography, Morgan State University, Baltimore, MD, July 16, 1966.

106. Howard University *Hilltop*, January 1951, March 12, October 15,1951.

## Chapter 4

1. William C. Stancik and R. Cargill Hall, "Air Force ROTC: Its Origins and Early Years," *Air University Review* 35 ( July-August 1984):40–41. For information concerning the disarmament conference, see Ernest Andrade, "The United States Navy and the Washington Conference," *Historian* 31 (May 1969): 345–363; Thomas C. Hone, "The Effectiveness of the 'Washington Treaty' Navy," *Naval War College Review* 32 (November-December 1979): 35–59. Hereafter, ADC will be used for Air Defense Command, ConAC for Continental Air Command and AFROTC for Air Force ROTC.

2. GO 124, War Department, Washington, DC, October 25, 1945; Howard University *Hilltop*, October 24, 1947. Army Air ROTC PASTs were required to have obtained field grade rank, and be between the ages of twenty-seven and forty-eight with at least three years of active commissioned service and twelve months of overseas duty. They were further required to have a Bachelor's degree and above average efficiency ratings. See Stancik and Hall, "Air Force ROTC: Its Origins and Early Years," 43–44.

3. Fred D. Patterson to Secretary of War Robert P. Patterson September 10, 1946, LTG C. P. Hall to Army Air Force Commanding General, September 16, 1946, BG Leon W. Johnson to Director of Organization and Training Division, September 19, 1946, Secretary of War Robert P. Patterson to F. P. Patterson, September 26, 1946, RG 407, NA II.

4. Howard University *Hilltop*, April 15, 1948.

5. G. L. Washington, Survey of Post War Aviation Possibilities in Negro Land Grant Colleges, October 25, 1945, G. L. Washington, Supplement to Recommendations, Report to Conference of Land Grant (Negro) Presidents, October 25, 1945, Twenty-Third Annual Conference of the Presidents of Negro Land Grant Colleges, October 23–25, 1946, Chicago, IL, Center of Excellence for the Study of Kentucky African-Americans, Kentucky State University, KY, RG 107, NA II.

6. MAJ Robert A. Stevens to Charles H. Wesley, October 25, 1946 Marcus H. Ray to Charles H. Wesley, November 8, 1946, COL Monro MacCloskey to Charles H. Wesley, November 12, 1946, Charles H. Wesley to James C. Evans, December 31, 1945, February 10, 1948, Marcus H. Ray to Charles H. Wesley, August 5, 1946, MG John T. Lewis to Charles H. Wesley, n.d., RG 107, NA II.

7. Charles H. Wesley to James C. Evans, April 29, 1948, RG 107, NA II.

8. Memorandum, CPT Howard L. Baugh for James C. Evans, May 4, 1948, RG 107, NA II.

9. Memorandum, LTG I. H. Edwards for Assistant Secretary of the Air Force, December 5, 1947, Records of Assistant Secretary of the Air Force, RG 340, NA II. There were 192 officers assigned to Lockbourne Army Air Base while MacDill Field, Lockbourne Army Air Base and San Antonio had the largest concentration of enlisted men with 1581, 1862, and 3450 respectively. Hereafter, RG 340 will be used for Records of Assistant Secretary of the Air Force.

10. James C. Evans to John W. Davis, March 1, 1948, RG 107, NA II; Mike Tucker, "ROTC-A Training Ground for Tomorrow's Leaders," *Howard Magazine* 5 (Summer 1967): 25.

11. John W. Davis to Secretary of War Robert P. Patterson, February 6, 1946, COL D. R. Patrick to Army Service Forces Commanding General, April 8, 1946, Memorandum, COL A. Segarra for Executive of Reserve and ROTC Affairs, April 12, 1946, Executive of Reserve and ROTC Affairs to TAG, April 18, 1946, TAG to Fifth Service Commanding General, April 18, 1946, RG 407, NA II.

12. John W. Davis to Secretary of War Robert P. Peterson, March 15, 1947, Memorandum, James C. Evans for the Office of the Assistant Civilian Aide to the Secretary of War, March 24, 1947, Assistant Secretary of War Robert P. Peterson, April 3, 1947, RG 107, NA II.

13. Report of the Research and Planning Staff, Joint Army-Air Force Advisory Committee on ROTC Affairs to the Second Meeting of the Civilian Components Policy Board at Washington, DC, November 2–4, 1949, Records of the Assistant Secretary of the Air Force, RG 340, NA II. In addition to the chairman of the committee and the representative, the other membership included civilian educators from the Association of Land-Grant Colleges and Universities, the National Association of State Universities, the Association of Military Colleges and Schools, and from privately controlled colleges and universities as well as members from the Departments of Army, Navy and Air Force.

14. Memorandum, Marx Leva for Secretaries of the Army, Navy and Air Force, Chairmen of Personnel Policy Board, Civilian Components Policy Board and Service Academy Board, and Director of Medical Services, n.d., F. J. Lawton to Secretary of Defense, September 26, 1949, Records of Assistant Secretary of the Air Force, RG 340, NA II.

15. Statement of GEN John P. McConnell to Assistant Secretary of the Air Force Harold C. Stuart, November 23, 1949, Backup Data for the Proposed ROTC Act of 1949, December 14, 1949, RG 340, NA II.

16. Memorandum, R. M. Thurston for Assistant Secretary of the Air Force Harold C. Stuart, n.d., Assistant Secretary of the Air Force, RG 340, NA II.

17. Air Force Assistant Vice Chief of Staff to Commanding General of Continental

Air Command, May 17, 1950, Records of the Assistant Secretary of the Air Force, RG 340, NA II.

18. Gene M. Lyons and John W. Masland. *Education and Military Leadership.* Princeton: Princeton University Press, 1959, 102–103.

19. John W. Davis to Honorable Louis Johnson, July 7, 1950, Honorable Louis Johnson to John W. Davis, July 12, 1950, Memorandum, Chief of Staff for Secretary of the Air Force Louis Johnson, July 20, 1950, Secretary of the Air Force Thomas K. Finletter to John W. Davis, July 28, 1950, John W. Davis to Secretary of the Air Force Thomas K. Finletter, January 11, 1951, Assistant Secretary of the Air Force Harold C. Stuart to John W. Davis, February 2, 1951, Records of the Assistant Secretary of the Air Force, RG 340, NA II.

20. D. W. Dent to Honorable Louis Johnson, July 20, 1950, Honorable Louis Johnson D. W. Dent, July 24, 1950, COL Clarence D. Wheeler to D. W. Dent, August 2, 1950, Records of the Assistant Secretary of Air Force, RG 340, NA II.

21. Horace M. Bond to Honorable Thomas K. Finletter, July 20, 1950, Congressman J. Caleb Boggs to Honorable Thomas K. Finletter, March 6, 1951, A. J. G. Priest to Honorable Thomas K. Finletter, March 12, 1951, BG Robert E. L. Eaton to Congressman J. Caleb Boggs, March 14, 1951, Honorable Thomas K. Finletter to A. J. G. Priest, March 17, 1951, Congressman Edward Martin to Honorable Thomas K. Finletter, March 20, 1951, BG Robert E. L. Eaton to Congressman Edward Martin, March 27, 1951, Congressman Frances P. Bolton to Honorable Thomas K. Finletter, April 9, 1951, BG Robert E. L. Eaton to Congressman Frances P. Bolton, April 14, 1951, RG 340, NA II. Lincoln also graduated LT Purnell and LT Lee Rayford who served as combat pilots without the benefit of ROTC training.

22. Mary McLeod Bethune to Anna Rosenberg, April 12, 1951, Anna M. Rosenberg to Mary McLeod Bethune, May 2, 1951, BG R. L. Copsey to Mary McLeod Bethune, May 23, 1951, Records of the Assistant Secretary of Air force, RG 340, NA II.

23. R. B. Atwood to Secretary of the Air Force Thomas F. Finletter, January 8, 1951, Deputy Director of Training to R. B. Atwood, January 25, 1951, Senator Earle C. Clements to Anna Rosenberg, February 24, 1951, Memorandum, COL James F. Collins for R. M. Thurston, March 15, 1951, Memorandum, Anna M. Rosenberg for Secretary of the Air Force, March 19, 1951, Anna M. Rosenberg to Senator Earle C. Clements, March 19, 1951, Under Secretary of the Air Force John A. McCone to Senator Earle C. Clements, March 29, 1951, BG Robert E. L. Eaton to Senator Earle C. Clements, March 29, 1951, RG 340, NA; James C. Evans and Albert J. Parker, "ROTC Programs and Negro Youth," *Journal of Negro Education* 25 (Spring 1959): 134.

24. Memorandum, MG Earl S. Hoag for the Record, September 14, 1950, MG Earl S. Hoag to CONAC Commanding General, September 14, 1950, Memorandum, MG Earl S. Hoag for the Assistant Secretary of the Air Force, September 15, 1950, Harold C. Stuart to College Presidents, September 15, October 7, 1950, Mordecai W. Johnson to Harold C. Stuart, October 9, 1950, F. D. Bluford to Assistant Secretary of the Air Force Harold C. Stuart, October 14, 1950, Alonzo G. Moron to Assistant Secretary of the Air Force Harold C. Stuart, November 9, 1950, J. Irvin Washington to Assistant Secretary of the Air Force Harold C. Stuart, November 16, 1950, Records of the Assistant Secretary of the Air Force, RG 340, NA II. Others who attended the meeting were MG K. P. McNaughton, Director of Training; MG W. E. Todd, Office of the Assistant for Programming; BG R. L. Copsey, Deputy Special Assistant for Reserve Forces; COL Daniel S. Campbell, Deputy Special Assistant for Reserve Forces; COL Llody P. Hopwood, Deputy Director of Personnel Planning; COL N. C. Ambrosion, Office of the Assistant for Programming; LTC Marshall N. Strickler, Deputy Chief, AFROTC Division, Office of the Special Assistant for Reserve Forces; MAJ Morgan S. Tyler,

Executive, Office of the Special Assistant for Reserve Forces; L. Eugene Hedberg, Special Assistant for ROTC Affairs; and George J. Nagy, Office of the Assistant for Programming, RG 340, NA II.

25. Memorandum, BG Edmund C. Lynch for Assistant for Programming, March 30, 1951, Records of the Assistant to the Secretary of Air Force, RG 340, NA; Stancik and Hall, "Air ROTC: Its Origins and Early Years": 45.

26. MG Earl Hoag to Assistant Secretary of the Air Force, January 25, 1951, Memorandum, MG Earl Hoag for Chief of Staff, January 25, 1951, BG Harlan Parks to Vice Chief of Staff, n.d., Records of the Assistant Secretary of the Air Force, RG 340, NA II.

27. COL Daniel S. Campbell to Assistant Secretary of the Air Force, March 29, 1951, Memorandum, COL George H. Krieger for Record, March 31, 1951, Memorandum, COL W. S. Steele for Record, April 13, 1951, Memorandum, COL Daniel S. Campbell for Honorable Finletter, April 16, 1951, News Release, Office of Public Information Department of Defense, Washington, DC, April 20, 1951, Memorandum, BG R. L. Copsey for COL Steele, April 28, 1951, Records of the Assistant to the Secretary of the Air Force, RG 340, NA II. Members of the panel of educators were Raymond B. Allen, President of the University of Washington; Carl E. Borgman, Dean of Facilities at the University of Nebraska; Frank H. Bowles, Director of the College Entrance Examination Board; J. E. Buchanan, President of the University of Idaho; Henry Chauncey, President of Educational Testing Service; Dana M. Cotton, Secretary of New England Association of Colleges and Secondary Schools; Vincent J. Flynn, President of Alabama Polytechnic Institute; and Frederick D. Patterson, President of Tuskegee.

28. W. S. Davis to Congressman J. Percy Priest, April 11, 1951, J. A. Barksdale to Congressman J. Percy Priest, April 13, 1951, Congressman J. Percy Priest to Secretary of the Air Force Thomas K. Finletter, April 16, 1951, Memorandum, Jack O. Crawford for the Record, April 23, 1951, Records of the Assistant Secretary of the Air Force, RG 340, NA II; Tennessee A and I State University Meter, November 1958; "Historical Summary of Tennessee State University," *Tennessee State University Bulletin*, 42 (November 1961): 3.

29. Alonzo G. Moron to Assistant Secretary of the Air Force Harold C. Stuart, November 9, 1950, J. Irvin Washington to Assistant Secretary of the Air Force Harold C. Stuart, November 16, 1950, F. D. Bluford to Secretary of Defense Thomas K. Finletter, April 24, 1951, W. S. Davis to Secretary of Defense Thomas K. Finletter, May 1, 1951, F. D. Bluford to Assistant Secretary of the Air Force Harold C. Stuart, October 14, 1950, RG 340, NA, Records of the Assistant Secretary of the Air Force, RG 340; GO 72, Headquarters, Fourteenth Air Force, Robbins AFB, Georgia, June 1, 1951. The first officers commissioned at Tennessee A and I in 1953 were LT James Caruth, Charles D. Howard and Alex Turner, Jr., and by August 8, 1954 eight others were commissioned. They were LT David A. Taylor, Sidney O. Davis, Willie L. Jones, John P. Landry and Joseph L. Anthony in June 1954; James L. Bates, Jesse L. Wilson and William J. Reed in August 1954. See "Recapitulations from the Department of Air Science," Tennessee A and I State University *Bulletin* 42 (September 1954):14; Tennessee A and I State University *Meter*, January 1955. In 1961 the first Regular Air Force commissions were awarded to LT Ronnie Peoples and Edward Moon. See the Tennessee A and I State University *Meter*, April 15–30, 1961.

30. Lawrence A. Davis to Secretary Thomas K. Finletter, May 3, 1951, RG 340, NA II. Hereafter Arkansas AM and N will be used for Arkansas Agricultural, Mechanical & Normal College.

31. Maryland State College *Maroon and Gray*, October 21, 1951; Ruth E. Wennersten, "The Historical Evolution of a Black Land Grant College: The University of Maryland Eastern Shore," Unpublished Thesis, University of Maryland, College Park, MD, 1976, 92–93.

32. James C. Evans and Albert J. Parker, "ROTC Programs and Negro Youth": 134.

33. Baltimore *Afro-American*, March 20, 1938; Memorandum, MAJ O. C. Talbot for Earl D. Johnson, RG 335, NA II; June 26, 1951, History of the NROTC, NROTCU-FAMUINST 5400.2H, FAMU NROTC File, July 20, 1992, FAMU, Tallahassee, FL. This program was later extended to include sixty-six Naval ROTC detachments nationwide plus five Naval ROTC detachments at Maritime Academies. Hereafter, NROTC will be used for Naval ROTC.

34. LT Commander Edward S. Hope to Chief of Bureau of Personnel, January 1947, RG 107, NA II. In addition to Tuskegee, LT Commander Hope visit Prairie View A and M and Phyliss Wheatley, Jack Yates and Washington High Schools in Houston, TX; Dillard University, Xavier Preparatory, Gilbert Academy and Washington High School in New Orleans, LA; Alabama State and Washington, Loveless and St John's High School in Montgomery, AL; Parker High School, Veteran's School and the Business Men's Group in Birmingham, AL; Morehouse, Clark and Washington High Schools in Atlanta, GA; Tennessee A and I, Fisk and Pearl High School in Nashville, TN; Johnson C. Smith University and Second Ward and West Charlotte High Schools in Charlotte, NC; Atkins High School in Winston-Salem, NC; Dudley High School in Greensboro, NC; Palmer Institute in Sedalia, NC; North Carolina State College in Durham, and Hilldale High School in Durham, NC; Shaw University and Washington High School in Raleigh, NC; Armstrong and Maggie Walker High Schools in Richmond, VA; and Dunbar, Armstrong and Cardoza High Schools and Phelps Vocational High School in DC. Hereafter LCDR will be used for LT Commander.

35. Southern Field Division, National Urban League, Second Report on the Status of Participation of Negroes in the Navy ROTC Examination sponsored by the Southern Field Division, 1950; Howard University *Hilltop*, October 22, 1948, RG 107, NA II. Institutional visitation by LT Gravely included Armstrong High and Virginia Union University in Richmond, VA, Booker T. Washington High in Norfolk, VA, Norcum High in Portsmouth, Phoenic High in Hampton, VA, and Booker T. Washington, Carver Vocational High, and Morris Brown in Atlanta, GA; visitations by LT Reagan included Winston-Salem Teachers College, Atkins High and Carver High in Winston-Salem, NC, Dudley High in Greensboro, NC, Lincoln High in Chapel Hill, Washington High, Shaw University, and Saint Augustine College in Raleigh, NC, North Carolina State College and Hillside High in Durham, NC, Dunbar High in Lexington, NC, Washington High in Reidsville, NC in addition to organizational meeting sponsored by the W. D. Hill Boys Club of Raleigh, the YMCA of Winston-Salem, and the Avery Boys Club; LT Nelson visited Gaudet High, Booker T. Washington, Xavier Prep School, and McDonald High in New Orleans, LA, Landry High in Algiers, LA, Edward Waters and Stanley High in Jacksonville, FL, Fisk and Tennessee State A and I in addition to giving presentations to the National Urban League board, and the Negro American Veterans in Nashville.

36. Baltimore *Afro-American*, March 20, 1948.

37. Baltimore *Afro-American*, July 17, 1948. In September 1947, Floyd L. Bolton of St. Louis, Missouri enrolled in Illinois Polytechnic Institute, Gerald E. Thomas of Natick, Massachusetts, was accepted into the University of Nebraska. Forrest L. Flewellen of Columbus, Ohio was a sophomore at Ohio State University and Lonnie A. Marshall of the same city was a senior in the College of Engineering at Ohio State University. Alonzo J. Fairbanks of St. Louis, Missouri was attending Wisconsin University and Earl L. G[C]arter of New York City was a collegiate student. Commissioned in 1947 and assigned to duty were Ensign Norman T. Matlock of Akron, Ohio and commissioned at the University of Pennsylvania, Ensign Frederick A. Mosby of Morgantown, West Virginia and commissioned at the University of Rochester, Ensign James E. Ward of Philadelphia, Pennsylvania and commissioned at Princeton University.

Ensign Edward T. Bowser of East Orange, New Jersey in January 1948 but elected to remain at the university until June to receive a bachelor of science degree in architecture. He was also awarded the Princeton University Most Outstanding NROTC Award.

38. Henry I. Shaw, Jr. and Ralph W. Donnelly, *Blacks in the Marine Corps* (Washington: History and Museums Division, Headquarters, U.S. Marine Corps, 1975), pp. 48, 56; Baltimore *Afro-American*, August 28, 1948. LT Branch was selected for the V-12 program at Purdue University and became a member of the dean's list. He earned a degree in physics from Temple University and taught in the Philadelphia Public School System for 35 years. In 1997, the Marine Corps dedicated a building in his honor at Camp Lejeune in North Carolina. See "First Black Marine Officer Frederick C. Branch Has Base Building Named in His Honor," *Jet* 92 (August 4, 1997): 18.

39. Debra Newman Ham, *The African American Odyssey* (Washington: Library of Congress, 1998), p. 93; Florence Murray, ed., *The Negro Handbook, 1949* (New York: Macmillan Co., 1949), p. 278; Campbell C. Johnson, *Fifty Years of Progress: Armed Forces* (Pittsburgh: Pittsburgh Courier, 1950):3; Baltimore *Afro-American*, July 10, 1948. He was born on June 10, 1920 in Virginia; his father was a deceased WWI veteran and his mother, Charlotte H. Chambers, was employed as a clerk in the Department of the Army in Washington, DC. Chambers was valedictorian of his class and Cadet Colonel of the Washington Cadet Corps at Dunbar High School. He received an award for academic achievement and was recognized as the outstanding junior for the year.

40. James C. Evans to LT Dennis D. Nelson, February 26, 1948, James C. Evans to John W. Davis, March 1, 1948, Horace M. Bond to James C. Evans, April 6, 1948. James C. Evans to Horace M. Bond, April 12, June 28, 1948, RG 107, NA II; Baltimore *Afro-American*, March 20, May 8, 1948.

41. Baltimore *Afro-American*, July 17, 1948.

42. The President's Committee on Equality of Treatment and Opportunity in the Armed Services, The Pentagon, Washington, DC, April 26, 1949.

43. The President's Committee on Equality of Treatment and Opportunity in the Armed Services, The Pentagon, Washington, DC, April 25–26, 1949. Hereafter, PNS will be used for Professor of Naval Science.

44. The President's Committee on Equality of Treatment and Opportunity in the Armed Services, The Pentagon, Washington, DC, April 26, 1949.

45. Howard University *Hilltop*, January 12, 1949, November 10, 1950, February 18, 1953.

## Chapter 5

1. Gene M. Lyons and John W. Masland. *Education and Military Leadership* (Princeton: Princeton University Press, 1959), 104–105.

2. Memoranda, BG Robert E. L. Eaton for Secretary of the Air Force Thomas K. Finletter, January 19, February 6, March 14, 22, April 25, May 2, June 6, 1952, Records of the Assistant Secretary of the Air Force, RG 340, NA II. Vinson was also concerned with the combat effectiveness of the F-86 against the MIG-15 and the operational readiness of the 95 Wings expected by June 30, 1952.

3. COL Daniel S. Campbell to Assistant Secretary of the Air Force, March 29, 1951, Frederick D. Patterson to Assistant Secretary of the Air Force Harold C. Stuart, May 9, 1951, Memorandum, L. Eugene Hedberg for Record, February 8, 1952, Thomas K. Kinletter to College and University Presidents, February 19, March 10, 1952, Records of the Assistant Secretary of the Air Force, RG 340, NA II.

4. Second Army Commanding General to TAG, June 12, July 8, 1952, TAG to RROTC, June 18, 1952, LTC Oliver G. Kinney to Chief of Ohio Military District, June 26,

1952, Second Army Commanding General to Chief of Ohio Military District, 23, 1952, 2LT David M. Nelson to Second Army commanding general, June 30, 1952, RROTC to TAG, July 25, 1952, RG 407, NA II.

5. Mordecai W. Johnson to Assistant Secretary of the Air Force Harold C. Stuart, July 19, 1950, G. Frederick Stanton to Harold C. Stuart, August 3, 1950, Records of the Assistant Secretary of the Air Force, RG 340, NA II.

6. Assistant Secretary of the Air Force Harold C. Stuart to Mordecai W. Johnson, August 23, 1950, Mordecai W. Johnson to Harold C. Stuart, August 29, 1950, Records of the Assistant Secretary of the Air Force, RG 340, NA II.

7. MG N. B. Harold to Commanding General of the Air University, October 31, 1952, Mordecai W. Johnson to Assistant Secretary of the Army Fred North, September 17, 1952, Mordecai W. Johnson to Assistant Secretary of the Air Force for Management James T. Hill, Jr., Mordecai W. Johnson to Secretary of the Army Robert T. Stevens, July 23, August 25, 1954, MG F. W. Farrell Summary Sheet on Request that 60–40 Ratio Between Air Force and Army ROTC Students at Howard Operate Flexibly, August 10, 1954, Assistant Secretary of the Army James P. Mitchell to Mordecai W. Johnson, August 12, 1954, RG 335, NA II. In 1953 at Howard, the Army and Air Force ROTC percentage was 50 for each detachment but at Tuskegee the percentage was 45–55 and 54–46 at North Carolina A and T College. However, the percentage of AS-IV students who applied for flight training by May 15, 1953 was 38.18 percent or 10 students for North Carolina A and T and 28.57 percent or 2 students for Tennessee A and I. See TAG to Commanding Generals of Second and Third Armies, October 7, 1953, RG 407, NA II. During this controversy, Howard experienced the tragic loss of three of its AFROTC cadre, MAJ W. T. Mattison, CPT A. H. Manning and CPT C. R. Taylor, who were aboard an AF C-45 transport aircraft en route from Selfridge Field to Bolling AFB when the aircraft crashed on January 28, 1951 in Oak Harbor near Toledo, Ohio. MAJ Mattison joined the cadre in June 1949 and had graduated from Arkansas State College before joining the 332nd Fighter Group at Lochbourne Air Base where he became the director of operations and training. CPT Manning also joined the cadre in June 1949 and had served in the 332 Fighter Group. He graduated from South Carolina State College and entered the AF in 1942. CPT Taylor was a graduate of Clark University in Atlanta prior to serving in the AF and was assigned to Howard in June 1951. Each of the officers had distinguished combat service during World War II. See Howard University *Hilltop*, January 31, 1951.

8. MAJ Jack L. Paxton to Chief of Army Field Forces, July 17, 1952, Frederick D. Patterson to Assistant Secretary of the Army, September 5, 1952, September 17, 1952, RROTC to TAG, October 9, 1952, TAG to Frederick D. Patterson, October 27, 1952, RG 407, NA II.

9. Lyons and Masland, *Education and Military Leadership*, 107–108.

10. MG N. B. Harold to Air Force Chief of Staff for Reserve Forces, January 13, 1954, RG 340, NAII.

11. MG William E. Hall for MG N. B. Harold, January 27, 1954, RG 340, NA II.

12. Memorandum, MG E. S. Wetzel for Chief of Staff, February 1, 1954, Memorandum GEN Thomas D. White for Assistant Secretary of the Air Force, February 5, 1954, Memorandum, COL Robert H. Warren for Assistant Chief of Staff for Reserve Forces, February 5, 1954, Memorandum, BG William S. Stone for the Assistant Secretary of the Air Force for Management, February 8, June 10, 1954, Memorandum, Assistant Secretary of the Air Force H. Lee White for GEN Thomas D. White, March 31, 1954, Memorandum, Assistant Secretary of the Air Force H. Lee White for Assistant Secretary of Defense, April 12, June 17, 1954, Memorandum, MG N. B. Harold for Assistant Secretary of the Air Force for Management, June 3, 1954, Memorandum, Assistant

Secretary of the Air Force H. Lee White for Deputy Chief of Staff for Personnel, June 30, 1954, RG 340, NA II. Also see Stancik and Hall, "Air Force ROTC: Its Origins and Early Years," pp. 47–48.

13. MG William F. McKee to Commanding General of Continental Air Command, May 17, 1950, Frederick D. Patterson Papers, Hollis Burke Frissell Library, Tuskegee University, Tuskegee, AL.

14. LTC George S. Roberts to Frederick D. Patterson, March 28, September 26, 1950, I. A. Derbigny to LTC George S. Roberts, April 27, 1950, Frederick D. Patterson Papers. Cognizant that additional administrative requirements increased efforts to improve the ROTC Department, MAJ Elmer Hatton requested additional staff since the department was divided into two separate AFROTC and Army ROTC branches. Army ROTC only had one-third of previously assigned personnel. See MAJ Elmer Hatton to Frederick D. Patterson, May 26, 1950, Frederick D. Patterson Papers.

15. Lyons and Masland, *Education and Military Leadership*, 110, 118, 228.

16. Howard University *Hilltop*, January 13, 1950, March 12, October 15, 1951.

17. Howard University *Hilltop*, February 18, 1953.

18. LTC Sandra Williams Ortega Retirement Ceremony Brochure, September 23, 1994, Morgan State ROTC Files, Morgan State University, Baltimore, MD; Women in Military Service for American Memorial Foundation *Register*, Winter 1995–1996.

19. Walter L. Hawkins, *African American Generals and Flag Officers* (Jefferson: McFarland & Co., 1993), pp. 120–121.

20. Tennessee State University *Bulletin* 42 September 1954, p 14; South Carolina College *ROTC Fact Sheet*, October 22, 1991.

21. LTG Walter L. Weible to Chief of Staff, June 27, 1956, BG C. J. Hauck for Assistant Secretary of Defense for Legislative and Public Affairs, June 27, 1956, RG 335, NAII.

22. Memoranda, Carter L. Burgess for Secretaries of Army, Navy and Air Force, July 9, 1955, MG Donald P. Booth to Chief of Staff, September 28, 1955, RG 335, NAII.

23. U.S. Congress Senate Hearing before a Subcommittee of the Committee on Armed Services, U. S. Senate, Eighty-Fourth Congress, Second Session on H. R. 5738: An Act to Authorize Flight Instruction during Reserve Officers' Training Corps Programs, and for other Purposes, June 8, 1956 (Washington: Government Printing Office, 1956), 7–9; Memorandum, Francis R. Jones for the General Counsel, December 19, 1960, RG 335, NAII; Army Regulations 145–350: *Reserve Officers' Training Corps*, Headquarters, Department of the Army, Washington DC, September 12, 1961.

24. Stancik and Hall, "Air Force ROTC: Its Origins and Early Years," pp. 48–49.

25. Lyons and Masland, *Education and Military Leadership*, 179–183, 203. Hereafter GMS will be used for General Military Science.

26. Memorandum, Special Assistant for Reserve Forces Elvis J. Stahr, Jr. for Secretary of the Army, April 1, 1952, RG 335, NA II, TAG to Commanding Generals of Alaska, Caribbean, Pacific and Continental Armies, Chief of the Army Field Forces, October 28, 1953, RG 407, NA II. The Department of the Army estimated that an equipment saving on a typical conversion from BM to GMS for Signal Corps, Antiaircraft Artillery and Infantry would be reduced from $1,041,600 to $222,900, for Armor from $376,750 to $210,000, and for all of the 11 other branches from $1,793,840 to $891,600.

27. MG Hugh M. Milton, II to William J. L. Wallace, October 28, 1953, RG 407, NA II.

28. Organization and Training Division to Chief of Army Field Forces, June 19, 1953, TAG to Second Army Commanding General, June 24, December 4, 1953, TAG to Third Army Commanding General, June 24, August 26, October 2, 1953, March 31, 1954, COL K. P. Jones to Chief of Army Publications Service Branch, June 25, December

15, 1953, GO 58, Department of the Army, Washington, June 24, 1953, F. D. Bluford to Chief of North Carolina Military District, August 13, 1953, 1LT J. M. Smith to Third Army Commanding General, August 14, 1953, TAG to RROTC, September 2, 1953, LTC Louis F. Springer to TAG, September 4, 1953, MG Hugh M. Milton, II to Fulton G. Clark, September 28, 1953, MG Hugh M. Milton, II to Robert P. Daniel, September 28, December 7, 1953, MG Hugh M. Milton, II to E. B. Evans, September 28, 1953, MG Hugh M. Milton, II to Alonzo G. Moron, September 28, December 7, 1953, MG Hugh M. Milton, II to Sherman D. Scruggs, September 28, 1953, MG Hugh M. Milton, II to William J. L. Wallace, September 28, 1953, E. B. Evans to MG Hugh M. Milton, II, November 6, 1953, Robert P. Daniel to MG Hugh M. Milton, II, November 23, 1953, GO 94, Department of the Army, Washington, DC, December 22, 1953, TAG to Fourth Army Commanding General, December 2, 15, 1953, LTC Lynch to Chief of Publication Branch, April 27, 1954, GO 31, Department of the Army, Washington, DC, May 3, 1954, RG 407, NA II; Memorandum, MG John A. Klein for Assistant Secretary of the Army (M&RF), July 10, 1956, RG 335, NA II. The chairman of the Reserve Forces Policy Board, Milton G. Baker, also recommended the elimination of kitchen police duty for cadets during summer camps. Baker visited summer camps conducted at Fort Lee, Fort, Benning and Fort Belvior and urged the discontinuance of the policy would increase the prestige of the cadet corps. Assistant Secretary of the Army Hugh M. Milton, II explained the policy had been proven sound and profitable from a training standpoint. The policy also provided cadets with appropriate mess management training, and summer camps were the only place where practical instruction in mess management was available for cadets. See Memorandum, Milton G. Baker for Assistant Secretary of the Army (M&RF), October 2, 1956, Assistant Secretary of the Army Hugh M. Milton, II for Assistant Secretary of the Army, October 2, 1956, RG 335, NA II.

29. William J. L. Wallace to MG Hugh M. Milton, II, March 9, 1954, RG 407, NA II.

30. Memorandum, Assistant Secretary Hugh M. Milton, II for Secretary of Defense, November 1955, RG 335, NA II. There were 42,700 MS II deferred, 16,000 MS III and 14,000 MS IV. Although MSI were not eligible until successfully completing one academic semester or quarter, their total was 65,000. Also included in the total were 3,100 MSIV cadets who had completed their ROTC training but lacked the required academic credits to receive their commissions.

31. Robert P. Daniel to Secretary of the Army Robert T. Stevens, April 28, 1954, Assistant Secretary of the Army Hugh M. Milton to Robert P. Daniel, May 7, 1954, Executive for Reserve and ROTC Affairs Summary Sheet on Policies affecting Negro Land Grant Colleges, June 9, 1954, RG 335, WNRC; Memorandum, MG Reuben E. Jenkins for Chief of Staff, August 23, 1961, Memorandum, Assistant Secretary of the Army Karl D. Johnson for Chief of Staff, October 4, 1961, RG 335, NA II; James C. Evans and Albert J. Parker, "ROTC Programs and Negro Youth," *Journal of Negro Education* 25 (Spring 1956):132–133. The other military participating in the meeting were MAJ A. J. Parker of the Department of Defense; Dr. Herbert J. Moss (OASD M&P), BG Philip F. Lindeman, COLs Thomas D. Meier and Douglas B. Murray (RROTC), LTC Thomas R. Bruce (ACofS, G1), LTC Philip E. Smith (ACofS), and Dr. R. K. Davenport (TAGO) of the Department of the Army.

32. Executive for Reserve and ROTC Affairs Summary Sheet on Policies Affecting Negro Land Grant Colleges, June 9, 1954, RG 335, NA II.

33. Ibid.

34. Hugh M. Milton to Robert P. Daniel, June 21, July 28, 1954, Robert P. Daniel to Hugh M. Milton, June 26, August 2, 1954, Memorandum, BG Philip F. Lindeman for Assistant Secretary of the Army, July 9, 1954, RG 335, NA II.

35. Memorandum, Hugh M. Milton for the Army Chief of Staff, May 20, 1954, RG 335, NA II.

36. Lyons and Masland, *Education and Military Leadership*, 117.

37. Memorandum, MG Ralph A. Palladino for the Assistant Secretary of the Army (MP&RF), November 14, 1957, RG 335, NA II.

38. Memorandum, MG Frederick M. Warren for the Undersecretary of the Army, May 14, 1960, LTC Allan E. Wilmot to ARROTC, July 20, 1960, LTC Marlow, Summary Sheet the Secretary of the Army, on Plans for Elimination, Adjustment, and Realignment of Detachments within the Senior Division ROTC Program, August 17, 1960, RG 335. Hereafter, CRROTC will be used for Chief of the Army Reserve and ROTC Affairs.

39. Summary Sheet, MG Frederick M. Warren to Assistant Secretary of the Army, August 17, 1960, RG 335, NA II.

40. Memorandum, Frank G. Millard for Memorandum for Assistant Secretary of the Army (MP&RF), December 3, 1957, MG Ralph A. Palladino for Assistant Secretary of the Army (MP&RF), January 15, 1958, MG Ralph A. Palladino to Secretary of the Army Cyrus R. Vance, August 10, 1962, RG 335, NA II.

41. Samuel D. Stroman, A Descriptive Study of the Relationship of (RQ) Scores, Summer Camp Standings and Cumulative Averages to Service School Orientation Courses Standings of Howard University Army Graduates, Unpublished MA Thesis, Howard University, Washington, DC, 1964, pp. 3–8, 11–15. For another assessment of ROTC which reveals similar problems, see Norris R. Capers, A Descriptive Study of the Relationship of Certain Variables to College ROTC Success of Army Cadets at Predominantly Black Institutions of Higher Education, Unpublished EED Dissertation, George Washington University, Washington, DC, 1974.

42. Robert L. Turman, A History of the Development and Operation of the Army Reserve Officers' Training Corps at the Agricultural and Technical College of North Carolina, Greensboro, North Carolina, Unpublished MS Thesis, Agricultural and Technical College of North Carolina, Greensboro, NC, 1962.

43. Tennessee State University *Bulletin* 43 (May 1965): 4; Tennessee State University *Meter*, October 1954, January 1956, May 15–31, September 15–October 1961. LTC Baugh graduated from Virginia State and entered pilot training at Tuskegee where he joined the 99th Fighter Squadron in 1942. He also served with Howard's AFROTC prior to joining the Air Science program at Tennessee State University. Included among the other cadre assigned to the university were CPT Isaac Gilliam, CPTs Arthur D. Graves and James O. Hill with commissions from Tuskegee Institute, CPT Robinson T. Dickerson who graduated from West Chester Teachers College in PA, CPT Albert J. Price who graduated from OCS, CPT Eldridge F. Williams with previous service with the 332nd Fighter Wing at Lockbourne AFB, CPT James Caruth who graduated in the first Tennessee State University AFROTC class and decided to leave the AF and pursue civilian enterprises in Clarksville, TN, CPT Otis C. Russell, and MAJ Claude M. Dixon who graduated from Southern University. See Tennessee State University *Meter*, October 1–15, 1961, Tennessee State University *Bulletin* 44 (May 1957): 44.

44. Tennessee State University *Meter*, February 1–15, 1962.

45. CPT James V. Hood to CARROTC, May 11, 1960, CWO to CARROTC, May 12, 1960, CPT V. M. St. Peter to Chief, US Army Reserve and ROTC Affairs, May 19, 1960, file 326.6, bx 800, RG 335, WNRC. During the period of August 1955 to June 1959 and ranked 1st through 12th with the highest percentages of graduates in the lower third or failing the officer basic course were South Carolina State A and M (91.8), North Carolina A and T (86.4), Tuskegee (83.5), Central State (82.1), Prairie View A and M College (81.6), Morgan State (77.5), Florida A and M College (76.9), Lincoln (76.0), Virginia

State (72.4), Hampton (71.2), West Virginia State (70.9), and Southern A and M (69.6). Howard was ranked 15th (62.0) and none of its graduates failed the officer basic course.

46. Memorandum, GEN G. H. Decker for Assistant Chief of Staff for Reserve Components, January 25, 1960, Memorandum, COL Leon F. Lavoie for the Record, June 23, 1960, LTC Allan E. Wilmot to CARROTC, July 20, 1960, CARROTC to Assistant Secretary of the Army, July 29, 1960, Undersecretary Hugh M. Milton to Samuel Dewitt Proctor, August 16, 1960, RG 335, NA II. The CARROTC also recommended the withdrawal of the Centenary College ROTC detachment at the end of the academic year.

47. Samuel D. Proctor to Undersecretary Hugh M. Milton, August 18, 1960, RG 335, NA II.

48. Memorandum, Hugh M. Milton for Army Chief of Staff, September 7, 1960, Memoranda, MG Frederick M. Warren for Undersecretary of the Army, September 12, 23, 1960, Memorandum, MG Ned D. Moore for the Assistant Secretary of the Army (MP&RF), November 21, 1960, Memorandum MG Frederick M. Warren for Assistant Secretary of the Army (MP&RF), November 28, 1960, Memorandum, Duncan Hodges for Assistant Secretary of Defense, December 2, 1960, RG 335, NA II.

49. William J. L. Wallace to Hugh M. Milton, September 3, 1960, RG 335, NA II.

50. Felton G. Clark to Hugh M. Milton, September 2, 13, 1960, RG 335, NA II.

51. Undersecretary Hugh M. Milton, to Senator Sam J. Ervin, September 6, 1960, Samuel D. Proctor to Undersecretary Hugh M. Milton, September 7, 13, 1960, Undersecretary Hugh M. Milton to Governor Luther Hodges, September 8, 1960, Memorandum, MG Ned D. Moore for the Assistant Secretary of the Army (PM&RF), November 21, 1960, Samuel D. Proctor to MG Walter B. Yeager, January 6, 1961, RG 335, NA II.

52. Felton G. Clark to Undersecretary Hugh M. Milton, October 12, 1960, RG 335, NA II.

53. William J. L. Wallace to Undersecretary Hugh M. Milton, September 28, October 25, 1960, MAJ Edward D. Hinkson to William J. L. Wallace, September 23, 29, 1960, William J. l. Wallace to MAJ Edward D. Hinkson, 28, 30, 1960, RG 335, NA II.

54. Memorandum, MG Ralph A. Palladino for the Undersecretary of the Air Force, Assistant of the Army, and Assistant Secretary of the Navy, October 6, 1960, Undersecretary of the Army to Samuel D. Proctor, October 28, 1960, Undersecretary of the Army to Charles W. Wesley, October 28, 1960, Undersecretary of the Army to George W. Gore, Jr., October 28, 1960, Undersecretary of the Army to E. B. Evans, October 28, 1960, Undersecretary of the Army to Benner C. Turner, October 28, 1960, Memorandum, COL George H. Rochman for the Record re: Undersecretary of the Army Briefing, November 20, 1960, RG 335, NA II.

55. Charles Wesley to Undersecretary Milton, November 8, 1960, file 326.6, bx 799, RG 335, NA II.

56. Memorandum, LTC Rieder W. Schell for CARROTC, April 2, 1957, NA II. South Carolina State College was authorized by the Constitutional Convention of 1896 which enacted provisions that permitted the State Legislature to sever its interest with Claflin University and provide funds for a state land grant college. Initially called the Colored Normal, Industrial, Agricultural and Mechanical College of South Carolina. The General Assembly redesignated the institution South Carolina State College in 1954. Its ROTC detachment was also on probation for the 1956 academic years because of the low production of 20 commissioned officers the previous year.

57. Benner C. Turner to Undersecretary Hugh M. Milton, November 19, 1960, RG 335, NA II.

58. CRROTC to Assistant Chief of Staff for Reserve Components (ACSRC), February 23, 1961, CRROTC to Chief of Staff, Army, February 23, 1961, Undersecretary

of the Army, February 23, 1961, CRROTC to Undersecretary of the Army, February 23, 1961, Memorandum, CRROTC for the Undersecretary of the Army, April 7, 1961, Undersecretary of the Army Stephen Ailes to Samuel D. Proctor, May 2, 1961, Undersecretary of the Army Stephen Ailes to Felton G. Clark, May 2, 1961, Undersecretary of the Army Stephen Ailes to William J. L. Wallace, May 2, 1961, CRROTC to J. Francis Pohlhaus of the NAACP, May 26, 1960, RG 335, NA II. The institutions together with the length of time by academic year since detachments on probation had failed to meet the production standard were: North Carolina A and T (1955–56), University of California at Santa Barbara (1956–57), Centenary College of Louisiana (1956–57), Eastern Washington College (1958–59), Georgia State College of Business Administration (1957–58), Lincoln (1956–57), Midwestern University (1956–57), West Virginia State (1957–58), Arkansas Polytechnic College (1959–60), Southern A and M (1959–60), Northeast Louisiana State College (1959–60), California State Polytechnic Institute (1959–60), University of Chattanooga (1959–60), and University of Wichita (1959–60).

59. Performance of Lincoln Graduates at Army Branch Schools, Department of Military Science, Lincoln University, Jefferson City, MO, n.d., ROTC Files, Ethnic Studies Department, Lincoln University Library, Lincoln, MO.

60. COL Nathaniel P. Ward III to Jerome H. Holland, February 24, 1964, LTC Osceola Thornton to [Hampton Institute] Colleague, February 26, 1964, Jerome H. Holland to COL Nathaniel P. Ward III, March 6, 1964, Jerome H. Holland to LTC Osceola Thornton, March 8, 1964, March 17, 1965, LTC Osceola T. Thornton to Hugh M. Gloster, March 19, 1964, LTC Osceola T. Thornton to Douglas Gold, March 31, 1964, LTG John S. Upham to Jerome H. Holland, April 6, 1964, Marie V. Wood to LTG William Train, November 25, 1954, LTC Osceola Thornton to Commanding General of XXI Army Corps, September 15, 1964, Hampton Battalion Cadets to Jerome H. Holland, April 25, 1965, Military Science File, Hampton University Archives.

61. U. S. Comptroller, Report to the Congress of the United States: Retention of Uneconomical Detachments in the ROTC Program, October 1964 (Washington: U. S. General Accounting Office, 1964), 1–2, 4.

62. Memorandum, CRROTC for the Assistant Chief of Staff (MP&RF), March 20, 1961, Memorandum, Deputy Assistant Chief of Staff for Reserve Components for Secretary of the General Staff, June 14, 1960, Memorandum, CRROTC for Secretary of the Army, June 17, 1960, RG 335, NA II. For analysis of Tennessee State University's AFROTC, see James R. Coles, Jr., Relative Value of Scholastic Grades, "Psychological and background factors in predicting the success of Air Force ROTC Cadets in Passing the Air Force Officers Qualifying Test at Tennessee Agricultural and Industrial State University," Unpublished MS Thesis, Tennessee Agricultural and Industrial State University, Nashville, TN, August 1960, passim.

63. Lyons and Masland, *Education and Military Leadership*, 124–125, 170.

64. Memorandum, Assistant Secretary of Defense Charles C. Finucane for Secretary of Defense, September 11, 1960, Memorandum, MG Frederick M. Warren for Assistant Secretary of the Army (MP&RF), September 16, 1960, MG Frederick M. Warren to Secretary of the Army, July 20, 1961, Undersecretary of the Army Memorandum, Stephen Ailes for the Assistant Secretary of Defense (Manpower), March 15, 1962, RG 335, NA II.

65. Samuel D. Stroman, *A Descriptive Study of the Relationship of (RQ) Scores, Summer Camp Standings and Cumulative Academic Averages to Service School Orientation Course Standings of Howard University Army ROTC Graduates*, Unpublished MA Thesis, Howard University, Washington, DC. 1964, pp. 3–8, 11–15. For another assessment of ROTC which reveals similar problems, see Norris R. Capers, *A Descriptive Study of the Relationship of Certain Variables to College ROTC Success of Army Cadets at*

*Predominantly Black Institutions of Higher Education*, EDD Dissertation, George Washington University, Washington, DC, 1974.

66. James A. Hurd, *A Survey of Attitudes of ROTC Cadets, Faculty, and Administrative Officers toward ROTC Programs at Howard University*, Unpublished MS Thesis, Howard University, Washington, DC, 1965, pp 5–9, 96–104.

67. LTC Osceola T. Thornton to the Hampton Institute Faculty, February 26, 1964, Jerome H. Holland Papers, Hampton University Archives.

68. LTC Osceola T. Thornton to Hugh M. Gloster, March 19, 1964, LTC Osceola T. Thornton to Douglas Gold, March 31, 1964, LTG John S. Upham, Jr. to Jerome H. Holland, April 6, 1964, Marie V. Wood to LTG William F. Train, November 25, 1964, LTC Osceola T. Thornton to Second Army Commanding General, September 15, 1964, Jerome H. Holland to LTC Osceola T. Thornton, March 17, 1965, MG F. H. Britton to Jerome H. Holland, April 29, 1965, Jerome H. Holland Papers, Hampton University Archives

## Chapter 6

1. MAJ Jesse J. Makes to James C. Evans, November 3, 1961, LTC Arthur H. Booth to James C. Evans, November 6, 1961, LTC Osceola T. Thornton, to James C. Evans, November 6, 1961, MAJ Edward D. Hinkson to James C. Evans, November 6, 1961, LTC Howard L. Baugh to James C. Evans, November 20, 1961, LTC James A. Hurd to James C. Evans, January 3, 1962, James C. Evans Papers. Hereafter, PAS will be used for Professor of Air Science and PMS for Professor of Military Science.

2. Memorandum, James C. Evans for Ralph Dungan, April 4, 1961, James C. Evans Papers.

3. Memorandum, LTC John T. Martin for Record, September 25, 1962, James C. Davis Papers. The roster of senior active duty Army officers comprised COLs Clarence M. Davenport, ART; COL James D. Fowler, INF; John F. Harris, MC; Stanford R. Hicks, ORD; Campbell C. Johnson, INF; and Melvin W. Ormos, QM. The Air Force officers were COLs Nelson S. Brooks, William A. Campbell, George G. Evans, Edward C. Gleed, Elmer D. Jones, Hubert L. Jones, Vance H. Marchbanks (Medical Corps), and George S. Roberts. A roster submitted by LTC Willard C. Stewart extended the list with the inclusion of COLs Thomas J. Money, T. B. Smith, Eugene F. Tyree and Dudley W. Stevenson. See Memorandum, LTC Willard C. Stewart for James C. Evans, August 13, 1963, James C. Davis Papers.

4. MAJ Lawrence D. Goode, North Carolina A and T to LTC John T. Martin, August 6, 1965, LTC Osceola T. Thornton to LTC John T. Martin, August 9, 1965, MAJ George M. Hampton to LTC John T. Martin, August 20, 1965, James C. Evans to Judge Edward Gourdin, September 2, 1965, LTC Jesse J. Mayes to James C. Evans, September 10, 1965, LTC Reginald E. Crocker to LTC John T. Martin, September 10, 1965, LTC Raymond K. Dewberry to LTC John T. Martin, September 22, 1965, LTC Arthur N. Fearing to LTC John T. Martin, October 1, 1965, MAJ Walter R. Mebane to LTC John T. Martin, October 1, 1965, LTC Roger S. Walden to LTC John T. Martin, October 1, 1965, CDR Thomas D. Parham to James C. Evans, October 26, 1965, David Youngblade to LTC, ret, Jesse R. Liscomb, November 2, 1965, James C. Evans Papers, Archives Branch, MHI, CBPA.

LTC (Chaplain, ret) Lewis M. Durden provided Evans a roster of active duty Chaplains which consisted of LTC John W. Handy with the Army Chaplain Board at Fort Meade, MD; LTC Cauthion T. Boyd with HQ, 2nd Army at Fort Meade, MD; LTC Douglas Hall at Fort Dix, NJ; LTC Lee A. Cousins with Army Materiel Command in Washington, DC; LTC George W. Williams; LTC Gray G. Johnson at Fort Benning, GA;

MAJ Joseph A. Davis at Fort Monmouth, NJ; MAJ Ezra Everett at Aberdeen Proving Ground, MD; CPT Thomas A. Strahand at Fort Benning; CPT John A. Deveaux, Jr. in Santa Domingo and MAJ William Calbert with the Chaplain School. The retired Chaplains were LTC John A. Deveaux, pastor of Quinn Chapel AME Church in Steubenville, Ohio; LTC Elmer P. Gipson, president of Morristown College in Morristown, TN; LTC Andrew L. Johnson, Chaplain at Tuskegee Institute; LTC Osborne E. Scott, field representative for the American Leprosy Foundation; LTC Rufus A. Cooper, graduate student at UCLA; LTC Pliny Jenkins, Methodist minister in San Francisco, CA; LTC Beverly Ward, Presbyterian minister in Pasadena, CA; LTC Robert A. Bryant in Colorado Springs, CO; LTC Brannon J. Hopson in Philadelphia, PA; LTC William B. Crocker in Roanoke, VA; LTC Warren J. Jenkins (USAF) in Savannah, GA; LTC Theodore Owens (USAF), AME minister in Chatham, VA; LTC Charles S. H. Hunter, AME minister in Tampa, FL; LTC A. S. Hankerson (USAF) in Tacoma, Washington. LTC Lewis M. Durden was executive vice president of the Lighthouse Life Insurance Company and Lighthouse Securities and Investment company in Shreveport, LA. See LTC Lewis M. Durden to James C. Evans, October 20, 1965, James C. Evans Papers.

Evans informed COL West A. Hamilton that the ROTC unit at Prairie View State College by August 31, 1965 had commissioned more than 600 officers. See James E. Evans to COL West A. Hamilton, August 31, 1965, James C. Evans Papers.

5. LTC Edward D. Hinkson to James C. Evans, August 2, 1962, James C. Evans Papers.

6. LTC L. W. Cracken to James C. Evans, August 8, 1962, James Evans Papers.

7. Memorandum, CRROTC for the Assistant Chief of Staff (MP&RF), March 20, 1961, Memorandum, Deputy Assistant Chief of Staff for Reserve Components for Secretary of the General Staff, June 14, 1960, Memorandum, CRROTC for Secretary of the Army, June 17, 1960, RG 335, NA II. For analysis of Tennessee State University's AFROTC, see James R. Coles, Jr., *Relative Value of Scholastic Grades*, "Psychological and Background Factors in Predicting the Success of Air Force ROTC Cadets in Passing the Air Force Officers Qualifying Test at Tennessee Agricultural and Industrial State University," MS Thesis, Tennessee Agricultural and Industrial State University, Nashville, TN, August 1960, passim.

8. Secretary of Army Stephan Ailes to Jerome H. Holland, January 13, 1965, LTG W. H. S. Wright to Jerome H. Holland, January 15, 1965, Military Science file, Hampton Archives, Hampton University, Hampton, VA; Christian K. Arnold, ed., *Proceedings of the Association of State Universities and Land-Grant Colleges 77th Annual Convention*, Washington, DC, November 10–13, 1963, 60; TAG to Commanding Generals of Alaska, Hawaii and ZI Armies, and Antilles Command, US Army of Southern Command, NC A and T ROTC Records.

9. LTC Samuel F. Sampson to LTC Willard C. Stewart, November 24, 1965, James C. Evans Papers.

10. LTC Reginald E. Crocker to LTC John T. Martin, July 20, November 30, 1965, LTC Reginald E. Crocker to 3rd Army Commanding General, November 2, 1965, 3rd Army Assistant Adjutant General to Chief of the Office of Reserve Components, November 9, 1965, Chief of the Office of Reserve Components to LTC Crocker, November 19, 1965, James C. Evans Papers.

11. LTC Reginald E. Crocker to LTC John T. Martin, November 30, 1965, James C. Evans Papers.

12. James C. Evans to COL Frederic Davison, James C. Evans Papers.

13. COL E. M. Shaffer to Commanding General of Alaska, Pacific and Army Forces of Southern Command, June 4, 1968, James C. Evans, MHI, CBPA.

14. James C. Evans to COL Hyman Y. Chase, August 20, 1968, James C. Evans Papers.

15. James C. Evans to COL DeWitt Cook, March 21, 1969, James C. Evans Papers.
16. Clarence A. Miller, Procurement and Retention of Black Officers: A Research Report, U.S. Army War College, Carlisle Barracks, Pennsylvania, April 7, 1972, 35–41. The respective totals of African American officers commissioned through ROTC programs from fiscal year 1966 to 1971 were 352, 365, 382, 430, 430 and 424.
17. Elizabeth C. Duran and James A. Duran, "Integration in Reverse at West Virginia State College," *West Virginia History* 45 (1984): 63–69.
18. Miller, Procurement and Retention of Black Officers, 48–51.
19. Miller, Procurement and Retention of Black Officers, 54–56. In addition to COL Hurtt, officers assigned to the cadre of Morgan State University consisted of LTC Grady A. Culpeper, MAJ Charles T. Birt, MAJ Clarence Cheatham, CPT Nicholas Lagattula, and CPT Charles W. McClain, Jr. See the Baltimore *Afro-American*, October 19, 1968.
20. Baltimore *Afro-American*, January 21, 28, February 18, 1967. Cadet Franklin D. Taliaferro of Culpepper, VA became the most decorated cadet in the Virginia State College history. See the Baltimore *Afro-American*, April 29, 1967. Hereafter SNCC will be used for Student Nonviolent Coordinating Committee
21. Michael Chalfen, "'The Way Out May Lead In': The Albany Movement Beyond Martin L. King, Jr.," *Georgia Historical Quarterly* 79 (Fall 1995): 560–598; Glenn L. Eskew, "Bombingham: Black Protest in Post-War Birmingham, Alabama," *Historian* 59 (Winter 1997): 371–390; David L. Garrow, "The Voting Rights Act in Historical Perspective," *Georgia Historical Quarterly* 74 (Fall 1990): 377–398; Steven F. Lawson, "Martin L. King, Jr., and the Civil Rights Movement," *Georgia Historical Quarterly* 71 (Summer 1987): 242–260; Mamie E. Locke, "The Role of African Women in the Civil Rights Movement in Hinds County and Sunflower County, Mississippi," *Journal of Mississippi* 53 (August 1991): 229–239; Charles H. Martin, "The Civil Rights Movement and Southern Black Defendants," *Georgia Historical Quarterly* 71 (Spring 1987): 25–52; Kenneth O'Reilly, "The FBI and the Politics of the Riots, 1964–1968," *Journal of American History* 75 (June 1988): 91–114; Kenneth O'Reilly, *"Racial Matters": The FBI's Secret File on Black America* (New York: Free Press, 1989), passim; Christopher Strain, "We Walked Like Men": The Deacons for Defense and Justice," *Louisiana History* 38 (Winter 1997): 43–62; Timothy B. Tyson, "Robert F. Williams: 'Black Power,' and the African Freedom Struggle," *Journal of American History* 85 (September 1998): 540–570; Timothy B. Tyson, *Radio Free Dixie: Robert F. Williams & the Roots of Black Power* (Chapel Hill: University of North Carolina Press, 1999), passim; Nikolas Kozloff, "Vietnam, the African African Community, and the Pittsburgh New Courier," *Historian* 63 (Spring 1999): 520–538.
22. Ingrid Monson, "Monk Meets SNCC" *Black Music Research Journal* 19 (Fall 1999): 187–200; Bernice Johnson Reagon, "Let the Church Sing 'Freedom,'" *Black Music Research Journal* 19 (Spring 1999): 105–118. Among the other musicians and prominent artists who performed Joan Baez, James Baldwin, Paul Bley, Count Basie, Nat "King" Cole, Ron Carter, Ruby Dee, Miles Davis, Ossie Davis, Sammy Davis, Jr., Eric Dolphy, Bob Dylan, Duke Ellington, Billy Eckstine, Don Friedman, Lorraine Hansberry, Coleman Hawkins, Roy Haynes, Mahalia Jackson, Ahmad Jamal, Quincy Jones, Abbey Lincoln, Herbie Mann, Thelonious Monk, J. C. Monterose, Gerry Mulligan, Odetta, Gary Peacock, Ben Riley, Max Roach, Jackie McLean, Charlie Shavers, Zoot Sims, Frank Sinatra, Frank Stozier, Billy Taylor, Clark Terry, Sarah Vaughan, and the SCNN Freedom Singers. The only jazz musician arrested was Al Hibbler during the Birmingham campaign.
23. Harry Edwards, *Black Students* (New York: Free Press, 1970), 45–54; Clifton E. Marsh, From Black Muslim to Muslim: *The Resurrection, Transformation and Change of*

*the Lost-Found Nation of Islam in American, 1930–1995* (Landon, MD: Scarecrow Press, Inc., 1996), 60–63.

24. Edwards, *Black Students*, 62–64.

25. Stokely Carmichael, *Stokely Speaks: Black Power Back to Pan-Africanism* (New York: Vintage Books, 1971), 61–62, 69; Baltimore *Afro-American*, March 23, May 11, 1968; Morgan State College *Spokesman*, March, April, May, October 18, 1968, January 10, May 9, 1969. The first Coppinites in the program were Isaac Ballard, Paul Chiles, Jeffrey Covington, Monroe Davis, Paul Smith, Franklin Travis and the first to complete the two-year program for commissioning was Travis. See Morgan State College *Spokesman*, April 15, December 16, 1965, January 25, 1966. For a list of Morgan faculty who joined the Maryland academic community and endorsed a letter to President Lyndon B. Johnson protesting the Vietnam War, see Morgan State College *Spokesman*, April 13, 1965.See Morgan State College *Spokesman*, April 1, 1967.

26. Morgan State College *Spokesman*, April 13, 15, December 16, 1965, January 25, 1966, April 1, 1967.

27. Baltimore *Afro-American*, April 1, 1967.

28. Baltimore *Afro-American*, May 6, 27, 1967. Huey Newton of the Black Panthers considered the inclusion of white members, SNCC who helped to initially formulate policies was a mistake. See Philip S. Foner, ed., *The Black Panthers Speak* (Philadelphia: J. B. Lippincott Co., 1970), 56–57.

29. Jack Bass and Jack Nelson, *The Orangeburg Massacre* (Mercer University Press, 1984), 4–7; Baltimore *Afro-American*, March 11, 1967

30. Baltimore *Afro-American*, March 29, April 1, May 20, 1967; New York *Times*. January 8, 11, 20, February 1, 21, April 11, 29, May 1, June 5, 21, 1967, July 7, 1970.

31. Hugh M. Gloster to Faculty of Hampton, May 2, 1967, Rudolph F. Pierce and Kenneth A. Murphy to Jerome H. Holland, Marie Wood, Hugh M. Gloster and LTC Ernest Johnson, May 2, 1967, Hugh M. Gloster to Rudolph F. Pierce, May 5, 1967, Jerome H. Holland to Rudolph Pierce, May 8, 1967, Jerome H. Holland to Dennis Montgomery, May 8, 1967, Jerome H. Holland to Kenneth Murphy, May 8, 1967, Jerome H. Holland Papers, Hampton University Archives; Baltimore *Afro-American*, May 7, 1967; Marsh, *From Black Muslims to Muslims*, pp. 59–60.

32. Secretary of the Army Stephen Ailes to Jerome H. Holland, January 13, 1965, LTC Ernest B. Johnson to Jerome H. Holland, May 4, 1967, Jerome H. Holland to Arthur Howe, Jr. and members of the Board of Trustee of Hampton Institute, May 9, 1967, Jerome H. Holland to LTC Osceola Thornton, LTC Ernest Johnson et. al, June 26, 1967, Jerome H. Holland to Albert Berriam, May 3, 1968, Jerome H. Holland to Norman E. Hodges, May 21, 1968, LTC Clarence T. Cummings, Jr. to Jerome H. Holland, December 19, 1969, Jerome H. Holland Papers, Hampton University Archives.

33. Hampton Institute *ROTC Bulletin*, November 1967; LTC Ernest B. Johnson, Howard V. Young, Jr., and Valmore R. Goines, May 9, 1968, Jerome H. Holland to Members of the Faculty-Staff, May 15, 1968, Jerome H. Holland to Alexander Strawn, Thomas Hawkins, Amalete Moore, Theotis Holland, LTC Osceola Thornton, and LTC Ernest Johnson, George O. Roberts to Jerome H. Holland, May 22, 1968, Norman E. Hodges to Jerome H. Holland, May 22, 1968, Gordon B. Cutler to Jerome H. Holland, June 3, 1968, Charles B. Harding to Jerome H. Holland, June 10, 1968, Jerome H. Holland to Albert Berrian, Edward Kollmann, and Edgar Thomas, June 24, 1968, Albert H. Berrian to Division Directors and Department Chairmen, July 25, 1968, Department of Military Science File, Hampton University Archives.

34. Lawrence Gordon, The AFROTC Program at Tennessee State University, MS Thesis, Tennessee State University, May 1971, pp. 51–53, 99; Tennessee State University *Meter*, April 29, May 9, 1968; Baltimore *Afro-American*, April 8, 1968

35. Tennessee State A and I University *Meter*, May 1967.

36. *Delaware State College Catalogue, 1958–1959*, 10, 72, *Delaware State College Catalogue, 1964–1965*, 95–96, *Delaware State College Catalogue, 1968–1969*, 17, *Delaware State College Catalogue, 1973–1973*, 52–53; Luna I. Mishoe, *Delaware State College President's Report, 1967–1968*, 7. Two freshman volunteer courses composed the previous ROTC program which was taught by LTC Samuel M. Arnold. Delaware State College Catalogues had listed LTC Arnold as the visiting ROTC PMST for more than a decade but in the 1969 edition his name does not appear in the listing of visiting staff.

37. Southern University and A and M College *Digest*, October 17, November 1, 1968, September 9, 1969.

38. Harry Edwards, *The Revolt of the Black Athlete* (New York: Free Press, 1969), pp. 39–114, 169–170, 174–75.

39. Baltimore *Afro-American*, May 6, 1967, May 3, October 18, 25, 1969; *New York Times*, October 19, 1969; Virginia State College *Statesman*, December 3, 1969.

40. Maxine D. Jones and Joe M. Richardson, *Talladega College: The First Century* (Tuscaloosa: University of Alabama Press, 1990), 211, 220–241.

41. Howard University *Hilltop*, April 7, 14, 21, 1967; Baltimore *Afro-American*, April 1, 15, May 20, 1967.

42. Howard University *Hilltop*, April 28, May 12, 19, October 13, 27, November 10, 17, 1967.

43. Howard University *Hilltop*, October 5, November 10, 17, December 1, 1967; Baltimore *Afro-American*, January 28, May 17, 1969, New York *Times*, May 9, 1969.

44. Virginia State College *Statesman*, April 24, October 8, 1968.

45. Ileana S. Brown, *History of the Air Force Air Force Reserve Officers Training Corps, 1 July 1967— 30 June 1968* (Montgomery: Office of Information, AFROTC, 12 August 1968), 47–48.

46. Lawrence Gordon, *The AFROTC Program at Tennessee State University*, MS Thesis, Tennessee State University, May 1971, 65–65a; Jackson State College *Blue and White Flash*, May 1971; Tim Spofford, *Lynch Street: The May 1970 Slayings at Jackson State University* (Kent: Kent State University Press, 1988), passim; "South Carolina State University Honors Orangeburg Massacre Victims," *Jet* 99 (February 26, 2001): 8

47. Morris J. Mac Gregor, *Integration of the Armed Forces, 1940–1965* (Washington: Center of Military History, 1981), 569–571.

48. ROTC Files, University of Arkansas, Pine Bluff, Arkansas.

49. South Carolina State College ROTC Fact Sheet, October 22, 1991. The South Carolina State College ROTC program had graduated 1751 commissioned officers by 1991 with 15 commissioned in 1991.

50. James C. Evans to Lawrence A. Oxley, May 15, 1969, James C. Evans Papers; Jackson (MS) *Daily News*, November 30, 1968; Jackson State College *Blue and White Flash*, February 1969; *Military Science at Jackson State University*, Army Reserve Officers' Training Corps, Jackson State University, Jackson, MS, n.d. MAJ Joseph Creasy, who was selected as APMS on February 28, 1969 was replaced by, LTC Leo M. Roberts who became the PMS on September 8, 1969. The fifteen cadets were commissioned in 1971 and though Milton Austin was first to receive a commission as 2LT the highest ranking graduate was Eddie Cain. After the program was extended to females, MAJ Della P. Burke and MAJ Martha McRavin-Oliver respectively became the first commissioned officers to return to Jackson State as APMSs. An alumnus and non-ROTC graduate to serve in the cadre was LTC Silvanius Johnson. The unit by September 1994 would graduate 546 officers. See Jackson State College *Catalog, 1971–1972*, 40; "Jackson State University Army Reserve Officers' Training Corps 'Tiger Battalion' Profile," *U. S. Army Cadet Command 19th Annual Historically Black Colleges and Universities Conference*,

Jackson State University, Jackson, MS, March 28–30, 1995, 87. The African American colleges conference began as a forum in 1977 when six Presidents of African American colleges met at South Carolina to discuss their requirements and efforts to provide quality ROTC officers. Before the establishment of the ROTC unit, detachments had been formed at the University of Mississippi, Mississippi at Starkville, and Mississippi Southern University.

51. LTG William F. Train to Jerome H. Holland, May 9, 1967, Roger T. Kelly to Presidents of Colleges and Universities Having ROTC Detachments and Professors of Military Science, April 29, 1969, Holland Papers, Hampton University Archives.

52. Miller, *Procurement and Retention of Black Officers*, 45–47, 52–53.

53. Miller, *Procurement and Retention of Black Officers*, 3, 68.

54. *Norfolk State University Spartan Battalion* (Norfolk: Norfolk State University Department of Military Science, n.d.), 1; Virginia State College *Stateman*, October 12, 1964.

55. *Fort Valley State College ROTC Handbook*, 1–2. In August 1977, the college was authorized additional cadre who were assigned to the Albany campus.

56. GO 4, Headquarters, Department of the Army, Washington, DC, January 28, 1971; Memorandum, CPT Clarence H. McNeill for the Record, HQ, Third U.S. Army, Fort McPherson, GA, January 25, 1971, Alcorn A and M College ROTC Files, Alcorn A and M College, Lorman, Mississippi.

57. "Military Department," Alabama A and M *Normalite* 3 (1919): 63–72. The unexpected arrival of LTs William H. Thompson and William R. Smalls on October 13–14, 1918 surprised the college administrators but with their cooperation the officers organized a unit of 154 soldiers by October 28, 1918.

58. Alabama A and M University *Campus Intercom Bulletin*, January 28, February 12, 1971; Richard D. Morrison, *History of Alabama Agricultural and Mechanical University, 1875–1992* (Huntsville: Liberal Arts Press, 1994), 241.

59. Alabama A and M University *Maroon and White*, October 11, 1971; Huntsville *News*, October 12, 1971; Huntsville *Times*, October 12, 14, November 8, 1971; Huntsville *Times Valley*, October 13, 1971, Nashville *Tennessean*; October 13, 1971; Birmingham *Post-Herald*, October 13, 14, 1971. Other grievances involved the installation of handles on cafeteria doors, providing travel for cheerleaders to attend out-of-town athletic events, selection of a new band director, permitting female students to have off-campus dates escort them to their dormitories, elimination of a sign-in roster for visiting students from other campuses, and adding an additional serving line in the dining hall. Students also protested the smoking ban policy, the lack of entertainment in the recreation center, and the extension of the academic year by three weeks with the same scheduled holidays. They also advocated a birth control course or birth control clinic, reduced bus fares to athletic events, elimination of guests paying fees when staying with students living on campus, improving security officer facilities, improving dormitory equipment and facilities, revision of class absence policies and an improved procedure revision in university policies.

60. Morrison, *History of Alabama A and M University*, 240–243. Anti-ROTC activities did not deter LTC John H. Redd and his cadre from accomplishing their mission. Cadet Brigade Commander Isaac Brown attended the Advanced Summer Camp at Fort Bragg where his outstanding performance earned him the designation of a distinguished military cadet. He had the highest overall performance in his battalion and was ranked fourth among all cadets attending the camp. Eighteen other students attended the Basic Summer Camp at Fort Knox and all who successfully completed the training were eligible for enrollment into the advanced ROTC curriculum. The cadets commissioned on May 20, 1973 were LT Isaac Brown who was assigned to the Finance Corps with a two

year detail to Infantry at Fort Bragg. LT Larry C. Lauderdale was assigned to the Signal Corps and selected to complete airborne training at Fort Benning in Georgia. However, LT Clifton Miller, commissioned into the Quartermaster Corps, was among nine cadets who completed the first four-year ROTC program at the university.

The Third Army commanding general also approved three-year scholarships that were presented to Lloyd Holloway, Hugh B. Grant, Jerry W. Smith, Delarie Parmer and George L. Preyer. The cadre in addition to LTC Redd consisted of MAJs Stephen H. Lee and Charles Nelson, CPTs Denneth G. Baskett and Winston S. Leonard, SMAJ David Smith, MSGT James Warmley, 1SGT George Schumake, SSGT Bruce A. Tidwell and SPEC Walter J. Yarn. For meritorious service prior to their assignment, Richard D. Morrison presented LTC Redd with the Meritorious Service Medal, MAJ Lee with the Army Commendation Medal and SMAJ Smith with the second Oak Leaf Cluster to the Army Commendation Medal. See "On Campus—ROTC Program Has Successful First Year," Alabama A and M University Normal *Index* 50 (Fall 1972–73): 14; Greensboro (AL) *Watchman*, May 29, 1975; Memorandum, LTC Redd for Henry Ponder, May 1973, Archives Collection, Alabama A and M University, Huntsville, AL; Huntsville *Times*, October 19, 1971. For additional concerns of Morrison, see Richard D. Morrison, *Walking in the Wilderness: An Autobiography of Richard David Morrison* (Huntsville: Liberal Arts Press, 1994), passim.

61. J. D. Boyd to TAG, June 26, 1967, History of Alcorn A and M Army ROTC Unit, n.d., Institutional Fact Sheet, A and M College, Lorman, MS, n.d., COL L. B. Mattingly to Deputy Chief of Staff for ROTC, February 12, 1971, LTC Charles D. Randal Annual ROTC Report, 1973–1973, in Alcorn A and M College ROTC Files, Lorman, LA; Alcorn A and M College *New Alcorn Herald*, May 1971, Alcorn A and M College *Alcorn Kadet*, April 1973. After 1942, applications were submitted in January 1946, June 1947, October 1950, June 1954, January 1955, September 1958, June 1966, June 1967 and October 1969. Other cadre personnel were MAJ Oscar C. Mack, CPT Harvey J. Bailey, CPT Quarlie Jackson, CPT John F. Affeldt, CPT Joseph M. Tyson, SGM Edward Crook, Jr., SFC Johnny W. Mitchell, SFC Leonard Bauduin, and SSGT Willis Chappell. The secretaries were Carrie L. Rose and Lynn Blackman. See SO 53, HQ, Third U.S. Army, Fort McPherson, GA, March 15, 1971, SO 64, HQ, 3rd Squadron, 11th Air Cavalry, March 30, 1971, SO 97, HQ, U.S. Army Training Center and Fort Campbell, Fort Campbell, KY, April 19, 1971, SO 212, HQ, Third U.S. Army, Fort McPherson, GA, September 30, 1971, GO 277, HQ, U.S. Continental Army Command, Fort Monroe, VA, June 14, 1973, Mississippi *Enterprise*, October 28, 1972, May 13, 1973, Vicksburg *Evening Post*, May 7, 1973, Vicksburg *Sunday Post*, May 20, 1973. The first commissioned officers were LTs Larry D. Beamon, Signal Corps; Ronald A. Byrd, Air Defense Artillery; Franklin Gales, Armor; Timothy R. Major, Signal Corps; and James C. Stubbs, Military Intelligence Corps. BG Edward Greer who officiated the first commissioning ceremony was the Deputy Commanding General of Fort Leonard Wood. See Alcorn A and M College *Alcorn Kadet*, April, September 1973.

62. Virginia State College Reserve Officers' Training Corps (ROTC): 32 Years of Outstanding Service to the Nation, Virginia State College Military Science Department, Virginia State University, Ettricks, Virginia.

63. Grambling State University ROTC History, ROTC Detachment File, Grambling University, Grambling, LA.

64. Saint Augustine's College *Pen*, 1.

65. George A. Sewell and Cornelius V. Troup, *Morris Brown College: The First Hundred Years, 1881–1981* (Atlanta: Morris Brown College, 1981), 163. Commissioned during commencement were LTs James Bender, Larry Drummer, Ervin Jenkins, Tontina Redwine and Raymond Walker.

66. CDR Gerald E. Thomas to Chief of Naval Operations, May 22, 1969, March 2,

1970, Post-46 Command File, Naval Historical Center, Washington Naval Yard, Washington, DC; Baltimore *Afro-American*, December 30, 1967, March 30, 1968. Under Secretary Charles F. Baird was the keynote speaker during the ceremony held on May 19, 1968. Other attendees included Rear Admiral Herbert H. Anderson, US Navy Assistant Chief of Naval Personnel, BG Leo J. Dulacki, Assistant Director of Personnel in Headquarters, USMC, and Earl Rudder, President of Texas A and M University. Immediately after his arrival on April 1, 1968, LT Gordon E. Fisher was assigned as the Navigation and Operations Instructor, SKCS Charles E. Siebott reported for temporary duty having served with CPT Brady's NROTC staff at Harvard University, and YNC Enneth H. Ingerson who had served with the NROTC at Purdue University similarly reported, all arriving by April 3, 1968. CDR Gerald E. Thomas, reported on April 14, 1968 and became the Executive Officer.

CPT Brady graduated from the Naval Academy and served on destroyer duty until February 1945 when he was selected for flight training. He volunteered for duty at Prairie View College to help organize the NROTC unit.

CDR Admiral Thomas was born on June 23, 1929 in Natick, MA, attended the University of Nebraska before transferring to Harvard University where he entered NROTC and was commissioned an Ensign in July 1951. He served as Engineer Office aboard the *USS Newman K. Perry* and in the Gunnery and Operations department aboard the *USS Worcester*. CDR Thomas completed the Russian Language Course at the US Naval Language School in Anacostia prior to his assignment at the National Security Agency at Fort Meade, MD. In 1963 he was transferred to the Bureau of Naval Personnel to head the College Training Program Section in the Officer Promotion Branch where he assisted in administering the NROTC, Navy Enlisted Science Education (NESEP), Reserve Officer Candidates (ROC), and the Merchant Marine and Chaplain programs. He additionally served as a member of the President's Board for Racial Equal Opportunity where he was responsible for making and assisting in the implementation of recommendations for achieving racial equality in the Navy. A graduate of Naval War College in Newport, RI, the recipient of a Masters of Science in International Affairs from George Washington University and a Ph.D. in Diplomatic History at Yale University in 1970, CDR Thomas commanded the *USS Bausdell* prior to his assignment at Prairie View College. His promotion to the rank of Rear Admiral on January 30, 1974 made him the second African American to attain the rank. See Rear Admiral Gerald E. Thomas File, Naval Historical Center, Washington Naval Yard, Washington, DC, Boston *Globe*, March 6, 1974, Chicago *Defender*, April 13, 1974, "Profiles of the Fleet: Two Stars for Gerald Thomas," *ALL HANDS* (April 1974): 40–41. LTCDR R. A. Frederick replaced CDR Thomas as the executive officer at Prairie View A and M. Polly Elmore, a junior majoring in sociology, became the first Miss Prairie View A and M NROTC on October 17, 1968.

67. CPT Warren H. Lowans to Director of Naval History, February 16, 1971, February 25, 1972, CDR Reeves R. Taylor to Director of Naval History, March 9, 1973, Post-46 Command File, Naval Historical Center, Washington Naval Yard, Washington, DC, Baltimore *Afro-American*, May 9, 30, 1970, Washington *Star*, October 16, 1970. CPT Lowans was relieved on April 31, 1972 by LDCR Donald O. Burrell who served as acting commander until the assignment of CDR Reeves R. Taylor on July 15, 1972.

CDR Taylor was born on March 6, 1929 in Providence, RI to John E. and Cleone Ramsey Taylor. He attended Brown University prior to graduating from the Naval Academy in 1953. Completing flight school and serving in several capacities abroad the *USS Columbus*, *USS Ranger* and *USS Wasp*, he also served as a US representative to the Reconnaissance Group of NATO Standardization Committee, served as commander of an aircraft unit abroad the USS Kitty Hawk, and became advisor and Special Assistant for Minority Affairs to the Commander-in-Chief of the US Atlantic Fleet prior to his assignment at Prairie View. See CDR Taylor's biography in reference files on Blacks in the Navy/Military, Naval Historical Center, Washington Naval Yard, Washington, DC.

LCDR Burrell initially enlisted in the Navy in 1946 and after thirteen years was among the early Master Chief Petty Officers in the Navy. Rejecting an LDO appointment in favor of the Navy Enlisted Scientific Education Program (NESEP), he graduated with a degree in electrical engineering from the University of Kansas. On November 22, 1963 after completing Officer Candidate School at Newport, RI and receiving a commission as LT (jg), he served in several capacities which included instructor at the Nuclear Power School at Mare Island, as electronics warfare officer aboard the *USS Oklahoma City*, and operations officer aboard the *USS Gridley* before his assignment as executive officer of the NROTC unit at Prairie View. See "Profiles of the Fleet: Now He's Exec of NROTC at Prairie View," *ALL HANDS* (June 1954): 58–59. Hereafter, SECNAV will be used for secretary of the Navy,

68. Washington *Post*, March 1, 1971.

69. Baltimore *Afro-American*, March 30, October 30, 1971; CDR Donald A. Griffin to Director of Naval History, March 3, 1972, Post-46 Command File, Naval Historical Center, Washington Naval Yard, Washington, DC; Baton Rouge *Morning Advocate*, October 6, 1971; New Orleans *News Leader*, October 13, 1971; Southern University and A and M College NROTC Unit History, Southern University, Baton Rouge, LA; Change of Command, Naval Reserve Officers Training Corps Unit, Southern University, Baton Rouge, LA, November 1, 1984. Others who attended the dedication ceremonies included Rear Admiral R. A. McPherson, Commander of the Eighth Naval district, Mayor W. W. Dumas of East Baton Rouge, COL William L. Beach, Director of the Eighth Marine district, CPT R. A. Hartman, Bureau of Naval Personnel, Director of Officer Education, and CPT E. E. Wilson, Commander of Tulane University NROTC.

The NROTC cadre included CPT S. J. Pitts as Marine Officer Instructor, LT James L. Bowen as Freshman Officer Instructor, QMC William E. Thrift as Assistant Navigation and Operations Instructor, SSGT James Shells (or Shales) as Assistant Marine Instructor, SKI F. L. Swift as Supply Assistant, and Chief Willie I. Banks as Administrative Assistant. The first Miss ROTC at Southern University was Sietta Simon and the NROTC unit's first issue of *Floating Jaquar* was published on September 22, 1971. See CDR Donald A. Griffin to Director of Naval History, March 3, 1972, Post-46 Command File, Naval Historical Center, Washington Naval Yard, Washington, DC.; Baton Rouge *Morning Advocate*, April 3, September 8, 1971; Southern University *Campus Digest*, July 31, 1991, Baton Rouge *Sunday Advocate*, August 1, 1971; CITY News Leader, August 22, September 5, 1991

70. CDR Virgil V. McGee to Director of Naval History, January 9, 1972, February 27, 1973, Post-46 Command File, Naval Historical Center, Washington Naval Yard, Washington, DC., Clyde W. Hall, *One Hundred Years of Education at Savannah State College, 1890–1990* (East Peoria, IL: Versa Press, 1991), 94–95. The principal speaker during the ceremony was James E. Johnson, Assistant Secretary of the Navy for Manpower and Reserve Training. Other guest included RADM Edwin M. Rosenberg, Commander of Naval Reserve Training, BG Eugene M. Lynch, Commanding General of Fort Steward-Hunter Army Airfield, Georgia Representative Jesse Blackshear, Savannah Mayor John Rousakis, Regent H. Peterson, University System of Georgia, Henry Ashmore, President of Armstrong State College, COL Charles B. Jiggetts (USAF), Office of Telecommunication Policy, Office of the President, CPT R. G. Hartman, Director of Officer Education Division, Bureau, COL R. H. Jones, representative of the Commandant of the Marine Corps, CDR Robert C. Powell, Commander of Coast Air Station at Savannah, CDR J. Baumgartner, CDR of the *USS Barracuda*, James Yates,

President of the Navy League of Savannah, Marcuss Stubbs, former Alderman of Savannah, CPT F. Spencer, member of Chatham County Board of Education, Daniel Washington, President of Savannah State College Alumni Association, LT Wayne Jones, CDR of the Naval Reserve Training Center at Savannah, and Roy Jackson, President of Savannah State College Student Government Association.

Other cadre of the NROTC unit were LCDR Joseph J. Hutton as Executive Officer, CPT Frederick L. Jones as Marine Officer Instructor, LT David O. Dinwiddle as Sophomore Instructor, LT Oswald L. Mikell as Freshman Instructor, QMC G. W. Perry as Navigation Instructor, YNI Nathaniel Breaker as unit Yeoman, SSGT Johnny L. Morris as Drill Instructor, SK2 David M. Walls as Unit Storekeeper, and Lynda Gordon and Mildred Paige as Secretaries.

71. Hall, *One Hundred Years of Education at Savannah State College*, 95; "U.S. Navy's Blue Angels Selects First Black Pilot," *Jet* 69 (November 4, 1985): 16.

72. Baltimore *Afro-American*, September 16, December 30, 1972; CDR Raymond A. Lambert to Director of Naval History, February 27, 1973, Post-46 Command File, Naval Historical Center, Washington Navy Yard, Washington, DC; Durham *Morning Herald*, October 28, 1972; *Bulletin of North Carolina Central University* 7 (June 1973): 166. Commander Lambert was born in New York, New York on September 16, 1932. He graduated from North Carolina A and T with a Bachelor's degree in chemistry and soil chemistry and entered the Navy in October 1956. Assigned to the Officers Candidate School in Newport, RI where he was commissioned an Ensign on February 28, 1957, he later completed the Naval Flight Training Course at the Naval Air Station in Pensacola, Florida. Promoted to the rank of Commander in January 1971 and attached to the U.S. Naval Academy as a Chemistry Instructor and the Associate Chairman of the Chemistry Department, he was reassigned on July 1, 1972 to establish the NCC NROTC unit. The other cadre assigned to the unit by December 31, 1972 were CDR Clifford W. Gibson as Executive Officer, CPT George H. Walls, Jr. as the Marine Officer, LTs Wallace M. Elton and Donald R. Rentschler as Assistant Professors, QMC Franklin W. Longson as Assistant Reference Librarian, Yeoman First Class Andrew Jason, Jr. as Personnel and Administrative Assistant, and SSGT Eugene Bowden as Assistant Marine Instructor. Gilda R. Bell was the secretary and Robert L. Davis the chief storekeeper. The NROTC dedication was conducted by Chancellor Albert Whiting on October 27, 1972 at the Duke Auditorium. Among the attendees were Secretary of the Navy Warner, Rear Admirals Samuel Gravely, Jr., Frank Corley, H. J. Kossler, and CPT (Chaplain) Thomas D. Parham.

73. Leedell W. Neyland, *Florida Agricultural and Mechanical University: A Centennial History — 1887–1987* (Tallahassee: Florida A and M University Foundation, 1987), 410–11, Baltimore *Afro-American*, September 16, December 30, 1972; NROTCU-FAMUINST 5400.2H, FAMU NROTC, Tallahassee, FL, JULY 20, 1992. Commander Hacker later obtained the rank of Rear Admiral and served as the commander of the Naval Training Center at San Diego prior to retiring in 1988. Among the distinguished midshipmen are Ensign Robert Hill, who became the first commissioned officer in March 1975 and during the following year Ensign Bobby Johnson became the first Marine Corps officer commissioned. Other achievements of the FAMU NROTC include Ensign Jeffrey Young as the first ECP commissioned in June 1979, the assignment of Ensign Harold Lomas as the selectee of the Nuclear Power Program in February 1976, Ensign Carol Skiber as the unit's first female aviator in December 1978. SSGT Robert Winchester, the unit's first MECEP officer in August 1989, became the first MECEP commissioned in December 1991. CPT Williams after his retirement became Inspector General for the State of Florida.

74. Interview with LT Roger D. Hardy, NROTC Detachment, Morehouse College, Atlanta, GA, August 3, 1994.

75. Ileana S. Brown, *History of the Air Force Air Force Reserve Officers Training Corps, 1 July 1967 — 30 June 1968* (Montgomery: Office of Information, AFROTC, 12 August 1968), 48.

76. *North Carolina A and T State University Air Force ROTC Detachment 605 Directory of Commissioners Since 1953* (Greensboro: A and T AFROTC Detachment 605, June 1987): 1; North Carolina A and T State University, *AFROTC DET 605 Directory of Commissioners Since 1953* (Greensboro: A and T AFROTC, June 1987): 1, CPT Huey B. Scott to First ROTC Region Commander, April 4, 1975, LTC Franklin N. Horton to North Carolina A and T PMS, April 9, 1975, Cross-Enrollment Agreement for the Establishment of Army Reserve Officer Training Corps Instruction at Elon College, August 1, 1975, BG F. Cecil Adams, Jr. to North Carolina A and T PMS, July 28, 1980, NCA and T ROTC Records, Greensboro, NC.

77. James H. White, *Up From a Cotton Patch: J. H. White and the Development of Mississippi Valley State College* (Itta Bena: Mississippi Valley State College, 1979), 102.

78. Levi Watkins, *Fighting Hard: The Alabama State Experience* (Detroit: Harlo, 1987), 123–124; Levi Watkins, *Report of the President of Alabama State University, 1962–1981* (Montgomery, AL: Office of University Advancement, 1981):11

79. Ileana S. Brown, *History of the Air Force Reserve Officers Training Program, 1 July 1971 — 30 June 1972* (Montgomery: Office of Information, AFROTC, October 10, 1972), 65–68.

80. Grambling AFROTC Detachment 331 History, Grambling University, Grambling, LA; Grambling University *Gramblinite*, April 30, May 14, September 10, 17, 24, 1971, February 25, May 4, July 30, September 8, 29, 1972. LTC Frederick who was subsequently promoted to COL had graduated from North Carolina College and Syracuse University. Other cadre included CPT John H. Sparks who graduated from Tuskegee Institute and Oklahoma State University; CPT William L. Ivy who graduated from the USMC and was previously assigned to Minot AFB as a B-52 instructor pilot; SSGT Easton A. Somers who was transferred from Holy Cross College where the detachment had been deactivated; SSGT Lee Roy Burrell who was transferred from Little Rock AFB to replace SSGT Somers; and SSGT Leon Riley who was assigned to perform recruiting duties until transferred to Louisiana State University in February 1974. Carrie Johnson, a resident of Monroe, was employed as secretary and was a graduate of Robinson Business School.

81. Fayetteville State University *Voice*, September 30, 1972, May-June 1974. Franklin Melvin, Conrith Davis, Bernard Taylor, Frank Douglass, Jr., Johnny Jones, and Bobby H. Washington completed the summer encampment at Gunter AFB in Montgomery, Alabama and Ronnie Smith trained at Forbes AFB in Topeka, Kansas.

82. Baltimore *Afro-American*, March 30, 1968, January 17, 1967, May 31, June 14, 28, September 20, 1969, June 13, 1970, June 10, 17, 1972, January 2, July 1–7, 1973. West Point in 1969 commissioned Cornelius M. Cooper, Rene G. Copeland, Sheridon H. Groves, James A. Minor, Jr., Jerome R Hackett, Michael F. Steele, Francis F. Tabela and Michael M. Williams. The Naval Academy graduated the highest number of African Americans in 1972 with the commissioning of Edward A. Burnette, Alfred B. Coleman, Walter L. Crump, Jr., Eugene Llody W. Keaser, Eugene Lovely, Matthew T. Madison, Julius McMillan, Nelson M. Jones, Charles H. Rucks, Earl M. Smith, Roland B. Staton and Julius S. Tindall. This accomplishment was duplicated the following year with the commissioning of Larry W. Calhoun, Kerry H. Caliman, James H. Campbell, William G. Evans, Homer L. Faust, Jr., Wayne M. Fernard, James E. Jackson, Larry W. Jones, Richard D. Samuels, Rodney L. Schockley, Robert D. Watts and Ernest C. Young. The Naval Academy expected to graduate twelve more in 1974, thirty-three in 1975 and an incredible sixty in 1976.

83. Baltimore *African American*, August 26, September 23, 1967. LTs commissioned officers were LTs Robert Harris, Robert Gibson, Raymond James, Roland Livington and Irving Evans.

84. J. S. Durkee to COL Howard, December 29, 1924, January 28, 1925, J. S. Durkee to Secretary of War John W. Weeks, January 17, 1925, Secretary of War to J. S. Durkee, February 9, March 7, 1925, LTC John A. Wagner to TAG, March 13, 1926, TAG to 5th Corps Area Commanding General, April 2, 1926, COL R. B. Parrott, April 15, 1926, 3rd Corps Area Commanding General to TAG, February 14, 1925, April 21, 1926, MAJ Charles D. Cable to TAG, March 1, 1938, files 000.862, 322.94, RG 94, NA; Logan, *Howard University*, 217–18; Howard University *Hilltop*, January 25, 1928, October 17, 1934, April 13, 1939. Wilberforce had a band which consisted of eighteen members.

85. Redstone Arsenal *Rocket*, May 3, 1972

86. Howard University *Hilltop*, March 18, 1929, March 3, 1933; "Virginia State College Reserve Officers' Training Corps (ROTC): 32 Years of Outstanding Service to the Nation," Virginia State College Military Science Department, Virginia State University, Ettricks, Virginia; Virginia State College *Statesman*, May 3, 1967; Morgan State University *ROTC Alumni News*, June 15, 1999. The first retreat performed at Howard University was performed by Cadet CPT Frank S. Clark, III, and Cadets Vernon Archer, William Birch, Robert Johnson, Marvin Killibrew, and Augustus Symonette. See Howard University *Hilltop*, November 10, 1960.

87. Howard University *Hilltop*, March 18, 1929, April 11, October 15, 1951, March 25, 1955, March 25, 1956, November 10, October 12, 1961, March 16, 30, 1962, December 17, 1968; Tennessee A and I State University *Meter*, May 1954; Alcorn A and M College *New Alcorn Herald*, April 1972. CPT Spencer was promoted to the rank of MAJ after the company was assigned to the 372nd Infantry Regiment during World War I but at the age of sixty-five he retired from the Maryland National Guard and died in 1929.

88. Tennessee State University *Bulletin*, 42 (September 1954): 14; Tennessee State University *Bulletin* 42 (May 1955): 25.

89. Howard University *Hilltop*, October 24, 1947, February 10, 1950, Jan 25, 1951. The first cadets initiated by the charter members were Robert M. Alexander, James Bourne, James Brody, Robert B. Burke, Marcus Cannady, Howard Davis, Nathaniel Fairfax, Gerand L. James, Otto Jordan, William O'Neil, Chester R. Redhead, Robert Strange and Herbert Saunders. Rangers were also formed at Alcorn A and M. See Alcorn A and M College *New Alcorn Herald*, September 1972.

90. Alcorn A and M *Kadet*, November 1971.

91. Sherrie Tucker, "The Prairie View Co-Eds: Black College Women Musicians in Class and on the Road during World War II," *Black Music Research Journal* 19 (Spring 1999): 93–126.

92. Wilberforce University *Forcean*, 1941, 106; Tennessee State University Bulletin 42 (September 1954): 14; CPT Warren L. Lowans to Chief of Naval operation, February 25, 1972, Post-46 Command File, Naval Historical Center, Washington Navy Yard, Washington, DC; Lincoln University *ROTC Newsletter*, October 1961; *Alabama A and M Yearbook, 1972*; South Carolina State College ROTC Fact Sheet, October 22, 1991; Florence M. Read, *The Story of Spelman College* (Princeton: Princeton University Press, 1961), 297–299; Martha S. Putney, *When the Nation was in Need: Blacks in the Women's Army Corps* (Metuchen, NJ: Scarecrow Press, 1992), passim; Janet Sims-Wood, "We Served America Too!": *Personal Recollections of African Americans in the Woman's Army Corps during World War II*, Unpublished Ph.D Dissertation, Union Institute, Cincinnati, OH.

93. *Army ROTC: Alabama State A and M University* (Normal: Military Science Department, n.d.); 7. The founders of the Persherettes were Mary Ellen Boone, Andrea

Coverdale, Billie Ann Davis, Rose Keith, Sue Poole, Gloria Richardson, Lillian Yearwood and Sylvia Julian who also was elected Miss Pershing Rifles. The author is indebted to Gloria Richardson Marrow for giving the names of these students who also were sorors in the Alpha Gamma Chapter of Delta Sigma Theta.

94. John F. Potts, *A History of South Carolina State College* (Orangeburg: South Carolina State College, 1978), 142; *South Carolina State ROTC Fact Sheet, October 22, 1991*; "Virginia State College Reserve Officers' Training Corps (ROTC): 32 Years of Outstanding Service to the Nation," Military Science Department, Virginia State University, Ettricks, VA., 7–8, 10; Department of Military Science, Supplementary Year End Report, School Year 1973–74, Hampton Institute ROTC File, Hampton University Archive, Hampton University Library, Hampton, VA; Jackson State College *Jacksonian 1973*, 68; Jackson State College *Blue and White Flash*, December 1972; Jackson *Daily News*, July 22, 1973, May 7, 1976. Commissioned in the class were LTs Vera Joyce Wright, Della R. Powell, Joslin G. Martin, Deborah Louise, and Joslin G. Martin, Carolyn Fay Washington, Janice M. Brooks, Annie L. Hannah, Carrie B. Brown, and Shirley Ann Bolton. In addition to Jackson State, officials at the ROTC Regional Headquarters, FT Riley, KS, stated that Pennsylvania State University was also scheduled to graduate ten women officers.

95. Alcorn A and M College *Alcorn Kadet*, November 1971, March 1972.

96. Fayetteville State University *Voice*, September 30, 1972; Press Release, Office of Public Relations, July 9, 1973, Military Science Department Records, Alcorn A and M College, Lorman, MS; Columbia (GA) *Progress*, July 19, 1973.

97. History of ROTC at Southern University & A and M College, ROTC Files, Southern University & A and M College, Baton Rouge, LA.

98. Baltimore *Afro-American*, June 2, 1973; Martha S. Putney, *When the Nation was in Need: Blacks in the Women's Army Corps* (Metuchen, NJ: Scarecrow Press, 1992), 149. For additional information concerning African American personnel, see Janet Sims-Wood, *"We Served America Too!": Personal Recollections of African Americans in the Woman's Army Corps during World War II*, Unpublished Ph.D Dissertation, Union Institute, Cincinnati, OH.

99. Tennessee State University *Meter*, August 1970; "The University AFROTC Open to Women," Tennessee State University *Bulletin* 50 (1973): 2.

100. Baltimore *Afro-American*, February 24, May 19, 1973.

101. Grambling A and M AFROTC Detachment 311 History, Aeroscience Department, Grambling University, LA.

102. Baltimore *Afro-American*, March 30, October 30, 1971; CDR Donald A. Griffin to Director of Naval History, March 3, 1972, Post-46 Command File, Naval Historical Center, Washington Naval Yard, Washington, DC; Baton Rouge *Morning Advocate*, October 6, 1971; New Orleans *News Leader*, October 13, 1971; Southern University and A and M College NROTC Unit History, Southern University, Baton Rouge, LA; Change of Command, Naval Reserve Officers Training Corps Unit, Southern University, Baton Rouge, LA, November 1, 1984. Others who attended the dedication ceremonies included Rear Admiral R. A. McPherson, Commander of the Eighth Naval district, Mayor W. W. Dumas of East Baton Rouge, COL William L. Beach, Director of the Eighth Marine district, CPT R. A. Hartman, Bureau of Naval Personnel, Director of Officer Education, and CPT E. E. Wilson, Commander of Tulane University NROTC.

The NROTC cadre included CPT S. J. Pitts as Marine Officer Instructor, LT James L. Bowen as Freshman Officer Instructor, QMC William E. Thrift as Assistant Navigation and Operations Instructor, SSGT James Shells (or Shales) as Assistant Marine Instructor, SKI F. L. Swift as Supply Assistant, and Chief Willie I. Banks as

Administrative Assistant. The first Miss ROTC at Southern University was Sietta Simon and the NROTC unit's first issue of *Floating Jaquar* was published on September 22, 1971. See CDR Donald A. Griffin to Director of Naval History, March 3, 1972, Post-46 Command File, Naval Historical Center, Washington Naval Yard, Washington, DC.; Baton Rouge *Morning Advocate*, April 3, September 8, 1971; Southern University *Campus Digest*, July 31, 1991, Baton Rouge *Sunday Advocate*, August 1, 1971; New Orleans *News Leader*, August 22, September 5, 1991.

103. Baltimore *Afro-American*, June 19–13, 1973.

104. "Marine Corps Names Its 1st Black Female Colonel," *Jet* 81 (February 3, 1992): 26.

105. "Coast Guard Officers," *Jet* (May 30): 24; "People: Andrea Parker," *Jet* (July 30): 19.

106. ROTC Files, Southern University and A and M College, Baton Route, LA; The Rocket, June 1995.

107. *Morgan State University Magazine* (Spring/Summer 2000), 12–17; Baltimore *Afro-American*, July 14–20, 2001. Another Morgan State officer commissioned in 1971 is MG William Ward who has an assignment with the Joint Chiefs of Staff with an excellent opportunity to earn the rank of LTG. GEN. Roscoe Robinson, Jr., commissioned at the USMA, GEN Colin Powell, commissioned at the City College of New York, and GEN Johnnie E. Wilson, who was commissioned through OCS, are the other African Americans to attain the rank of Four-star General in the U.S. Army.

# Bibliography

## Manuscript Collections

Alcorn A and M College, Lorman, MS.
Military Science Department Records.
Alabama State University, Montgomery, AL.
AFROTC File.
Central State University, Wilberforce, OH.
ROTC File.
Florida Agricultural and Mechanical University.
Army ROTC File.
Naval ROTC File.
Fort Valley State College, Fort Valley, GA.
ROTC File.
Grambling University, LA.
Aeroscience Department Files.
ROTC Detachment File.
Harry S. Truman Library, Independence, MO.
Philleo Nash Papers.
Hampton University Archive and Library, Hampton, VA.
Ralph P. Bridgman Papers.
Jerome H. Holland Papers.
Malcolm S. MacLean Papers.
Army Specialized Training File.
Department of Military Science File.
ROTC File.
U. S. Naval Training School File.
Howard University Moorland-Spingarn Research Center, Washington, DC.
J. Stanley Durkee Papers.
Thomas M. Gregory Papers.
Campbell C. Johnson Papers.
Jackson State University, Jackson, MS.
ROTC File.
Kentucky State University Center of Excellence for the Study of Kentucky African-Americans, Frankfort, KY.
Conference of the Presidents of Land Grant Colleges Papers.

Lincoln University, Jefferson City, MO.
  ROTC File.
Morehouse College, Atlanta, GA.
  NROTC File.
Morgan State University, Baltimore, MD.
  Beulah Davis Collection.
  ROTC File.
National Archives II, College Park, MD.
  Records of the Adjutant General's Office, 1780s -1917, Record Group 94.
  Records of the Adjutant General's Office, 1917-, Record Group 407.
  Records of the Army Ground Forces, Record Group 337.
  Records of the Army Staff, Record Group 319.
  Records of the Office of Education, Record Group 12.
  Records of the Office of the Secretary of the Air Force, Record Group 340
  Records of the Office of the Secretary of War, Record Group 107.
  Records of the Office of the Chief Signal Officer, Record Group 111.
  Records of the Secretary of the Army, Record Group 335.
  Records of the War Department General and Special Staffs, Record Group 165.
  Records of the Veterans Administration, Record Group 15.
  Selected Documents Relating to Blacks Nominated for Appointments to the U.S.
    Military Academy During the 19th Century, 1870-1887, National Archives Microfilm
    Publication Pamphlet Describing, M1002.
Norfolk State University, Norfolk, VA.
  ROTC File.
North Carolina A and T University, Greensboro, NC.
  ROTC Records.
Prairie View State University, Prairie View, TX.
  ROTC File
  NROTC File.
Southern University and A and M College, Baton Rouge, LA.
  ROTC Files.
  NROTC Files.
St. Augustine's College, Raleigh, NC.
  ROTC File.
Tennessee State University, Nashville, TN.
  AFROTC File.
Tuskegee University Hollis Burke Frissell Library, Tuskegee, AL.
  Robert R. Moton Papers.
  F. D. Patterson Papers.
United States Naval Historical Center, Washington Navy Yard, Washington, DC.
  Files on Blacks in the Navy/Military.
  Post-46 Command File.
United States Army Military History Institute, Carlisle Barracks, PA.
  Benjamin O. Davis Papers.
  James C. Evans Papers.
University of Arkansas at Pine Bluff, MO.
  ROTC File.
Wilberforce University, Archives and Special Collections, Rembert E. Stokes Learning
  Center, Wilberforce, OH.
  Executive Board Minutes.
Yale University Library, New Haven, CT.
  Henry L. Stimson Papers.

## Public Documents

79th Congress, 1st Session, Senate Report 203, *Reserve Officer's Training Corps Credits for Military Training While on Active Duty, April 24, 1945.*

## Annual Reports

*Reports of the Adjutant General, 1918, 1920.*
*Report of the Chief of Staff, 1919.*
*Reports of the Secretary of War, 1937, 1941.*

## University Bulletins, Catalogues, and Yearbooks

Alabama A&M *Maroon and Gold.*
*Alabama A and M Yearbook.*
*Bulletin of North Carolina Central University.*
*Catalogue of State Agricultural and Mechanical College of South Carolina.*
*Delaware State College Catalogue.*
Jackson State College *Catalog.*
Lincoln University *Quill.*
Lincoln University *ROTC Newsletter.*
Maryland State College *Maroon and Gold.*
Prairie View State University *Purple and Gold.*
Prairie View State University *Panther.*
Tennessee State *Bulletin.*
Tuskegee Institute *Crimson and Gold.*
Tuskegee Institute *Tuskeanna.*

## Interview

LT Roger D. Hardy, NROTC Detachment, Morehouse College, Atlanta, GA, August 3, 1994.

## Unpublished Manuscripts

Brown, Ileana S. History of the Air Force Reserve Officers' Training Corps, July 1, 1967-June 30, 1968. Montgomery: U.S. Air Force University, August 12, 1968.
_____. History of the Air Force Reserve Officers' Training Corps, July 1, 1971-June 30, 1972. Montgomery: U.S. Air Force University, October 10, 1972.
Capers, Norris R. A Descriptive Study of the Relationship of Certain Variables to College ROTC Success of Army Cadets at Predominantly Black Institutions of Higher Education. Unpublished Ed.D Dissertation, George Washington University, Washington, DC.
Coles, James R. Relative Value of Scholastic Grades: Psychological and Background Factors in Predicting the Success of Air Force ROTC Cadets in Passing the Air Force Officers Qualifying Test at Tennessee Agricultural and Industrial State University. Unpublished MS Thesis, Tennessee Agricultural and Industrial State University, Nashville, TN.
Gordon, Lawrence. The AFROTC Program at Tennessee State University. Unpublished MS Thesis, Tennessee State University, Nashville, TN, May 1971.
McQuire, Phillip. Black Civilian Aides and the Problems of Racism and Segregation in

the United States Armed Forces: 1940-1950. Ph.D dissertation, Howard University, Washington, DC, 1975.

Satneck, Walter J. History of the Origins and Development of the Delaware State College and its Role in Higher Education for Negroes in Delaware. New York University, New York, NY, 1962.

Simms-Wood, Janet. "We Served America Too!": Personal Recollections of African Americans in the Woman's Army Corps during World War II. Unpublished Ph.D Dissertation, Union Institute, Cincinnati, OH.

Stroman, Samuel D. A Descriptive Study of the Relationship of (RQ) Scores, Summer Camp Standings and Cumulative Averages to Service School Orientation Courses Standings of Howard University. Unpublished MA Thesis, Howard University, Washington, DC.

Testimony before the President's Committee on Equality of Treatment and Opportunities in the Armed Services. Washington, DC, April 26, 1949.

Turman, Robert L. A History of the Development and Operation of the Army Reserve Officers' Training Corps at the Agricultural and Technical College of North Carolina, Greensboro, 1962.

Wennersten, Ruth E. The Historical Evolution of a Black Land Grant College: The University of Maryland Eastern Shore. Unpublished Ed.D. Dissertation, University of Maryland, College Park, 1976.

## Newspapers, Magazines, and Journals

Alabama A&M *Normalite.*
Alabama A&M *Normal Index*
Alabama A& M University *Campus Intercom Bulletin.*
Alcorn A&M College *Alcorn Kadet.*
Alcorn A&M College *New Alcorn Herald.*
*Army Times.*
Baltimore/Washington *Afro-American.*
Baton Rouge *Morning Advocate.*
Baton Rouge Sunday Advocate.
Birmingham *News.*
Birmingham *Post-Herald.*
*Boston Globe.*
Chicago *Defender.*
Chicago *Tribune.*
Charleston *Gazette.*
Cleveland *Gazette.*
Columbia (GA) *Progress.*
Durham *Morning Herald.*
Fayetteville State University *Voice.*
Grambling University *Gramblinite.*
Greensboro (AL) *Watchman.*
Hampton Institute *ROTC Bulletin.*
Houston *Informer.*
Howard University *Hilltop.*
Howard University *Journal.*
Huntsville *Times.*

Huntsville *Times Valley.*
Jackson (MS) *Daily News.*
Jackson State College *Blue and White Flash.*
Jackson State College *Jacksonian.*
*New York Times.*
New Orleans *News Leader.*
Mississippi *Enterprise.*
*Morgan State University Magazine*
Morgan State College *Spokesman.*
Morgan State University *ROTC Alumni News.*
Nashville *Tennessean.*
North Carolina A&T College *Register.*
Philadelphia *Tribune.*
Pine Bluff *Commercial.*
Southern University and A and M College *Digest.*
Southern University *Campus Digest.*
Saint Augustine *Pen.*
Tennessee A&I State Normal School *Bulletin.*
Tennessee State University *Meter.*
Tuskegee *Student.*
Vicksburg *Evening Post.*
Vicksburg *Sunday Post.*
Virginia State College *Statesman.*
Washington *Post.*

Washington *Star.*
Wilberforce *Forcean.*

Women in Military Service for American
Memorial Fount *Register.*

## Books

Bacote, Clarence A. *The Story of Atlanta University: A Century of Service, 1865-1965.* Atlanta: Atlanta University, 1969.

Bass, Jack, and Jack Nelson. *The Orangeburg Massacre.* Macon: Mercer University Press, 1984.

Biggs, Bradley. *The Triple Nickles.* Hampden, CT: Archon Books, 1986.

Black, Zella J. *Langston University: A History.* Norman: University of Oklahoma, 1979.

Brisbane, Robert H. *The Black Vanguard.* Valley Forge: Judson Press, 1970.

Carmichael, Stokely. *Stokely Speaks: Black Power to Pan-Africanism.* New York: Vintage Books, 1971.

Cole, Glen, Jr. *The African American Experience in the Civilian Conservation Corps.* Gainesville: University of Florida, 1999.

Cox, Thomas C. *Blacks in Topeka, Kansas, 1865-1915.* Baton Rouge: Louisiana State University Press, 1982.

Davis, Benjamin O., Jr. *Benjamin O. Davis, Jr: American.* Washington: Smithsonian Institute Press, 1991.

Davis, Walter M. *Pushing Forward: A History of Alcorn A. & M. College and Portraits of Some of its Successful Graduates.* Okolona, MS: Okolona Industrial School, 1938.

Edwards, Harry. *Black Students.* New York: Free Press, 1970.

_____. *The Revolt of the Black Athlete.* New York: Free Press, 1969.

Fletcher, Marvin E. *America's First Black General: Benjamin O. Davis, Sr., 1880-1970.* Lawrence: University of Kansas, 1989.

Foner, Philip S., ed. *The Black Panthers Speak.* Philadelphia: J. B. Lippincott Co., 1970.

Goggins, Latharus. *Central State University: The First One hundred Years, 1887-1987.* Wilberforce: Central State University, 1987.

Greene, Robert E. *Black Defenders of America, 1775-1973.* Chicago: Johnson Publishing Co., 1974.

_____. *Who were the Real Buffalo Soldiers?* Fort Washington, MD: R. E. Greene, 1994.

Dyson, Walter. *Howard University: The Capstone of Negro Education, 1867-1940.* Washington: Howard University Graduate School, 1940.

Flipper, Henry O. *The Colored Cadet at West Point.* New York: Arno Press, 1969.

Hall, Clyde W. *One Hundred Years of Education at Savannah State College, 1890-1990.* East Peoria, IL: Versa Press, 1991.

Ham, Debra Newman, ed. *The African American Odyssey.* Washington: Library of Congress, 1998.

Harlan, John C. *History of West Virginia State College, 1891-1965.* Dubuque: William C. Brown Co., 1969.

Hawkins, Walter L. *African American Generals and Flag Officers.* Jefferson: McFarland & Co., 1993.

Janken, Kenneth R. *Rayford W. Logan and the Dilemma of the African-American Intellectual.* Amherst: University of Massachusetts Press, 1993.

Jakeman, Robert J. *The Divided Skies: Establishing Flight Training at Tuskegee, Alabama, 1934-1942.* Tuscaloosa: University of Alabama Press, 1992.

Johnson, Charles Jr. *African Americans in the National Guard: Recruitment and Deployment during Peacetime and War.* Westport: Greenwood Press, 1992.

Jones, Edward A. *A Candle in the Dark.* Valley Forge: Judson Press, 1967

Jones, Maxine D. and Joe M. Richardson. *Talladega College: The First Century.* Tuscaloosa: University of Alabama Press, 1990.

Lindsey, Donal F. *Indians at Hampton Institute, 1877-1923*. Chicago: University of Illinois Press, 1995.

Lloyd, Grant. *Tennessee Agricultural and Industrial State University, 1912-1962: Fifty Years of Leadership Through Excellence*. Nashville: Tennessee A&I State University Press, 1962.

Logan, Rayford W. *Howard University: The First One Hundred Years*. New York: New York University Press, 1969.

Lyons, Gene M. and John W. Masland. *Education and Military Leadership*. Princeton: Princeton University Press, 1959.

MacGregor, Morris. *Integration of the Armed Forces, 1940-1965*. Washington: Center of Military History, 1981.

Marsh, Clifton E. *From Black Muslim to Muslim: The Resurrection, Transformation and Change of the Lost-Found Nation of Islam in America, 1930-1995*.Landon: Scarecrow Press, 1996.

Marshall, Albert P. *Soldiers Dream: A Centennial History of Lincoln University of Missouri, 1866-1966*. Marceline, MO: Walsworth, 1966.

Marszalek, John E. *Assault at West Point: The Court-Martial of Johnson Whittaker*. New York: Collier Books, 1972.

McGinnis, Frederick A. *A History and Interpretation of Wilberforce University*. Blanchester, OH: Brown Publishing Co., 1941.

Miller, Edward A. *Gullah Statesman: Robert Smalls from Slavery to Congress, 1839-1915*. Columbia: University of South Carolina Press, 1995.

Morrison, Richard R. *History of Alabama State Agricultural and Mechanical University, 1875-1992*. Huntsville: Liberal Arts College, 1994.

_____. *Walking in the Wilderness*. Huntsville: Liberal Arts Press, 1994.

Murray, Florence, ed. *The Negro Yearbook, 1949*. New York: Macmillan Co., 1949.

Nalty, Bernard. *Strength for the Fight*. New York: Free Press, 1986.

_____, and Morris J. MacGregor, eds. *Blacks in the Military: Essential Documents*. Wilmington, DE: Scholarly Resources, Inc., 1981.

Neyland, Leedell W. *Florida Agricultural and Mechanical University: A Centennial History, 1887-1987*. Tallahassee: Florida A&M University Foundation, Inc., 1987.

O'Reilly, Kenneth. *"Racial Matters": The FBI's Secret File on Black America*. New York: Free Press, 1989.

Potts, John. *A History of South Carolina State College, 1896-1987*. Orangeburg: South Carolina State College, 1978.

Putney, Martha S. *When the Nation was in Need: Blacks in the Women's Army Corps during World War II*. Metuchen Scarecrow Press, 1992.

Read, Florence M. *The Story of Spelman College*. Princeton: Princeton University Press, 1961.

Richardson, Joe M. *A History of Fisk University, 1865-1946*. University, AL: University of Alabama Press, 1980.

Sanders, Gaston O. *The Prairie, 1926*. Prairie View: Senior Class of Prairie View State Normal and Industrial College, 1926.

Sandler, Stanley. *Segregated Skies: All-Black Combat Squadrons of WWII*. Washington: Smithsonian Press, 1992.

Savage, W. Sherman. *The History of Lincoln University*. Jefferson City: Lincoln University, 1939.

Schall, Keith. *Stony the Road: Chapters in the History of Hampton Institute*. Charlottesville: University of Virginia Press, 1977.

Schneider, James G. *The Navy V-12 Program: Leadership for a Lifetime*. Boston: Houghton Mifflin Co., 1987.

Scott, Emmett J. *Scott's Official History of the American Negro in the World War*. New York: Arno Press, 1969.

Shaw, Henry I., Jr., and Ralph W. *Blacks in the Marine Corps.* Washington: History and Marines Division, Headquarters, U.S. Marine Corps, 1975.

Shubert, Frank N. *On the Trail of the Buffalo Soldiers, 1866-1917.* Wilmington, DE: Scholarly Resources, 1995.

Spofford, Tim. *Lynch Street: The May 1970 Slayings at Jackson State University.* Kent: Kent State University, 1988.

Tyson, Timothy B. *Radio Free Dixie: Robert F. Williams & the Roots of Black Power.* Chapel Hill: University of North Carolina Press, 1999.

Uya, Okon E. *From Slavery to Public Service: Robert Smalls, 1819-1915.* New York: Oxford University Press, 1971.

Vincent, Charles. *A Centennial History of Southern University and A&M College.*

Watkins, Levi. *Fighting Hard: The Alabama State Experience.* Detroit: Harlo, 1987.

West Virginia State College. *The History of the Military Science Department, West Virginia State College.* Institute: West Virginia State College, 1968.

White, James H. *Up From a Cotton Patch: J. H. White and the Development of Mississippi Valley State College.* Itta Bena: Mississippi Valley State College, 1979.

Wilson, Edward N. *History of Morgan State College, 1868-1967.* New York: Vantage Press, 19.

Wolters, Raymond. *The New Negro on Campus: Black College Rebellions of the 1920s.* Princeton: Princeton University Press, 1975.

Womack, William M., Sr. *Double V: The Civil Rights Struggle of the Tuskegee Airmen.* East Lansing: Michigan State University Press, 1994.

## Articles

Andrade, Ernest Jr. "The United States Navy and the Washington Conference." *Historian* 31 (May 1969).

Atkins, James A. "Negro Educational Institutions and the Veterans' Educational Facilities Program," *Journal of Negro Education* 17 (Summer 1948).

Atwood, R[ufus] B. "The Future of the Negro Land-Grant College," *Journal of Negro Education* 27 (Summer 1958).

_____. "The Origin and Development of the Negro Land Public College, with Especial Reference to the Land-Grant College," *Journal of Negro Education* 31 (Summer 1962).

Bigglestone, W. E. "Oberlin College and the Negro Student, 1865-1940," *Journal of Negro History* 56 (July 1971).

Brown, Willis L., and Janie M. McNeal-Brown. "Langston University: The Early Years," *Chronicles of Oklahoma* 74 (Spring 1996).

Chalfen, Michael. "'The Way Out May Lead In': The Albany Movement Beyond Martin L. King, Jr." *Georgia Historical Quarterly* 79 (Fall 1995).

Chase, Hal S. "Struggle for Equality: Fort Des Moines Training Camp for Colored Officers, 1917," *Phylon* 38 (December 1978).

"Commissions for Howard University Men as Reported at Time of Going to Press," *Howard University Journal* 15 (October 17, 1917).

"Coast Guard Officers," *Jet* (May 30).

Davis, John W. "The Participation of Negro Land-Grant Colleges in Permanent Federal Education Funds, 7 (July 1938).

Duran, Elizabeth C., and James A. Duran. "Integration in Reverse at West Virginia State College," *West Virginia History* 45 (1984).

Eskew, Glenn L. "Bombingham: Black Protest in Post-War Birmingham, Alabama." *Historian* 59 (Winter 1997).

Evans, James C. "Adult Education for Negroes in the Armed Forces," *Journal of Negro Education* 14 (Summer 1945).

_____, and Albert J. Parker. "ROTC Programs and Negro Youth." *Journal of Negro Education* 25 (April 1956).

Garrow, David L. "The Voting Rights Act in Historical Perspective." *Georgia Historical Quarterly* 74 (Fall 1990).

Hone, Thomas C. "The Effectiveness of the 'Washington Treaty' Navy." *Naval War College Review* 32 (November-December 1979).

"Jackson State University Army Reserve Officers' Training Corps 'Tiger Battalion,' Profile," *U.S. Army Cadets Command 19th Annual Historically Black Colleges and Universities Conference.* Jackson State University, Jackson, MS, March 28-30, 1965.

Jenkins, Martin D. "Current Trends and Events of National Importance in Negro Education: Enrollment in Institutions of Higher Education for Negroes, 1944-1945," *Journal of Negro Education* 14 (Spring 1945).

_____. "Current Trends and Events of National Importance in Negro Education: Enrollment in Institutions of Higher Education for Negroes, 1945-1946," *Journal of Negro Education* 15 (Summer, 1946).

_____. "Current Trends and Events of National Importance in Negro Education: Enrollment in Institutions of Higher Education for Negroes, 1947-1948," *Journal of Negro Education* 17 (Spring 1948).

Johnson, Charles. "The Army, the Negro and the Civilian Conservation Corps: 1933-1942." *Military Affairs* 26 (October 1972).

Kozloff, Nikolas "Vietnam; the African Community, and the Pittsburgh New Courier," *Historian* 63 (Spring 1999): 520-538.

Kuebler, Edward J. "The Desegregation of the University of Maryland," *Maryland Historical Magazine* 71 (Spring 1976).

Lawson, Steven F. "Martin L. King, Jr., and the Civil Rights Movement." *Georgia Historical Quarterly* 71 (Summer 1987).

Lightfoot, George M., Alaine Locke and Martha MacLear, "Howard University in the War: A Record of Patriotic Service," *Howard University Record.* 13 (April 1919).

Locke, Mamie E. "The Role of African Women's in the Civil Rights Movement in Hinds County and Sunflower County, Mississippi." *Journal of Mississippi* 53 (August 1991).

Lyons, Gene M., and John W. Masland. "The Origins of ROTC." *Military Affairs* 23 (Spring 1959).

"Marine Corps Names 1st First Black Female Colonel," *Jet* 81 (February 3, 1992).

Martin, Charles H. "The Civil Rights Movement and Southern Black Defendants." *Georgia Historical Quarterly* 71 (Spring 1987).

Martin, William H. "The Land-Grant Functions of the Negro Public College," Journal of Negro Education 31 (Summer 1962).

Monson, Ingrid. "Monk Meets SCNN." *Black Music Research Journal* 19 (Fall 1999).

O'Reilly, Kenneth. "The FBI and the Politics of the Riots, 1964-1968." *Journal of American History* 75 (June 1988).

"People: Andrea Parker," *Jet* (July 30).

"Professional News," *Journal of the National Medical Association* 35 (November 1943).

"Profiles of the Fleet: Now He's Exec of NROTC at Prairie View." ALL HANDS (June 1954).

"Profiles of the Fleet: Two Stars for Gerald Thomas." ALL HANDS (April 1974).

Putney, Martha S. "The Formative Years of Maryland's First Black Postsecondary School," *Maryland Historical Magazine* 73 (June 1975).

Reagon, Bernice Johnson. "Let the Church Sing 'Freedom.'" *Black Music Research Journal* 19 (Spring 1999).

Reid, Herbert O., and James N. Nabrit, "Remedies Under Statutes Granting Federal Aid to Land Grant Colleges," *Journal of Negro Education* 17 (Summer 1947).

Schneider, James G. "'Negroes Will Be Tested!'-FDR," *Naval History* (Spring 1993).
"Special 'G.I.'" *Prairie View University Bulletin* 37 (February 1946).
Spivey, Donald. "Crisis on a Black Campus," Chronicles of Oklahoma 59 (Winter 1981-1982).
Stancik, William C. "Air Force ROTC: Its Origins and Early Years," *Air University Review* 35 (July-August 1984).
Strain, Christopher. "'We Walked Like Men': The Deacons for Defense and Justice." *Louisiana History* 38 (Winter 1997).
Tucker, Sherrie. "The Prairie View Co-Eds: Black College Women Musicians in Class and on the Road during World War II." *Black Music Research Journal* 19 (Fall 1999).
Tyson, Timothy B. "Robert F. Williams: 'Black Power,' and the African Freedom Struggle," *Journal of American History* 85 (September 1998).
"U.S. Navy's Blue Angels Selects First Black Pilot," *Jet* 69 (November 4, 1985).
Wennersten, John R., and Ruth Ellen. "Separate and Unequal: The Evolution of a Black Land Grant College, 1890-1930," *Maryland Historical Magazine* 72 (Spring 1977).

## Pamphlets

*Army ROTC: Alabama State A and M University*. Normal: Military Science Department, n.d.
Arnold, Christian K., ed. Proceedings of the Association of State Universities and Land-Grant Colleges 77th Annual Convention, Washington, DC, November 10-13, 1963.
*Fort Valley State College ROTC Handbook.*
Grambling AFROTC Detachment 331 History, Grambling University, Grambling, LA.
Hampton Normal and Agricultural Institute. *Act of Incorporation, By-Laws, Extracts from the Code of Virginia, Etc. for the Use of the Trustees.* Hampton: Hampton N&A Institute, 1922.
Howard University. *Reserve Officers' Training Corps Regulations, Howard University Unit 331.* Washington, DC, November 31, 1919.
Johnson, Campbell C. *Fifty Years of Progress: Armed Forces.* Pittsburgh: Pittsburgh Courier, 1950.
Lincoln University. *ROTC Handbook.* Jefferson City: Lincoln University, July 1962.
Marshall, Albert P. *Soldiers' Dream: A Centennial History of Lincoln University of Missouri, 1866-1966.* Walsworth: Marceline, MO, 1966.
*Military Science at Jackson State University*, Army Reserve Officers' Training Corps, Jackson State University, Jackson, MS, n.d.
Miller, Clarence. *Procurement and Retention of Black Officers: A Research Report*, U.S. Army War College, Carlisle Barracks, Pennsylvania, April 7, 1972.
Mishoe, Luna I. *Delaware State College President's Report, 1967-1968.* Dover: Delaware State College, 1968.
*Norfolk State University Spartan Battalion.* Norfolk: Norfolk State University Department of Military Science, n.d.
*North Carolina A&T State University Air Force Detachment 605 Directory since 1953.* Greensboro: NCA&T AFROTC Detachment 605, June 1987.
NROTCUFAMUINST 5400.2H, FAMU NROTC, Tallahassee, FL, July 20, 1990.
South Carolina State College ROTC Fact Sheet, October 22, 1991.
*Tawawa Remembrances.* Wilberforce: Wilberforce Class of 1914.
U.S. Comptroller, *Report to the Congress of the United States: Retention of Uneconomical Detachments in the ROTC Program, October 1964.* Washington: U.S. General Accounting Officer, 1964.
U.S. War Department. *Army Specialized Training Bulletin* 9 (December 1944).

_____ *Training Camps for Reserve Officers' Training Corps.* Washington: Government Printing Office, 1918.

*Virginia State College Reserve Officers' Training Corps (ROTC): 32 Years of Outstanding Service to the Nation.* Virginia State College Military Science Department, Ettricks, Virginia, n.d.

Watkins, Levi. *Report of the President of Alabama State University, 1962-1981.* Montgomery, AL: Office of University Advancement, 1981.

# Index

287